SLATS

THE LEGEND & LIFE OF
JIMMY SLATTERY

SLATS

THE LEGEND & LIFE OF
JIMMY SLATTERY

RICH BLAKE

NFB
BUFFALO, NEW YORK

Published by NFB, Buffalo New York.

NFB is an imprint of No Frills Buffalo/Amelia Press
119 Dorchester Road
Buffalo, NY 14213

For more information visit
nofrillsbuffalo.com

First edition. Printed in the United States of America.

ISBN: 978-0-6924114-3-8

Cover design by Tony Zajkowski.

Interior design and layout by Mulberry Tree Press, Inc.

Slats: The Legend & Life of Jimmy Slattery is a work of non-fiction.

*Dedicated to my father, Tom Blake,
who introduced me to Slats at an early age,
and who inspired me to write this book.*

My candle burns at both ends;
It will not last the night;
But ah, my foes, and oh, my friends—
It gives a lovely light!

—Edna St. Vincent Millay

CONTENTS

PREFACE

IN JUNE OF 1925, the midway point of the decade that roared, few things in American life were more popular than boxing—and no boxer transfixed fans like Jimmy Slattery. Sleek, handsome, only twenty years old, Slattery took New York City by storm, bursting into rarified territory as the fight game's crown prince.

Tex Rickard, maestro of Madison Square Garden and creator of champions, had declared Slattery to be the finest boxer he had ever seen. He was steering the light heavyweight toward a shot at Jack Dempsey's heavyweight title. That same month, the *Chicago Tribune* ran a multi-installment feature on Slattery, "The Boy Who Has Everything," which was nationally syndicated. In the series, the native son of Buffalo, N.Y., was heralded as a coming champion by virtue of his uniquely complete collection of weapons—a hard punch, blazing speed, clever defense, dazzling footwork and ring intelligence bordering on wizardry—a blessing of talents that led famed sportswriter Hype Igoe to dub Slattery "the darling of the boxing gods." Probably fifty boxing writers were working in New York City right then—and virtually all of them predicted Slattery would add poundage, graduate to heavyweight and win the title, likely within a year or two.

Dempsey himself had conceded as much. On an extended and unpopular hiatus from ring activities, Dempsey referred to Slattery as "the fellow who will take my crown." The unexpected remark was widely repeated in newspapers around the country during Slattery's dizzying springtime ascension.

Meanwhile, the boy prodigy was being fawned over by former heavyweight champion James J. Corbett, one the most famous living Americans of the day. Iconic symbol of the Gay Nineties, popular vaudeville performer, lecturer and a widely read boxing commentator, Corbett had followed Slattery's rise from the time he first emerged as a gangling welterweight. "Slattery is the most perfect fighting machine I ever saw," Corbett said in one interview. In June of '25, Corbett told the *Associated Press* "it would not surprise me if Slattery succeeded Dempsey as ruler of the heavy-weight division."

Fans had never seen anyone like Slattery. He was a ghost; no one could lay a glove on him. With his statuesque physique and dark hair slicked back, "Slats" more resembled a silent movie star than a pugilist. He fought in a fast, fluid, totally unique manner—arms dangling loose at his sides, dancing on his toes, avoiding punches with a deft tilt of the head before snapping his right like a cobra. Slattery's sheer artistry left the hardboiled men at ringside mesmerized and the old-timers convinced they had just seen the second-coming of Corbett.

Earlier that spring, Slattery, arriving in Boston for a fight, was met at the train station by a fan delegation that included a brass band. Appearing on one of Rickard's all-star boxing cavalcades held in May of '25, Slattery by far shined the brightest. The spectacular fashion in which he knocked his opponent across the ring, somersaulting, jolted the sell-out throng into a tizzy and remained the talk of New York for days.

Considered so far ahead of everyone else in the game, Slattery drew comparisons to Man O' War. When he fought in Yankee Stadium, Babe Ruth sat ringside.

The metropolitan area's famous warm-weather boxing season was only just heating up. Rickard and rival promoter Humbert Fugazy were scrambling to sign Slattery to appear on their outdoor cards. Because of his tender age, not yet 21, Slattery, under New York State law, could not participate in bouts of more than six rounds. Realizing that over a short distance the Buffalo speed boy was invincible, top contenders unapologetically steered clear. Fugazy was having trouble finding a suitable opponent—no one wanted to fight Slats. And yet no program was complete without Slattery on it. Fugazy would have settled for anyone he could find, even a glorified sparring partner. Gotham fans so badly wanted to see the kid in action, the opponent was inconsequential.

"Perhaps there is nothing paralleling Slattery in all the archives of Fistiana," wrote Ed Hughes of the *New York Telegraph*. "Slattery in a remarkably short space of time rose to the heights of ring glory without being knocked off his feet."

Amidst the onslaught of publicity and adulation, Slattery personified the riotous pace of the era. Flush with tens of thousands in ring earnings, naturally magnetic and always smiling, he pursued leisurely activities with a volcanic intensity, whether it be racing around in his Ford, playing a game of football, competing in a dance marathon or staying out all night in an "anything-goes" speakeasy.

Manager and mentor Red Carr, an ex-boxer and veteran of the Great War, was continually challenged to devise new ways to keep his boy from careening out of control. Two childhood pals, Skitsy Fitzgerald and Joe Hickey, served as Slattery's faithful corner men and formed the nucleus of an entourage that came to include their large waterfront gang, assorted sycophants, hangers-on and an inexhaustible supply of female admirers.

That spring, Slattery was a comet, the rage of the nation. Never was anyone so assuredly fated for ring supremacy. Although largely forgotten over the years and never until now fully chronicled, the story of Slattery's staggering ride is both a remarkable reflection of the period in which he lived—and just plain remarkable. And it had all been set into motion five years earlier by a fairly ordinary occurrence: two teenage boys squaring off on a South Buffalo street corner.

ONE

A Legend is Born

BY ALL ACCOUNTS, the instigator of Jimmy Slattery's first important fight had it coming. Harp Griffin was a hulking, sixteen-year-old ruffian. Weighing more than 200 pounds, Griffin, leader of his own gang of Elk Street toughs, not only would have been a fearsome character for any adolescent to face down, but, at that size, he numbered among the most imposing figures in the entire neighborhood.

They say it happened on Valentine's Day in 1920. Slattery had been walking along Elk, near St. Stephen's Church, shadowed by his two best pals, Skitsy Fitzgerald and Joe Hickey. The boys had just visited a nearby candy store. One year younger and 100 pounds lighter than his tormentor, Slattery must have looked like an easy mark: quiet, spindly, clutching a box of chocolates. Whether Griffin strong-armed Slattery, or employed more stealth-like tactics, is unclear. But the candy was snatched, and when demand for its return was voiced, Griffin issued the dare that has served as prelude to so many fistic entanglements: "*Make me.*"

James Slattery was born on August 25, 1904, the second son of John "Sloak" Slattery and his wife, Mary. At the time, the family lived in the upper half of a rickety wood-frame dwelling at 323 Fulton Street, between Alabama and Hamburg streets in a section of Buffalo called the First Ward. Mary gave birth at home. On his birth certificate, Slattery's middle name was listed as Edward, Sloak's reply when the doctor asked. Ten days later, the child was baptized James Joseph (mom's choice) by Father Daniel O'Brien at St. Brigid's Church. Years later, Slattery would inexplicably begin signing his name as James Patrick.

The Slattery's would soon become more connected with St. Stephen's Parish, which encompassed an adjacent, partly Polish neighborhood situated between—and cut off by—two railroad bridges. A few blocks north, there was yet another separate industrial/residential neighborhood, "the Hydraulics"—its name was derived from the man-made Hydraulic Canal, a marvel of a millrun that once powered half a dozen textile factories. Household products magnate John Larkin built a huge headquarters that towered over this section's main thoroughfare, Seneca Street. For many decades, the area was synonymous with overcrowding, poverty and epidemic. Stubbornly cloistered residents of the First Ward, entirely Irish, were sticklers when it came to recognizing who was, and who was not, part of their community as defined by precise boundaries. They could instantaneously spot an interloper from bordering neighborhoods. Most people knew to stick to their own territory.

Sloak moved his family around the south side of the city, as struggling residents typically did when overdue rent piled up. They intermittently lived in the heart of the Old First Ward, and on its outskirts. For a long stretch of Jimmy's childhood, his family lived in Holy Family Parish, several miles from the waterfront in a then nascent suburban community known as South Buffalo. Yet the Slattery family's connection to the First Ward transcended street or parish divisions, such was the esteem held for Sloak.

In his younger days, back when bouts were staged at halls and theaters, Sloak Slattery made a name for himself as a boxer. He was even more famous for his charm and sincerity. Sloak was old-country loyal, a friend to all. Born in 1870, he'd grown up in a community of lakefront squatters living in cottages at the foot of South Michigan. He came to know every speck and contour of the jigsaw shoreline—comprised of wharves, slips, quays, docks, grain elevators and assorted industrial sites, as well as a vast web of railroad switching yards, trunk lines, coal bins, freight sheds, passenger depots and miles upon miles of tracks and trestles.

Sloak's father, John Slattery, Sr., emigrated from Ireland to Buffalo during the middle part of the 19th Century. The name Slattery comes from the Gaelic *slantra*, meaning strong. The clan was prominent on the West Coast, especially in County Clare. Not much is known about John Slattery except that he died unexpectedly when Sloak was still very young. Sloak's mother, Ellen, remarried a one-armed lake captain, Matthew Boardman, a native of Chicago and one of the pioneers of the strange and wonderful little colony of "sea-wall squatters." The 100 or so hearty inhabitants of the narrow peninsula strip—cordoned off by a lakeshore road, grain elevators and a railroad coal dock—were led by a rebellious Great Lakes sailor named John Hoolihan. To survive, he and fellow shanty dwellers battled fierce December gales and those who would contest their sovereignty, namely the railroad companies, the city and the federal government. Living closely together in this world of their own, these rogues often battled one another, as well. After Ellen Slattery Boardman was widowed for a second time, she stayed on the beach raising Sloak, his two brothers (one of whom died young) and two daughters she had had with Captain Boardman. They lived next to Hoolihan, his wife and their eleven children. Over the years, the families fought like "Kilkenney cats," as one exasperated magistrate put it.

Slight of build and pugnacious as a teenager in the 1880s, Sloak inherited his nickname from his uncle Joe, a saloonkeeper and waterfront overlord. Joe, the original Sloak Slattery, deserves some mention.

A short, stout, powder keg of a man, Joe could be amiable one moment and raising his fists or a pistol the next. He was a longtime pal of neighborhood strongman William "Fingy" Connors, the boss of the saloon bosses controlling the docks. Joe became a top Connors henchman and one of the most feared enforcers of the contract system for controlling the supply of labor. From his Ohio Street hotel/bar, he doled out railroad freight handling jobs to the patrons of his establishment. No one dared interfere with his arrangement with the railroad. In 1888, Joe shot a man in the leg during an argument in the bar. Police were called, but in the end the victim declined to testify.

With Fingy Connors as his backer, Joe boldly ran for the New York State Assembly as a Republican. He lost the race to a 28-year-old incumbent, William "Blue-Eyed Billy" Sheehan. The saloon bosses began to lose their grip.

In the summer of 1899, the waterfront boiled over. Workers of all stripes—freight handlers, ore handlers, stevedores, grain scoopers and coal heavers—rose up. Buffalo's labor strife made national headlines. Joe Slattery called in scab labor and punched out a Polish union leader who went to the police (and who, similarly, later declined to testify).

But the dockworkers won out. Labor unions flourished. Within a decade, some of the same insecure Irish immigrants who would have once considered themselves lucky just to have a job—even one amounting to indentured servitude—would ascend to become policemen and firemen and find even higher-paying management jobs with railroad, steel and lake freighter companies.

At the turn of the century, Buffalo was exploding as a transshipment hub. More Irish were pouring into the First Ward. They cherished their homeland yet were determined to reclaim a new version of it. If an Irish immigrant made it to Buffalo, he or she was warmly received and looked after by friends or relatives. The newcomers almost immediately found work. In turn, they wrote letters home, sharing highlights and whatever money they could spare, so that kin and friends could join them. Entire hamlets wound up transplanted to the First Ward.

The Irish had been coming to North America from the time it was first being settled. Around the start of the American Revolution, an estimated 200,000 Irish called the Thirteen Colonies home. Half of George Washington's rebel army was Irish. When the first Irishman arrived in Buffalo in 1815, the town was little more than a tiny, creek-side trading post in the process of being rebuilt after being burned to the ground during the War of 1812. Within a decade, Buffalo had soared to international relevance as the linchpin connecting the Western half of the United States with the Eastern Seaboard via the Great Lakes and the newly completed 363-mile Erie Canal. Roughly 3,000 Irish workers helped dig that ditch. Some settled in Buffalo. More immigrant workers came to the city in later years when the Erie Canal was enlarged and additional barge canals were built. Then the railroads came. Work was abundant. Between 1820 and 1840, some 300,000 Irish immigrants arrived in the U.S. And this was *before* Ireland's potato crop failed. By the second half of the 19th century, there were nearly one million people who were born in Ireland but living in America. About 6,000 of them lived in Buffalo.

They clustered around the waterfront, unloading the grain from the bellies of freighters that came from Chicago by way of Lake Michigan and the Detroit River. This dockside district emerged as the city's first voting precinct when such lines were drawn. It formed a Democratic political bastion. Many First Ward residents lived on top of each other in ramshackle cottages. Countless saloons sprang up. The labyrinth of streets could be a magical place—filled with generosity and camaraderie, not to mention inadequately drained sewage. They could also be mean. Fist fights were a way of settling disputes, large and small. Fighting was also done for laughs or as a spectacle on which to be wagered or sometimes for no discernible reason whatsoever.

In New York City, during the "No Irish Need Apply" era, the Irish mixed fighting with politics. One of the chief leg-breakers on the Tammany Hall payroll was John Morrissey, a native of Ireland who was raised in the Erie Canal town of Troy, N.Y. Morrissey went on to become one of the first internationally recognized bare-knuckle boxing champions, even as he continued to crack skulls for Boss Tweed. Growing up in Troy, Morrissey had learned how fists could be currency. Canal boats, called bullheads, were in constant competition for rights of way, often leading to heated bottleneck situations along the towpaths. Each boat captain employed his personal enforcer, usually some muscular barge hand. You didn't always have a neighbor or a pal on the Erie Canal—sometimes you had an iron-fisted barge "bully" in your face. Nightly, going town to town, these brawlers would put their talents to further use beating on each other in the saloons. Each canal town had a champion, part athlete, part folk hero.

Boxing was in a primeval stage during the 1880s. Prizefighting was outlawed in New York State during much of the decade. Small-town rings were pitched with stakes driven into the ground and ropes strung from posts whilst a designated lookout kept watch for the local sheriff. Still, bouts had been taking place in Buffalo since its birth. The city's waterfront was awash with illicit fights that took place above bars, in back rooms, back alleys, isolated piers, floating barges and forest clearings. On Canal Street, a mere two-block cobblestone lane, there were nearly 100 saloons, brothels and boarding houses catering to lake-faring transients. It was an unimaginably ruthless place, a lawless enclave of mayhem and murder. Countless bodies ended up in the canal. Bare knuckle contests were the live entertainment of the day. There were also cockfights, dog fights, dog-on-cat fights, dog versus rat—even rat against rat, for those who preferred an all-vermin affair. Extra disturbing were the "gouging matches," in which men (of questionable mental health) grew out and sharpened their fingernails to engage in contests that routinely ended when one of them lost an eye.

By the 1890s, however, Buffalo was also a breeding ground for modern, refined pugilism. The gloves were going on. Legitimate boxing, as sport, was allowed at athletic clubs, which sprang up all over most major cities, even as rural Christians expressed disgust. Exhibition matches, governed by more civilized rules, were staged at theatres and social clubs. The Bijou Theater on Main Street hosted some of these boxing matches, as did the Black Rock Athletic Club, which doubled as a bowling alley. Southside boxing venues included Kilgallon's Hall and the Home Pastime A.C. on Elk Street.

No records exist to chronicle Sloak's boxing career in the 1890s. One *Buffalo Times* article asserts that he was "well-known in his younger days for sports achievements, especially in the ring." Some accounts indicate Sloak embarked on boxing barnstorming tours that took him to Pennsylvania and Ohio. It appears Sloak played his fair share of baseball, too. He certainly was a knowledgeable boxing fan. At a time when most Americans only cared about heavyweights, Sloak worshiped the little fellows like himself, such as fast-punching Packy McFarland and the immortal featherweight Young Griffo. Sloak followed the big fellows, too. He delighted in reciting the trail of Irish/Irish-American champions from Paddy Ryan to John L. Sullivan—America's first genuine celebrity—to James J. Corbett to Bob Fitzsimmons (actually a Cornishman of Irish descent), who took the title from Corbett on St. Patrick's Day 1897. That fight took place in the first outdoor arena built specifically for a boxing match.

Right around that time, Corbett, nearing retirement, agreed to fight Kid McCoy in Buffalo under the auspices of the Hawthorne Athletic Club. Western New York was becoming recognized as a ravenous fight region. The club was planning to build a 10,000-seat outdoor arena in Cheektowaga, just east of the city. But the fight never happened. Either local law enforcement learned of the production and shut it down, as some boxing historians believe, or, alternatively, Corbett's curious deal with a small upstate club created so much suspicion that the bout was moved to New York City.

The Hawthorne A.C. did eventually stage a 20-round world lightweight championship fight in a renovated cattle stockade in July of 1899. This was at a time (between 1896 and 1900) when boxing was briefly re-legalized in New York State. In the first championship fight ever held in Buffalo, local wonder boy Frank Erne defeated George "Kid" Lavigne of Saginaw, Michigan. Erne, a native of Switzerland, won over his adopted hometown as a clever teenager fighting rivals like Curly Supples in venues like the Court Street Theater. In 1901, Erne defended his title against Joe Gans. The fight took place in Fort Erie, Ontario, and lasted only a few seconds. Gans laid out Erne with a single punch. The outcome was known all over the world; not only had Gans delivered one of the fastest knockouts ever, but in doing so, he had become the first recognized black champion. After briefly bringing national attention to Buffalo, Erne faded from boxing. Boxing was later outlawed again.

If matches were held they were strictly limited to private clubs under the laughable pretense of "educational seminars." Nevertheless, various new athletic clubs opened up all over Buffalo to stage boxing "exhibitions" exclusively for members. No other sport, apart from baseball, seemed to matter.

One can only imagine, against this backdrop, the allure boxing must have held for the young Sloak Slattery. But as he neared his 30th birthday, Sloak hung up the gloves and went to work, full time, as a day laborer on the docks. Though powerful in body and spirit, Sloak stood only 5'6", and barely weighed 130 pounds. He married late, at age 32, taking for his bride a taller, heavyset woman by the name of Mary Hickey, who was five years his junior. This was not an uncommon kind of pairing, as some diminutive Irishmen were mindful of fortifying their offspring. The union was soon blessed with the births of two boys: John, Jr. in 1903, and Jimmy the following year. The family lived in a back, upstairs flat on Fulton Street. And with a wife, two toddlers and a third child on the way, Sloak was forced to think about a career beyond the seasonal work on the Buffalo waterfront.

Sloak took a Civil Service test and, in 1906, landed a low-rung position with the Buffalo Fire Department, assigned to Engine No. 20—the fire boat *W.S. Grattan*, docked at the foot of Ohio Street. Grain dust was known to spontaneously combust and wooden structures on the water's edge were like tinderboxes. The fire boat, one of the first of its kind, used a steam-fuelled pump that sucked up water from the lake. Sloak's job was stoker, working below deck shoveling coal into the boiler. He would later help get his brother Patrick a job as a stoker, too. It was a filthy, sweaty way to earn $1,400 per year, especially in the heat of the summer, although in the winter, Sloak likely would have been grateful to be down below making steam.

Winters in Buffalo could be harsh at the start of the 20th Century, harsher in some ways than the ones that have garnered the city its arctic reputation in more recent decades. Indoor plumbing was unheard of, and trips to the outhouse were less than comfortable. For Sloak, frigid winter mornings would begin with a trek outside, in long underwear and galoshes, to gather up a load of coal to fire up the stove. Awaiting him on the back stoop would likely have been a thin film of coal dust mixing with the freshly fallen snow—a familiar sight to Ward residents. Coal dust from the Lehigh Valley Railroad's roundhouse and fuelling station was a pretty awful facet of life on Fulton Street and throughout the St. Stephen's section. As the coal was poured from giant gondolas into locomotive hoppers, black clouds rose into the air and were carried off by the wind blowing in from the lake. Coal dust blackened residents' clothes. It got in their eyes. It got in the foam of their beer. In addition to bordering the sprawling railroad yard, St. Stephen's parish sat in the shadow of the giant Husted Milling Company. Residences and factories sat side by side. It was a hard, noisy, sometimes foul place, once described by the *Buffalo Times'* Willis Wilber:

> *A maze of crooked streets, railway tracks, viaducts and ramshackle buildings . . . glimmering yellow lights flashing dully through the fog sweeping up from the harbor. Swarms of children. Gossiping women. Men with dinner pails and odorous pipes. Dingy churches and halls blackened by the smoke of years. Dingy houses . . . the hard life of the sailor, the longshoreman and the scooper.*

Close to the lakeshore, the First Ward was—despite all that—a terrific spot in the summertime. When he was still just a toddler, Jimmy Slattery, visiting his grandmother on the Seawall peninsula, took naturally to the water, scarily so. The incredible sight of a three-year-old splashing way out toward the horizon is said to have baffled even the lifelong watermen of the beach community. Jimmy's mom also grew up near the water with her parents and five brothers, as well as a few Irish boarders. Sloak's stepsister, Ellen, married Edward Fitzgerald, and they had a son, Willie, who was Jimmy's age. Family stories place Jimmy and Willie together as babies rolling around in the Lake Erie sand. They were cousins and the closest of friends. Willie eventually became known as "Skitsy."

In 1908, the Slattery family moved to O'Connell Street, near Our Lady of Perpetual Help Church and School. Jimmy attended first grade there. He was known as a bright, energetic kid. As a tot, Jimmy sped about the family flat—once, when he was about age three, bounding out of an open second-floor window and crashing to the ground as his frantic mother chased after him. Luckily, his injury was limited to a broken left shoulder. A doctor set the bone and rigged a sling; the event had no lasting effects beyond the fact that the child, a natural lefty, was forced to use his right hand.

One of the earliest known photos of Jimmy Slattery, around that age, shows him in a fighter's pose, outfitted in boxing gloves and a thick wool sweater at least two sizes too big, making him appear ridiculously broad shouldered and skinny legged. He looked like a pint-sized Bob Fitzsimmons (known for his scrawny lower quarters and incongruously monstrous upper torso forged during his blacksmithing days). Little Jimmy donning gloves may have been a wonderfully cute photo. But Sloak would teach his boys—a third brother, Joe, had come along, as had two girls, Mary and Helen—to use their fists. Boxing lessons were given by the age of six. In the Ward, as Sloak well knew, if you couldn't fight you didn't survive. Dad Slattery brought his pups to boxing shows and to local gyms to watch fighters train.

The most popular Irish fighter in the First Ward at the time was a welterweight, Paddy Lavin. He had come to Buffalo from County Kildare in 1900 as a teenager—supposedly ousted by British authorities for associating with Sinn Féin rebels. A known bootlegger, Lavin died under mysterious circumstances around the start of Prohibition.

The best known fighter in America at this time was heavyweight Jess Willard. The Kansas farm hand, at 6'6" tall and weighing 235 pounds, was considered one of the largest men to ever step inside a boxing ring. He would emerge as redeemer to white America, wresting the heavyweight title from Jack Johnson—black and widely despised at a time of Jim Crow segregation. Following that 26-round battle in Havana, Cuba, in April of 1915, the press portrayed Willard as invincible.

But one year prior to becoming champion, Willard was in Buffalo training for a fight at the First Ward Athletic Club. His trainer, Ike O'Neill, was a Buffalo native. Sloak took Jimmy down to get a look at Big Jess, at the time just one of several "White Hopes" to rise up from the heartland.

Decidedly underwhelmed by Willard's clumsy sparring, Sloak, as one version of the story goes, knelt down, pulled his young son close and told him, "I'm going to train you to beat bums like that fellow Willard." Surely, Sloak was being brash to the point of absurdity. But the little nine-year-old believed him.

★ ★ ★ ★ ★

Around this time, Sloak was promoted to Pump Engineer and transferred to Engine No. 22, a horse-drawn brigade located in the heart of Buffalo's East Side (German and Polish) community. Like many Irishmen at that time, Sloak had transitioned from low-skill laborer to a civil servant, now earning nearly $2,000 a year, enough to send his kids to St. Stephen's school. Sloak moved his family to 362 Marilla Street off of South Park Avenue, which was a ten-minute street-car ride from the First Ward. The rise of the steel industry south of Buffalo spurred development and boosted incomes. Families were branching out to be closer to those jobs. For the Slattery family, Marilla Street was located in an entirely residentially zoned section that was spacious, tree-lined, and quieter.

It is quite possible that when Slats was growing up, no one, besides Sloak, would have taken him to be a fighter. To the contrary, some kids thought Slattery was a sissy. Although he was a boxing fan and an admirer of the tough kids who brawled frequently in the streets of South Buffalo, he appears to have tried to keep his head down. "Even in the street battles of the boys his age he was never conspicuous," Billy Kelly of the *Buffalo Courier* once wrote. "When rivalries were settled in hand-to-hand conflict, Slattery managed to be absent."

Call it pride or prescience, but Sloak always conveyed to his son that the boxing game was rightfully his for the taking, and that one day he would make a name for himself. Sloak seemed to have genuinely believed in his son's destiny even as the boy gravitated more toward baseball and football. "Here's the future champion of the world!" Sloak would declare, plopping his son on a bar stool, whenever he returned to the old neighborhood to visit a relative's tavern.

Eventually, Sloak got his hands on a beat-up punching bag from a fellow fireman and fastened it to a post in his backyard. Early on, it was evident to him that his Jimmy, whom he and his wife affectionately called "Shamus," had inherited some boxing talent. One oft-repeated yarn concerning Jimmy's earliest start in boxing goes something like this: Sloak grew tired of Jimmy and his older brother John constantly squabbling. The boys seemed too old to spank, so Dad Slattery fit them with boxing gloves and told them to have at it. Jimmy clobbered his big brother and eventually, supposedly, every other kid on the block. It's been said that the Slattery backyard on Marilla became an afterschool boxing playground; Sloak secured extra pairs of 4-ounce leather gloves so that multiple matches could be happening at once. Picture screaming kids clambering around, dirt swirling, Sloak, the happy referee, bouncing about, laughing, shouting pointers and slapping his knee. Accounts of the backyard boxing are prominent in several stories about Jimmy Slattery's formative years that were written during his rise to fame, including a lengthy 1930 series penned by the *Buffalo Times*' Wilber, and another in 1925 by nationally syndicated *Chicago Herald* writer Sid Sutherland. Each contains a reference to a favorite phrase Sloak would cry out during these melees: "Fight ye little devils! Fight!"

In time, kids from many blocks around congregated at the Slattery home. Even adults came to watch. Seldom were the crowds larger than when father and son mixed it up. "The Slatterys are at it again!" was the cry that would ring out in the neighborhood. If Jimmy got out of line, Sloak took him outside and made him put on the gloves. The old man wasn't afraid to knock his son silly. If the boy swung sloppily or wide, Sloak punished poor form with lethal force. When Jimmy went down, Sloak leaned over him, taunting: "If you think you're a man, then get up and fight like one!" It wasn't unusual for Jimmy to give as much as he got, and these backyard affairs could get raucous with crowds of onlookers hysterically howling with delight at the sheer unbridled violence that the Slatterys freely perpetrated against one another. Wrote Wilber: *"No mercy was given, nor expected. Dad and son went out for blood every time the gloves were laced."*

At one point, according to neighborhood lore, a Protestant priest, whose church was across the alley behind the yard, finally had enough. "You're ruining South Park Avenue!" was the sermon he delivered to the congregation along the Slattery fence. Sloak's responsorial rebuke: "To hell with South Park!"

Sloak made sure his boys were properly educated at St. Stephen's grammar school, a three-story stone and brick building on the corner of Elk and Euclid Place, back in the old neighborhood. Here Pastor Tom Barrett and the Sisters of Mercy taught reading, writing and arithmetic—as well as the mystery, magnificence and wrath of God Almighty, a concept that all of St. Stephen's would come to feel on June 24, 1913.

Just before 4:00 P.M. that day, grain dust ignited at the Husted feed mill down the street from the church. The ensuing explosion killed 33 workers, and injured 80 others. It tore apart the facility and caused considerable damage to surrounding property. For days, the stunned parish struggled to identify the dead and comfort those who lost loved ones.

That Jimmy continued to attend St. Stephen's kept him tethered to the old neighborhood. He marched off to the I.R.C. street car that carried him to school early each morning, a floppy wool cap on his head, the top button of his white shirt secured, the tips of his withered collar curled up. Jimmy and his cousin/best friend Skitsy began to pal around with a boy named Joe Merrick, who also went by Joe Merritt. After his mother died, Joe moved to Euclid to live with his grandmother, Bridget Hickey. He eventually became known as Joe Hickey. Before long, the three were inseparable. Skitsy was the cut-up. All three played sports. But here is where Jimmy truly set himself apart. He sprinted, knocking out the 100-yard dash in ten seconds; he played baseball, a second baseman who also pitched. The three spent long, endless summer days at Lanigan Park, where baseball games went morning until night. Jimmy and his cohorts would have no shortage of adventures. Giant sand piles stored for cement making on the bank of the ship canal proved ideal for "king of the mountain," a game that always held an element of real danger—the possibility of accidentally tumbling into the fetid muck of the Ohio Street Basin where several children had drowned. Tugboats and grain elevators cried out for exploration and were perfect for jumping off into the river during the summer.

Slats and Skitsy sold the *Buffalo Evening News* in the afternoons on Main and North Division. If the boys weren't playing sports or hawking papers, they went to the movies or just hung around Elk Street. Now and again the boys would sneak into the pro boxing matches at the Broadway Auditorium. They followed a young knockout artist named Jack Dempsey on a tear in the latter part of 1918. Slattery had snuck into the Aud on the December night Dempsey knocked Gunboat Smith to the canvas nine times. Dempsey's first national headlines had come in a fight against Carl Morris held in Buffalo ten months earlier.

By age 15, Slattery, bony and feeble-looking, having not fully realized his initial adolescent growth spurt, was nevertheless trying his luck at amateur boxing. And he'd surely had at least a few street fights before that Valentine's Day he ran into Harp Griffin—just not the kind that people talked about for decades to come.

Slattery and his pals had gone to a favorite spot of his mother's, a candy store near St. Stephen's. Likely it was Marren's Ice Cream & Candy Store, No. 802 Elk, across the street from the church. Legend holds that Slattery bought his mother a box of chocolates. By this time, the family was back living on Fulton Street. Although Slats had always attended St. Stephen's School, he may have been mistaken as an outsider. Then again, Harp Griffin bullied all the kids; maybe it was just Slattery's turn.

The scene that unfolded on Elk Street that Valentine's Day was never forgotten. It was passed down from father to son, like an epic poem or creation myth. Cy Kritzer, writing years later in the *Buffalo Evening News*, described it like this:

> *The Ward never saw anything like what happened in the next 25 minutes. A crowd of nearly 200 gathered before the fight was over. The stripling cut the bully to ribbons, left him begging, enough, enough . . .*

Joe Hickey, eyewitness to the fisticuffs, would, six decades later, provide an account to the *News'* Frank Wakefield. Hickey said that he had never seen his companion so livid, before or since. On impulse, Slattery had unleashed a furious bombardment of punches. He took a few good shots, too.

In Wakefield's 1984 article, Hickey placed the fight in front of Gene Murphy's Service Station at the corner of Elk and Louisiana. But another boyhood friend of Slattery's, the late Abe Gallivan, a legendary Buffalo bartender, always insisted that the fight had occurred in a vacant lot at the corner of Smith and Elk, near St. Stephen's (according to Noel Burke, who knew Gallivan). Regardless of the precise location, the import was unmistakable: Slattery had a gift.

Spent and bloodied, Slattery caught his breath amidst a battery of backslaps from amazed onlookers, including one young man who volunteered to escort him to a nearby boxing gym for a proper assessment. Slattery had pictured himself following his father's footsteps into the fire department. But now he wondered if perhaps he had a different calling. With his two best buddies by his side and a parade of jubilant neighborhood kids in tow, Slattery trotted over to the Newsboys' Gym, downtown on Franklin Street. Here, he would meet the person who would forever change his life.

TWO

RED

I N THE SPRING OF 1918, Paul Carr found himself flat on his back, unable to move. The 23-year-old boxer from Buffalo's West Side lay in a cramped bunk on a slow-moving ocean vessel headed for the biggest fight ever staged—the Great War.

Quiet and unassuming, Carr belonged to the 108th Engineers, part of the Army's 33rd Division en route to the French port city of Brest, first stop for hundreds of thousands of servicemen pouring toward the Western Front. The United States had declared war on Germany one year earlier. Arriving better late than never, the American Expeditionary Forces supplanted decimated British and French troops trying to hold back the Kaiser's offensive.

Their ride over was the *Minnesota,* an iron battle tub embarking from Hoboken, New Jersey. Its crossing was difficult and protracted, a result of dangerously stormy seas, engine problems and a zigzag course deliberately plotted to thwart German U-Boats.

During the voyage, when he wasn't battling queasiness, Carr managed to take in a few sparring sessions with some crewmen who dabbled. Otherwise, much of his punching and jabbing took place in the confines of an imaginary ring. Daydreams of disseminating rights and lefts passed the hours and helped blunt two ever-present adversaries, one being seasickness (conditions were so rough that entire teams of horses washed overboard) and the other being fear (the men had all heard stories of poison gas).

Carr made friends easily. His habitual shadow boxing was endearing. The young soldier was a tightly coiled 120 pounds, his body well-conditioned from an adolescence spent hustling newspapers and hanging around gymnasiums. His nose had been broken but wasn't too disfigured; his piercing blue eyes gave him an owl-like intensity. But Carr's most striking feature was his thick crop of fiery hair. Naturally, everybody called him Red.

After 33 days at sea, the *Minnesota* concluded what should have been a two-week trip. Red and his unit spent another full day on a train bound for Bordeaux. Arriving in camp, they were issued gas masks and informed of an AEF-sponsored boxing tournament about to get underway. When Red and his pals arrived, murmurs began to spread through the rows—apparently, a U.S. entrant had unexpectedly begged off his match with a superb French welterweight. Were there any volunteers?

"Come on Red!" his buddies cried, shoving him toward some officers asking around for willing souls. "Here's your fighter!" one of them shouted. "He'll lick the Frenchman!"

Just like that, Red Carr was returned to the roped-square about which he'd been dreaming. For three rounds, Red, a featherweight giving away 20 pounds, endured a relentless barrage of jabs and crosses, any one of which might have flattened him. It wasn't pretty, but he went the distance. "I had never seen so many gloves before," Red would recall later.

Afterwards, Red was invited to join the Army's boxing team, which meant he'd eat better and avoid a lot of mundane drills. Boxing would be a part of his daily life. He took it as a good sign.

★ ★ ★ ★ ★

Eleven years earlier, Red had crossed the Atlantic going in the other direction. He was born Paolo Carriero in 1894 in rural Avigliano in Southern Italy. His father, Angelo Vito, immigrated to the United States around 1904. He was part of a wave of displaced members of Southern Italy's agrarian class suffering from crop failures and unfair land practices, a situation mirroring the one in Ireland five decades earlier. Just as the Irish population in America exploded in the middle of the 19th century, Italians began arriving en masse in the latter part. Some 14,000 came to Buffalo between 1880 and 1900. Some found work along the docks and in the steel plants, but more commonly, Italians went into business for themselves, selling fruit and homemade goods from push carts. They cut hair, made clothes and cobbled shoes. Angelo made his living doing construction work and selling newspapers. He came over first and eventually saved up enough to send for his children (Red's mother had died when he was still a toddler). With a quarter in his pocket, Red arrived in Buffalo just a few weeks shy of his 13th birthday. He'd traveled by steamer, and then by train, along with an uncle, his 10-year-old brother and two sisters. Red's mother had died when he was still a toddler. Angelo later remarried (that wife died, too) and was raising his family in a small, wood-framed house on Busti Avenue, the beating heart of Buffalo's Lower West Side, which was also home to a fairly large Irish community. The influx of "darkies" and "dagos" did not occur without some hostilities. Gangs of Irish kids and Italian kids waged frequent wars in the yard behind the Gas House, pummeling each other with sticks, rocks and tin cans.

Red and his younger brother, Domenico, both went to Public School No. 2. They attended Mass every Sunday at St. Anthony's. After school, the boys sold newspapers with their father along one of the busiest stretches of Main Street, where all the major street car arteries intersected. Right nearby stood the 10-story Ellicott Square Building, one of the most expansive office complexes yet built, as well as the Iroquois Hotel, among the finest anywhere. Newsboys worked every intersection along Main Street. In an era long before television and just before radio, Buffalo had six dailies—two morning papers and four in the evening—as well as weeklies printed in both German and Polish.

The popular depiction of an early 1900s newsboy—a gritty urchin in a floppy cap shouting headlines with the bombast of a carnival barker—wasn't far off. The cries of the newsboys (*"Ex-tree!"*) were a part of the downtown cacophony that included honking automobile horns, clacking cable cars, screeching police whistles and the rhythmic clip-clop of horse-drawn trucks. New York City newsboys made headlines when they went on strike. The industry—from William Randolph Hearst down to the guy running the corner newsstand—felt the pinch.

Buffalo newsboys, many of them orphans, were a colorful bunch, with names like Gus, Mullet and Kootch. "Megaphone" Gibbs, who could shriek louder than a steam whistle, worked Main and Clinton. Petey Smith, a.k.a. the "German Cyclone," worked Main and Eagle. Many pedestrians and shopkeepers viewed newsboys as a scourge. They traveled in unruly packs, and smoked and cursed and rolled dice. Others in the community felt sorry for them.

In 1903, a small cadre of Buffalo newsstand owners gathered a delegation of about 100 newsboys in a room in the Bachmann News Company building on Ellicott Street. They proposed the creation of an association. Each boy would contribute 15 cents per week into a fund. If one of them got sick, he would be cared for. Plans called for a clubhouse and a gymnasium, a place of their own that was not a pool hall or a saloon. The leader of the newsboys was Moxie Brechtel, a big-eared, bug-eyed 31-year-old. He'd been selling papers on the street since he was five. Through his determination and an uncanny ability to sell papers, Brechtel came to eventually own his own newsstand and then rose to a well-paying job with the *Buffalo News* working in circulation. He put $40 into the kitty and was promptly selected to head up the newly chartered Newsboys' Benevolent Association. The organization, steered by about 80 newsstand operators, eventually comprised more than 300 members.

Society women took up the cause. Within a few years, the association had $4,000 in its coffers, enough for a down payment on a three-story building previously owned by the Children's Aid Society. On Christmas Eve, 1910, the Association finalized the purchase of what would become the Newsboys' Home on 29 Franklin Street across from police headquarters. By 1912, it had been fully converted into a proper dormitory, with a library, lounging rooms, and a dance hall. The third floor was turned into a fully outfitted gym—pulleys, speed bags, a heavy bag, belly boards, medicine balls, ample sparring areas and clean showers. A grimy hole-in-the-wall boxing gym it was not.

The Newsboys' Home sponsored basketball and baseball teams. They held boxing competitions, too. Fighting came naturally. Friction between Irish and Italian newsboys had resulted in some memorable street clashes over the years. A newsboy had to scrap to hold on to his turf. Foreign-looking Italian kids were treated like dogs. With his crimson hair and light complexion, Red assimilated better than most and could have passed as an Irish lad. His uprooting had come during crucial formative years, allowing for easier adoption of a new tongue and dialect, unlike Angelo Vito, who struggled with the language. Still, numerous indignities were endured. Once, while selling papers, Red and his brother were booted off a busy corner, according to a story Red had told to his son, the late Paul Carr, Jr. Some older fellow had shooed the youngsters away like back-stoop vermin. The boys never forgot.

Red loved sports. At around age 13, he became fascinated with boxing, which, alongside baseball, was the most popular American pastime. Red watched fights at the Superior Athletic Club, which staged weekly "exhibitions." Following a brief period of legality in the late 1890s, prize-fighting was banned in New York State between 1900 and 1911—except in private clubs on a membership basis.

Red was a natural athlete. He played handball at the YMCA. On the baseball field, he impressed with his mitt. But boxing was his passion. By the time Red was 15, he'd insinuated himself into a regular gig doing odd jobs at Allie Smith's gymnasium on Broadway Street on the East Side.

Although a large segment of the country still considered prizefighting to be, like drinking alcohol, a shameful activity, the sport, nevertheless, was more popular than ever. In 1911, boxing was briefly re-legalized in New York and limited to 10-round bouts. The ban's lifting came with one other major caveat: no decisions. The only way a competitor could be declared victorious was if he knocked his opponent out. The measure was a response to widespread fight fixing. The no-decision bouts (and the wagers placed on them) were settled instead by "newspaper decisions." The no-decision era brought boxing out of saloons and small clubs and into larger arenas such as Buffalo's Broadway Auditorium, a Civil War-era Armory refurbished into a civic gathering hall that sat several thousand. Well-known fighters from around the country appeared there under the auspices of local athletic clubs. Red was swept up in the craze. He went to Allie Smith's gym every day, toting towels and water pails, cutting tape off fighters' hands after workouts, mopping floors, and anything else that needed to be done. Even-tempered and in his early 30s, Smith piloted several locally based contenders such as middleweight slugger Willie "K.O." Brennan. Another fighter Red got to know hanging around the gym was newcomer Rocco Tozzo, a short, stocky Italian newsboy who later changed his name to Rocky Kansas.

Red loved Smith's gymnasium. Amidst the din of smacking gloves, Red studied techniques and practiced shadow boxing. His brother Domenico, who now went by Luke, began hanging around the gym, too.

One day, the two boys, a little bit older and a lot more proficient with their fists, happened to run into the fellow who had once cast them off while they were selling newspapers.

"Hey, mister, do you remember us?" Red asked, innocently enough. "We were here one time selling papers and you kicked us off this corner."

"Nope," the guy replied. "I don't recall."

"Well, I do," Red countered, dropping the guy with a hard smack to the chin. Luke threw in a shot for good measure while he was on his way down.

★★★★★

The first time Red ever laced up his gloves to scrap for money was above a First Ward saloon called Metzger's on Michigan Avenue. He was nineteen at the time. His opponent was another Italian boy fighting under the name of Patsy Klein, an alias possibly chosen to invoke the reputation of either Irish Patsy Cline, the famous child prodigy from New York City, or Patsy Kline the top-ranked featherweight from North Jersey.

About 100 males had crammed themselves into a sweaty spare room, fathers and sons, dockworkers and railroad men, placing wagers, puffing on five-cent Phillies and reeking of liquor. The signature heavy cigar cloud produced a nickname for these kinds of unsanctioned matches— "smokers." Red won his bout. He left Metzger's that night with a buck and a half, collected in a hat, a busted nose and his first taste of the prizefighter's life. The experience had left an impression on him, and it's not unfair to say that his impression was this: What Red really wanted was to become a trainer/manager, like Allie Smith, with his own stable of prospects.

In 1915, Red represented his first fighter, Dick Clancy, a fellow newsboy. At the time, Red hawked the *Buffalo Evening News* on the corner of Main and North Division. All winter and through the spring, Red stalked the head of the Queensberry Athletic Club, a jovial, dapper newspaperman named Charlie Murray. In addition to promoting fights on behalf of the Q.A.C., Murray was sports editor for the *Buffalo Commercial*. Red used to spot Murray en route to the Hotel Iroquois where he conducted business and rendezvoused with out-of-town boxers contracted by his club. Following Murray inside, the scruffy newsboy in ear muffs and squeaky rubber galoshes would draw glares of consternation from lobby attendants, but Murray apparently found him amusing. Buffalo's biggest boxing promoter finally gave Red a break. Murray put Red's boy Clancy on a Q.A.C. card at the Broadway Aud. Clancy got pummeled in a bout that had to be stopped. Murray was not pleased. Red's foray as a boxing manager was temporarily stymied.

Red, through it all, continued to box. He trained in the gym at the Newsboys' Home alongside a tough little teenager named Ed Moran, a newsboy who had moved to Buffalo from Scranton, Pennsylvania. Moran was living with his mother and her new husband in the steel mill section south of the city. Taking his stepdad's name, Moran fought as Jimmy Goodrich. He took up boxing while working a paid apprenticeship at Lackawanna Steel. Only 5'4", Goodrich entered into some Saturday night smokers as a way to make an impression on a ball-busting plant foreman who was making his life hell. During a steel workers' strike, Goodrich boxed to make ends meet and later stuck with it. Red was fighting more regularly, too. He was also involved in running the Newsboys' Gym and organizing local amateur matches. Soon, he started handling Goodrich. Red's brother Luke joined his stable, as well. Things were beginning to fall into place. But then forces well beyond his dominion interrupted.

★★★★★

The assassination in August 1914 of Archduke Franz Ferdinand, heir to the throne of the Austro-Hungarian Empire, set off a cascade of strategic alliances across Europe and Russia. Within a few weeks, Germany had declared war on France and Belgium, causing Great Britain to declare war on Germany. In May of 1915, a German submarine torpedoed the passenger liner *Lusitania* off the coast of Ireland—killing 128 Americans. Two years later, America declared war on Germany. The Army's finger-pointing Uncle Sam poster sent a powerful message to young men everywhere—the fate of the free world depended on them. Red enlisted. He signed up on May 27, 1918, in Room 215 of the Federal Building in downtown Buffalo. Some guys went for adventure. Red joined out of allegiance to his new country.

"My father always said that the thing he was most proud of in his life was his military service," the late Paul Carr, Jr. once recalled.

Most details of Red's fourteen months overseas were not recorded, although over the years he occasionally hinted in newspaper interviews at having been involved in some harrowing situations trucking food and ammunition to the front lines. "He once told a story about how he had to teach himself to drive in the darkness of the Argonne Forrest—after an ambulance driver had been shot," said Red's niece, Judy Beecher. These supply runs were made in the black of night, often under incoming shell fire and the constant threat of poisonous gas. Authoritative histories of the "war to end war" rightly mention the efficiency and bravery of the Transportation Corps.

After the Armistice with Germany was signed on November 11, 1918, more than one million U.S. soldiers remained in Europe on peace footing. Another three million were headed back home. Red, an acting Sergeant, was put in charge of the regimental boxing program at Camp Covington in Marseille, the official embarkation facility for doughboys coming through at a rate of a few thousand per day. During this post-Armistice period, the A.E.F., seeking to buttress morale and keep the soldiers busy, held a series of boxing tournaments at bases throughout France, culminating in a finals event in Paris in April 1919. A U.S. Marine, Gene Tunney of New York City, achieved some notoriety by winning the light heavyweight division. A few weeks later, the A.E.F. staged another boxing show at the lavish seaside Hotel du Palais in Biarritz, France, near the Spanish border. In addition to running the boxing program, instructing fighters and arranging bouts, Red also competed as a featherweight. Many years after the war, *The American Legion Magazine* published a photograph showing Red in the ring in Biarritz. The grainy black-and-white image was snapped May 15, 1919, by an army mechanic named George Boller. Leading with his right and on the prowl, Red appears menacing, if a bit pale, as numerous rows of soldiers cheer him on. His unnamed foe has his back to the camera. It's not known who won. In the shot, the referee, as well as a number of spectators, don wide-brimmed, inverted-bowl helmets, probably to keep the sun off their brows.

Returning to Buffalo that summer, Red resumed fighting and became a fixture at the Newsboys' Gym. He bought his own newsstand on Main and North Division. Charlie Murray came by that newsstand often, especially on Tuesday mornings during the winter boxing season. Red continued to stalk the promoter inside the Iroquois, touting his latest prospect, burly middleweight Johnny Paske. Murray used to snatch up all the papers and retreat to the hotel's shoeshine stand to devour what each sports page had to say about the Q.A.C.'s Monday Night boxing shows at the Broadway Auditorium.

Helping Murray run the club's affairs was another prominent sports editor, the *Courier*'s Billy Kelly, a force of nature all his own. Kelly, a former Western Union messenger boy, was a rabid sportsman who poured his enthusiasm into boosting area golf and bowling and his most beloved pastime—horse racing. A jack of all beats, Kelly was most knowledgeable about baseball after many long seasons traveling with the minor league Bisons. But by 1919 boxing had become by far Buffalo's favorite sport. Together, Kelly and Murray forged a reputation for boxing exhibitions run both honestly and civilly.

The Q.A.C.'s main rival, the Velodrome Athletic Club, put on equally respectable Friday Night Fights at the Broadway Aud. That club was run by two *Buffalo Times* sportswriters, Eddie Tranter and Bob Stedler.

Buffalo's enterprising promoters employed a nifty work-around to the state law banning prizefighting, functioning as private clubs with a few thousand dues-paying members—and authorities never trifled with them.

As the Q.A.C.'s matchmaker, Murray endeavored to show the best-known boxers in the country. He liked to claim that he was the first promoter in the east to properly exploit the mighty Kansas farmer Jess Willard, who would later become champion. Many champions of the day, including Jack Britton, Freddie Welsh, Benny Leonard and Harry Greb, had thrilled fans in Buffalo over the years. "C.J. Murray on Boxing" was a regular column in the *Commercial*. No dedicated fight fan ever missed it. Oozing charisma, ready with a firm handshake in any setting, regardless of whom he was greeting, Murray seemed to know everyone—from the guy at the newsstand to the governor of the state. He knew top-rung boxers and has-beens, singers, producers, famous writers, sports celebrities, politicians, bankers and businessmen. Detroit automobile mogul Henry Ford was a personal friend of Murray's. So was George M. Cohan, whose patriotic songs (such as "Yankee Doodle Dandy") had become national treasures. Murray was not a man of any significant wealth, although he carried himself as if he were. His favorite possession was his shiny diamond ring. Although he was always launching new promotions—marathon bicycle races were among his specialties—many of his events were not profitable. However, even if he took a financial bath, Murray never complained. When he needed a sizable bridge loan to see through one of his productions, he could put the touch on any number of rich pals who gave him what he needed without hesitation or stipulations.

Although Murray had an office at the *Commercial,* he was rarely ever there. He preferred to be out and about, holding forth at the Iroquois. Billy Kelly used to ask Murray why, with so much on his plate, he didn't just rent out some space. "I keep my office in my hat," was Murray's stock reply.

Born in the First Ward, Charles J. Murray attended his first boxing match in 1896. It was held at the Lyceum Theater on Washington Street. The 11-year-old sat captivated as Young Griffo and Jack Everhardt fought 20 rounds to a draw. Murray took home the roar of that crowd in his bone marrow. At age 14, he broke into the newspaper business. At the end of the Spanish-American War, the *Buffalo Enquirer* dispatched the intrepid youth to New York City to cover the hero's welcome for Admiral George Dewey. Murray later landed a position in the sports department. By age 16, he was promoting boxing matches for the paper.

In the summer of 1905, Murray put on an automobile race at the Kenilworth Race Track, the first such event in Buffalo's history. It was designed as a two-day competition. Impressive crowds came the first day to watch nationally known driver Barney Oldfield attempt to set a record for speed. On the second day, a lesser known driver lost control of his machine on a turn, flew over a fence and down a muddy embankment. He was killed. Though not at fault, Murray endured a national backlash. He never forgave himself.

Still, he kept right on promoting. In 1909, Murray got a hold of one of the first-ever fight films—the heavyweight battle in Reno, Nevada, between James J. Jeffries and Jack Johnson—and creatively cut an "exhibition rights" deal, allowing him to show the breathtaking moving pictures in a Buffalo theater.

Murray eventually became sports editor at the *Commercial*. Around 1910, he started promoting boxing matches for the Buffalo Athletic Association, which later merged with the Q.A.C. run by the *Courier's* Kelly.

Continuously looking for new ways of entertaining the public, Murray arranged for his friend Cohan to make appearances on Buffalo stages. It was Murray who helped popularize professional wrestling (when it was a true sport) and helped make stars out of the Zbyszko brothers, Stanislaus and Wladek. Murray took enormous pride in his signature contribution to the entertainment landscape, the wildly popular Six-Day bicycle races. Once, when a famous cyclist, Norman Hill, was injured in a hellacious crash, Murray personally paid for multiple surgeries Hill needed to repair his broken back. Murray never drew attention to his charitable act, but word got around.

That was Murray's way. If a boxer broke his hand or jaw, Murray made sure he got proper care, and also paid the bill. He raised $22,000 for the war-stamps effort, putting on an outdoor boxing show in Lafayette Square. After a tragic dock explosion on the Niagara River, he put on a benefit boxing show to aid the stricken families. He was extraordinary at his job—networking, closing deals, executing contracts, and at the same time always mindful of the need for intriguing, competitive matchups. When

Tex Rickard came east in 1916 to take control of Madison Square Garden, he tried to recruit Murray to be his matchmaker.

But it wasn't until 1918 when Murray's true claim to fame arrived. That was the year he gave a then relatively unknown western slugger his first exposure in the East. Murray had taken a gamble and matched the 23-year-old heavyweight from Manassa, Colorado, against an aging giant named Carl Morris. The bout represented a dramatic steppingstone for that unknown western slugger—Jack Dempsey.

Before a packed Broadway Aud in February of 1918, Dempsey battered Morris. It was, for Dempsey, a significant rung on a rapid climb up the boxing ladder marked by a noteworthy string of exhilarating knockouts, some of them coming only seconds after the opening bell. On July 4, 1919, in Toledo, Ohio, Dempsey annihilated heavyweight champion Jess Willard and took hold of the title. But Dempsey's run had started in Buffalo, and he never forgot the break Murray had given him.

With the crowning of a new champion—a ferocious giant slayer—America's obsession with prizefighting was entering into a new era; indeed, a national romance was budding.

Red's enthusiasm for boxing, meanwhile, was beginning to wane. He'd fallen in with some unscrupulous handlers inclined to put their own financial interests ahead of his development—which is to say, they over-matched him.

In the first half of 1920, Red fought seven times, losing three, winning two by knockout and two by newspaper decisions. Red's final fight was a six-rounder in Niagara Falls for a $30 purse. His foe was a well-traveled Philadelphian named Harry Boyle. For the first few rounds, Red took the fight to Boyle and appeared to be on the verge of winning. But towards the end, he grew tired and wound up taking a beating. The fight was called a draw, but Red knew he had lost by a mile. A foggy week nursing sore ribs gave him time to reflect.

When the wheels in his head finally stopped spinning, Red had some clarity: Prizefighting was too dangerous—for him. He was hanging up the gloves to focus on becoming a manager. He became re-energized. "There is nobody braver than a hungry manager," Red would insist. "Outside the ring you don't get punched."

Jimmy Goodrich now fought regularly in Buffalo under Red's direction. Goodrich had the right mix of skill and dedication. Like Red, he didn't drink or smoke. He had exemplary work habits. In winter, Goodrich, determined to get in six miles of road work every day, fashioned a home-made rubber suit for training.

Red also had high hopes for his middleweight, Paske. With his cauliflower ears and beetling brow, Paske was a pug straight out of central casting. He could also hit like a mule kicked.

With the passage of the Walker Law in 1920, boxing in New York State was, yet again, re-legalized, this time for good. Attendance swelled. The sport was coming into its own. And whenever Murray turned up at his newsstand, Red talked up Paske. Murray agreed to give Red one more chance. Murray put Paske on a Q.A.C. show at the Broadway Auditorium against a hard-punching Western New York favorite, Bobby Sullivan. It was a risk. Sullivan, in the midst of a K.O. rampage, easily could have put Paske's fledgling career in reverse. But Paske made the most of the opportunity, knocking Sullivan out in the second round. In an outdoors rematch at the baseball park one week later, Paske knocked Sullivan out once again. Paske was now a main-bout fighter.

His influence expanding, Red took control of the Newsboys' Gym. He trained side by side with his charges, trading blows and working up a sweat—Red wasn't going to be the kind of manager who chirped out pointers from a folding chair. At age 25, Red had his stable brimming with prospects.

One February afternoon, a skinny Irish kid from the First Ward walked into the gym seeking an evaluation. Red politely looked him over, but didn't see much.

He would.

THREE

PRELIMINARY BOY

O<small>N THE NIGHT OF HIS PROFESSIONAL</small> boxing debut, Jimmy Slattery showed up at the Broadway Auditorium about one hour early. It was the Monday after Thanksgiving, 1921. He was scheduled to go four rounds, the curtain-raiser of a five-bout program beginning at 8:15 P.M. Rested, fit, more than a little excited, the seventeen-year-old approached the side entrance around the corner from the marquee.

Packed into street cars, a large delegation of First Ward boosters was on its way. Buffalo's Queensberry Athletic Club had been staging top-rate boxing programs fairly regularly for more than a decade. Q.A.C. Monday Night Fights had become an enjoyable ritual to kick off the week. Slattery grew up sneaking in with his friends. Now he was on the card.

"Not so fast," said the man at the door, taking one look at the reed-thin, delicate-looking lad. "You're no fighter."

Presuming Slattery to be some sly hustler, the doorkeeper refused to let him in. Such a harsh putdown on what was to be a momentous occasion might have caused another teenager to stressfully plead his case. Slattery just walked away.

It was hardly the first time Slattery had been rebuffed in his effort to become a professional boxer. Two years earlier, in the exhilarating aftermath of his triumph over the bully, Slattery had been corralled by a captivated curbside spectator who took the teen to go meet Red. That onlooker was Ed Manning, a 23-year-old tool-and-die factory worker who lived on Harvey Place in St. Stephen's Parish. And so it was, Red Carr would recall, that Jimmy Slattery showed up at the Newsboys' Gym looking for a tryout with some fifty neighborhood kids trailing behind him.

Usually around this juncture, the typical Jimmy Slattery origin story makes a sharp turn, from avenging the harassed children of St. Stephen's straight into professional boxing. But his journey to the ring was hardly instantaneous.

Red was acquainted with Manning, a clean-cut fellow, active in youth sports, so the manager agreed to take a look at his discovery. Red doled out a few words of encouragement to Slattery and even welcomed the boy to train in his gym. Beyond that, though, Red wasn't about to devote any more of his attention to the fifteen-year-old. Since returning from overseas, Red was busy running Newsboys' Gym and looking after his expanding stable of pro boxers, all while still operating one of the busiest newsstands in the city. The truth: "Red didn't think Slattery had what it took to make it in boxing," recalls Tom Carr, Red's nephew. "He thought he was too scrawny to be a fighter."

Still, once he got his toe in the door, Slattery started showing up at Newsboys' every day. He had always liked the atmosphere of a boxing gym—the musty smell, the hypnotic cacophony of bags being smacked. Right then, local wunderkind Frankie Schoell (pronounced "Shell") was coming into the national lightweight picture. Slattery idolized him and would often be scrounging for the nickel it cost to stand in Bert Finch's gym and watch Schoell spar.

Having ceased his parochial schooling after completion of the seventh grade, Slattery was, to borrow a Horatio Alger line, "shifting for himself." And the world he had entered might well have seemed scary. Disease and death were part of life down in the Ward. Anarchist bombings and lynch mobs were being added to the national lexicon of dread. Then there were all the soldiers coming back from the war, some maimed, passing through Buffalo in droves, catching westbound trains and lake steamers, and carrying with them a new horror: Spanish Influenza. In the fall of 1918, during the height of the epidemic, more than 100 flu deaths were recorded in one single day in Buffalo. The city was quarantined.

Slattery at some point enrolled in Masten Park High School in Buffalo, but it does not appear that he ever finished. By 1919, about one year prior to his famous fight with bully Harp Griffin, Slattery was employed in a shipyard hammering rivets alongside his older brother, John. They liked the work but the pay wasn't great, about twenty cents for a six-hour shift.

One day after work, Slattery met up with Skitsy Fitzgerald and Joe Hickey, who were cooking up an interesting scheme. An enormous amateur boxing tournament was being put on by the Automobile Club of Buffalo. The best part: they were handing out prizes—silver and gold watches which could be pawned for five times what Slattery made in a day as a riveter. Never mind that he was merely a mite, barely 100 pounds; Slattery's friends were certain he could do well.

Despite backyard bouts galore and the forecasts of his father, Slattery still didn't consider himself that strong of a boxer. Although he was an avid boxing fan, he still preferred and excelled in, baseball and football. Reminiscing once about his amateur debut, Slattery claimed he needed to be cajoled into the ring. "Skits and Joe egged me on," he told a newspaper scribe in 1924. "I never wanted to go into the boxing game, but my pals urged me, and I fell for it."

Skitsy would be manager; Joe would serve as trainer, chief second and sparring partner. Not content to peddle the *Evening News*, Skitsy saw the amateur circuit as a promising racket. It was true that amateurs were in some regard placed upon a pedestal compared to paid athletes. But everyone knew those watches could be sold for a buck.

Skitsy was a shrimp. With his smallish skull surmounted with a choppy brush cut, he somewhat resembled a newly hatched chick. He tried to dabble with the gloves, fighting as "Kayo Fitzgerald." But an encounter with a crusher named Joe Korey one night in Niagara Falls, N.Y., convinced Skitsy he was better suited for the corner. Slattery was the talent, Skitsy was convinced. And the Automobile Club tournament was the venue to try him out. But he was far from the only one with that notion. Dozens of boys from all over the city showed up at the Superior Gym on Oak Street for sign-ups. The trio returned to the House of Slattery to cram in some training. It was a few weeks before Christmas, too cold to box outside. So the boys bolted upstairs to the Slattery brothers' room, turned the beds on their sides and removed the dressers. The result was a cozy rumpus area where they could practice.

The Auto Club tournament, billed as "the Amateur Championship of Western New York," served as the entertainment portion of a long evening program. This was one of the country's oldest and largest organizations dedicated to motorists' interests. Total membership exceeded 3,000. The annual gala, held at the Elmwood Music Hall, kicked off with the election of club directors. After voting, attendees and guests settled in for their smoker—two dozen little hellions knocking the crap out of each other for a few hours.

Such shows played partly for laughs, although usually one or two boys emerged as worthy of keeping an eye on. The tournament received the support of the local chapter of the Amateur Athletic Union and the Q.A.C., which provided the ring and the gong, and necessary supervision. Bert Finch, prominent manager, helped run the affair.

One day prior to the event, Slattery, accompanied by his inseparable seconds, had gone down to Finch's gym to weigh in and be examined by a doctor. At 107 pounds, he was definitely among the puniest competitors, but was cleared to compete in the lightest of the five weight classes—flyweight, 112 pounds and under. Each entrant was listed on a sheet by both given name and fighting name. Slattery picked "Bo's'n Slattery," which was the name of a fictitious lake sailor featured in the colorful columns of *Courier* marine editor Walter C. Kelly.

That night, Monday, December 15, 1919, Slattery was matched against a West Side kid, Al Paul. The experience was unforgettable. For the first time, Slattery was inside an actual ring, before a crowd of probably about 1,500 people. Beaming nervously in a borrowed bathrobe, the youngster won the three-round bout by decision. Paul is said to have given him a tough fight. It took everything Slattery had. But that was all for the night; Slattery had injured his hand and did not continue on in the tournament.

Not exactly bitten by the boxing bug, but finding he could do the same thing the other boys did in the ring *only faster*, Slattery stayed with it. He entered more tournaments during the winter of 1920, much to the dismay of his mother. Like all moms, Mary Slattery feared the disfigurements associated with boxing. But when her son returned home from matches without black eyes, she warmed up. Soon enough, Mary was a member of the support team. She stitched him trunks and training tights. She welcomed indoor sparring sessions and gave her son a liniment rub down afterwards.

Around this period, boxing in Buffalo was growing like wild weed (as was Slattery, who added ten pounds to become a bantamweight by the spring). Weekly amateur boxing shows began to be staged by the Parkside Wheeling Club at their hall on Genesee Street in the heart of downtown Buffalo. Also popular were the outdoor boxing cavalcades held at historic Fort Ontario, a few hours away in Oswego, N.Y. Slattery didn't always emerge victorious, but he was acquiring confidence, along with some other experimental nicknames, such as "Young Slattery."

Amateur competitions, trimming the neighborhood bully, gaining entry (albeit barely) into Red Carr's stable—these accomplishments had all positioned Slattery on the path. But without a manager, an aspiring boxer had little hope of breaking in. It took the seedling months to garner even a droplet of Red's attention.

Slattery's first days hanging around the gym were uncomfortable—no one wanted him there. One account, provided in 1923 by the *Courier's* Billy Kelly, paints Slattery as a wallflower. Between Red's stable of pro fighters, out-of-towners and assorted drop-ins, there wasn't much room, not even for one extra little twerp.

"Can I fool around a little bit?" Slattery would ask Red, who couldn't refuse. Told to stay out of the way, Slattery tried to be as inconspicuous as possible. He would shadow box off in a corner, work out with pulley weights or practice on the light and heavy bags. He watched. He mimicked. A shy boy then, he would try to ask questions, which constituted interference and got on Red's nerves. Probably because he didn't feel welcome, Slattery never sparred with anybody, which annoyed the other fighters who razzed him— *"hey kid, why don't you put on the gloves and do some actual fighting!"* Just a boy amongst men—men who made their living dishing out and enduring punishment—Slattery was understandably leery, content merely to mix it up with the punching bag. Even a boy just three years older, like Red's welter-weight prospect, Benny Ross, who was just turning pro after a brief stateside hitch in the Navy, would have seemed like a worldly elder.

Finally, one day, according to Kelly, the other fighters insisted Slattery go a few rounds with somebody, anybody. Whomever he faced (possibly it was Ross) it didn't go well. Embarrassed, Slattery stopped going to News-boys' for a few days. But eventually he returned.

During that summer of '21, Slattery could often still be found outside religiously practicing with his father—Sloak letting loose, neighbors hur-rying over when they heard the cry: *"The Slatterys are at it again!"* By this time, the family was back living in the St. Stephen's section of the Ward, renting No. 589 Fulton, around the corner from the church. Everyone liked Slattery. With his smiling Irish eyes and affable spirit, not to mention his growing fistic reputation, "Slats" came to be the leader of a gang of a dozen or so St. Stephen's boys. Every boy on the block also wanted to box with Slattery. Sloak would call for them, and there was no shortage.

Slattery continued to compete in tournaments sponsored by fraternal orders looking to discover the best boys to represent Western New York in state and national Amateur Athletic Union competitions. Red was involved in choosing and coaching the local A.A.U. squads. But Red barely noticed Slattery's amateur exploits. Sportswriters, scouts, matchmakers—not one of them ever saw anything special in the boy. Some used to sneer at his nonchalant fighting style, arms dangling at his sides. Slattery's approach was dismissed as unsound. *One of these days,* the ring-wise regulars snickered, *that lad is going to get his head knocked off.*

At the gym, Slattery was still being scoffed at. But he kept coming. Week after week, he was there almost every day.

One day, when Benny Ross tried to point out that "the skinny Irish kid was a clever little scrapper," Red tuned out.

Slattery, as far as Red was concerned, just wasn't cut out for the ring. He was too frail, his technique, terrible. Whatever success he had had, Red wrote off as owing to inferior competition.

But down in the Ward it was another story. Slattery was becoming widely admired by both the young and the old. He'd punched out every boy who dared to test him. In the Ward, every block had its own champion. The neighborhood was teeming with toughs. Slattery defeated them all—except one. And as it turned out, these two boys were about to clash.

★★★★★

Arthur "Artie" Colpoys, a popular, wide-framed boy, started coming to the Newsboys' Gym around the same time as Slattery, just another fifteen-year-old looking to get into the game. It didn't take Red long to realize that Colpoys had skill to match his size. Only one out of one hundred promising teenage boys ever made it up from the amateurs to the pros and even then they likely would never graduate beyond maybe appearing in one of the four-round preliminary bouts. Of those, only one in one hundred preliminary boys ever advanced to the level of contender. The way Red saw it, Colpoys, not Slattery, was the one worth developing.

For contests bearing no official records, the Slattery-Colpoys affairs—there were two fights, possibly three—remain legendary in some South Buffalo circles.

Details, locales and circumstances vary, depending on the sources, ranging in this case from tattered newspaper accounts plucked from scrapbooks and Colpoys family stories passed down word of mouth, to neighborhood tales that have taken on lives of their own. The versions differ in large and small ways. Some versions place the most famous of these fights in the summer of 1919, although it seems more likely to have occurred in the summer or fall of 1920. A few things are certain, however: first, that the two were friends; and second, that Colpoys was a formidable battler.

In one of the more colorful (but improbable) versions of the episode, Sloak Slattery takes his 11-year-old warrior to a neighborhood smoker featuring an experienced fighter named Art Colpoys. When the opponent is a no-show, Sloak volunteers his son as an unlikely substitute. Slattery takes a beating but gets hooked on fighting, so this story goes. It's a cute yarn, repeated in some official tributes to Slattery—but also wildly implausible.

Even more dramatic is a version provided in a syndicated newspaper series from 1925. In this enthusiastic narrative, Slattery and Colpoys, both leaders of their own gangs, nurture an unspoken inclination to leave open the question of who was tougher, out of mutual admiration. Eventually, an argument arises and escalates into a vicious brawl in an empty lot on the banks of the Ship Canal.

"*There, surrounded by their partisans, the two pals hopped to it,*" wrote columnist Sid Sutherland. "*They say it was a brutal thing, both lads biting and gouging and kicking and dashing their little knuckles into each other's faces until they were blind and helpless . . . toppling over, they called it a draw.*"

Don Colpoys, Art's nephew, says he never could put his fingers on any precise details. But as he understands the broad strokes, having heard many stories over the years, the bout was arranged by a group of First Ward guys who saw potential in Slattery, but who sensed he was getting too big for his britches and thus required a beating. Plus, the matter of determining the First Ward's toughest kid needed to be settled.

Red, meanwhile, would many years later recall a somewhat different, and yet possibly compatible, set of circumstances leading up to the fight: he personally set it up, wanting to teach Slattery a lesson—and to rid himself of the little pest once and for all.

Said Red: "I tossed him into the ring with a boy named Colpoys. He could hit hard and I figured he would give that fresh punk a couple of shots in the belly and that would be the end of him."

In one of his many other chronicled remembrances, Red has the pair meeting twice, both times in his gym. In several other instances, Red corroborates what appears to be the actual venue: the Larkin Auditorium.

The grandiose theater was located on Seneca Street in the Hydraulics section of Buffalo. It was built by the Larkin Soap Company to show moving pictures showcasing their household products—toiletries, utensils, furniture; you name it—to employees, merchants and ladies clubs from around the country. The company was proud of its comfortable, state-of-the-art facility. Red helped the Larkin Men's Club put on amateur boxing. There's evidence pointing to at least one definitive Slattery-Colpoys showdown happening at the Larkin hall.

In a newspaper interview several years afterwards, Slattery himself refers to his wild fight with Colpoys as having been at "Larkin's place." Also mentioning the Larkin connection is *Buffalo Times* scribe Willis Wilber. In Wilber's telling, the two pals *approached Red* with the idea of him putting them in a preliminary bout in one of his amateur programs. Certainly, it was a match the First Ward Irishmen would want to see. If filling the 750-seat Larkin hall was the goal, Red could do worse.

What was to transpire wasn't child's play. Each boy prepared for the serious business of fighting. In bed early, they were up at dawn for roadwork conducted on coal- and grain-dusted streets. When fight night came, the boys and their gang of mutual friends paraded to the showdown. They would box three, two-minute rounds. Slattery's recollection was that they were both competing as lightweights (135-pound limit) matched in one of several bouts scheduled for that evening.

"Little boys with small gloves tied to their wrists," wrote Sutherland in his 1925 account, "but with fierce, ruthless light burning in their eyes."

Opened just a few years prior, the Larkin Auditorium was part of a sprawling complex of factories and warehouses, but inside it would have seemed quite the plush environment for blood sport. Like a church, it had two long sections of rows, separated by a wide center aisle, which ran from the back of the house to the front center stage where a regulation ring was erected. Sloak, along with a group of friends from the firehouse, sat in the back.

"The moment the fight started," Slats once recalled, "we both let go with left hooks. And I know mine went astray."

His opponent's did not. Colpoys rocked him. A scene of bedlam erupted.

Slattery was sent flying into an impromptu cartwheel and collapsed in a heap as the audience burst into a raucous tizzy that shook the hall. With Sloak bellowing obscenities and Skitsy hollering "get up!" repeatedly, Slattery somehow scrambled to his feet.

"I did get up," Slattery would recall. "Only to have Colpoys nail me again."

Struck in the head by a hard right, Slats twirled into a sort of gymnastic handstand and somersaulted across the canvas. Once again, he rose, only to find Colpoys right on top of him, his powerful right hand primed to knock him silly. *Thwap!* Down again. It's said Artie Colpoys floored Slats five times in that opening round. The last knockdown left him flopping on his belly like a reeled-in trout. But, as luck would have it, the bell saved him.

Skitsy and Joe dragged their pal back to the corner. Slattery later joked that he thought "the Larkin roof had caved in." Desperate to revive their woozy pal, the frantic duo dumped a bucket of cold water on Slats' head. They furiously toweled him off, yelling and slapping him about the face. Skitsy was jumping around so hysterically that he accidentally tumbled out of the ring.

Leaving his corner for round two, Slats regained his senses. The whole predicament infuriated him. "What a riot of punches followed!" he later recalled, describing his boiling-mad, spasmodic explosion of haymakers. In the remaining two rounds, according to multiple accounts of the watershed battle, Slattery proceeded to completely turn the tables. As it turned out, he *could* take a punch and had stamina to spare. His legs were sturdy, his feet nimble from countless backyard mills. In the third and final round, Slattery swarmed and supposedly rendered such a savage attack on Colpoys that the audience fell into stunned silence.

It was a fight Slattery never really wanted. Art Colpoys was his friend. When it was over—when Artie went down to stay—Slats was relieved and exhausted.

Sitting flabbergasted in the audience that night was a young Larkin company tour guide named Roy Stadel, who years later would end up becoming instrumental in Buffalo's Golden Gloves tournaments. Stadel would later describe the bout as "one of the most grueling battles I have ever witnessed."

"Slattery was skinny, but he was willing," Red would say. "And fast as lightning."

The young manager was amazed at how fleet afoot the lanky kid was—Red's eyes could barely follow him. Watching Slattery take everything Colpoys could dish out and come back to win, Red decided maybe he did have himself a future prospect after all.

But there was work to be done. Slattery's hands-dangling-low fighting style needed to be corrected, Red knew that much for sure. Pals kept asking Slattery, when was he going to turn professional? Slats would inquire as to when he could get a real fight. Red assured him he wasn't ready.

When disapproving parents Henry and Delia Colpoys got wind of their son's ring foray, they put an end to it. Slattery's mother, on the other hand, fashioned a green silk robe with an embroidered shamrock on the back. Skitsy remained manager, Hickey worked the corner. Red still was not formally involved as Slattery's handler but was working with him on his technique, and monitoring his progress in the gym.

Professional boxing was by now fully legalized in New York State. The sport exploded with frequent programs at the Broadway Aud—Murray's Q.A.C. putting on its Monday night cards, rival Velodrome A.C. staging shows on Fridays—and amateur boxing tournaments popping up everywhere.

Heading into the holidays, several charity tournaments were organized under the supervision of the Q.A.C. These shows, generating upwards of $5,000 for a variety of worthy causes, were sponsored by the Larkin Men's Club, the Elks Club, the Niagara Association (of the Amateur Athletic Union), the Lockport A.A.U., and the Buffalo Auto Club. Absurdly wiry and still growing, Slattery entered all of these events, competing in the 135-pound division. He won most of them. Two weeks before Christmas, Elks Local No. 23 put on a holiday boxing tournament at the Broadway Aud. Attendance was sparse, only around 1,000 people. By comparison, the pro boxing events usually drew about 5,000. Still, for a 16-year-old kid, the opportunity to perform in that ring was a thrill.

An immense fortress standing in the heart of Buffalo's fast-growing black community, the Aud held a special spot in the hearts of locals. The facade was castle-like, harkening back to its origins as an armory at the time of the Civil War. Major renovations came in 1911, including construction of a window-encircled "monitor" roof. Inside, it was cavernous but cozy, with dazzling incandescent electric light bulbs draped over ceiling truss beams high above rows of wooden chairs. Always lining the top of the house was a constellation of shadowy faces, nervy children, dozens of them, peeking in through the sky lights. Originally, the facility was used for civic gatherings, public hearings, political rallies and assorted conventions. But it was boxing that turned the arena into a hallowed place. Given the opportunity, Slattery showed he was right at home.

During the Elks event, Slattery tore through the field, standing out as the most talented boxer, by far, in any weight class. In the finals, having nothing left to prove, he refused to lay a glove on his opponent, Harry Ryan, a friend. Of course, Ryan wanted no part of Slattery. The referee, Dick Nugent, bewildered, tossed them both out of the ring for stalling.

In the finals of the Niagara District A.A.U. tournament, held two days before Christmas, Slattery floored his opponent in the first round, earning himself a gold medal and a slot on a six-man squad dispatched to New York City to compete in a statewide tournament to take place just after New Year's. The delegation included another St. Stephen's boy who fought for the Orioles club under the alias Billy O'Day. Also making the trip was Stanley Joynt, hailing from the nearby steel town, Lackawanna.

On the night of Sunday, January 2, 1921, the boys gathered in the DL&W passenger terminal at the foot of Elk Street to receive some final instructions from chaperones, including Red Carr, before boarding an overnight train. The New York State Amateur Championships were being staged by the Metropolitan Association of the A.A.U. at the storied Madison Square Garden. It was New York's most beloved spot.

Opened in 1890 and located on Madison Avenue and 26th Street, the Garden was among the most recognizable landmarks in the city. Its majestic tower, adorned with the statue of Diana, Goddess of the Hunt, was a notable feature of the city's ever-expanding skyline. At the time, the stretch of Broadway emptying into Madison Square Park drew society people and degenerates alike—a great place for people watching. For three decades, P.T. Barnum's old barn had been home to circuses—the elephants invaded for a few weeks each year but the smell never left— bicycle races, political rallies, speeches, debates and orchestra concerts— the Garden was not just an auditorium; it was the mirror reflecting the mood and passions of the city. And yet promoter Tex Rickard, who came

East in 1916, had since transformed the Garden into something else alto-gether: the national cathedral of boxing.

For Slattery and his cohorts, the excitement grew more intense as their train chugged toward Albany. The boys peered into the frigid night and imagined the faces of their competition. New York City police and fire departments would be well represented by the best amateurs in their ranks. The New York Athletic Club was a breeding ground for promising prospects. The young black champions of Harlem's St. Christopher Boys Club would be toughest of all.

To pass the time and keep their minds off of hunger pangs—Red had Slats and Billy trying to make 125 pounds—the pals played rummy. Billy blew on his harmonica. He and Slats were friends who played football together. They both cut their hair the same way, like Dempsey, shorn on the sides, thick on top, slicked back with styling cream.

On Monday, January 3, 1921, Slattery stepped into the same vener-ated ring where just two weeks earlier Jack Dempsey had fought. Slats squared off against an older, more experienced bantam, Edmund Riley, a St. Christopher's boy. The crowd of 5,000 might have seemed sparse con-sidering the Garden sat 12,000. However, that 5,000 New Yorkers showed up for the preliminary phase of a marathon two-night tournament (one that ended up spilling over into a third night) was actually quite impres-sive. In prior years, the state finals had been staged at the N.Y.A.C., which could accommodate only around 1,000 people. In a lively contest, Slat-tery lost a close, three-round bout by decision. "Riley had to fight every inch of the way," the *Buffalo Evening News* reported. A Slattery right hook to Riley's mid-section shook him up right before the final bell. Had it gone four rounds, the outcome might have been different, the paper said. All in all, Slattery had done well.

Slattery was making a name for himself. A few names, really. He con-tinued to try out monikers. "Jimmy Slats" was one. All of his friends called him Slats. Many adults knew him as Shamus, an old nickname used by his parents and their friends ever since he was a tyke. "That's our Shamus," older First Ward residents would say when they saw Slattery's name in print.

After his New York appearance, Slattery took one month off from the amateur circuit to heal an injured hand. He then promptly won a Q.A.C. charity boxing tournament held in February of 1921 to raise money for the starving children of Europe. Later that spring, Slattery was among those chosen to represent the region in the A.A.U. national tournament held in Boston. Curiously, his parents forbade him from attending. Supposedly, his father didn't relish the idea of the young boy roaming freely in such a large town as Boston, according to published recollections of a local amateur who did make the trip. (Some early fable-tellers describe Slats as a model boy who did not drink or smoke or curse—although a boy from the Ward surely would have found his share of mischief by age sixteen, whether loitering on Elk Street or under the Jack Knife Bridge.)

Regardless, Red no longer could ignore the possibility he had something special, and so he set about the task of altering the boy's lackadaisical technique. Recalling an icon of yesteryear, Red tried an idea. Dressed in fighting togs, Red got in the ring and showed Slattery the upright stance used by Gentleman Jim Corbett, the first gloved champion.

"Look here," Red instructed his pupil, striking a pose: Left arm, straight out, lead weapon; right arm, cocked, held close to the chest; back, arched; shoulders, squared—totally opposite from the typical boxer's hunching crouch. Slattery took to the throwback approach. Red, reluctant to tinker too much with Slattery's natural, effortless form, allowed the boy to experiment. Slats would continue to develop a unique style all his own.

That summer of '21, Slattery turned seventeen. He would ask Red when he might get a real professional fight. Red said not yet.

For one thing, a fighter had to be eighteen to get a boxing license in New York State. But Slattery's age was not the reason Red had balked. He could have contravened that rule.

Professional boxing was an exceptionally difficult way to make a living. Red, having recently hung up his gloves, knew firsthand how dangerous a boxer's lot could be—both physically and psychologically. You had to be a little crazy to do it. At that moment in time, Slattery probably could not have picked a more competitive profession. An estimated 100,000 pro fighters were earning a living with their fists in the U.S. at the start of the 1920s, more than at any other period. Buffalo alone was home to at least 100 licensed boxers.

Only a decade earlier, prizefighting had been frowned upon by a large, Puritan-minded portion of the general public who saw it as barbaric, lowly and deservedly outlawed. Now, even as Prohibition took effect, banning the sale of alcohol, boxing was spreading everywhere (as was drinking, for that matter). Every city was churning out contenders and a crop of amateurs moving up behind them. New York City was becoming the center of the boxing universe and sought to monopolize the sport. San Francisco remained the sport's Western headquarters. Chicago was the Midwestern boxing capitol. In cities large and small, gymnasiums and fight clubs were ubiquitous. Not unlike houses of worship, each part of town had at least one, and attendance spiked weekly. Boxing flourished in Baltimore and Boston, Milwaukee and Minneapolis, Philadelphia and Pittsburgh, New Orleans and St. Louis. Scranton, Pennsylvania, due to its proximity to New York, was a major fight town. In Western New York, ring action was abundant in Jamestown, Olean, Elmira, Lockport, Niagara Falls and Rochester, as well as in nearby Fort Erie, Ontario and Erie, Pa.

Young boys on every street in every town wanted to be prizefighters, and most every prizefighter wanted to be champion—or at least considered a contender. Some accepted their station as journeymen, taking what purses they could, fighting whomever, fighting often; others were being groomed, matched selectively with a singular purpose by managers believing that the only things standing between their fighter and Jack Dempsey's title were a few lucky breaks.

Impossible odds confronted any teen hopeful in 1921. James Slattery had a better chance of being elected to Congress than of ever being mentioned in the same breath as Dempsey, whose knockout victory that summer over Frenchman Georges Carpentier captivated people all over the world.

Not only was it the first sporting event to be broadcast by radio, it was one of the first major broadcasts, period. Sports in modern society would never be the same. Dempsey-Carpentier drew more than 90,000 spectators, making it at the time the most heavily attended athletic event ever staged. The fans packed into Boyle's 30 Acres, a bowl-shaped arena, built entirely of wood, in Jersey City, N.J. To lure such a fervent throng—and generate such unprecedented gate receipts—the fight had needed mass appeal. To stoke that, promoter Tex Rickard had needed both a hero and a villain. His hero was "Gorgeous Georges," the debonair world's light heavyweight champion seeking to wrest the world's heavyweight championship from the villainous Dempsey, a scowling, bearded menace with murder in his right hand.

Rickard's ensuing "Million-Dollar Gate" had punctuated, emphatically, the start of what would come to be called the "Golden Era of Sports."

And no sooner had attendees tucked away their 15-cent souvenir programs than followed the tidal wave of speculation over who might lift Dempsey's crown.

The mauler was not exactly a popular champion. Dempsey had been cast as a savage brute and, on top of that, a wartime slacker. By the end of the summer of '21, Dempsey had run out of worthy challengers, save for the awesome black heavyweight Harry Wills. Sadly, Wills was denied his shot by a boxing establishment disinclined to alienate white fans.

Rumors of a Dempsey–Jess Willard return match surfaced. Willard, despite previously having been beaten to within an inch of his life by Dempsey, and retired, nevertheless was seen as the best possible challenger. However, the proposed rematch never materialized.

Outside the now distinctly uninteresting heavyweight division— Dempsey would not defend his title again for two more years—boxing storylines were more compelling, the level of competition, in every division, unprecedented.

Among the light heavyweights, Carpentier still held the public's adoration—and the world title in that division.

The middleweights of the era were extraordinary—the best being a walking fury named Harry Greb, the "Pittsburgh Windmill."

Irish-Americans still ruled in the ring, mainly in the smaller divisions. Featherweight champion Johnny Kilbane and welterweight champion Jack Britton were both of authentic Irish stock. But as the '20s began, both were approaching the end of their careers.

Indeed, it appeared the Irish stronghold on boxing was waning, while Italian and Jewish fighters were ascendant. Gone were the mythic Irish icons. John L. Sullivan had died in 1918. He'd spent the final years of his life as a teetotaler promoting the Dry Movement. Dempsey liked to claim some Irish roots on his father's side, but he wasn't viewed as Irish.

Meanwhile, perhaps as many as 1,000 Jewish and Italian boxers were plying their craft in New York in 1921. Arguably the best boxer of the era, lightweight champion Benny Leonard, was a product of a Jewish tenement slum.

One Irish sports writer lamented that for roughly every 100 fighters he observed in local clubs in 1921, only around one-quarter were Irish boys, the rest were Jewish and Italian. Crowds filled neighborhood boxing clubs for the specific purpose of cheering on a fellow countryman. Matches were deliberately set along ethnic lines: Italian versus Irish, Irish versus Jewish, Jewish versus Italian, all lucrative equations. "Hebrews and Italians may crowd the Irish off the map," wrote referee and ex-fighter Jack Skelly in the May 7, 1921 issue of the weekly *Boxing Blade*.

Among the top Italian fighters in the country was Buffalo lightweight Rocky Kansas, considered a logical challenger to Leonard. Born Rocco Tozzo, Kansas was short (5'2") but stocky. Newspapermen tried to christen him "Little Hercules" but the sobriquet never really quite stuck.

Kansas got his first taste of boxing just as Red Carr had—as a newsboy hanging around Allie Smith's gym. Toiling locally during the no-decision/club membership era, Kansas burst onto the national scene in the winter of 1921 with a first-round knockout of Milwaukee's best, Richie Mitchell. Kansas was a clean-living family man who only really strove for recognition in his hometown. Along with international notoriety in the lightweight ranks came fatter purses, which rose from $1,500 to $15,000 as he moved to the front of the line. He got his crack at Leonard's lightweight championship in the summer of '21. But it was not to be. "Fighters like Leonard come once in a lifetime," Kansas used to say. "But why did he have to come along in mine?"

Kansas was perhaps Buffalo's most famous fighter during pugilism's coming-out period, but there were several others who were nationally known. Among them: Jimmy Duffy, the "Duke of Lockport," a veteran lightweight and welterweight from the nearby Erie Canal town of Lockport, N.Y., whose epic battles with the likes of Packy McFarland and Freddy Welsh were engraved into ring lore. Willie "K.O." Brennan (not to be confused with New York City heavyweight Bill Brennan) gained publicity for the hectic pace at which he performed. He once fought six times in eight days, including two tilts with the Pittsburgh Windmill. When he did pause from the ring it was to go fight on the front lines in France.

The most exciting young prospect in Buffalo was Frankie Schoell, a twenty-year-old German-American lightweight from Buffalo's East Side. Schoell was known for his crafty defense and a punishing left jab to the stomach. Outside the ring, he dressed in fancy three-piece suits and donned fedoras with colorful bands. He drove a fast automobile and carried a thick roll of bills earned by betting his end of the purse on himself.

Slattery attended many of Schoell's important victories on the way up. Slats would push his way to ringside so he could study his idol's footwork and then go home to try to emulate his style. In the summer of 1921, Schoell fought Kansas, who took a 12-round decision and extinguished some simmering questions in Buffalo about youth versus experience, science versus brawn (and German versus Italian).

Though relatively new on the scene, Red Carr was rising fast. His middleweight, Johnny Paske, was becoming a regular headliner at the outdoor fights held at the Buffalo baseball park. Red's lightweight, Jimmy Goodrich, had cemented his rise, knocking out veteran Herman Smith. But Red was enjoying success on other fronts, as well. His newsstand on Main and South Division was the busiest in Buffalo. So was his gym. His stable of boxers was growing—Nate Lewis and Bud Ridley had defected from Allie Smith and signed with Red, joining Paske and Goodrich and Red's brother Luke. To top it all off, Red was newly engaged to his childhood sweetheart, Margaret Nagle, who lived around the corner from his newsstand. Red had known her since she was in pigtails. It was a good time to be Red Carr. As summer wound down, Red was in talks with Murray to arrange a match between Paske and K.O. Brennan, likely to produce a big payday.

Of all the men behind Buffalo's boxing scenes, Murray was the singular driving force, always looking to amplify the city's reputation as a fight town. He'd lobbied aggressively, but ultimately unsuccessfully, to have Buffalo host the December 1920 fight between Bill Brennan and Dempsey. Murray was in the catbird's seat when boxing was legalized in New York State with the passage in April 1920 of the Walker Law. The bill's champion, flamboyant state senator Jimmy Walker, believed an independent regulatory troika could take measures to reduce, if not eliminate, match fixing. The newly formed New York Boxing Commission, chaired by elderly physical fitness aficionado Billy Muldoon, handed out about thirty licenses to club promoters. One of the first ones went to Murray. Within hours of the law taking effect on September 1, 1920, Murray was on a train home, his suitcase stuffed with stacks of applications for boxers, managers, trainers, seconds, timekeepers, referees, judges and physicians. His weekly cards kept drawing more impressive crowds. Murray's vision of Buffalo as an internationally recognized boxing bastion was coming true. Between September 1920 and September 1921, Kansas rose to become the top lightweight challenger while Schoell entered the national conversation. Total attendance figures in Buffalo surpassed one half million. But then, what should have been a time for Buffalo's boxing community to celebrate was shockingly interrupted.

On the morning of September 8, 1921, Allie Smith—fight manager known to thousands, founding father of the local game, and mentor to Red Carr—killed himself. Said to be despondent over a falling out with K.O. Brennan, the 46-year-old had put a .32 caliber revolver to his head and squeezed the trigger. His landlady found him slumped on his bed, still breathing. An hour later, Smith was dead.

It is believed Smith was beset by some consequential, but not insurmountable, financial woes, about which he occasionally groused. He was losing his fighters to Finch and Carr. A sibling of Smith's would relay to city detectives that the deceased had been sulking over Brennan's decision to cut ties. What might have seemed like just a business decision to some was, to Smith, a mortal blow. The fight game was taking off and leaving him behind. His entire life's passion had turned against him.

As Smith was being carried out to a waiting ambulance, a messenger boy showed up with a telegram. It was from a Wilkes-Barre, Pennsylvania promoter offering Smith a match.

★★★★★

Slattery, around this time, was starting to feel like maybe the amateur circuit was the right place for him. He felt at home with the pure athletes. He enjoyed the status he'd earned there. But his friends kept prodding him. Soon enough, so would Red.

In the autumn of 1921, Johnny Paske walked into the Newsboys' Gym feeling worn out. He'd just lost a bruising fight. "I don't feel so good today," Paske told Red. "I think I'll spar with that skinny kid."

He motioned toward Slattery, who sprang up, ready to go, unfazed by the extra weight advantage Paske had in his shoulders, neck and arms. At first Red didn't notice what was going on in the ring. When he eventually did glance over, the sight astonished him: Slattery was dominating his star middleweight. Lithe, fluid, darting gracefully, Slats fired off punches from all angles and could not be touched. Finally, Paske waved him off, flustered.

"That kid is the funniest thing I was ever up against," Paske huffed to Red.

Red told him to hit the showers. Then he turned to Slattery.

"Hey Slats," Red said. "If you want, I'll get you that license."

★★★★★

Slattery was turning pro. That night, Red went over to the Slattery home to confer with Sloak and seek his consent to be manager of record, empowered to engage promoters. The next day, Sloak came to Newsboys' Gym to sign papers giving Red control of his son's boxing affairs. Skitsy stepped aside as manager, but he would stay in the fold as trainer. Slats insisted. Joe Hickey would also be one of his seconds. Slattery never signed anything. The arrangement he made with Red was cemented with a handshake.

Within a few days, Red helped Slats get a license. No one asked to see proof of Slattery's age. He wrote down he was born in 1903 (instead of 1904), paid the $5 application fee, and the license was issued October 25, 1921.

Red got Charlie Murray to agree to insert Slats on an upcoming Q.A.C. boxing program in one of the four-round preliminaries. His debut was set for November 28, the Monday after Thanksgiving. He would perform at the Aud in the curtain-raiser on a program headlined by Frankie Schoell.

Although Red touted his boy to Murray using a variety of superlatives, the veteran promoter was ambivalent. To Murray, Slattery was merely "Red's skinny Irish boy." When they met, Slattery told the promoter that he wanted to use the fighting name "Jimmy Slats." Murray told him he thought Jimmy Slattery was a perfectly good fighting name and to stick with it.

Murray matched Slats against the second greenest local kid he could find, a featherweight named Jack Casey, who was being groomed by Lockport Jimmy Duffy. Retired from the ring at age 32, Duffy was in a transitional phase. Less than a decade earlier, he had been the region's top ring attraction. But a serious auto accident had stolen his foot speed and the war had stolen years, and by the start of the new decade he was settling into a second career as a Niagara County sheriff's deputy. In his final fight, Duffy (not to be confused with "Oakland Jimmy Duffy") was knocked out in the first round by Kansas. Still, Duffy kept his fingers in the game as a manager, and when Murray proposed Duffy's protégé be matched against Red Carr's skinny Irish kid, Duffy accepted on the spot.

Thanksgiving came and Buffalo feasted on boxing. Around 7,000 people filled the Aud for a special Thursday Night program featuring former light heavyweight champion Battling Levinsky versus journeyman Captain Bob Roper, a strange character who wore black trunks adorned with a skull and crossbones, and who was known to climb into the ring with a live snake around his neck.

The following Monday, Slattery went to the gym about 11:00 A.M. Wearing shorts over tights and a dark, sleeveless undershirt, Slats took in a light work-out—jump rope, belly bends, some shadow boxing. At 2:30 P.M., he went over to the Aud to be examined by a Boxing Commission-appointed physician, Dr. Louis Kaiser, and to weigh in. He was 132 pounds. So willowy he was during this stage of boyhood, Slattery would later quip that he must have resembled "a tall jockey."

Red told Slats to be at the building by 7:00 P.M., about an hour before the opening gong, and to use the fighters' entrance around the corner from the main doors.

Slattery got there on time. He carried a small travel bag packed with a green robe, homemade green, shamrock-adorned trunks, wine-red gloves and a well-worn pair of borrowed Everlast boxing shoes. But when the man at the door told him to scram, Slats moved along, unconcerned. He knew another way in.

Slats fastened his bag across his shoulder and hopped the six-foot wrought-iron fence that surrounded the property. Then he scurried across a lawn toward a set of four enormous stone pillars that fortified the side of the building. The pillars' terraced design made them ideal for scaling. They led right up to the edge of a steeply slanted roof that could be traversed so long as it was not too icy. At the very top there was a separate, flat section of the roof—and a ring of double windows, any one of which could be pried open. From there, it was a short climb across a ceiling beam connecting to the balcony. As he shimmied across, Slattery could have snuck a glimpse down at the ring, some 50 feet below. Once he made it from the rafters to the balcony area he was home free. Finally, he made his way back to the dressing room area.

The building had begun to fill up. Smoke clouds were beginning to form, despite a ban Charlie Murray was aggressively trying to enforce. After Slattery was introduced, cheers from a large First Ward contingent echoed throughout the Aud. A lopsided contest ensued. Slattery's quick-ness and long-range left allowed him to be the aggressor. Duffy's boy Casey spent much of the fight ducking and covering. According to the *Courier*'s Billy Kelly, who gave the scrap a few summary lines in the following day's morning paper, Slattery won "every minute of every round." More than 3,000 people witnessed it.

Afterwards, Red handed the boy his end, two $20 bills—the equivalent of $120 today—the most cash he'd ever held.

Slattery broke into an elated grin, reveling in his newfound racket: "Forty beans! Ha! This boxing game is soft!"

The crowded trolley zipped down Broadway toward Exchange Street. By Slattery's side were his best pals, his brothers, and the rest of his gang. He couldn't wait to get another fight. The whole evening had been a blast, a blur—he barely had time to take it all in.

His ride had only just begun.

FOUR

UNBEATABLE

SLATS WON HIS NEXT PROFESSIONAL FIGHT, and the next one, and the next one after that. He even knocked out a couple of boys. Local ring connoisseurs dismissed them as pushovers.

Prominent among Slattery skeptics was, in fact, promoter Charlie Murray. A dim view by such an influential force would have dashed the hopes of any youngster trying to break into the game. Yet Murray continued to put the seventeen-year-old First Ward boy on his boxing programs—purely to attract the Irish.

The matchmaker fancied himself able to spot a coming champion. Not only did Murray claim to have discovered Jack Dempsey, he also took credit for putting Jess Willard on the map.

After one of Slattery's early fights, Murray pulled manager Red Carr aside in the dressing room in the basement of the Broadway Auditorium. "Red, I have always respected your judgment—until now," Murray said. "That Slattery boy will *never make it* as a fighter."

Slats, meanwhile, enjoyed a prominent booster in Billy Kelly, the Irish-American sports editor at the *Courier*. In December of 1921, the paper called Slattery "the best prospect to debut in a local ring since Frank Erne." The Swiss-born, Buffalo-reared Erne was lightweight champion for a brief period at the turn of the century. He'd since faded into obscurity.

Slattery was given a chance to ring in 1922 with a bang. Murray matched him in the curtain-raiser of a nearly sold-out matinee January 1. Boxing on New Year's Day was becoming a Buffalo tradition with several memorable bouts showcasing local rivalries in recent years. For this latest installment, Murray crafted a main event that played on contrasts: veteran warhorse K.O. Brennan versus agile colt Frankie Schoell. Conceding 14 pounds in a catch-weight affair, brash Schoell wasn't waiting to have the torch passed to him; he was taking it. Brennan, 34, in likely his final appearance, wanted one last taste of glory.

A record crowd was expected—more than 6,000 fans bought tickets in advance at Snyder's, a Main Street cigar store that doubled as a ticket depot. Work crews erected new bleacher sections in the rear of the house. On the day of the event, floor seats were packed with political and business leaders, fifty rows of white males in suits and ties, hats resting on their knees, some of the men undoubtedly feeling the effects of the night before. This was no back room smoker. Literally. The club had just kicked off a vigorous "No Smoking" campaign with support of the fire department. Spectators in the upper sections refused to comply, producing a high, hazy cloud dome splendidly fractured by winter sunbeams coming in through the skylight windows.

Just prior to the start of the main bout, the crowd spotted a trim, middle-aged gentleman stepping into the ring. Despite his gray hair, he was recognizable to many. It was Frank Erne. When Billy Kelly, acting as ring announcer, bellowed the ex-fighter's name, fans rose in an extended ovation. The 46-year-old Erne was on hand to commemorate becoming Buffalo's first boxing champion nearly a quarter-century earlier. Erne had made a clean break from the sport, landed a cushy job on Wall Street and never looked back. Though he considered the scientific boxing of his era a dying craft, Erne had told Kelly that he was looking forward to seeing Schoell, known for sharp defensive techniques.

The New Year's Day boxing show was one to remember. In the wind-up, a wiry featherweight, Joey Joynt, drew howls with his feisty stand against Benny Ross. In the finale, Schoell dominated the bigger, slower Brennan.

As for Slattery's four-round opener, it largely went unnoticed.

Slats won easily—too easily. Opponent Joe Morey, disadvantaged in all possible ways, particularly in height and reach, could not lay a glove on Slats, whose peculiar style and at times half-hearted effort made for a lame contest.

Still, so long as Slattery kept winning fights—strictly four-round affairs—his large group of friends and neighborhood admirers would come out to shout his praises as though he were a world champion. And Murray would keep putting him in the ring.

Ever the clever matchmaker, Murray was clearly attempting to spark a rivalry between Slattery and a Cheektowaga greenhorn, Tommy Sayers.

Slattery and Sayers met three times in nine weeks. Slattery prevailed each time, winning every round, unleashing a level of punishment on Sayers that would have made an ordinary boy wither. It wasn't until after the third Sayers bout, when Slats demonstrated total superiority, did Murray decide that Red's skinny Irish kid could move up the line.

Red was grooming his prodigy carefully. Left to his own inclinations, Slats would have fought three times a week—for the money. Red had him going once or twice a month. The manager deliberately avoided overmatching his budding prospect, stoking the newcomer's confidence while at the same time avoiding any scenario in which a more seasoned pro might hand him a humiliating defeat. Slats gladly took any fights arranged for him, trusting Red's inclination to proceed gradually, although the impatient teenager often would nag his manager to hunt bigger game.

"Take it easy, Jimmy," Red would say. "Knock off the punks first. Get the experience."

Among Slattery's early adversaries other than Sayers that spring of '22 was Carl Dietz of Jamestown. Slattery was still gangly, but he was gaining weight. He may not have looked imposing but, as Dietz soon learned, he hit hard. In the first round, Slattery knocked Dietz senseless. When the bell clanged to start the second round, Dietz's manager, Tommy Moore, flung a crimson-soaked towel into the center of the ring.

Those who regularly attended the Q.A.C. shows couldn't help but notice how Slattery kept improving with each outing. At the Newsboys' Gym, Slattery made a point to spar with heavier, stronger, older fighters, including some of the black boxers who had come to Buffalo from the south. Red let whomever train in his gym, whether a black migrant or some washed-up palooka looking for a break. Increasingly, his gym teemed with a new constituency: little First Ward boys come to watch their neighborhood hero, Slats.

On fight night, Slats slicked back his dark brown hair with styling cream so that it gleamed under the lights. When he trained, Slattery's wavy mop was thick and unkempt. He wore sparkling emerald-green trunks, a nod to his Irish roots. He didn't yet own boxing shoes. He still wore a pair borrowed from his pal, Billy O'Day, who had quit the game to join up with a grain elevator crew. Since Slattery was earning decent cash, he offered to purchase the good-luck shoes—he hadn't lost a fight while wearing them.

"How much do you want?" Slattery inquired.

His friend hesitated for a moment and finally said, "gimme ten bucks."

Slats completed the transaction without a second thought. It was the seller who had remorse.

As the spring of '22 became the summer, Slattery was fighting twice a month, roughly every other week—which was all that Red would allow. Talk of creampuff opponents didn't bother the manager, who knew it was better to endure cries of "set-ups" than to rush his boy along. But Red had reached the point where he needed to get a proper sense of what the kid had in him, and what Red had in the kid.

Thus far, Red's plan had been to only let Slats box opponents of equal experience, and to never go more than four rounds. It was time to step up.

With Sloak's consent, Red sought out a six-round bout versus a more seasoned opponent: tenacious Joey Joynt. Murray loved it—Joynt, the favorite son of the steel mill district, against Slattery, the favorite son of the flour mill district—a surefire way to pack the Aud.

No one would have ever used the term "pushover" to describe Joynt. Born in Scranton, Pennsylvania, Joynt was a toddler when his family moved, along with practically everyone else in Scranton, to the Buffalo area around the time Lackawanna Steel did. The lakeside community south of the city instantaneously became a blast furnace of boxing talent. Rival athletic clubs staged weekly smokers. Joynt's older brother, Jack, fought regularly and became a boxing instructor in the Navy. Another brother, Stanley, had forged a reputation as a local amateur, traveling with Slats and the rest of the A.A.U. contingent to Madison Square Garden in 1921. Of all the Joynt brothers, though, it was Joey who was making the most noise. He'd become known around Western New York following a memorable bout at the Aud against a rival featherweight from Lackawanna.

The affair had been arranged by a committee of steelworkers who came to Murray asking for his help putting a controversy to rest. It seemed that around the different sections of the plant there were two groups: those who supported Joynt and those who supported Joynt's arch enemy, Joey Eagan (not to be confused with the Boston-based fighter Joe Eagan). Tensions were building as rival factions taunted one another from week to week. The fighters themselves kept trading victories in men's club smokers, with neither youth emerging as superior. The matter had to be settled once and for all. Murray obliged. To his delight, the Joynt-Eagan grudge match drew a mob of steel workers. Ironically enough, nothing got settled; the six-round bout ended in a draw. Fans, however, generally seemed won over by Joynt's fighting spirit, and he was invited to join the Bert Finch stable which included Schoell.

Joynt was soon sparring with Schoell and appearing regularly at the Aud. In the spring of 1921, Joynt was part of an entourage that traveled to the Angler's Club in Grand Island, N.Y., where Schoell set up his training camp to prepare for a championship bout with Benny Leonard. The excitement already surrounding Schoell's training camp intensified when Joynt, while out for a stroll one morning prior to a sparring session, stumbled on the bloated corpse of a suspected bootlegger washed up on the banks of the Niagara River. Local lawmen descended and questioned everybody in the camp for hours, causing a local stir. In the end, the Schoell-Leonard fight never came off—the champion pulled up lame with a hurt thumb and refused to reschedule.

What Joynt stumbled upon when he got into the ring with Slattery was no corpse—it was a very live human form. Few had expected Joynt to have much difficulty handing Slats his first loss. But in two consecutive bouts fought over the course of a few weeks, Slattery twice defeated the Lackawanna boy.

Their rematch was particularly lopsided. With a straight, accurate jab that he never stopped firing, Slattery punished Joynt for five brutal rounds. In the sixth, he caught Joynt with a right cross to the chin—landing the blow in a perfect spot, or, in boxing vernacular, *right on the button*. Joynt toppled to the canvas. At the count of eight, he got to his knees, then struggled to his feet, barely able to stand upright. During the fight's last remaining minute, something curious happened: Slats, seeing that Joynt was delirious, moved in close and forced a steadying clinch; he was holding the helpless boy up, and did so for the remainder of the fight, occasionally throwing harmless punches in his vicinity, careful not to connect.

The crowd saw what was happening. Murmurs of dismay morphed into appreciative applause. For the first time anyone could recall, a fighter was actually cheered for refusing to go for the kill.

Slattery won over a new batch of admirers that night and kept his record (13-0-0) unblemished, gaining some elevation in the local game, moving up from preliminary boy into a "semi wind-up" attraction, which connoted a boxer of some promise. It meant more attention, more publicity; and it meant a slot on a special summertime boxing program that July which was how Slats came to be featured on the undercard of one of the strangest heavyweight title fights in boxing history.

★★★★★

That spring, Jimmy Slattery's young life was unfolding like some splendid Irish fairy tale. Around the same time, Jack Dempsey was living an unbelievable male fantasy.

In early April 1922, the heavyweight champion booked passage on the Aquitania, a luxury liner bound for Europe. A flock of gushing New York City showgirls gathered at the pier to bid him bon voyage. More pretty females awaited him on deck, including songstress Alma Gluck and the feather-adorned Broadway dancers, the Dolly Sisters. Famed movie director D.W. Griffith was also on board. He hosted the champ in his plush cabin—brandy, cigars and worldly conversation—a long way from Dempsey's transient young adulthood hopping freight trains and scrapping in mining town saloons.

Dempsey had to be pinching himself. As Roger Kahn explains in his biography, *A Flame of Pure Fire*, Dempsey was young, handsome and world heavyweight champion—anything he wanted was his for the taking. In Paris, Dempsey went out for long strolls on the boulevards to marvel at beauty and to be marveled at. He traveled all over Europe. He visited Buckingham Palace, sipped tea with Dukes and Earls. He went to the most famous art galleries, stayed in the finest hotels, ate the most sumptuous meals, and sampled the best wine and cigars. He experienced things he never would have imagined. He did it all, anything and everything—everything, that is, except step into a ring and defend his title.

It's not that Dempsey didn't want to fight; greed, politics, and circumstances beyond his control were making the staging of his next bout near impossible. Boxing at that time was suffering from a dearth of heavyweight contenders other than Harry Wills, who was being denied a shot at the title. Dempsey always maintained he wanted to fight Wills, but pointed to the fact that neither his manager, Jack "Doc" Kearns, nor promoter Tex Rickard, believed the public would support a contest that put the heavyweight title in jeopardy of going to a black man. Publicly,

Rickard insisted he wanted to stage Dempsey-Wills but then never followed up, blaming Kearns for asking for too much money, and blaming the New York Boxing Commission for over-regulating the price of tickets. Chairman Billy Muldoon stuck by his claim to be saving the sport from cancerous greed. Years later, Muldoon, sensitive to lingering accusations he had concocted the ticket-price clampdown, would cryptically allude to larger political forces calling shots.

And so it was that the search for someone to challenge Dempsey, viewed as unbeatable, continued on, with no end in sight, much to the dismay of impatient fans hungry for a title fight. This should have been New York's time to shine—the sun at the center of the boxing universe at the dawn of the golden age. The Big Town had its enormous population, more than a dozen daily newspapers, hundreds of top fighters pouring in from all corners of the map and the world's most prestigious arena. Moreover, New York's fight game had solid structural and political underpinnings provided by the newly formed Boxing Commission.

The Anti-Saloon League could not be stopped but anti-boxing forces had been quelled. Rickard had devised a clever pamphlet campaign aimed at cementing the sport's legitimacy in the eyes of Albany lawmakers at a time when the newborn Walker Law was coming under attack. Enlisted in this lobbying push was a young sportswriter named Nat Fleischer, who seized the project as a springboard to launching, in February 1922, *The Ring Magazine*. Fleischer ran the magazine from an office in the Garden that he shared with Rickard's head of publicity, Ike Dorgan. Rickard himself—"Creator of Champions"—was featured on the cover of the debut issue (20 cents).

But all was not well. Boxing had major problems.

In early 1922, Rickard was arrested on charges he had sex with underage girls. Friends rallied to his side and the world-famous sports promoter vehemently proclaimed he was the victim of a shakedown. While he was ultimately found not guilty, Rickard was emotionally spent and quietly ceded control of the Garden to circus showman John Ringling.

Meanwhile, an unsavory odor (beyond circus elephant dung) hung over the Garden: Rickard's ticket master, Mike Jacobs, operating out of the Hotel Normandie on 38th & Broadway, was pioneering the practice of "scalping." Legions of "flim-flam" artists soon got in on the action and negative publicity piled up. Fans were paying ever-more exorbitant admission fees, even as Muldoon railed against piggish monetization.

To make matters worse, the Commission itself was under attack for a range of alleged improprieties, which forced the fledgling entity to disband and reconstitute under a new umbrella, the New York Athletic Commission (although the sport's ruling body would still be known as the Boxing Commission). Meanwhile, the Boxing Commission's policy of not recognizing titles won outside the state incensed boxing supervisors in the 17 states that had created boxing commissions in the likeness of New York's, and together comprised the National Boxing Association (which the New York Boxing Commission refused to join).

Muldoon had it right—boxing was no longer a sport. It was a business. Fans lamented the influence of money and pined for the old days when fighters met for sheer pride and glory—forgetting, perhaps, the rampant match-fixing at the start of the century.

But even if the public could forgive corruption and commercialism, one thing it simply could not tolerate was an idle heavyweight champion gallivanting around Paris.

Dempsey's manager, Doc Kearns, knew boxing was a business and could see that business was imperiled. He had to show the public that Dempsey's traipse across Europe had not made him soft. Kearns knew just the right person to enlist in his campaign to rehab the champ's public image: Charlie Murray.

When Kearns came knocking, the Buffalo promoter was, indeed, more than happy to arrange a special exhibition show at the Broadway Auditorium. It was set for July 24, 1922. To stir public curiosity, Murray announced Dempsey would battle two local boxers, each for a few rounds, but would not reveal who those fighters would be.

He then set out to find the best big men available—no easy task, as Buffalo, for whatever reason, possessed a shocking paucity of decent heavyweights. Kearns was busy lining up other exhibitions around the East Coast and purported to be in talks with numerous parties for the arranging of a hectic schedule of title defenses, which helped sate the public temporarily. Murray had spent years trying to get Dempsey to defend his title in Buffalo. At least the champ was coming to town, even if the fight didn't mean anything.

Murray secured the finest possible lodging for Dempsey and his entourage at the Hotel Iroquois. On the afternoon of the match, Dempsey invited Murray, Billy Kelly and some other friends to his suite for an informal reception. When the Buffalo scribes arrived, Dempsey was sprawled out on a massage table getting a rubdown from his trainer/man-servant, "Jerry the Greek." Dempsey's hands were soaking in a pail filled with a broth of salt and vinegar, a method for hardening his knuckles. Kearns was dressed in his signature dark shirt and bright tie. Once the group of visitors settled in, Murray and Kearns began to reminisce.

It had been 1918, back when Dempsey was a relative unknown, and Murray had needed to find an opponent for a fighter named Carl Morris.

Murray liked Morris. He packed the house. Area fans were always eager to see the 6'4", 240-pound Oklahoman, one of the original White Hopes.

A match between Morris and Fireman Jim Flynn was slated in Buffalo for the middle of February 1918. Kearns, master manipulator, got Chicago matchmakers to occupy Flynn so that he would be unavailable to fight Morris in Buffalo. Kearns, knowing that Murray would be scrambling to find a substitute, telephoned the Q.A.C. matchmaker out of the blue and positioned himself as a savior. He offered a replacement: Dempsey. Murray had vaguely heard of Dempsey, training out in Oakland and recently on a winning streak out West. But Murray had never seen him in person. He was hesitant to match this Dempsey against a giant like Morris without first laying eyes on the Westerner.

"Dempsey is a powerhouse," Kearns boasted over the telephone. "Trust me—you'll be putting on the next heavyweight champion of the world."

"How big is he?" Murray asked.

Embellishing, Kearns told Murray that Dempsey was well over 200 pounds, and 6'2".

But Dempsey only weighed 182 pounds and he was exactly six feet tall.

Reluctantly, Murray agreed to Kearns' proposition and invited them to take the train to Buffalo at his expense. He'd put them up at the Iroquois. The promoter liked to bring in out-of-town fighters ahead of time, so the public could watch them work out, something to generate interest. Murray, suddenly second-guessing himself, decided he needed to put his own eyes on Dempsey. It was late in the evening when Kearns and Dempsey arrived. A blizzard was raging in Buffalo. Murray trudged over and knocked on the door to their room.

"Where's your heavyweight?" Murray asked.

"Right there," Kearns motioned.

Dempsey was lying in bed in his underwear reading a newspaper. When he got up to shake hands, Murray nearly fell over. Dempsey must have looked two times smaller after Kearns' exaggerated description.

"What's going on here?" Murray yelled. "I thought you said you had a heavyweight—why, you don't expect me to put this little guy in the ring with Morris? My God, Morris will kill him!" Murray was furious—this was exactly what he feared. Dempsey's surprisingly high-pitched speaking voice did not help. "No, the public won't stand for this. I'll get booed out of town. The fight's off!"

Murray had cause for caution. Over the years, boxing had endured an epidemic of ring fatalities. Some of these incidents were flukes or freak accidents. Jess Willard once hit John "Bull" Young so hard that a piece of Young's jaw lodged into his brain. Nebraskan heavyweight Luther McCarty dropped dead in a Calgary ring. Boxing-related deaths—an estimated 40 of them had occurred in just the prior ten years, including 10 in 1917—created a backlash against the sweet science as intolerable savagery.

"I've never had a fighter killed in my club," Murray declared. "And I don't wish to see it happen now."

But Dempsey begged, cried and begged some more, until Murray simmered down. The Buffalo promoter agreed to give Dempsey his crack at the giant. It would not be their first encounter.

Dempsey had once outpointed Morris out in San Francisco. Before that, early in his career, Dempsey had been one of Morris' sparring partners, and got to know him personally. Dempsey would say later that of everyone he ever fought, he loathed Morris most of all. He found him to be condescending, and a cheapskate. Morris, for his part, knew Dempsey had a thing about seeing anyone before a fight. So, he decided to swing by Dempsey's dressing room to say hello. "Get out of here you cheap bastard or I'll flatten you right now!" Dempsey had yelled.

When they met in the ring, Dempsey pummeled the hulking Morris for five rounds. In the sixth round, Morris, realizing he was fighting a losing battle, tossed a ridiculously obvious low blow in order to get himself disqualified rather than lose a newspaper decision. Scared to death that, literally, Dempsey *would be killed*, Murray had hidden alone in the box office, afraid to watch. But in the end, Morris was disqualified and Dempsey got his headlines, opening the door to the path that would lead to his championship fight with Willard in Toledo, Ohio, in July of 1919. Dempsey never forgot the break Murray had given him on that cold and snowy night.

Now four years later, as Murray recalled his role "creating" the future champion, the gathering in the room at the Iroquois had a laugh as Kearns playfully teased Murray about that night.

"I thought you were going to pass out," Kearns chuckled.

"Well you told me on the telephone that your man was a powerhouse," Murray said.

"After my description, I suppose he must have seemed small," Kearns conceded.

After hanging around a little while longer, Murray wished the champ luck and left to nail down the evening's program—the exhibition was only several hours away yet the lineup still had not been finalized. Murray had to figure something out. His plan was to put Dempsey in the ring for a couple of rounds with one of Buffalo's best and most popular fighters, but he had not yet located anyone suitable. Murray had to pick the most qualified guy he could find, realizing that Dempsey never took it easy on anyone. One problem, though: Buffalo's biggest ring star, Frankie Schoell, was booked to appear at an event in Syracuse, which he refused to cancel. There was talk that he could motor back to Buffalo by automobile. He'd gladly take a crack at Dempsey—but only if he could get back in time. Johnny Paske was also being considered.

To round out the program's opening portion, Murray slated the First Ward boy, Jimmy Slattery, versus another local boy, Buddy Merritt. In teasing out the undercard in a newspaper story the day of the exhibition, Murray referred to that "hilarious Slattery," a nod to the teenager's odd boxing style and awkwardly lanky appearance. Murray was framing Slats as a novelty act.

Even going into a seemingly harmless exhibition bout, Dempsey battled nerves and self-doubt—overconfident he was not. The champ viewed every single second of ring combat as fearsome—a window in which to kill or be killed. At the sound of the bell, his innate courage would well up, causing him to relentlessly batter any foe—including his poor sparring partners—into submission. To distract himself from these thoughts and kill some time before the show, Dempsey took an automobile ride out to the countryside to inspect some prized German Shepherds. Just hours before the special Q.A.C. program was to begin, it was still unclear exactly who Dempsey would be fighting.

In prior exhibitions, Dempsey had boxed with his top sparring partners. However, because of Dempsey's inability to pull punches, the usual options, including Larry Williams, the New England light heavyweight champ, and Larry Renault, Canadian heavyweight champ, were spent. Dempsey's donning extra-padded practice gloves, the use of protective head gear—none of it had mattered. Finally, and just in time for the evening papers, the local Buffalo boxers were announced: Dempsey would go one round apiece with both Paske and Schoell, provided the latter could get there in time. Additionally, one of Dempsey's stablemates, West Coast light heavyweight Jimmy Darcy, would also box Dempsey for one round.

Lines formed down Main Street as fans raced to Snyder's, excited to get a glimpse of the champion. Some fans gave Schoell a puncher's chance of knocking Dempsey down.

The first bout went off at 8:15 P.M. and featured Roggie Lavin, one of Red Carr's boys and the nephew of Paddy Lavin, legendary First Ward boxer turned bootlegger/gambling parlor operator. The Ward's new boxing hero, Jimmy Slattery, fought in the second bout. He won decisively in six rounds. When he wasn't pumping left jabs into Buddy Merritt's cheeks, Slats coasted. In these moments, as he let up, visibly disinterested, members of the crowd rolled their eyes and grumbled.

After three more bouts, Dempsey finally came strolling down the center aisle toward the ring, the audience rising to its feet and letting out a cheer. Paske, looking rugged and ready, sat ringside in his fighting togs, his heart racing. Leaving Syracuse en route to Buffalo, meanwhile, was Schoell, racing his motor car along pitch-black country roads.

Just as he entered the ring, Dempsey was handed a telegram from the local office of the Boxing Commission: Billy Muldoon, embattled commissioner, had telephoned minutes ago—*Dempsey had to defend his title.* The ruling was that if the champ was setting foot in a prize ring within New York State, his title was considered to be on the line. As far as the state was concerned, there was no such distinction as "exhibition" and no fighter, by rule, could meet more than one foe in a 24-hour period. So there would be no multiple opponents, only one.

Dempsey, in other words, was about to officially square off with Jimmy Darcy for the world's heavyweight crown, at least in the eyes of New York's boxing regulators.

Jimmy Darcy was actually Valen Trambitas, a native of Romania. He wasn't known as a particularly hard puncher. But he did have the distinction of having once knocked down the indefatigable Harry Greb. No one really thought Darcy stood a chance to steal the title. The fans, disappointed that the local contenders were not going to get their shot, let out groans of disapproval when the change in the evening's card was announced. But the show went on. Clad in powder blue tights, Dempsey looked bronzed and chiseled. But he and Darcy donned overstuffed gloves, sixteen-ounce pillows that bordered on cartoonish. For a few rounds, the mankiller was content to show off his footwork and blocking skills, impressing fans with a flashy speed not considered his forte. But in the third round, Dempsey let loose with four lefts and a right, a crisp, effective combination that ended any delusions about Darcy having it within him to pull off a shocker. Seeing Darcy dazed along the ropes, the champ pounced, but then uncharacteristically let up. The exhibition tour still had a few more stops.

Dempsey got the decision, of course. Fans yelled for Dempsey to say something. He wanted to. Dempsey wanted it announced to the crowd that in two months he was going to fight Bill Brennan of New York City—for real, and for the title. Doc Kearns had supposedly just closed the deal. But that fight would never take place.

Dempsey was still champ. Nevertheless, for the first time in more than a year his title was hung out for the taking, peculiarly though not perilously. As the July 25th *San Francisco Chronicle* noted: "Had Darcy landed a lucky punch he would be the world's heavyweight champion today."

★★★★★

Buffalo's fight season all but shut down during the month of August before roaring back in September when weekly programs returned. Slats took off for Crystal Beach. During the fall of '22 he fought regularly, at least a couple times per month. He remained undefeated.

In some of these bouts, Slats looked sensational, prompting chatter that he was destined to be the next Philadelphia Jack O'Brien, a national curiosity in the Gay Nineties as a wily teenage fighter. When Slats met the Erie, Pennsylvania boy K.O. Kelly, he kayoed him in the second. A bout against local Sam Willert ended in the third when his corner tossed out a bloody sponge.

On other occasions, Slattery performed merely capably, even lackadaisically, as if he wasn't really all that interested in the manly art. He showed no zeal for assaulting his opponents. He lacked, the cognoscenti declared, true fighting spirit.

Chastising the First Ward boy, Bob Stedler of the *Buffalo Evening News* around this time wrote:

> *Slattery has a bad habit of letting things slide along when he is on top and while this might be alright with him it is not what the fans want. They expect a boxer to keep going and Slattery thus far fails to realize that important factor in the game. He has shown his bad habit in recent bouts and someone should put him wise to the fact that he is getting himself into disfavor with the fans.*

Red Carr had not exactly lost interest in Slattery. He still believed the Irishman was that rare thoroughbred. But as the year wore on, Red's attention turned to Harry Cook, a black lightweight new in town from New Orleans. Cook took the city by storm. Suddenly, Red's place was bustling with hundreds of black children eager to marvel at Cook, with whom Slattery was sparring regularly. Red let the two tear each other up. Slattery was never better than when he was sparring with someone bigger and stronger.

In nearly twenty fights, Slats had not yet met defeat; nor was there even a single draw on his record. Slats continued to needle Red about moving up in competition. He was about to get his wish. Red was taking his thoroughbred out for a romp.

"Sailor" Max Hoffman was an unquestionably tough kid from the East Side. He was cruising through all the top area welters and was considered to be among the most experienced opponents available for Slattery. Red knew Slats was hitting his stride. He'd knocked Cook around at the gym. In Syracuse, Slats had fractured an opponent's jaw. Red went to Murray, who envisioned a full house. The pride of Buffalo's Irish section was going to fight the pride of the Jewish section.

The bout, a six-round affair, was to take place on a mid-December evening at the Aud. Was the Irish boy legitimate? "The strenuous test which has long been asked at last has arrived," wrote the Buffalo *Commercial*.

As round one began, it seemed Slattery would have an easy time. He jabbed Hoffman, hard and often. But the Sailor treaded water and by the end of the round had managed to turn the fight, increasing his momentum during the second round. Prior to round three, Slattery leaned over in his corner and threw up. Skitsy offered Red an explanation: "Must be a stomach virus."

Sapped of energy, Slattery muddled through the third. He was losing. Hoffman slammed Slattery across the ring, bouncing him hapless into the ropes. In a panicky state of duress, Slats at one point even pathetically turned his back on Hoffman during the middle of a nasty exchange. In the crowd, the First Ward boosters themselves were about to vomit. *Maybe Slats had bitten off more than he could chew.* For the past year, the Irish fans who had come out to watch (and bet on) Slats had never been disappointed. Now the usually rowdy section was quiet.

When Slattery came back to the corner, Red didn't pull punches: "This fellow's licking you."

Catching his breath on his stool, Slats glowered up at his pilot.

Gesturing nonchalantly behind him with a head nod, Red continued with his assessment.

"Listen how quiet it is," he said. "Your friends think you're a goner."

Red had uttered the magic words. Slats proceeded to give Hoffman such an unholy pasting in the final two rounds they say those who witnessed it never were able to pry the disturbing scene from their memories.

Slattery's record remained spotless. He had passed the first of what would be a gauntlet of tests. The next one came immediately: Slattery was to face Benny Ross.

A big-chinned Jewish boy (real name, Samuel Rosenberg) from the Cold Spring section of Buffalo, Ross had stumbled into the game fooling around in Jack O'Brien's gym circa 1918. Ross, at the time, was an underage sailor assigned to the Philadelphia Navy Yards at the end of the war, during which time he was caught up in a drunken melee so absurdly out of hand it may have even helped bring about Prohibition.

Two of Ross's shipmates on the USS Minnesota had gotten thumped at a dancehall by servicemen from the USS Columbia. A mob had then poured off the Minnesota, found itself a dozen random Columbia sailors, and issued them beatings. Tensions culminated in an all-hands-on-deck Battle Royale on 12th and Market streets as police stood by helplessly. Through it all, Ross was throwing haymakers in all directions and had accidentally popped one of the top officers of the fleet. Ross was clearly a natural-born scrapper. At O'Brien's gym, Ross had made friends with a rising featherweight, Frankie Brown, who mentored him.

After the war, Ross had set up home base at the Newsboys' Gym and had climbed the local ladder as part of Red's stable. By this time, Ross had jumped to Hugh Shannon, one of the best-known Buffalo boxing managers, owing in part to his regular column in the weekly *Boxing Blade*, and later, in *The Ring Magazine*. Ross had shown well the night of the Dempsey exhibition. He was well-liked around town for his awkwardly delivered but deadly right cross.

Ross was being trumpeted nationally (by Shannon, in his column) as a coming star, and was in line to challenge Frankie Schoell, bidding for national welterweight supremacy. If Max Hoffman was a hop up, Benny Ross was a broad jump. Outside of the Irish neighborhood, stubborn skeptics were still not satisfied that the unbeaten Slattery had done anything more than bowl over a feeble parade of suckers. Now they complained Red was putting Slattery in over his head.

The night of the big test came. Slats climbed into the ring to a thunderous outcry from his supporters—it is believed every available male vocal cord in the First Ward was present and utilized that night at the Aud. Under the hot incandescent lamps, Slattery's emerald green trunks and burgundy-colored mitts vividly stood out against his pale limbs and the drab mat. The referee, W.J. Taggert, dressed in white slacks and a white, short-sleeved button-down, looked like an asylum attendant. It was appropriate. Bedlam was about to ensue.

At some point in his development, Slattery was bound to get *really* good. And indeed, it had started to happen. He was faster and stronger. Ross had a six-pound weight advantage, but while Slats was a lean 146 pounds, he had gradually added nearly 20 pounds since climbing through the Aud roof skylight 14 months earlier.

From the opening gong, Slattery was the aggressor. He caught Ross early with a blistering right that seemed to cost Ross his nerve. Playing the game not to lose, waiting for an opening that never came, Ross lurched and lumbered as Slats methodically piled up points, flinging his left from long range.

Becoming more brazen as the rounds wore on, Slats would step in close, land a quick blow and then instantaneously disappear from the spot, leaving Ross dumbfounded and out of striking distance. Finally, in the sixth and final round, with time running out, Ross threw a desperation right that smashed into Slattery's head. His lethal sledgehammer had connected. But as vicious as the shot was, Slats shrugged it off and kept up the furious pace straight through to the end of the round. Getting in close, the final seconds ticking, Slats concluded his demonstration with a torrent of left jabs to Ross's face, flung in a comical rapid-fire succession. The First Ward Irish were hugging and jumping and screaming and tossing their derbies into the air. Many in the crowd wore stunned looks on their faces. No one was more surprised than Ross.

Slats hadn't just put in a respectable showing, which would have been treated as a kind of victory; he had not merely hung tough with a far more experienced foe; nor had he squeezed out a close decision. Slats had utterly dominated the fight.

Among the spectators in the crowd that night was George Pierce, a Broadway producer who sat ringside with a party of fellow Gotham show-business impresarios. Pierce was beguiled by the eighteen-year-old wonder boy. He saw artistry, choreography, elegantly timed moves.

As Slattery was officially announced the winner, amidst a deafening out-pouring from the throng, Pierce yelled to his party, "This boy is going to go far!"

All of the showmen agreed that their friend Jim Corbett had to see this kid.

★★★★★

When James J. Corbett had snatched the world's heavyweight title from John L. Sullivan in New Orleans in 1892, prizefighting was transformed into the sport of boxing. Fading then was the era of outlawed bare-knuckle affairs conducted in back rooms and on barges. Corbett-Sulli-van was staged properly in a legitimate outdoor stadium under a set of agreed-upon rules, one of which stipulated the use of five-ounce gloves. In knocking out the champion, Corbett, a former San Francisco bank clerk and amateur actor, dealt a blow to the notion of boxing as barba-rism—technique had trumped brute slugging.

Slender, elegantly coiffed with his jet-black pompadour, a true dandy—possibly the last person on earth who could be considered capable of beat-ing the Boston Strong Boy—"Gentleman Jim" Corbett had shocked the world and shot to fame.

He toured the country, starring in a play, *Gentleman Jack*, the story of an unlikely prizefighter who became a champion. Although not the great-est test of his range, Corbett did impress audiences nightly by boxing a few rounds with any manly member of the audience who had the nerve to come on stage. Never once did any of these challengers so much as muss a single hair out of place. No one could lay a glove on Corbett, not even the local Irish maulers sneakily handpicked by Corbett's prankster pals.

At one point, Corbett and Sullivan toured together as a live exhibition, telling tales and doing some light sparring. Both men loved the high life and became friends. Following performances, while out on the town together, Sullivan liked to saunter into a saloon and announce loudly, "I'll lick any man in the house!" Whereby Corbett would pull him aside and scold him for being such a lout. Hoping to reverse the perception of prizefighters as undignified hell-raisers, Corbett strove to earn a reputation as an actor equal to the one he'd earned as a boxer. He was literally among the first motion picture actors when he boxed Peter Courtney of Trenton, N.J., in front of the whirring, embryonic "Kinetoscope" in 1894—although few people ever saw the experimental moving images; there just weren't yet exhibit halls. Audiences still flocked to musical theatre and vaudevillian variety shows; most weren't aware of Thomas Edison's moving pictures breakthrough.

Corbett, whose father, Patrick, had emigrated from County Mayo, had the Irish gift of storytelling. His colorful anecdotes recalling his adventures as heavyweight champ enthralled the adoring public. When silent movies did take off—studios were cranking them out in the New York City area before the industry shifted to Los Angeles—early producers had no use for Corbett's good-natured monologues. Still, he remained extremely popular despite the decidedly sour note on which his boxing career ended around the turn of the century.

Defending his title on St. Patrick's Day in Carson City, Nevada, versus old, bald, bow-legged Bob Fitzsimmons, Corbett had dealt the Cornishman uninterrupted punishment round after round. Then, just as it seemed Corbett was cruising to an easy victory, it happened: Fitzsimmons caught him off guard with a sharp hook to the solar plexus. The blow dropped Corbett to his knees, absconded with his breath and, ten seconds later, his title. Corbett was heartbroken.

He retired from the ring and opened a saloon on Broadway and 34th Street in Manhattan. Corbett desperately wanted to be taken seriously as a thespian. His dream was to perform on Broadway. But when he finally did, the production closed after only a 16-show run. Twice, Corbett put on a play based on his favorite novel, about a prizefighter, *Cashel Byron's Profession*, written by George Bernard Shaw—who tried to have it scuttled.

Eventually, Corbett was lured back into the ring. California rancher James J. Jeffries had taken the heavyweight crown from Fitzsimmons.

Corbett deduced that his scientific tactics and sheer stamina would be too much for the grizzly-bear Jeffries. Corbett sold his bar, signed papers for a 25-round title fight against Jeffries and entered a period of intense training. And he nearly did regain the title, coasting for 22 rounds until it happened again, another sudden reversal: he rode an unlucky bounce off the ropes straight into a lethal Jeffries barrage. Jeffries knocked him out.

A subsequent attempt, at age 37, to reclaim the title from Jeffries had proved not only unsuccessful but humiliating. The fight was halted in the 10th round. Soundly beaten, Corbett had made his way to a San Francisco restaurant afterwards. Jeffries and his entourage happened to be sitting inside. Summoning his acting talent, Corbett strode past them defiantly, struggling to keep his aching body firm and straight, his top hat tilting from the ostrich-egg-sized lump on his head. Jeffries and his cohorts burst out laughing.

Meanwhile, Corbett had been involved in a pair of controversial non-title fights widely suspected of having been faked so that Corbett could lose on a foul and pocket a rich sum. His reputation was tarred, but only for a spell. The public forgave him. Ultimately, the terrible ending to Corbett's boxing career was forgotten.

As the years rolled on, even as vaudeville began to surrender audiences to motion pictures, Corbett remained a top attraction. He toured with various troupes, regaling audiences with his humorous stories, which more often than not painted him in a deprecating light to show his common touch. He settled down with his wife Vera in a splendid, three-story home in the Bayside section of Queens. They never had any children. But Corbett made it a priority to be a positive fatherly influence on all the boys in the neighborhood. He rode the Long Island Railroad into Manhattan to meet with theater friends, always polite to anyone who approached, always dressed in a fine suit. His run as champ had been sweet while it lasted, but the roar of the fight crowd, as he liked to say, was no longer for him; he was one of them. He enjoyed simple pleasures. He loved to recite poetry or lines from his favorite roles. He tended to his hydrangeas, or just sat and relaxed with Vera on the front porch, smoking a cigar and looking out through the trees at the smooth, gray waters of Little Neck Bay.

As the 1920s dawned, Corbett, nearing his mid-50s, still enjoyed the role of celebrity. His syndicated column, Corbett's Corner, gave him a stage upon which to act as pugilism's conscience and its preeminent commentator. Corbett was convinced that the modern fight game was heading in the wrong direction. Back in his era, fans didn't have to wait so long to see the heavyweight champion defend his title. "Jack Dempsey would be better if he learned how to box," Corbett wrote.

In January of 1923, Corbett was touring the East—nine cities, three shows a day—along with Billy B. Vann, an old minstrel show veteran known for his musical comedy. By now, most of the old vaudeville houses already had been converted to movie theaters.

One Thursday afternoon, Corbett played to a full house at Shea's Theater on Main Street in Buffalo. When his bit was done, he hurried out the stage door and over to the nearby Hotel Iroquois.

To goose ticket sales for the act when it came to a new city, Corbett liked to summon local newspaper men who arranged for him to meet some unknown fighter, so the old master could hail the boy as a coming champion. Gentleman Jim had recently heard about this Irish lad Slattery, "the second coming of Johnny Kilbane," from his acquaintances in the theater world. He had reached out to Buffalo's best-known boxing scribes, Billy Kelly and Charlie Murray, and arranged for them to set up a publicity stunt disguised as a private boxing lesson.

The two promoters loved the idea. They of course enlisted photographers from their papers. Red told Slats to put on a shirt and tie and to head over to the Iroquois. So Slats trudged through the snow to the aging but still grand hotel, which was about to be shut down to make way for something bigger and better. When Slats got there, Kelly and Murray met him and led him into a large, stately meeting room. There to greet them was the great Jim Corbett, looking to impart some lessons.

For Slats, it must have seemed as if Zeus himself had climbed down from Olympus. Corbett was struck by something startling, too—there before him was a replica of himself as a younger man. A twinkle came into his eyes as Corbett gazed upon the tall, slender fighting specimen. Slattery just chuckled and shook his head, dumbstruck that such an icon had any interest in him.

"How much does he weigh?" asked Corbett, looking him over.

"He's just 145 pounds but still growing," Murray told him. "Probably he'll be a middleweight. Or maybe even a light heavyweight."

"Why my boy with your height, reach and strength, there shouldn't be a lad anywhere around to lick you," Corbett remarked as he patted Slattery on the shoulder. A cadre of photographers snapped away.

Slats squared his shoulders. His cheeks went flush. "Thanks, Mr. Corbett," he replied. "I'll try not to disappoint you."

"Well, get your coat off and let's get down to business," Corbett said, removing his suit jacket but keeping on his vest and necktie.

Slattery flung off his overcoat and sprung into a shadow boxing routine. In all of the excitement it never dawned on him to remove his rubber overshoes. Even with the galoshes flapping about, Corbett could see effortless, nimble grace. He was particularly impressed with the way the boy threw rapid-fire rights.

For the next half hour, the man who revolutionized the sport of boxing dipped repeatedly into his endless reserve of pointers, reeling off one valuable lesson after another. With a fatherly manner and his distinctive hyper-articulate speaking style, Corbett schooled Slats on a number of techniques, including how to: turn an enemy's left hook aside with a flick of the wrist just as the punch begins to unfurl; strike when the enemy leads; use uppercuts to steadily administer body blows; duck and sidestep; block and counter.

"Countering is the greatest asset in boxing," Corbett declared.

As for Slattery's irregular, upright, arms-at-his-sides stance, which fans and writers had dubbed the "weeping willow defense," Corbett validated the concept of relaxing when out of an opponent's striking range so as to conserve energy. But once in close, Corbett warned, a low-stationed right hand was useless. The instructor reached for Slattery's right hand coiled at waist level. "Your right should be held higher to block or strike," he advised.

"Never stay within reach of your man unless you are hitting," he continued. "Either stay away or stay in close. When you're in range—start firing."

Corbett, at 56, still looked as spry as ever. He urged Slats to train hard but not to overdo it. A young man is filled with natural vigor, so a few days of roadwork, five miles or so, as well as one hour of boxing a day—plus one day of rest—would be more than sufficient to put him in perfect condition. Make sure to eat one apple each day, he added.

When the private lesson was over, Slattery was genuinely inspired.

"Gee, Mr. Corbett," Slats gushed. "I didn't know there was one-tenth of this stuff in the game . . ."

Interrupting the youthful obsequiousness using a well-timed YES BUT, Corbett countered with his most important lesson.

"The big item today, son, is to remember to practice each day," Corbett said. "One hour a day. Don't ever think you're perfect. Practice, practice, *practice* . . ."

And one other thing, added Corbett: "Save your money."

It's said that Slats bolted out of that big ornate room at the Hotel Iroquois and raced back to the Newsboys' Gym, where he ditched his bow tie for boxing togs. He then proceeded to run through all of the drills he could think of, not taking off his gloves that gray winter afternoon until the electric bulbs of the nearby Main Street marquees started to twinkle. Over at Shea's, Corbett waited for the jugglers to wrap up so he could perform his act for perhaps the thousandth time.

For Slattery, everything was ahead of him, including another "test" just a few days away. It was yet another chance to prove to his doubters that his record—no losses, no draws—was no fluke. Slattery was matched against Mixer Mitchell, the pride of Central New York. The 25-year-old war veteran was enrolled at St. John's Military Academy in Manlius, N.Y. The press loved him—a studious gent boxing his way to law school, a pug every mother could love. In the ring, Mitchell liked battling in close with both fists flying. That's how he got the name "Mixer."

The fight had almost not happened. When told by telephone of the offer to take on an inexperienced waterfront kid in a six-round undercard bout, Mitchell's manager, Charlie Huck, told Murray to forget it. "Mixer is no prelim fighter," Huck insisted and hung up the receiver. Slattery, though coming along wonderfully of late, was still considered in the fight game to be as green as his signature trunks. He'd only been fighting professionally a little over a year. Champion at his weight in Syracuse, Mitchell had met all the top lightweights in Buffalo. But a few hours after declining the offer, Huck called the Buffalo promoter back. He'd talked it over with Mitchell, who was fond of the Buffalo fight scene and who wanted to conquer it by stripping the new darling of his undefeated status.

The fight was set for Jan. 22, 1923, at the Broadway Auditorium, under the auspices of the Q.A.C. For Slats, it was another trial by fire. He wasn't expected to win. But his stock was on the rise. Suddenly, improbably, he was in a position in which if he could pull out a victory it could put him in the same conversation as his idol, Schoell. Down in the Ward, folks were convinced they had a coming champion.

Slattery had never been more prepared for battle. He'd trained with a heightened sense of purpose. When the opening bell sounded, with Corbett's coaching fresh in his mind, Slats darted right toward his prey as the fans cheered his pluck. Mitchell, per his custom, waded right in, swinging both fists. Fearless, Slats slashed straight into the teeth of Mitchell's cyclonic assault.

Slats coolly stood his ground, smashing uppercuts into his opponent's ribs—exactly as Corbett instructed him. A jarring left hook sent Mitchell flying into the ropes. In a dazed panic, the Syracuse boy started throwing looping haymakers. Slattery, weaving more of Corbett's advice into his repertoire, made it a point to *counter*, beating Mitchell to the punch almost every time. Mitchell did manage to land a few shots during that furious first round, and when the bell sounded, Slattery's face was beet red from getting stung—but Slats led on points. In rounds two and three, Slats continued to show courage under duress, stepping directly into the maelstrom and delivering perfectly timed counterpunches. Mitchell would rush in toward Slats; Slats would jab him off like a fencer wielding a foil. During the third round, Slattery's stomach began cramping up. Before the start of the fourth, Slats informed Skitsy of his situation but since nothing could be done they kept it quiet from Red. Slattery continued on in severe pain, although no one would have guessed it.

The fourth round saw the pair go blow for blow, bouncing back and forth from one end of the ring to the other. When the chaotic round wound down to its conclusion Slattery was dictating the pace. Slattery pranced and flitted in and around his foe with the elegance of a ballet performer. By contrast, Mitchell lunged about as if fitted with cement shoes.

In the fifth round, as Mitchell staggered toward him, Slattery employed yet another Corbett move—the forgotten sidestep—and executed it to perfection, resulting in Mitchell having a collision with one of the iron ring posts.

The sixth and final round saw Mitchell finally land one of his desperation haymakers square on Slattery's chin. Slats barely winced, seemingly impervious, his trademark devil-may-care smile remaining intact until the final bell. The crowd was whipped up into a tremendous frenzy by the time Slattery was declared the victor, and the long, loud ovation spilled over into the start of the next fight on the program. Every human hand for fifty rows reached out to slap Slats on his back as he made his way down the aisle toward the rear of the house.

Not long after, Charlie Murray was interviewing Mitchell in his dressing room. "They told me I was fighting a greenhorn," Mitchell told him. "If he's a greenhorn, keep him away from me when he becomes seasoned."

Victory celebrations were soon underway in the old Ward. Late that night, the *Courier* switchboard operator received a call from Jim Corbett, who'd just completed a performance in Toronto. Corbett was curious to know how Slattery had fared and couldn't wait for the morning papers.

The Mixer Mitchell victory instantly lit the Slattery fuse.

But it fizzled out just as fast. Finding a suitable opponent for Slats got even harder. Fans increasingly clamored for the newest sensation, Slattery, to be matched against the old new sensation, Schoell. Neither camp wanted to test those waters. The mere idea of fighting his idol made Slats uncomfortable.

Meanwhile, Slattery's age was a problem. Despite pleading and cajoling from Murray, the State wouldn't allow any fighter under the age of 21 to go more than six rounds. It was Muldoon's personally crafted safety measure and he wouldn't entertain the notion of issuing any exceptions. But short bouts connoted, inherently, lesser importance, and Murray was asking main event fighters to put stature and earning power at risk. Not even Soldier Bartfield, the veteran Brooklyn battler known for his willingness to fight anyone, would stoop to an abbreviated preliminary engagement.

Asked what he thought about a six-round fight with Slattery, Bartfield's manager, Dan McKetrick, told Murray, "*not a chance.*"

Slats had outgrown his experience level, trapped at least momentarily by boxing bylaws. The burning question in Buffalo: Who next for Slattery?

Red needed time to figure it out. He suggested Slats take a break from his regular training regimen. Put the gloves down for a while, Red counseled. Slats didn't argue.

For the next few weeks, his main source of exercise was swinging a sledgehammer in the shipyard and playing winter sports. Red told him to eat what he wanted—just be a normal kid.

Sloak fully supported the plan. He always advocated that the best form of conditioning for a growing boy was an honest day's work, and Sloak still had a voice in the affairs of his son. People came to recognize that voice at ringside. If someone didn't share the belief that his boy was a future champion, the 52-year-old ex-pugilist was prepared to have a fight himself. Sloak had one good eye. The other was partly poked out, an accident he had suffered while fighting a blaze. His good eye remained fixed on the ring. Nobody dared try to talk to Sloak during one of his son's bouts. "Oh, I only go to see how far off the boy can win," he would tell fellow firefighters.

Sloak had been promoted and transferred to department headquarters, and now the house on Fulton became a sort of headquarters for training. A support system coalesced. Mom was in charge of liniment rubdowns. The younger sisters, Mary, now 13, and Helen, 11, prepared Jimmy fried eggs and bacon after his morning roadwork on canal towpaths and the lakeside turnpike heading out toward the steel plant. Sloak manned the telephone.

Normally not one to be enthralled by the trappings of modern conveniences, old Sloak did go ahead and join the one-fourth of city residents who in just a decade or so had subscribed to the New York Telephone system. The dawn of direct dialing meant that Sloak and Red could discuss his son's boxing affairs with regularity. The Slattery's humble abode hummed with so much activity, burst with such pride, was so often visited and pointed out, that it took on the properties of a lordly castle. In the neighborhood, Slats was hailed as a boy king. If he walked a few blocks to Mordeno Brothers barber shop on Elk Street, there would be, by the time he arrived, a parade of young boys in his wake. Never far off were his two corner men and best friends, Skitsy and Joe. Slattery's extended gang of pals totaled at least twenty guys. His upbeat personality, his very being, drew people to him. In return, he shared his celebrity (and his bankroll) freely—wherever he was, that was *the place to be*. It could be a St. Stephen's dance or an ice hockey game on a frozen pond or an outing to the Masque Theatre, the tiny motion picture house on Elk where Slats and his gang (and gaggles of girls) would go to see the latest Douglas Fairbanks swashbuckler picture—wherever he was, everyone wanted to be there to bask in his glow.

All of the downtown newsboys were dedicated followers of Slattery. They'd been pooling their income and wagering on him to win, riding his uninterrupted streak of ring success. "When I graduate to the big money, I'll be sure to take you all to the fight as my guest," Slattery would promise them.

Slats had saved enough of his earnings to purchase an old Model T, a crapshoot on wheels. Among its missing amenities were shock absorbers, which is why in addition to being nicknamed "Tin Lizzies" these cheap cars were also called "Bonecrushers."

Drawn to speed, friendly with most cops, Slats drove full bore with zero regard for safety or rules of the road. Some fans grew worried enough to write to the *Courier* imploring authorities to take Slattery's motor machine away for his own good.

Cars were re-shaping '20s society as never before, fuelling fanciful notions of freedom and leisure. The general mood of the day was turning almost giddy. Opportunities abounded. Ordinary people hatched "get-rich-quick" schemes bottling homemade hooch or playing the stock market, which was beginning to climb. The radio boom was underway. Broadcasting stations were popping up everywhere. More people could afford the latest $300 RCA receiver sets. New stores opened to sell typewriters, cameras, phonographs and other gadgets. After nearly two decades of mostly stagnant conditions, the American economy—as measured then by the performance of the 20 publicly traded companies comprising Charles Dow's tracking list—was on the upswing after bottoming in the summer of '21. The whimsy of the times was reflected in one of the earliest song crazes to ever sweep the nation— "Yes! We Have No Bananas."

Nothing, in light of the ethos of the time, could have seemed sillier than the law banning the sale of alcohol. Huge swaths of the population ignored the law. Prohibition embroidered lawlessness into everyday life. Speakeasies flourished. All over Buffalo, saloons boarded up the front and operated secretly in the back, or repurposed as purveyors of cola or birch beer or "near" (non-alcoholic) beer—and also sold booze in the back. Everyone in the First Ward knew what went on at Chick Evans' "soft drink emporium." At the same time, and for the first time, young women, flouting taboo, took a spot at the bar alongside men. One of the hottest nightspots for Buffalonians to partake in a drink was the "Big House," a rustic hotel-restaurant on the outskirts of the city. What had been built as a destination for well-heeled automobile enthusiasts had over the years evolved into a madcap haven for bootleggers, gangsters, bookmakers, gamblers, prizefighters, cops, high rollers and assorted other denizens. Anything went. Meanwhile, betting parlors flourished in Tonawanda and Niagara Falls, N.Y. Such "sports clubs" would have been an irresistible tug for any liberated youngster.

Sloak had been taking his son into First Ward saloons throughout boyhood. Cotter's watering hole was the main hub for the lake men and railroad workers who comprised the core of Slattery's fan base. The boxer was treated like royalty in there. Sloak never begrudged his son a beer or two. And make no mistake, Slats and his pals liked their beer. Apparently, Slats, Skitsy and Joe liked to venture to Chicago, hotbed of bordellos and burlesque shows. Rumors about Slattery indulging in the high life had been circulating for a few weeks that winter of '23. Such talk had started after he knocked off Benny Ross. That triumph set the tone for a particularly rollicking celebration. Slats no doubt would have been the toast of Joe Nelbert's roadhouse.

Local promoters Murray and Kelly were quick to dispel talk of Slattery taking up the "hot pace." They were cultivating a sensible image for Slattery. If Kelly had it correct, Slats was saving money to enroll in college. "We saw Jimmy Slattery starting on the right road to a prosperous and useful life," Kelly wrote that winter. "He was opening a savings account."

Shakespeare penned the line "primrose path of dalliance" to describe the easy road of sin relative to the more difficult path of the righteous. The so-called primrose path became sportswriter shorthand for the party lifestyle sweeping the country. Slattery's brief respite from the ring only furthered speculation that he had adopted some questionable pursuits. Had too much playtime dulled Slats' skills? Fans would soon find out.

★★★★★

On a Tuesday evening in the middle of that February of '23, Slattery was at home getting ready to go out to the movies when the telephone's bell rang . . . *brrrrrring, brrrrrring*. It was his manager. Plans for a long layoff were being scrapped.

"You're going to box next Monday night," Red informed him. "We start training in the morning."

"All right," Slats said.

Red hung up. It was about 8:30 P.M. He decided he wanted to review some match proposals that had come in the mail. The pile of letters was in his office at the gym. So he went over to retrieve them.

When Red got there, after 9:00 P.M., the normally frenetic Newsboys' Gym was closed and locked for the night. Red entered and turned on the lights. He didn't plan on staying long. All of a sudden, he heard somebody come in. Red was startled to see Slattery grinning sheepishly.

"What in the devil are you doing up here?" Red asked.

"I'm going to work out for an hour," Slats said. "Try out some new stuff."

"Wait, you didn't know I would be here—how the hell did you think you were getting in?"

Slats held out a key that he'd borrowed from Red's assistant, Mr. Fagan. Red shook his head. "Kid, you are a pip."

In late February of '23, Slattery took a decision over Ray Graham. He kept winning, kept gaining in popularity.

Stories about his dazzling performances circulated around the area. Every Irishman for 100 miles in every direction was infatuated. In isolated rural communities with large concentrations of Irish, such as Batavia, N.Y., fans revolved their entire week around the next Slattery fight, setting out early when the day arrived, either hitchhiking or hopping a freight train. To those of Hibernian heritage, a Slattery bout was magical, not to be missed. Fans who could only afford the cheapest tickets formed a rowdy little club called "the dollar boys." Every kid in the First Ward would spend the entire week digging up the price of admission and did they ever whoop it up when he won.

No longer discounted as a fluke, Slattery met every challenge put in front of him. With some two dozen straight victories under his belt, Slattery was now hurtling toward the top ranks and richer spoils.

The next test was Al Cross of Syracuse. He was among the best welterweights in the state. Cross had just scored a one-punch knockout of Nate Lewis, a legitimate first-rate talent. If Slats could beat Cross, he'd instantly be viewed as deserving a spot in the upper echelon of the division. Then there would be no more patient grooming or easy progression; a victory would propel Slats on a push for the summit—and there would be no turning back. First, though, he had to beat Cross. For that to happen, the fight had to be arranged.

Murray had signed Slattery for a long string of six-round fights paying Slattery a couple hundred dollars per fight. But Syracuse promoter Jack Lewis was offering Slats $500 to fight Cross ten rounds at his arena in Syracuse. Murray wasn't going to let that happen. (Neither was the Boxing Commission, bent on limiting Slattery to six rounds). Joe Netro, Cross's roly-poly manager, accused Slattery of ducking the match. Furious, Red Carr published a letter in the *Courier* on St. Patrick's Day 1923 calling on Netro to bring Cross to Buffalo for a six-round bout, something Cross was hesitant to do. Upping the stakes, Red tossed in a side proposition: a $1,000 wager to make it that much more tantalizing. Like a banking syndicate, around two dozen newsboys came to Red pledging to back the bet. Cross was now game. One of his handlers scouted Slattery as a wispy, soft puncher and told Cross winning would be a "cinch."

Cross was brawnier and more experienced by several years. He didn't expect the fight to last more than two rounds. As preliminary bouts went, Slattery-Cross was eagerly anticipated, at least as much as the main event, in which Cleveland middleweight Charlie O'Connell was facing Teddy Myers, pride of Buffalo's Polish community. Trains filled with well-to-do Clevelanders arrived all afternoon. Among the invading out-of-town throng was Tom McGinty, boxing promoter and bootlegger. An estimated 8,000 fans packed the Aud the night Slats fought Al Cross. Before the fight, Murray had maintenance crews working around the clock to put in rear- and additional side-bleacher sections in yet another reconfiguration of the arena. Not even 30 seconds into the fight, Cross blasted Slattery with a heavy lick square on the chin. The crowd gasped. Slats blinked his eyes, as if detonating. Working both fists at a speed no one could believe they were seeing, Slats flew at Cross. The fury of his onslaught lifted the crowd to its feet. Cross was hurt but he never went down, much to the disbelief of those who watched the punishment he endured for the full six rounds. When the final bell sounded, Cross later admitted, he was grateful to hear it.

When they shook hands in the ring, Cross conceded he'd taken the bout lightly. "The guy who told me you were a cinch gave me a bum tip," Cross told Slats.

As Slattery made his way back to the dressing room, the boisterous Tom McGinty could not contain himself. "You're another Jim Corbett!" McGinty shouted, slapping the youth on the back.

Slattery had aced another big test. Once again, the Ward went wild. All over Buffalo, Syracuse, Cleveland, even New York City—the question remained: *Who next for Slattery?*

Matchmaker Murray was constantly being asked. Fans came up to him wanting to know, "when is Slats fighting again?" People rang Murray's telephone. They wrote letters. Promoters weren't supposed to be directly involved in the affairs of any individual boxer but of course Murray showed interest, made inquiries and helped Red screen correspondence. No second-rate foes would do. Working the telephone as if it were invented specifically for him, Murray spoke with fight managers around the North-east. What he needed now was a top contender who stood a chance against this freakishly talented teenager, even someone to merely hold Slattery to a draw.

Red knew that a new chapter in his boy's career was beginning—the chance at ever bigger purses. Money had always motivated the kid. But Red worried things were moving too fast. If Slattery overreached, he could wind up badly hurt. All of that promise, finally coming true, could be snuffed out by a single punch, Red's worst fear.

He enjoyed watching Slats as much as the fans did. This flowering period was special to behold. "Slattery was like a ballet dancer," Red told an interviewer in 1930.

Slattery's impossibly graceful style, while exquisite to observe, was also terribly effective. As he flitted about, he seemed uniquely able to vanish at the exact moment an opponent unleashed, then, inexplicably, reappear elsewhere in the ring, like some playful ghost.

Slats was giddy upon hearing that efforts were underway to line up a fight against world famous Soldier Bartfield for big money. At 31, Bartfield was nearing the end of a long, respectable career.

Here was a guy who never held a title and yet was revered as one of the game's toughest characters. Bartfield was from the old school of fistiana, as the late boxing historian Hank Kaplan has noted. "The Soldier," Kaplan wrote, "did not care who the next opponent was, just where and how much?" Bartfield's oft-used quip: "Never mind who—what's the purse?" (In his heavy Brooklyn-Jewish accent it came out, "*vots the poise?*")

Born Jacob Bartfeldt in Lanczyn, Austria, he moved to Brooklyn in 1908 at age 16. A few years later, "Jake," as he was known, joined the U.S. Army, where he took up boxing. He wound up in the 13th Regiment National Guard Unit dispatched to the border to hunt for Pancho Villa, the Mexican revolutionary/bandit. Villa (not to be confused with Pancho Villa the Filipino flyweight who fought around that same time) had been antagonizing American cattle ranchers. Returning from the 1913 Mexican Border campaign, Bartfield faced a pantheon of grand masters—Benny Leonard, Harry Greb, Jack Britton, Battling Nelson, Mike O'Dowd and Mike Gibbons. The Soldier was a 10-to-1 underdog when he battered Gibbons for ten rounds at Ebbets Field in 1915. Anything but graceful, at times clumsy, Bartfield had no observable tendencies. He struck in funny, unexpected ways, even using a ridiculous yet effective backhand blow now and again. He was totally unpredictable—a punishment glutton—the monster in a bad dream, relentlessly pursuing no matter what you threw at him. A more discerning approach to picking his battles may have provided him a better record. As the years went by, Bartfield's rankings in the welterweight division steadily hovered above the middle and below the top. Still, a more game scrapper could not be found anywhere in all of boxing. And even Bartfield refused to fight Slattery.

Once the local fans heard talks were underway with Bartfield, they would not let up on Murray about landing the fight. Determined to give the people what they wanted, Murray, like a pit terrier, kept after Bartfield and his manager, McKetrick, who shared an office in Manhattan at 1465 Broadway with Dempsey's pilot, Doc Kearns. The McKetrick-Kearns stable was one of the foremost in the country. As far as McKetrick was concerned, Bartfield was never going to appear in a preliminary match in Buffalo. It was too much of a step down and there was too little to gain. Bartfield was angling for Georgie Ward; Ward was chasing Mickey Walker; Walker was welterweight champion of the world.

To fend Murray off, McKetrick enlisted Frank "Doc" Bagley, also one of New York City's best known managers. Operating out of Grupp's Gymnasium on 116th Street and Eighth Avenue, Bagley briefly handled the "Fighting Marine" Gene Tunney. Bagley had a kid he was pushing, a welterweight prospect named Jimmy Sullivan. Bagley told Murray that knowledgeable spies in Buffalo were certain Sullivan could beat Slattery.

Murray would always be suspected of orchestrating Slattery's rise. Whether he was knowingly selecting a soft opponent, or gullible to Bagley's claim, or maybe even just doing Bagley a favor, Murray made the match. Sullivan didn't show up. A few days prior, he had been injured in a bout in Philadelphia.

In his place, Bagley brought another boy, a newcomer named Tony Sarracco. Murray blanched. Bagley told Murray if the Italian kid didn't have a respectable outing he didn't have to pay them. Sarracco had no chance against Slattery—although, those who watched the fight closely would have spotted something intriguing: the Italian kid fought out of low crouch, and it gave Slattery trouble.

Murray kept after Bartfield. The promoter arranged for the Q.A.C. to do two things that were unprecedented just to pull this off. Even though Slattery was only permitted to go six rounds, it was Slattery the fans most wanted to see. So Murray proposed that the bout with Bartfield be staged as the finale—a six-round main event—turning the usual boxing format on its head. Secondly, Murray was offering ten times the amount that a boxer would typically get paid for six rounds of work.

Murray even had one last ace up his sleeve. Bartfield's in-laws were, lo and behold, from Buffalo. That April, when the Soldier came to town to visit, Murray took him around and cleverly planted a few seeds. Bartfield could wind down his career right here in the Bison City. The fans loved him. He'd be in line for a crack at Schoell. That could set up a title shot. Succumbing to Murray's charms, and a pile of money—probably $3,000— Bartfield agreed to fight Slats in the otherwise unheard-of six-round main event. Murray rang Red, who was having second thoughts. He was worried that a dangerous puncher such as Bartfield could ruin Slats' budding career. Murray was offering Slats $500.

"I'm advising you against it," Red told him. "But I won't stand in your way."

"For that kind of money I'll fight Jack Dempsey," Slats said. "And I'll beat him."

The battle Buffalo craved was a go—veteran versus phenom. Murray figured he could get 10,000 people to attend, and that the fight would draw at least $10,000 in gate receipts. So initially, he dubbed the event the "$10,000 Card." As the fight approached, Murray and Billy Kelly had the idea to completely reconfigure the usual program—they arranged six, six-round fights, including bouts featuring Jimmy Goodrich and Frankie Schoell, either of whom could have rightfully complained they deserved top billing. But they were in favor of letting Slats appear in the main event; they were rooting for him, along with everyone else. The Q.A.C. called it the "Big Six Show," a format creatively devised to accommodate Slattery's age.

As usual, the entire First Ward was present at the Aud that night. When it came time, Bartfield climbed through the ropes first. He was met by a smattering of cheers. Older fans would have found Bartfield a familiar sight. The old veteran had fought in Buffalo several times over the prior decade, including a series of bouts with Jimmy Duffy.

Bartfield, at 5' 8", was stocky and muscular, with thick, sturdy legs. His face was ruggedly handsome, but he had a mean, almost menacing, look about him. Picture (if you are of a certain age) "Ganz," played by James Remar, in the 1982 action-comedy *48 Hours*.

When sleek, smiling Jimmy slid under the ropes, the Irish throng stood up and let out a roar that shook the rafters. Sloak Slattery was sitting ringside with his other sons, John and Joe. Jimmy's mother was too nervous to attend. She knew the risk her son was taking climbing into the ring against one of the game's most dangerous battlers.

At one stage of the negotiations with the Bartfield camp, Murray sought permission from the state boxing regulators to allow Slattery to go ten rounds. Some righteous members of the local community got wind of this notion and, protective of the frail-looking youngster, lodged formal protests with boxing authorities, who were disinclined to issue any such waiver.

Before a packed house, the boy wonder banned from participating in ten-round affairs would only need six to issue Soldier Bartfield the worst beating of his life. And moreover, Slattery made it look easy.

He dropped Bartfield twice, cleanly, in the first and fourth rounds. In that opening round, as soon as the bell clanged, Bartfield rushed Slattery, both fists flailing, apparently intent on intimidating the youth early. Unflappable, Slats stepped right into the fusillade and proceeded to pump lefts and rights into his opponent's jaw, while the Soldier's wild swings kept missing. For the previous few months, Slattery had been disposing of challengers with such ease that cries of "set ups" continued to reverberate around town—but it wasn't supposed to be this way, not against Bartfield.

As the first round came to a close, Bartfield, withstanding a sickening amount of punishment to his head and body, kept pressing forward with grisly courage. Finally, he saw his chance to take one of his famous backhand swings. Darting out of the way with the reflexes of a startled deer, Slats retaliated with a sharp right to the chin. The Soldier fell. This was the first knock down of the evening and it sent the crowd into a frenzy. Bartfield collapsed in a sitting position in front of Slattery's corner, where Skitsy and Joe were jumping up and down. Right then, a brown derby was flung up from near the front row, arching high into the air, as a hoarse-throated Irishman (possibly Sloak) proclaimed, "*You've got him whipped Jimmy me lad!*"

But Bartfield got up. Slattery pounced and hammered him with a right that sent him careening into the ropes just as the bell sounded to end the first session. Bartfield trudged back to his corner, exhausted, shaking his head. He'd barely lasted one round with the youngster.

For the rest of the bout, Bartfield chased Slats around the ring. To use a phrase coined by Twenties' sports scribes, Bartfield may as well have been trying to trap lightning. He would throw a looping haymaker from an awkward angle, miss by a mile and then, snarling in disgust, keep pursuing as the crowd howled with laughter. Bartfield's lumbering movements made Slattery's speed seem all the more bewildering. Slats' overflowing cadre of pals and supporters were going wild and getting louder as the second and third rounds progressed and he piled on the points. Slats kept up a ferocious pace, shooting combinations so fast that fans couldn't believe their eyes. Bartfield's head was transformed into a speed bag. At the end of the fourth, Slats dropped Bartfield a second time. Again, he got up.

When the bell sounded to end the fourth, Bartfield was so wobbly that his legs crossed up, and he nearly toppled over while walking back to his corner. The old veteran continued to pursue Slattery in the final rounds. When the final bell sounded, Slats was still showering Bartfield with blows. The crowd was applauding both of them—Slattery for his brilliance, the Soldier for his raw determination. Slats came over to shake hands. Bartfield, his face and chest smeared with blood, cried out emotionally, "Hey kid, you can fight!"

"So can you, Jake," Slats told him, giving the old veteran a pat on the shoulder.

Slats raced back to his corner, calling out to Joe Hickey: "Hey can you duck out and telephone my mother that I won? She'll be anxious to hear."

Speaking with newsmen in his dressing room later, Bartfield pronounced: "If that kid is only 18 and still growing he'll be heavyweight champion some day."

In his dressing room, Slattery, as the legend goes, ran his fingers through the fat stack of bills Red handed him and declared: "I sure picked the right racket!"

That night the First Ward celebrated as never before, a long, ecstatic night for all to remember. They say Jimmy paid the tab and that come morning half the people in the neighborhood followed him all the way to his doorstep still cheering away.

Matchmaker Murray stuck with his "Big Six" cards, which he promoted as fast-moving, jam-packed carnivals of boxing. Never mind that they were a reverse-engineered conceit, designed to allow Slattery, still limited to six rounds, to be the club's star attraction.

Dog Bagley eventually did bring his rising star Jimmy Sullivan to Buffalo to face Slattery. Sullivan had no idea what awaited him. In just a few rounds, Slats, unfurling blows at breathtaking speeds, punched the New York City welterweight into a pitiful daze. Somehow, Sullivan stayed on his feet, but by the end of the fifth round, the referee urged Sullivan's corner to end it. Sullivan begged his manager not to stop the fight. Bagley wasn't exactly the overprotective type. He sent Sullivan back out.

Early in that sixth and final round, Sullivan slowed to a stagger. The dreadful moment approached—one final, gruesome wallop to put down a helpless foe. The crowd grew disturbingly quiet. But the violence never came. In the blink of an eye, Slats switched gears, easing from brutally efficient pulverizer into playful showboat, shadow boxing and spraying light taps to Sullivan's shoulders. Slattery wasn't taunting Sullivan; he was just allowing a game opponent to finish standing up. This display of merciful gallantry drew the applause of a few, at first, and then the clapping cascaded into a roaring ovation. Murray shook his head, bemused. Slattery sure was a rarity. The crowd was cheering him for *pulling his punches*.

Unable to speak, Sullivan smiled a "thank you" through his stupor as the final gong clanged. Bagley trotted across the ring to shake Slattery's hand.

"You're a damn fine sport," Bagley said.

"No use murderin' a fella," Slats would say later.

★★★★★

Slattery's fame was spreading. His talents were mentioned to a national audience when *The Ring Magazine*, in early May of 1923, delivered faint praise tacked on to the end of a brief item pegged to the decline of a once-promising Jamestown, N.Y. welter, Ray Graham, whom Slats had defeated back in February.

"Jimmy Slattery, Buffalo's fast-rising star, was the latest to give Graham a licking in a match at the Broadway Auditorium on Feb. 19," *Ring* reported in a summary of "Upper New York State News."

Had anyone noticed the stale blurb, it likely would have only barely registered amidst the sensational news breaking in the boxing universe that May.

At long last, Jack Dempsey, two years dormant, had announced he would defend his world's heavyweight title on the Fourth of July. The challenger would be Minneapolis-St. Paul journeyman Tom Gibbons, younger brother of legendary Mike Gibbons. Aging, lacking in prestige and not exactly the most deserved of the candidates, Gibbons, nevertheless, was a clever, scientific boxer, and not a completely illogical choice. But what created such a tongue-wagging stir was the proposed location for the fight—in some tiny town way out West in the middle of nowhere. Dempsey's manager, Kearns, was sticking it to Tex Rickard, back in control of the Garden and planning to put on boxing at the just-opened, magnificent Yankee Stadium. Kearns instead struck up an improbable deal with a group of oil field operators reimagining their cowpoke settlement of Shelby, Montana. Town fathers envisioned a gusher of publicity from hosting a championship fight. Kearns saw a handsome payday. He demanded $300,000, extracting one-third of it up front. Shelby's residents tapped all possible resources to get the money together and started scrambling to make arrangements. Roads needed paving. The little railroad depot needed to be expanded. A local lumberyard sprang for $80,000 worth of pine boards for the hasty construction of an open-air octagon. Kearns was busy, too. Dempsey needed sparring partners. Good ones; lots of them. Dempsey chewed up practice foes. Kearns would need to start lining up as many as he could possibly find.

The 20th Century Limited, crown jewel of American passenger rail travel—the "Greatest Train in the World," proclaimed the New York Central—came streaking through the Mohawk Valley toward Buffalo en route to Chicago. To accommodate a surge in prosperous travelers, the 20th Century was actually three trains, in sections, running a half-mile apart in a midnight convoy. When it left Grand Central Terminal, the lead engines were lined up nose to nose like powerful racehorses ready to burst from the starting stall.

Riding in a luxury Pullman car on this night in the middle of May, 1923, was Doc Kearns, a focal point of the nation as he attempted to pull off one of the most outlandish sporting schemes ever conceived. Kearns was heading west to rendezvous with the champ, who was doing some fly fishing on the Missouri River. The plan was to meet at a training camp being established on the grounds of an old roadhouse on the outskirts of Great Falls, Montana, some 90 miles south of the proposed site of the Independence Day spectacle. The Dempsey faction—Jack's brother, Johnny, the trainers, and a bull terrier mascot—were preparing the camp.

Meanwhile, Kearns put together a deep stable of sparring partners, 17 and counting. He still had his eye out for one more, someone fast, a consummate boxer.

All through the night, the garrulous forty-year-old fight manager had played cards with fellow passenger and lightweight champion Benny Leonard, on his way to a scheduled fight in Chicago. A corps of newspaper reporters tagged along, too. As the sun came up May 16th, the world's fastest train pulled into Buffalo's Clinton Street depot for a scheduled nine-minute stop to switch engines. Kearns put on his hat, and exited his quarters, a hotel suite on wheels. He walked down to the end of the platform. There, a local fight manager was waiting.

Before leaving New York, after giving Tex Rickard one last chance to match the Shelby offer ("I wouldn't pay a nickel to see Dempsey in there with Tom Gibbons," Rickard supposedly retorted), Kearns had wired Red Carr requesting to parley. Kearns had only a brief window to make his pitch.

The champ needed a speed boy to help get fine-tuned, Kearns explained. "Can you get Slattery out to Montana by next week?" he asked.

"No," replied Red. "I've got fights booked for Jimmy."

"Well, how soon can you get him out?"

Kearns was offering Slattery a weekly stipend, expenses paid and now, to sweeten the offer, he floated the possibility of a slot on the undercard of the championship match.

"How much if Slats fights in one of the preliminaries?" Red asked.

"Oh, I guess a thousand," Kearns replied.

Red pressed for a guarantee. Kearns hedged. Putting Slats on the Dempsey-Gibbons undercard shouldn't be a problem, he insisted. "I'll arrange it when I get there," Kearns said.

"Fair enough," Red said. "I guess he can start the first week of June."

"Gibbons is a fast fellow," Kearns said, shaking hands good-bye. "Jack must be right."

The steam whistle blew and Kearns hustled back to his seat. He slid open the window as the train pulled away and shouted to Red, "Get Slattery to Great Falls!"

Red walked down the platform, a little uneasy. He opened an envelope Kearns had handed him. Inside was a note. Kearns intended to leave it with the station master in case Red had not shown up. The note read, in part: "Be sure to send Slattery right away. Dempsey needs him."

★★★★★

Excitement was in the air—Buffalo's own Jimmy Slattery was going to officially join the Dempsey training camp. Slats couldn't wait to get out there. Red wasn't nearly as fired up.

"Say, Red," Slats said to his manager, "I might as well take Skitsy and Joe along, too."

Slats wouldn't think of embarking on such an epic adventure without his two best pals. Red, on the other hand, was perplexed.

"Take them where?" Red asked.

"Out to Montana."

"Are you nutty? Where do you think Montana is, across the river? Why the railroad fare alone costs a hundred bucks!"

"We ain't gonna pay no railroad fare," Slats countered. "We'll all go out in my automobile."

As the old sportswriters told it, Red nearly fainted. Along with Dempsey's murderous fists and Doc Kearns' manipulative meat hooks, Red could now add a treacherous, weeks-long road odyssey to his growing list of worries. Red would have to keep his boy busy.

★★★★★

Meanwhile, inside Buffalo's watering holes, Slattery was the only conversation that mattered. Supporters were split over whether he should take on Frankie Schoell. Slats didn't want the match. With little to gain, neither did Schoell.

Welterweight contenders wanted no part of Slattery. Slattery's style—go like hell for six rounds—was trouble for ten-round fighters accustomed to conserving energy in the early parts of bouts. Slattery was dangerous. For any contender knocking on the door of a title shot in the Garden, the risk of fighting Slats outweighed the reward.

But that's where Charlie Murray came in. He was continually angling for a way to play his golden ticket. "The Q.A.C. could hang Slattery's green robe on a ring post and draw a good crowd," one Buffalo sportswriter joked.

Murray had his eye on Johnny Griffiths of Akron, Ohio. Griffiths had just surprised the boxing world by winning a unanimous newspaper decision in Scranton over Mickey Walker, welterweight champion. For weeks, Griffiths' Chicago-based manager, Tommy Walsh, had been hounding Murray to make a match between Griffiths and Schoell. Sure, Murray said, he could arrange that, provided Griffiths first agree to fight Slattery in a short-distance bout. Walsh balked at first but recognized this would be a steppingstone to a Schoell bout. The Chicago manager capitulated, telling Murray as an aside, "and you know Slattery shouldn't feel bad losing to Griffiths."

In retrofitting his programs around Slattery, Murray had stumbled on to something fresh. The Q.A.C.'s cavalcade of shorter fights drew more fans than ever before. The brightest star in Murray's galaxy was now earning $1,000 per fight, a hefty sum for less than twenty minutes of work.

Even Slattery's closest friends were nervous about Griffiths. He was 29, in his prime. He'd fought in Australia and Europe. He'd just won a decision over the best welter in the business.

Prior to the bout, Slats came down with a shivering cold. He climbed into the ring that night with red, watering eyes, chills, and a runny nose. He weighed 150 pounds. Among the lingering unknowns about Slattery: could he take a punch? Few opponents had ever truly connected. What if Griffiths plastered him?

The opening gong was still audibly reverberating when the fans learned the answer. Griffiths rushed in and buried a savage left hook into Slattery's ribs. The punch was so potent it lifted Slattery off the ground and dropped him cleanly to the mat.

All of Slattery's most enthusiastic boosters—Sloak and his firehouse friends, the St. Stephen's gang, neighbors—sat frozen in horror. Skitsy yelled, "Get up!" It had been a while since he'd had to. Red must have thought his worst fears about overmatching the kid too early had come true.

Before the referee reached the count of three, Slats popped up. Griffiths hadn't hurt him. He'd set off a trip hammer.

With his ruddy nostrils flaring, and his jaw tightening into a grimace, Slats went berserk in a methodical way, if such a thing is possible.

Here is the description of the fight by the *Courier*'s W.A. Norman: "*It is doubtful Johnny Griffiths ever saw as many gloves coming his way—he took more punishment wrapped up in six rounds than most fighters take in twenty.*"

In the final round, Slats, normally uninterested in going in for the kill, let loose in an effort to kayo the "Ohio Flash," who somehow stayed on his feet. In his corner, afterward, exhausted, Griffiths declared: "That boy is the fastest I ever faced. By gosh, he's a wonder."

Fans would later laugh at how strange it looked to see a grown man being tossed around the ring by such a young boy.

Tommy Walsh went back to Chicago and spread the word—*there's this kid in Buffalo who's the best young boxer I've ever seen* . . . and in New York City, Doc Bagley was making similar remarks.

As popular as Slattery was in his hometown of Buffalo, he was almost even more beloved in Syracuse, where promoter Jack Lewis paid him a couple hundred bucks just to appear in the ring in street clothes to wave to the fans. They gave him a warm ovation when he was introduced as "Buffalo's $10,000 Drawing Card." When Slats showed up at the arena, the local press corps, to his surprise, swarmed all over him and later wrote columns calling him the next middleweight champion. The Syracuse scribes fussed about his "aw shucks" boyish manner. But, *Slats was just a boy*, two months shy of his 19th birthday.

As Slattery's recognition was growing, demand for his services began to grow, too. Pals from the neighborhood were still in awe that their Shamus was going out to train with Dempsey. "Bring on Frankie Schoell!" became a battle cry amongst Slattery's most ardent supporters. Slattery fanatics allowed themselves to dream large. *How amazing was Slattery going to be when he got even older?*

What a difference the past year had made. The boy Charlie Murray had said would never make it as a fighter was not only becoming the talk of the sport, but also Murray's meal ticket. All doubts over Slattery's abilities were dissipating, except for one last lingering knock against him, that being his decided lack of a knockout punch.

Eddie Tranter was sports editor of *The Buffalo Enquirer* and ran the Velodrome fight club, rival to the Q.A.C., which had Slattery signed up for the foreseeable future. Tranter wasn't buying in. When, Tranter kept asking publicly, was Slattery going to fight someone other than a set-up or a has-been?

Now there were plenty of managers from around the East who wanted to come to town to take their shot. The scent of Charlie Murray's "$10,000 Cards" was irresistible.

Operating out of an office at 1547 Broadway, on the corner of 46th Street, in Manhattan, Al Lippe, originally from Philadelphia, gained notoriety as a brazen trainer-manager always working an angle and constantly running afoul of boxing authorities. Lippe had no qualms traveling halfway around the world with his fighters if the purse was sweet enough.

For part of the prior decade, circa 1915, before New York City fully emerged as prizefighting's undisputed epicenter, the richest gates could be found in Sydney, Australia. Lippe had trekked there with his prized welterweight, Jeff Smith, whose fistic fandangos alongside his adventurous handler earned him the nickname "Globe Trotter." Whether dabbling in theatrical bookings for a broke ex-pugilist or arranging bouts between two fighters simultaneously under contract to him, Lippe was always in pursuit of a score, even if he drew some heat. In the early 1920s, Lippe had assumed control of the affairs of another well-known welterweight, K.O. Loughlin, an ogre-like power puncher from Bethlehem, Pennsylvania.

Willie Loughlin earned his nickname by winning his first 11 fights by knockout, a noteworthy feat and at the time one shy of a welterweight record for consecutive kayos. Loughlin twice did battle with arguably the best in the game, Benny Leonard, fighting above his weight. Both fights were held at the Camden Sportsmen's Club outside Philly. In one, Loughlin supposedly knocked Leonard down. The current welterweight champ, Mickey Walker, had, only a few years earlier at the start of his climb, supposedly begged off an engagement with Loughlin, respecting his renowned punch. "He's knocked out more good men than any welter alive today," Lippe would say of the 34-year-old.

Slattery hadn't knocked out anyone, at least not in a while. Knowledgeable fans and commentators were fixated on Slattery's conspicuous inability to deal knockouts with his right hand, which was kind of a tantalizing sub-plot when taking into account the widely held belief that the boy marvel owned all of the other weapons in a champion's arsenal. Such focus on a singular flaw was at least partially unfair: Slattery won many of his early contests by knockout or technical knockout, including a few first-round kayos when he was first entering the game in December of '21. He'd stopped several opponents in 1922 and the early part of '23. Relying predominantly on speed and his long left, Slattery had made a rapid ascent and had done so in dazzling fashion, doling out some sound thrashings along the way. Lately, though, there had been no clean incapacitations, even in situations when his foes appeared right on the verge of collapse.

For every naysayer there was someone ready to take the other side. Fight fans, particularly the Irish (and especially after a few whiskeys), enjoyed vigorously debating the merits of top fighters. One person who definitely believed—who had always believed—that Slattery was going all the way was Billy Kelly of the *Courier*. On Sunday, June 3, the day before Slattery was set to take on K.O. Loughlin, the *Courier* published a glowing feature story, "Rapid Rise of Slattery Gives Hope Buffalo May Have Champion."

The article, accompanied by a full page of action photos, painted the eighteen-year-old as a modest, neatly dressed, churchgoing, saintly son whose only other devotions (beyond the Lord and his mother and father) were his boxing pursuits—which were designed to afford him the chance to one day enroll in a university.

"Jimmy lives the right sort of life," Kelly wrote. "He is without harmful habits."

Kelly laid out his case that Slats was a coming champion, even urged his readers to save the paper so as to be able to pull it out later when his prediction had come to pass.

Wrote the *Courier*'s Kelly:

> To name the chief fighting qualifications that Slattery has is to name the qualifications of a champion. He has everything—speed, height, reach, natural fighting ability, brains, cleverness; he has been well handled, not rushed. He hits hard with either hand, is cool under fire, has an uncanny knack for avoiding punishment . . . he has no scars indicating his strenuous profession. Just now Slattery is growing fast and will soon graduate to middleweight and then light heavyweight . . . the best judges of boxers have unanimously declared Slats has all the qualifications of a champion. AND HE HAS NEVER BEEN DEFEATED.

The images of Slattery were enchanting. The Sunday *Courier* "Rotogravure" pictorials—thematic depictions of life in Buffalo—were savored each week by readers. The *Courier*'s artistic photographer, Wilbur H. Porterfield, working with advanced carbon processes and exceptional technical acumen, captured, in one portrait, the gleam in Slattery's eyes more reminiscent of a matinee heartthrob than ring warrior.

Just arriving in Buffalo from New York City on the morning the photos ran were Al Lippe and K.O. Loughlin. When Lippe saw the shots of the trim, boyish sprite, he immediately got in touch with the local promoter to ask for their end in advance.

Not a chance, Murray told him. "Why do you need your money up front?" he asked.

"Because," Lippe said, "I'm going to bet it all on my fighter."

Lippe scrounged up a bankroll and placed his wager, supremely confident his old warhorse would overwhelm the agile colt.

Anxiety gripped the Aud when the opening bell rang and K.O. Loughlin, employing all the subtlety of an angry caveman, charged Slattery with a double-fisted assault. Slats danced out of harm's way, a vanishing act that amazed the crowd and flummoxed the older, slower Loughlin. Just a single wallop was all he supposedly needed to end this matter, but he was going to have to find the boy first. The wild barrage continued. At about the half-minute mark, Loughlin clipped Slattery on the nose, a glancing blow. Slattery came to a dead halt, suddenly, defiantly. He stood in close, slugging, toe to toe, with the wild man. To the surprise of everyone, he landed a short, solid left hook to Loughlin's jaw. The old pro withered to the canvas. The crowd of 7,000 let out an awesome shriek.

Loughlin took nearly a full count but regained his faculties and rose to his feet. He rushed the boy again. Slats stepped aside and slammed a right. Again to the jaw, again Loughlin went down. Referee Walter Kelly, bent low, hollered the count straight into Loughlin's ear so it could be heard above the screaming throng. Once more, Loughlin staggered to his feet. They slugged a few more seconds; Slats got the better of the exchanges. Another Slattery hook connected and sent Loughlin sprawling back to the canvas—the fight was just one-minute old and the veteran warrior had been dumped three times.

Rising yet again, Loughlin began to lob desperation roundhouses, which Slattery calmly ducked. The youth, fighting with smiling eyes and a bouncy spring, then measured out a perfect right uppercut—a finishing punch, savage in its precision—and THUD, Loughlin was finished, out cold.

The fans went wild. They jumped and hugged and slapped each other on the back. Hats, hundreds of them, flew up into the air.

Slattery, like some knight of olden times, went to his knee, cradled the fallen foe in his long arms and carried him over to his corner, where Al Lippe stood paralyzed with shock. They say trainers had to revive both fighter and manager.

The spectators, already worked into a fantastic tizzy, saw the gesture and could not believe their eyes. Lungs emptied. For ten more minutes, Jimmy Slattery was cheered as no Buffalo boxer had ever been before. The roar of the crowd vibrated the steel girders holding up the roof, which seemed as if it was about to rip off so that the triumphant crescendo could spill out into the late spring evening and pierce the sky.

Mobbed, Slats marched in tedious half steps through the pandemonium to the dressing room area. He shook hands with everyone he saw, if only to keep moving.

Everybody wanted a piece of him. Promoters from around the country telephoned with propositions. Challenges issued by managers came in the mail each day. Red received telegrams, including the one from Dempsey's people in Montana: "*Send Slattery at once.*"

Welterweights for hundreds of miles in all directions were all gunning for Slattery. Everywhere, admirers sought out the dashing young prizefighter. Slats suddenly had friends he never knew he had. And they all seemed to be singing the same siren song that anti-Prohibition summer: "Come on, Slats, let's have a drink."

FIVE

WILL-O'-THE-WISP

THE QUEENSBERRY ATHLETIC CLUB ran its season long, similar to a school year, from early September straight through June. New York City area promoters were starting to hold more outdoor shows, and Matchmaker Murray couldn't compete with the abundance of warm-weather boxing cavalcades. Demand for quality fighters spiked. Buffalo's minor league ballpark was sometimes used for open-air boxing but it was dilapidated and hardly ideal. So in Buffalo, boxing was more or less shelved during summer.

Several semi-accomplished but not top-echelon opponents were lined up for Slattery during the 1923–24 campaign. None of them seemed capable of spoiling his perfect record. Slattery's win streak was approaching 40—as was one of his mediocre challengers, journeyman Joe Eagan. Nobody expected him to beat Slattery. Their match, scheduled for January of 1924, smacked of a set-up.

It's not as if Red deliberately sought subpar challengers. He contended, to the contrary, that he was hunting trophy game—which is why he and Q.A.C. promoters were lobbying the Boxing Commission to set aside the Under-21 rule limiting their nineteen-year-old prodigy to contests of no more than six rounds. Some fans objected to the concept of rushing Slattery while others ridiculed the idea that a strapping young lad required state-imposed protection. Murray was chummy with commissioners. But political winds were shifting in Albany. Reformers were seeking to outlaw boxing yet again. Slattery's request to fight longer bouts was denied.

Suddenly, Slats found himself in a tricky position: no one of any notoriety wanted to fight him, especially not over a short distance. Sloak reckoned his boy should go back to the shipyard until he turned 21. But Slats kept fighting regularly, whomever Murray could find.

Joe Eagan, an Irish-American middleweight from Boston (and not to be confused with the Lackawanna featherweight of the same name), began his career in 1909. Short, bald, chubby, Eagan had once climbed to the middle of the middleweight ladder, but had since slipped. Slats viewed the match as a soft practice session in front of another record crowd.

It actually didn't matter who Slattery fought. The fans came anyway—to see him win. Slattery's three-dozen straight ring appearances without a loss or a draw was one whale of a way to launch a career, but it wasn't necessarily a widely known streak at the time. Match outcomes were only just then starting to be properly recorded, owing predominantly to *The Ring Magazine's* Nat Fleischer, who pushed back against boxing managers who embellished such information. Even the most rabid followers of the sport probably would not have known that Slattery's was among the longest active unbeaten streaks in the U.S. in more than two decades. Granted, well-versed aficionados could rattle off the names of those fighters most associated with extended stretches of freakish invincibility: Harry Greb, right then; Stanley Ketchel a generation earlier. But few people would have been able to definitively point to the number of wins (42) that Jack Root strung together around the turn of the century, which, according to *Ring*, was the last time any U.S. boxer had enjoyed such a lengthy uninterrupted winning streak to start a career.

Regardless, Slattery was beginning to become known through word of mouth. In a 1923 letter to the Q.A.C., Tex Rickard informed his friends in Buffalo that fans were starting to ask him when he would show the upstate speed boy in his Madison Square Garden. Rickard was interested in possibly signing Slattery to a series of engagements, but was hampered by the state's age limit. Then right around that time, just as it seemed Slats might break into the Big Town, some troubling signs emerged. Something wasn't right. He'd won his final fight of 1923 to run his streak to 38 in a row heading into the holidays. But he looked ordinary, particularly in comparison to the thrilling heroics of six months earlier.

★★★★★

That previous June, Slattery's knockout of K.O. Loughlin had capped an unforgettable 1922–23 boxing season. For several days afterwards, mouths in Buffalo remained agape as a sensational yarn wound its way around town. Apparently, Slats, with two consecutive blows, had dislocated, and then reset, Loughlin's jawbone.

As the weather warmed up, so too did Slattery's prospects; it wasn't only Rickard making inquiries. Promoters in Albany, Rochester, Syracuse, Pittsburgh and Youngstown had all heard the talk of the "Irish Flash" that one had to see to believe. Outsiders—racketeers—came sniffing around the gym with offers intended to lure Slats away from Red. Slats flatly turned them all away, and did so with the kind of abrasive language and accompanying glare that led some of the interlopers to step lively. Meanwhile, goading propositions from rival managers arrived daily. Red made a point to review each letter and telegram from the stack, keeping a list of worthwhile names, tossing the rest. The list wasn't long.

Doc Kearns continued to wire Red, asking him to send his boy out west to join Dempsey's training camp. But Slats never did make it out to Montana. In the end, Red didn't want him to go. Neither did his family. It was just too far away.

As for the July 4th heavyweight championship fight staged in the tiny town of Shelby, Montana, it would rank among the most monumental fiascos in the history of sports. Dempsey, listless in training, beat—but never dominated—Tommy Gibbons in a tedious affair witnessed by fewer than 20,000 spectators, half of whom crashed the gates. Dempsey failed to knock Gibbons out. Financial overextensions bankrupted the town. Dempsey and his manager, along with an armed security detail, fled the scene as fast as they could by private train.

Back east, New York's outdoor season was in full swing. Rickard secured the rights to stage boxing matches at the newly opened Yankee Stadium, considered a Roman Coliseum for modern times. And with no Dempsey to exploit that summer and no legitimate challenger in sight, the sport's biggest promoter focused his energy on cultivating champions in the light heavyweight and middleweight classes. If someone were to make boxing interesting again they would have to emerge from one of these divisions. Rickard sensed Slattery, who had the frame of at least a middleweight and eventually, possibly, a heavyweight, was a budding star. But when the Commission turned down the teenager's formal petition to fight longer bouts, Rickard lost interest.

Fresh out of suitable opponents, stuck between rungs—the Big Town beckoning yet just out of reach—Slattery laid down the gloves for the summer. He resigned himself to working two months in the shipyard, Sloak's prescription for natural development. Red had a different idea. He knew the boy was still maturing. What he needed most was a relaxed, natural setting—sun, fresh air—conducive for amassing weight. Red was betting on a summertime growth spurt. So he suggested Slats knock off for Crystal Beach. He could do as he pleased—swim, play golf, sunbathe, make merry, eat like a horse. Slats controlled his schedule.

The Fort Erie, Ontario amusement park and vacation spot had been expanding over the past three decades as Buffalo's answer to Coney Island. Slattery completely took it over. Frolicking amidst a postcard-worthy panorama—white sand beach, tree-lined midway, picnic groves, boardwalk promenade, grand hotels, magnificent coasters, sideshows, a Ferris wheel—Slattery proved to be the most popular attraction.

He loved to swim. With a power stroke reminiscent of national swimming sensation Johnny Weissmuller, Slats splashed across the Lake Erie horizon. Back and forth he went, for hours at a time, traversing between the steamship dock and the newly built recreational pier, pausing at intervals to rest atop the wooden diving platform set out 100 yards from the shore. Like a merman lording over the bay, Slats would leap from his perch when he spotted a swimmer in distress. Even though there were actual lifeguards on duty, it was the prizefighter who would be credited with saving four people from drowning that summer. One was Florence Ryan of Ridge Road in Lackawanna. Slats saw her sink, dove in, cut a wake straight to her, and dragged her to the beach where she was revived. One has to wonder, though, whether any of these other imperiled swimmers also happened to be resourceful females, perhaps intending to make contact with the handsome boxer. The civic leaders of the beach community thought enough of his efforts to wage a campaign to award Slats a medal.

The heroics continued on the baseball diamond. That same summer, Slats pitched his amateur team to a championship in the Lanigan Playground League. Large crowds gathered for the games. Every boy in the First Ward age 6 to 16 wanted to pat Slats on the back as though he were Babe Ruth.

It wasn't exactly the lazy summertime layoff Red had envisioned for his protégé, but then Slats wasn't one to idle around his cottage. If he wasn't swimming laps or playing baseball, he was busy: testing the balloon tires of his new Ford automobile; playing handball in the upstairs gym at the Knights of Columbus on Delaware Avenue with his partner Jimmy Kearns; dabbling in politics, collecting signatures for a friend eying a city council seat; or just playing euchre with the boys. Toward the end of the summer, Slats visited Fort Erie Race Track, where he found picking ponies a hoot, but tricky. Finally, something the kid couldn't do. Probably for the best.

Of course, if there was one activity at which Slattery was singularly gifted—what he did better than anything else, even box—it was the way he danced. The Charleston craze was sweeping the country that summer of '23, after James P. Johnson's infectious jazz piano tune was featured in a hit Broadway show. The moves, frenetic swinging of arms and shuffling of feet, perfectly suited Slats. Decked out in stylish bell-bottom trousers and a crisp straw-woven hat (wide oval brim, short rise, a colorful band), his face deeply tanned, his shoulders broadened from his vigorous swimming regimen, Slattery commanded all eyes when he strutted into the Crystal Dance Hall, packed with youths. Their Charleston "marathons" were met with deep suspicion by adults, even law enforcement officials, who decried jazz as the devil's music and treated these dance-a-thons as thinly disguised orgies. Because the Charleston was performed in large groups, with the tall, handsome prizefighter naturally at the center, scores of Buffalo women for decades to come could tell their children and grandchildren that they once cut the rug with Jimmy Slattery.

Indeed, his skills in the manly art of lady killing were becoming legendary. Slattery was as charming as he was dashing. Quick with a smile or a tune, he was a magnetic force and had run smack into a sexual revolution. More young women were rejecting traditional subservient roles, spawning a "we can do whatever men do" rebellion symbolized by the bob.

Parents often never learn the true extent of the debauchery of their children once they roam free of supervision. Nearly a century on, how can we know what young Slattery was really like while socializing in private? "A dog in heat," says Bertha Hyde, a First Ward historian, citing a one-liner often repeated by her father, who knew Slats.

Perhaps the single clearest window on behind-closed-doors Slats, though, comes from a 2007 biography of First Ward resident Kay Griffin, who was Slattery's age and who traveled in the same circles. As told to her son, author Thomas Murphy, the book contains some precious, first-hand glimpses of the pugilist at play. While there were abundant speakeasies and roadhouse saloons, many gatherings during Prohibition took place inside private homes. Fictional Jay Gatsby partied in a mansion on Long Island's Gold Coast; Slats went to bashes thrown at impressive dwellings sprouting up on McKinley Parkway in South Buffalo. "At every party, at all times of the day or night, there was Slats, surrounded by girls and booze," Kay Griffin recalls. "He would be playing the harmonica and proclaiming 'if I could only play the piano for a living, I'd quit the fight game!'"

Fighting ten pounds heavier, now a full-fledged middleweight, and shooting punches faster than ever before, Slats kept piling up victories in the second half of 1923. He humbled brash Wally Hinckle from Philadelphia, knocking him out in the third round and then, in what was becoming a signature move, carrying the out-cold opponent back over to his corner. When past-his-prime Jack Perry from Pittsburgh came to town looking to revive his career, Slats relieved him of any further notions. When the West Virginian Johnny Vascher tried his luck, a left hook pointed him back to where he belonged. Jamestown manager Tommy Moore made it his life's calling to find the boy who could beat Slats and bring him to Buffalo to cash in. But Moore couldn't put it together.

That fall, Red finally did set up a ten-round bout for Slats in Toronto, where there was no age limit. In his first fight exceeding six rounds, Slattery easily beat Jack McFarland of New York City. McFarland spent most of the encounter cowering with his head down. Slats injured his right hand pounding the top of it.

Though he played hard at night, Slats faithfully did his morning roadwork, alternating between running and walking along the old Erie Canal towpaths all the way out to the steel plant in Lackawanna and then back again, roughly a seven-mile roundtrip. He worked out at Newsboys' Gym every day, or *almost* every day. Attending church at St. Stephen's with his family was important. But that did not make Sunday exclusively the Lord's Day. For Slats, Sunday was about football.

★★★★★

A versatile left/right end and far and away the fastest player on the field, Slattery was an integral member of the "Fighting Micks," an elite amateur football team affiliated with St. Stephen's Church. Nothing in the entire world delighted Slats more than playing in a game of football. While the professional game had not yet taken off, college football was exploding in popularity all across America, particularly in the Midwest. Factory leagues had been forming in Buffalo over the past two decades. The squad from

St. Stephen's won a city junior championship in 1922 and started off the autumn of 1923 with a string of lopsided wins.

These were tough boys, a fun-loving, close group of neighborhood pals, including quarterback Ebby Leary and his sturdy linemen, Jumbo McGloin and Lefty Cotter. Some powerful spirit seemed to overcome the gang whenever they pulled on those scarlet sweaters and fastened their flat-top helmets of moleskin and padded leather; call it a collective will to absolutely pulverize the other team. Theirs was an electrifying brand of eleven-on-eleven, part blood and guts, part razzle-dazzle. Home-field contests— two hours of continuous collisions—were played in Collins Park against teams from other sections of Buffalo, Lackawanna, Ontario and Rochester. Crowds of up to 5,000 people would gather, mostly to see Slattery, who looked like any other ordinary high school-aged kid in his uniform. But there was no overlooking him when he touched the ball. He contributed on offense in every conceivable way possible, scoring touchdowns, kicking goals, making end runs, receiving forward passes and, at least once per game, galloping 50-plus yards like he was another Red Grange.

The football of the 1920s was notoriously brutal. As for the rules of trench warfare—there weren't any. Many players resorted to tactics more suited for wrestling or boxing. Slats, however, always played clean. It was not uncommon for sore players to spend Mondays completely immobile. And yet, as if needing to provide additional proof of his superhumanity, Slattery, on several occasions, would play an entire game on Sunday, box six rounds on the Q.A.C.'s regular Monday night card with no sign of fatigue, and then report back to football practice on Tuesday.

Red Carr agonized over his fighter's passion for football, but didn't try to stop him—or, rather, couldn't. Nervous to the point of tears, Red would attend games, barely able to watch, knowing how at any moment a promising ring career could be ruined. One time, a fast-moving sequence sent Slattery flying out of bounds straight toward an iron fence surrounding the park. Only a deft, split-second wriggle move, almost as if Slats were performing an illusion—did he just pass right through those rods?—prevented a disastrous crash. Most fans missed Slattery's close call. Sensing doom, they averted their eyes.

At some point, though, Slats risked burnout—and Red took action. On November 2, 1923, Slattery traveled to Erie, Pa., and stopped his opponent cold in the second round. Afterwards, Red stopped his boy.

He told Slats he was taking at least a one month vacation from the ring. Training in the gym, also, would cease. No more matches were made for November or early December.

Slattery, not surprisingly, played hard during this "free" period, frequenting parties and his favorite nightspots, enjoying his status as the toast of the town. But he was back in the gym by the middle of December and the layoff evidently had not caused him to grow stale. One Saturday, about two weeks before Christmas, a crowd came rushing over to the gym, hearing of the spectacle that was the lanky Irish boy roughing it up with Lee Anderson, a famous black heavyweight in town from the West Coast. Slattery had been preparing for his next opponent, Nick Volpetti, a burly young policeman from Pittston, Pennsylvania, in the heart of the Scranton/Wilkes-Barre coal mining region. Volpetti, who lorded over the South Main Street Armory scene, fighting as "Kid Moon," was so hungry for a crack at unbeaten Slattery, and so certain he could win, that he wagered, with Red, his end of the purse. To get Slats ready for this tough fellow, Red had instructed the large, imposing Anderson to cut loose. What followed was one of the wildest sparring sessions anyone ever recalled, as if a bomb had gone off on Franklin Street. When it ended, Anderson was in shock, gasping: "There never was a boy like him."

Red's wager was never in doubt. Slattery took the decision. Yet, and no one denied this, Volpetti had given Slattery a terrific fight. Slats, favoring his right, didn't land many stiff punches. He took a few, though, including several to the gut. Volpetti laid more gloves on Slattery than any previous foe had. He'd slowed Slats down with those body punches. Finally, someone found a weakness.

Now, the reason a fighter needs to be in superb physical condition, as Jim Corbett preached, was to deliver, and absorb, the shock of heavy blows. And then there are the blows for which no one can prepare.

★★★★★

Christmas came along with a dusting of snow. A spirit of generosity also blanketed Buffalo. Mayor Frank Schwab staged a boxing show to raise money for his toy drive. Troops of charitable citizens—fraternal societies, church groups and business leaders—lugged baskets filled with dolls and other goodies to city orphanages. On the north side of the city, needy residents were invited to a free yuletide feast held at a roadhouse owned by Joe

Di Carlo and his wife, Minnie. Di Carlo was better known for other activities, and by his nickname. As his late father had, Di Carlo helped oversee the Buffalo branch of a large crime syndicate with tendrils in New York and Chicago. His alias: "The Wolf."

Down in the First Ward, residents tried their best to make sure the poorest families had some meat on their table. Slattery stuffed the stockings on Fulton Street. It was the happiest holiday season the Slattery family ever experienced. Or rather, it should have been.

Right before Christmas, Slattery traveled with his teammates to Rochester for an important gridiron contest against the Oxfords. The St. Stephen's football squad was looking to cap another dominating season. In the middle of the game, Timmy "Lefty" Cotter, playing center, collapsed after a violent play. He'd broken his neck. All the players stood around him, helplessly staring down, speechless. Cotter never got up.

A few days later, at his funeral, the whole team, all together, grim-faced and wearing their red and white colors, filed into St. Stephen's Church. Slattery, still visibly shaken, was a pallbearer.

Lefty's death hit Slats hard. Perhaps what started out as a salve for his heavy heart devolved into a destructive booze jag, which might explain why there are stories placing Slats on a barstool on the afternoon of January 14, 1924, just a few hours before his fight with Joe Eagan. One variation of the oral history, an oft-repeated rumor heard long ago by a Slattery descendant, has the boxer out all night, and the entire next day, boozing at the Big House, the infamous bootlegger's hangout on Genesee Street. Red, years later, would concede that on at least one occasion Slats had fought while inebriated—although he never specified when.

Even before the Eagan fight, Red was in the uncomfortable position of having to refute stories of Slattery's high living, talk that Slats had, in the parlance of 1920s gamblers, "hit the toboggan." Red's bold counterclaim: if anything, his fighter had been over-training.

Stepping into the ring that night against Eagan, Slattery allegedly took one look at his opponent's round belly and snickered, "Holy smoke, will I ever get a razzing for fighting this fat setup."

Indeed, nothing seemed out of the ordinary; not at first. For three hectic rounds, the kid from the First Ward chased the old-timer from Boston about the ring, a ceaseless attack that Eagan was content to merely survive. Slats poured it on. Eagan covered, dodged and clinched or scampered away. Many fans figured the fight would not last more than three rounds. But it did.

In the fourth round, Slats sputtered, short on breath. Halfway through the round, Eagan changed strategy, suddenly going from timid prey to aggressive tormentor. Bobbing, shifting, cleverly spinning away, reaching deep into his mixed bag of veteran's tricks, Eagan seized the momentum. A pair of low blows left Slats doubled over and gasping. In the fifth, when it seemed Slats returned to form, Eagan locked arms, forcing clumsy, infighting. Slats was shooting punches straight down, his rangy arms unable to graze Eagan, who used his compact size to keep close, peppering Slats with short jabs to the midriff. What little gas Slats had left was sapped by those body punches.

The sixth and final round turned ugly. Tangled in the ropes, looking foolish, Slattery became a paper sack in Eagan's clutches. Stamina that Slattery surrendered seemed to flow into Eagan. At one point in the final stretch, it was Eagan chasing a pathetic, retreating Slattery about the ring. When Eagan connected with a terrific body smash from behind, Slats stumbled in pain as the mortified crowd yelled "*No!*"

When the decision went to Eagan—and when, for the first time, it wasn't Slattery's arm being raised in triumph—the crowd sat silent. No one booed. They knew Eagan deserved the verdict.

In his dressing room, Slattery was torn up. As much as his body ached physically, his inner turmoil was worse.

"The fans expect too much," he sulked afterwards. "They must think I'm a Jack Dempsey."

Skitsy and Joe tried their best to cheer him up. Pity the poor sucker unlucky enough to meet Slats next time—Slats would annihilate him and then all would be forgotten. This became their rallying cry.

"It was the best thing that could have happened to him," Red would say.

Sloak, too, agreed that an old-fashioned whipping might have been a godsend.

Offering fatherly consolation, Charlie Murray, who had a daughter but no sons, took Slats aside. Murray told him about the time that Dempsey got kayoed by Fireman Jim Flynn. This had been early in Dempsey's career and the setback only served to light a fire in the belly of the future champion.

"All the greats have tasted disappointment at some point early in their rise," Murray explained. "Like I always say—if you can't take the bitter with the sweet, then get out of the game."

Neither Murray, nor Red, was overly concerned with Slattery's loss to Eagan. They didn't expect it to seriously interrupt his climb. But those rumors—Slats was a lush, hurtling downward—persisted.

Slats, as it turned out, did have a potentially career-wrecking flaw no one quite knew about: fragile hands. He kept re-injuring his right, which caused him to favor it, and which was the reason why so often he would punch an opponent daffy but not floor him. Injury-prone mitts had nearly ended the promising career of Gene Tunney a few years earlier. But the New York City based light heavyweight had found a remedy—three months at an Ontario lumber camp. Chopping wood for hours a day, days on end, hardened his hands. Tunney soon returned to the ring and reignited his dream to someday become champion.

Despite his sore right hand and the sting of his first professional defeat, Slats was back in the ring just four days later in Syracuse. Red normally didn't allow his boy to box on such short rest, but he knew Slats needed to wash away the bitter taste of the Eagan loss. Slats took on Central New York favorite Al Cross, over whom he had owned a previous decision. Cheered on by a sizable delegation of supporters who'd come down on the afternoon train, Slats knocked Cross out in the third round. However, the ligaments behind his fingers were badly bruised in the process. After seeing the right hand swollen, Red declared that Slattery would be taking another month off. Murray looked for a way to keep the youngster out of trouble. The idea was to get Slats out of Buffalo, away from the Big House, away from his large gang of pals. His handlers weren't just putting his injured hand on ice; they were putting *him* on ice. Slattery was heading for the mountains.

★★★★★

On Sunday, January 28, 1924, Jimmy Slattery was present at St. Stephen's Church for the baptism of Helen Kearns, the newborn daughter of Jimmy Kearns, his close friend and handball partner. Slattery was Godfather. After mass, he returned home to finalize plans for a trip to the Adirondacks. He filled a trunk with his heaviest sweaters, wool socks, ice skates, a cap and mittens, just not the kind he usually wore. No boxing would take place where he was going. Later that frigid evening, Red Carr and a phalanx of folks from the neighborhood, a hundred or so, mainly from Fulton and nearby Euclid streets, marched Slats down Elk Street to the train station. His trusty seconds were coming along on the journey. Hockey sticks in hand, Skitsy and Joe helped lead the impromptu parade.

The rumor going around the neighborhood was that Slats was being sent away to a lumber camp in the deep wilderness. In actuality, he was embarking on a three-week stay at the extravagant Lake Placid Club. Murray and some well-heeled associates in New York City had arranged the stay. The exclusive, very WASPy resort was in the midst of an attempt to kindle a wintertime tourist season; playing host to a well-known prizefighter (even if he happened to be Catholic) would bring a spark of publicity.

Founded in 1895 by Melvil Dewey, head librarian for the State of New York and inventor of the Dewey Decimal System, the Lake Placid Club sat perched on a walled-off ridge on the eastern shore of Mirror Lake. During its first decade of existence, Dewey's mountain house and surrounding complex functioned solely as a summer retreat for society types and wealthy bankers who came from Manhattan and Connecticut. Recreation centered on the lake—swimming and boating; later, golf and tennis. In the winter of 1904–05, Dewey kept the grounds partially open to accommodate some outdoors adventurers who sought the enlivening mountain air, Norwegian-style skiing and woodsy snowshoe expeditions. In the ensuing years, Lake Placid, both the club and the village, steadily gained a reputation as a breeding ground for winter sports. Right as Slattery was arriving, village residents were celebrating news coming out of France, where the first-ever Winter Olympics were being held. Local speed skating hero Charles Jewtraw had claimed a gold medal.

The boys got into town late on a Sunday evening. They rode the New York Central to Plattsburgh, then switched to a Delaware & Hudson train right into Lake Placid. A driver in a Desoto limousine met them at the depot and drove them to the club about one mile away. The grounds had evolved over the years into a sprawling enclave of cedar chalets, cottages and clubhouses overlooking the lake. Back home, as Slats well knew, the rumor mill placed him "on the toboggan." Now here he was surrounded by a dozen actual toboggans, their chutes aimed at the frozen lake, an expansive shroud of ice and snow. Swirling in all directions out on the lake was a carnival of wonderful wintry pastimes: hockey games, dogsled races and, of course, skijoring—in which thrill-seekers (or people simply trying to get somewhere in a hurry) are towed on skis, either behind a horse or an automobile.

Slattery, indulging his lust for speed, took to the slopes. He was a natural at downhill skiing. It's not clear if Red ever would have authorized the trip had he known Slats was going to try out the ski jump on club-owned Mt. Whitney. A pet of the bellhops, maids, socialites and outdoors-types alike, Slats fell into a routine: Up at 6:00 A.M. to begin the day with a brisk walk around the three-mile perimeter of the lake. Next, Slats chopped fire wood for one hour under the supervision of his trainers and one of the groundskeepers. Hockey games went all day, on the lake and also on the tennis courts, which were converted into a rink. The stationary engineer, whose main job was to operate the coal furnace that powered the resort, had figured out a way to flood the surface with steaming boiler room water for maximum smoothing. Afternoons were packed with outdoor exercise, skiing—downhill and cross country—as well as snowshoe hikes. The boys ate like never before in their lives. Breakfast was sometimes served outside, right on the slopes, as the cooks fired up portable iron griddles for making flapjacks topped with butter that was hand churned at the club's own creamery, and also by healthy dollops of fresh Adirondack maple syrup. For dinner—an array of thick steaks and chops, ribs and roasts, always accompanied by soup, potatoes, vegetables, biscuits, an endless supply of milk and, best of all, the most delicious ice cream and milkshakes any of the three friends had ever tasted. Slats packed on the pounds, despite all of the activity. The gossip now spreading back in Buffalo was that Slats had reached 176 pounds—a coming heavyweight! Maybe he was on a collision course with Dempsey, after all.

Early in their stay, temperatures dropped to 40 below. But by the middle of February, the weather turned milder. A blinding winter sun would follow Slattery around on his new favorite activity—snowshoeing across the rolling meadow behind the club. Slats trekked for hours, through the woods, deep into the mountains, until light began to fade and the winds picked up. His face turned dark from the sun, as if he had been frolicking in the tropics, not the tundra. At night, the boys slept alongside a roaring fireplace with the windows thrown open and blankets piled high—Slats would recall how he never slept better. He vowed to make a pilgrimage to this winter paradise every year for the rest of his days. "We were in bed by 8:00 P.M. each night," insisted Joe Hickey, when they arrived back in Buffalo. It's not inconceivable, however, that at some point Slattery and his pals checked out the rollicking scene across the lake at the Northwoods Inn. Slattery would have stayed in Lake Placid all winter if it were up to him. But Red had summoned him home. He was heading back into the gym to resume boxing workouts. Interesting developments were unfolding. The question of who would be Slattery's next opponent had been settled. In trying to line up a worthy challenger these past few months, his handlers had been out big-game hunting. They'd bagged their prize.

He was a handsome, ripening fighter, a mere boy, sporting a near-perfect professional record, the talk of fistiana. No, not Jimmy Slattery. William L. Stribling, Jr., of Macon, Georgia, was another nineteen-year-old taking the country by storm that winter of '24. Sure, Slats was causing a commotion in Western New York and had been the subject of a few brief write-ups in the boxing magazines. Stribling, however, was a genuine American celebrity.

Known as W.L. to family, dubbed "Young" by scribes, or, simply, "the boy," Stribling captivated the nationally syndicated feature writers and enthralled "the creator of champions," Tex Rickard. Bolstering all of the fascination was the boy's delicious back-story: raised by a family of traveling acrobats; reared carefully since birth to be a boxing champion. Since he was still only a senior in high school there was, naturally, no shortage of "student by day, boxer at night" items, although by far the most colorful characters in the homespun storyline were the boy's faithful entourage—that is, his parents.

Willie and Lillie, better known as "Pa" and "Ma," never strayed far from their son's elbow. The press devoured their antics. Firmly directing his boy's boxing affairs, Pa was a round-faced, dark-haired, intense-looking, albeit stumpy little man in his late 30s; Ma, usually in a fancy fur or frilly hat, was much taller, physically imposing, and sort of pretty. As her son's trainer and chief second, Ma was right at home in the male-dominated fight game. She was known for her shrill outbursts during matches, usually aimed at the ref, always hurled from a nearby seat and never the actual corner itself. For all the strides women were making in everyday life, they were strictly forbidden from the ring.

Ma skillfully played the newspapermen. If photographers milled about, she would square her shoulders and hoist her brawny 165-pound pride and joy into her arms, comically cradling the oversized bundle. Pa, likewise, knew how to make a splash. In his sleepy drawl, he'd charm reporters with talk about how within a year or two the boy would become light heavyweight champion, add the necessary poundage, take Dempsey's heavyweight title, and then leave the fight game to pursue a university degree, probably at Yale. "Pa, we never agreed to that," moaned the boy one day after reading tales of his supposed interest in becoming a surgeon.

But the primary reason for W.L. "Young" Stribling's burst to fame was, undoubtedly, that lifeblood of prizefighting—*controversy*. The prior autumn, with the light heavyweight title at stake, its holder, New York City Irishman Mike McTigue, ventured to South Georgia for what was billed as the greatest battle ever to be fought in Dixie. To Northerner McTigue, a native of County Clare, Ireland, and his manager, Lower East Side character Joe Jacobs, the contest merely represented a hefty payday for taking on a schoolboy. But when the fight ended in a draw, bedlam had erupted. Fantastic accounts circulated around all parts of the country, particularly in the Northeast, concerning pistol-toting Klansmen and a strange, twice-reversed referee's decision. Seizing the headlines, Pa launched a barnstorming tour across the country and began talks with Rickard about a potentially lucrative rematch with McTigue at the Garden—provided, of course, the state Boxing Commission granted a dispensation allowing an underage fighter to box more than six rounds. With Jack Dempsey transplanted to Los Angeles to pursue a career in silent pictures, Stribling, overnight, became the biggest drawing card in boxing.

Slattery, it should be pointed out, was hardly an unknown. That there existed at this time not one, but two boy prodigies provided a boxing subplot that sweetened the formative years of a plump and privileged Columbia University literature major around the same age as Slattery and Stribling. Abbott Joseph Liebling, who would one day master the boxing essay, years later recalled in one of them how "in my young manhood there were two wunderkinder." Slattery, he wrote, was "a boy Mozart, a honeydew melon." Stribling was remembered for being overcautious, the result of doting parents.

How these precious jewels were handled became a subject for debate. As closely as their paths had paralleled, the youngsters had come up in contrasting ways. Red remained adamant that Slattery only box twice per month during the long season, with summers off and additional intervals of rest as needed. Pa Stribling lined up as many matches as he possibly could, always insisting that the best preparation was inside the ring, even as experts warned against burnout. As a result, Stribling had boxed nearly three times as many rounds as Slats over the previous two-and-a-half years, fighting more frequently and in longer bouts.

Pa Stribling made no apologies. He himself once dreamed of becoming a prizefighter. Born in Bainbridge, Georgia, William L. Stribling, Sr. ("Willie") had been a miserable store clerk, failed insurance salesman and frustrated photographer before embarking on a more fanciful quest. Willie grew up worshipping Gentleman Jim Corbett. At one time, he took up dedicated gymnasium training only to learn that he didn't have the skills to succeed in the ring. And besides that, his arms were way too short. Satiating his inner athlete and showman, Willie joined a vaudeville troupe. What's more, he convinced his young bride to come along with him. The couple reinvented themselves as acrobatic performers, intertwining comedy skits and monologues alongside rudimentary handsprings, tumbles and assorted feats of human equilibrium. Soon they were traveling the country. They played on the same circuit as W.C. Fields. Willie even once shared the footlights with his hero, Jim Corbett.

On the day his first son was born, the day after Christmas, 1904, Willie Stribling printed up theatrical handbills that announced: *"Born to Mr. and Mrs. W.L. Stribling Sr., a future heavyweight champion of the world."*

Ma came up with agility exercises while the child was still rolling around in his crib. The boy was placed under a strict nutritional regimen—no sweets. When he was four, little W.L. started performing on stage with his parents and baby brother, Herbert. The novelty act evolved into a humorous, boxing-themed domestic farce. To open, Pa worked a punching bag and delivered oration on the finer points of pugilism until, eventually, Ma cut in, berating him for ignoring his household chores. The splendid finale: the two kiddies, in oversized gloves, staging an adorable bout that culminated with W.L. taking an exaggerated dive. Crowds howled. The act was a smash hit. The family toured the United States and elsewhere—Europe, South America, even China. By the time W.L. was 11, the act came to include a new twist. Nightly, Pa offered a $10 cash prize to any boy (close to his son's weight) who could come up on stage and survive three rounds. The prize got claimed only a handful of times. W.L. became highly skilled at dodging punches.

Eventually, the Striblings put down roots in Macon, Georgia. Their nomadic lifestyle made the family extremely close, and they'd experienced some incredible adventures together. But W.L. fancied being a regular kid. His first love, as it turned out, was basketball. (Pa forbade him from playing football.) W.L. became the star of the Lanier High School hoops team. He also became sweethearts with classmate Clara Kinney. Regarding this relationship, W.L.'s parents could not have disapproved more.

Senior year was just getting underway when the boy learned he was going to get the opportunity of a lifetime.

For roughly two years, W.L., at the insistence of his father, had been boxing professionally, mainly in Atlanta, and was racking up an impressive record, losing only three fights out of almost 80. At 18, moving up from one weight class to the next, Stribling became a popular attraction in Atlanta, similar to the way Slattery shot to popularity in Buffalo. In what was surely an audacious gambit, the head of the American Legion Post in Columbus, Georgia, a retired Army major named John Paul Jones, wired the reigning light heavyweight champion with a challenge and $8,500 in guaranteed money; the 30-year-old Irishman had to take it seriously. McTigue's manager, Jacobs, a.k.a. "Yussel the Muscle," was a sly, wisecracking Jewish-American who used (and possibly coined) such phrases as *we wuz robbed.* Jacobs wasn't coming back without the crown. He negotiated an insurance policy—McTigue got to bring his own referee, Harry Ertle of Newark, N.J.

Some 10,000 fans turned up at the outdoor arena in Columbus, including soldiers stationed at nearby Fort Benning. This was also the Deep South, stronghold for the then suddenly resurgent Ku Klux Klan, exploding in ranks on the back of an anti-bootlegging platform, to go along with its vehement stances against blacks, Jews, Catholics and urban elites. If there were Klansmen lurking about, of course, it's not as if they were decked out in hooded garb. Very much conspicuous near ringside, though, was a sizable contingent of military police, local law enforcement and armed, private security detectives hired by Major Jones. Fans had roamed from across Georgia and neighboring Alabama. Most had never been to a boxing match. The local kid was a bronzed, finely chiseled, picture-book specimen next to the pale, crinkled northerner.

Round after round, Stribling appeared to dominate. When the final gong sounded, Ertle, the sole decider, was in a bind.

After some nervous hesitation, Ertle pointed to both fighters at the same time and called a draw. The crowd was not having it. Irate fans raced toward the ring. Stribling sunk distraught into the chair in his corner. Pa and the

Major rushed Ertle, pleading with him to do something quickly—*did he not see the enraged mob closing in*? The Newark officiator only had one move left to make. He went over and raised Stribling's arm. The angry mob dispersed. A few hours after the chaotic conclusion, Ertle, by this time safe in his hotel, issued a statement cementing his original verdict. He admitted to wavering out of panic. The fight was a draw. McTigue retained his title. The prophecy that Young Stribling would become a boxing champion had been fulfilled—for a few hours, anyway.

All of the sudden notoriety was thrilling for the high school senior. Having grown up on stage, Stribling took it in stride. He was hailed as "The Georgia Peach" and an "All-American Boy." But not all the attention would be favorable.

In New York, Stribling was being feted by Rickard, who was seeking to secure the boy a license and permission to fight 10-round bouts. Rickard had Stribling appear before the Boxing Commission at their offices in the novel-looking Flatiron Building, a three-sided structure constructed to fit a narrow, triangular section of Broadway down the street from Madison Square Garden. Later that night, Stribling sat ringside during a match as Rickard's guest. Rickard had the teen sensation formally introduced between preliminary bouts. "Ladies and gentlemen," cried the ring announcer, Joe Humphries, "please welcome, the marvel of Georgia . . ."

To Stribling's horror, some members of the audience drowned out the remarks by chanting "Ku Klux! Ku Klux! Ku Klux!"

Then, back home, Stribling was ruled ineligible to play basketball. He'd missed too much school.

And while he continued to garner headlines, with some in the press lionizing him, other writers questioned Stribling's fighting spirit. He was a gifted boxer. No one argued that. But sometimes it seemed his heart just wasn't in it.

★★★★★

Promoters cleaned up in Buffalo when showing black fighters, whether in black-versus-white or "all-black" affairs. Among the most recognized black boxers of the day, and probably the blackest, was Battling Siki from Senegal by way of France. By November of 1923, Siki (real name Louis Phal) had relocated to New York City, and Rickard matched him in the Garden against another top black contender, Kid Norfolk. Siki briefly had reigned as the world's light heavyweight champion—losing the title under dubious circumstances to McTigue. Agnostic to pain, Siki was known for raw courage inside the ring. But it was his eccentricities outside the ring that won him more attention. Supposedly, Siki would strut up and down 42nd Street, a pet monkey on his shoulder, dressed in garish French formal wear—purple satin cape, red gloves, silk top hat—squirting a water pistol, tossing peanuts, catcalling at females and generally sharing his own brand of whimsy. He loved the speakeasies, hundreds of which had popped up in Manhattan. It was said no amount of booze could quench his thirst.

Q.A.C. matchmaker Charlie Murray had traveled to the Metropolis to attend the Norfolk-Siki battle. If Siki won, Murray wanted to sign him for a match in Buffalo. Before the night's program began, Murray went to call on his rival, and pal, Rickard, in his lair high atop the famous Garden Tower. While Murray waited, one of Rickard's underlings introduced the Buffalo promoter to a friendly little man from down South—Pa Stribling.

The crowd at the old barn was sparse that night. Sitting together at ringside, Murray and the Southerner got to conversing.

"What's next for your boy?" Murray inquired.

"Well, it looks like he will have to pass on fighting in New York," Pa replied. "My son's age prevents him from anything except six-round bouts."

"Funny," Murray said. "We have that same issue with one of our local boys."

He explained how this boy accepted the condition placed upon him and, in spite of it, had gained quite a following.

"Turns out the fans like the spirit and the speed of the short-distance bouts," Murray said.

Soon, Pa realized how similar these two boys were. In drawing contrast, Murray may have let it slip that his boy was on the scrawny side and prone to poor habits—not much of a threat.

"Don't tell anyone I told you that," Murray added. "We can't have people thinking that I let you steal one. But, seeing as both boys are bound by the same limit, let's have them fight."

Pa was definitely interested. He knew Buffalo, cherished fond memories of the place. A quarter-century ago, at age 14, he had run off to find adventure at a world's fair held in Buffalo. He ended up working as a midway barker not too far from the pavilion where President McKinley got shot.

"What kind of seating does this club of yours have?" Pa inquired.

Murray pointed out how Q.A.C. shows were held at the city's largest auditorium and that the match would draw well. Pa was on board, sort of.

"Well, Mr. Murray," Pa said. "If we should change our minds about boxing in New York, I'd like nothing better than to take you up on this idea."

Whipping out a for-promotional-use fighter's photograph from his suit pocket and flipping it over, Murray hastily scribbled a contract. Pa wanted $3,000, guaranteed money. A steep price for six rounds, Murray remarked. But he acquiesced. Pa signed the makeshift document. Murray tucked it away.

After the fight, Murray caught the midnight train to Buffalo. He never did talk shop with Siki, who lost a 15-round decision in a bout so brutal it ended with the flamboyant warrior choking on his own blood. Over the course of the next year or so, poor Siki went broke and became a beacon for trouble—exploited by shady fight game figures, ostracized by the Boxing Commission and harassed by immigration authorities looking to deport him. The once proud champion, who for some inexplicable reason always tied his shoelaces backwards, declared that he was quitting the fight game and moving to Cuba. Before he could do so, however, Siki was shot to death in Hell's Kitchen. That too was never explained.

Because the Boxing Commission denied Stribling's plea for exemption from the six-round limit, the gate swung open for rival Newark promoter Babe Culnan to stage the McTigue-Stribling rematch. Rickard, convinced Stribling was the future of boxing and his new meal ticket, pushed ahead. But Pa Stribling was leaning toward a title fight in Newark, to be held at the First Regiment Armory, provided he and Culnan could come to terms.

Murray, meanwhile, kept hounding the Stribling camp, waving around his signed contract. He even filed a formalized version of it with the Commission. The Q.A.C. was claiming first dibs on Stribling's debut in New York State, which put Murray at odds with Rickard—but that wasn't unusual. Pa, meanwhile, kept Murray at bay while putting his boy through a grueling schedule. In early December of 1923, Murray received a telegram from Pa Stribling. It read: *"The boy has injured his back. All bouts called off for three weeks."* Then Pa proceeded to accept a few more matches in the South. Young Stribling found himself looking forward to the holidays, especially spending time with his girl, Clara. But on the day after Christmas—his 19th birthday—Pa ordered bags packed and put them on a train headed north, to Summit, New Jersey.

The family would be taking up temporary residence at a health farm owned by former lightweight champion Freddie Welsh. Stribling would be training for a New Year's Day fight against Brooklyn middleweight Dave Rosenberg at the Armory in Newark. A few years earlier, the Welsh farm had become known around the world as the training quarters for Jack Dempsey prior to his "Million-Dollar Gate" title defense against Georges Carpentier at Boyle's Thirty Acres.

No law in New Jersey prevented an underage fighter from going more than six rounds. But the state did have its own unpopular rule. Official decisions could not be rendered in the event both fighters finished upright. Newspapers published decisions to settle gambling interests. But to truly win a fight under Jersey rules you had to do it by knock out.

Stribling-Rosenberg ticket sales were brisk. It was a test-run to see how the teenager would play in the Metropolitan area—and indeed fans were excited to get a glimpse of the famous Georgia Peach.

At the hilly, 162-acre farm, snow fell. The southern boy wasn't accustomed to such a winter wonderland. As soon as they arrived, W.L. and his younger brother borrowed some sleds and were having a riot; Pa took notice and, allowing one last run, ordered them into the gymnasium.

Pa wasn't the only one keeping close tabs on the boy fighter. Newspapermen followed Stribling's every move. Jack Dempsey, who had just purchased his Hollywood dream mansion, came back East for a visit. The champ, himself trailed by reporters, specifically stopped by the Welsh farm to inspect the boy who might one day take his crown. When Dempsey delivered glowing compliments, the press pounced on them. Stribling, regardless of whether his back really was strained, felt worn down. He'd fought four times in five weeks, bouncing from Georgia up to New England, back down to Florida and Tennessee before shooting back up north to Jersey. He was battling the lingering effects of a bout with bronchitis. Mostly, he was lovesick.

On New Year's Day, 1924, Stribling met Rosenberg, once a middleweight titleholder. Both fighters finished on their feet. The newspaper decision went to Stribling.

When the Stribling's returned to Macon, the schoolboy boxer learned some bad news: he was being expelled from Lanier High School for chronic absenteeism. Pa threw a tantrum and threatened community leaders that if the matter wasn't sorted out he was moving the family to New Jersey. The school board welcomed Pa to attend its next meeting to argue his son's case, but the Striblings were hustling to catch another train, this one bound for South Florida.

At the Miami Cycledrome, W.L. Stribling kayoed New Yorker Mike Nestor. Jack Dempsey watched at ringside. "That kid will be champion one day," Dempsey told reporters afterwards.

A few nights later, Stribling met the "Ohio Iron Man" Norm Genet in West Palm Beach. Stribling liked to lock arms with his opponent, and pummel him coming out of the clinch. During one of these clinches, the referee ordered the pair to break. Stribling threw a punch after the command. When he did it again, the ref disqualified him. Pa lost it. He jumped into the ring and punched the ref. Another scene of mayhem nearly erupted, but things settled down when W.L. was able to subdue his dad. Not long after, Florida authorities moved to ban professional boxing.

In early February, with Slattery sojourning in the Adirondacks, Murray and Red Carr went gunning for Stribling. To build momentum, they enlisted a cadre of boxing's most influential voices—celebrated writers such as Damon Runyon and Hype Igoe—who supported a clash between the finest young prospect in the South and the finest in the North. One key ally was elderly boxing commissioner Billy Muldoon, who actually fought in the Civil War. Muldoon even came up with a clever moniker for the proposed fight: "Battle of the Age." Even Rickard backed off his claim that the Garden be the first to show Stribling in New York.

By the long-distance telephone, Pa informed Murray that as long as his terms—$3,000, guaranteed—were met, and provided that the still-to-be-scheduled rematch with McTigue did not pose a conflict, then, yes, he would honor his contract to fight the Slattery boy. Murray went ahead and penciled in Feb. 25th, and began promoting the event full-steam, selling tickets at raised prices. While Murray knew nothing was set in stone until the Striblings actually arrived in Buffalo, it did appear as if he had landed the fight of the year.

With one week to go, Murray was nervous. W.L. Stribling fought bouts in Savannah and Cincinnati, and then Pa took him to Newark to finalize the terms of the McTigue rematch with promoter Babe Culnan, who was thinking of slating it for the end of March.

"That works for us," Pa said. "We've just got one prior commitment to fight some guy in Buffalo."

"What guy?" Culnan asked.

"Some local fellow named Slattery," Pa said.

Culnan grimaced. Pa may not have heard much about Slattery, but the Jersey promoter sure had, and immediately he started to worry about waning interest in a Stribling-McTigue title bout should the Southerner get beat in Buffalo. Culnan added a condition: if Stribling lost any fight prior to the McTigue title fight, he would relinquish his shot.

Pa Stribling went ahead and signed the papers. Then he wired Charlie Murray to let him know they were catching the next train to Buffalo.

The fight was on! Murray had pulled it off. What's more, the Stribling's $3,000 guarantee represented a mere one-tenth of the gate he envisioned drawing. Tenacity and bold vision had prevailed. But what else was compelling the famous family to visit the shores of Lake Erie?

On a snowy morning, Friday, February 22, Murray stood waiting at a taxi stand across from the New York Central Railroad's Exchange Street station. The welcome party included Billy Kelly and some other Q.A.C. associates, assorted newspapermen and Hiker Foley, who ran the taxi stand. Foley saw them first. "Over there," he said, pointing out Ma, Pa and the boy, as well as some other members of their group, which included a top Atlanta boxing promoter who had tagged along to check out a few Buffalo boxers. Additionally, Pa, perhaps feeling a little in over his head, had asked Culnan to come work the corner. As the entourage made its way down the platform to the waiting taxis, a crowd began to form—fellow rail travelers, passersby; it wasn't an awestruck mob but rather a slowly expanding collection of quietly curious residents. They'd heard so much about these Striblings. The crowd swelled larger, encircling the taxi, which couldn't budge. Pa jumped out and said a few words, dispatching everyone with a thank-you, followed by his go-to line: "I can tell you this much, it'll be a fight." A half-hearted cheer let out, and the taxi pulled away.

They were heading for the nearby Hotel Statler, where Murray had booked a suite on the 11th floor. Pa instructed the driver to make an unplanned detour: "Take me to No. 92 Seneca Street. I want to get a peek."

Flush with nostalgia, Pa pointed out for his loved ones the very boarding house where he roomed during the summer of the Pan American Exposition. That was the summer that shaped his destiny, when he met those acrobats while sweeping the floors of the Japanese exhibit hall. They had befriended him and taught him a few of their tricks. "The place hasn't changed a bit," Pa said, gazing out the window at the old soda shop he used to hang around, perhaps unaware they had cruised into an area very close to Slattery's First Ward stronghold. "And that's all I drank by the way," Pa added.

They continued to the hotel. Plans were in place for a police escort to and from the ring. Vicious rumors were floating all over town that W.L. Stribling was a full-fledged Klansman—and this at a time when the rampant spread of the hooded order was feared and loathed in the north. Pa was always talking up the boy's intended academic pursuits; he needed to control the narrative. In the Statler suite, the boys relaxed and Ma washed up, while Pa tended to a backlog of correspondence—cards, telegrams and telephone messages—all the trappings of a busy man in an unprecedented age of heightened communication. In a few hours, W.L. was set to make an appearance at Bert Finch's gym on Main and Franklin, around the block from Newsboys' Gym. Stribling would work out there for the next few days. Finch planned to pack the place at a nickel a head. Plans were also laid, weather permitting, for the family to make an excursion to Niagara Falls on the Sunday before the Monday night fight.

"You know I still have friends in Buffalo," Pa said, holding up a stack of mail.

One of the letters was unsigned. "*I hope Young Stribling comes to Buffalo,*" read the anonymous missive. "*Someone needs to knock the block off this stuck up Irish kid.*"

Not everyone in town idolized Slattery. Someone, apparently, had it in for him.

★★★★★

While still up in the north woods, Slats was getting the Buffalo papers, so by the time he emerged—at 165 pounds, not as much as rumored, but still his heaviest—he knew the opportunity of a lifetime awaited him. Back at Newsboys' Gym, Slattery's regular workouts drew crowds jammed to the doorway. Slats, despite a winter storm, kept up his roadwork, happily power hiking along the lake in a heavy wool sweater, his only complaint being that he missed his snowshoes.

Stribling's workouts at the Finch gym were also drawing crowds. Slattery's buddies would go watch Stribling, then race back around the corner to Franklin Street to report to Red, who was putting his own boy through an absolute gauntlet. Red enlisted burly Johnny Paske to simulate Stribling's patented clinch maneuvers, which used brute force to lock up, then toss aside, a combatant at will, followed by a quick, dangerous hook. Red devised his most rigorous training program yet, sending Slats in against a rotating carousel of sparring foes, one after the other, until Red ran clean out and had to messenger around town for more. Red was seeing the crystallization of what they'd been working toward ever since the little pip first turned up at his gym. Following the last of these brutal training sessions, he declared: "Slats is at his best."

Skitsy Fitzgerald was frightened. He knew something Red didn't. Skitsy had come to the gym early. Slattery's 16-ounce training gloves hung on a peg on the wall. Pillowy due to the extra-padding, the mitts had stiffened overnight, covered in a crust of the Vaseline that sparring partners slicked on their headgear. Intent on softening the leather, the dutiful trainer pulled one of the gloves over his hand when he felt something sharp. Wincing, he removed his fingers, dripping with blood. Skitsy peered into the glove and made a startling find. Somebody—perhaps a sick prankster or a jealous rival—had planted a razor blade inside the socket. Skitsy knew a fighter's hand, even wrapped in bandages and tape, could be severely damaged by such a devious trap, specifically because of the intensity with which a trainer routinely thrusts the glove over the exposed fingers. Spooked but profoundly thankful he'd bothered to check the gloves, Skitsy decided to keep quiet. It would be several years before he ever mentioned the incident to anyone.

★★★★★

After church on Sunday morning, Slattery got in one hour of roadwork followed by some shadow boxing and jump rope. Then he lingered around Newsboys' for a while before returning home to Fulton Street. At their hotel drawing room, the Striblings were holding another press conference, during which time Pa mapped out the boy's future with his usual certainty. "He'll enter college as champ," the elder Stribling predicted. As for the fight, 24 hours away, there were no forecasts other than Pa's usual line—"it'll be a fight."

The local papers had been teeming with stories and photos of Ma and Pa Stribling, much to the displeasure of Slattery's father. Sloak had stomached just about all he could take. That night before the fight, Slats stayed at home, reported the *Courier*'s Billy Kelly in his morning column. Throughout the day, nervous electricity permeated the frosty air—*could Slattery win?* That was all anyone could talk about. The odds makers did not think so; Stribling was a heavy betting favorite. The battle of the 19-year-olds attracted national interest. More than two dozen sportswriters from across the country were set to cover the fight, many coming from New York City. Murray had enlarged the press rows to accommodate all of them. He also oversaw the weigh-ins at 2:00 P.M. and then huddled with the Aud's head custodian, as well as a team of builders putting the final touches on what Murray termed "total bleacherization" of the hall, with the ring pitched in the center. Dignitaries, sports celebrities, well-to-do fight fans—all kinds of folks from around the East Coast, Midwest and Canada—poured into the city by rail. One of the official judges was Jimmy Collins, the famed Boston Red Sox third baseman of a generation earlier and a Buffalo native now back home raising a family. On hand to personally oversee the proceedings was esteemed Boxing Commissioner James Farley, a political dynamo with Tammany ties who'd helped Al Smith become New York's governor. Farley assigned Ed Purdy, a New Yorker who'd never seen Slattery fight, as referee. Decisions in New York State were rendered by a quorum of three, the referee and two judges. The second judge, also picked by Farley, was Patsy Haley, a former professional lightweight and, like Purdy, a resident of New York City. Having two out-of-town deciders was done deliberately to stamp out any perception of hometown bias should the fight be close. Haley, however, was hardly a stranger. He'd moved to New York when he was 18—from Buffalo.

Area fans arrived in clusters. Various men's clubs—Elks, Larkin, Orioles, Eagles, and Knights of Columbus—bought blocks of tickets. The entire St. Stephen's football team attended together. An estimated 11,500 people would fill the Aud that night. It was Buffalo's biggest gate. The Q.A.C. had increased ticket prices, with the cheapest bleacher seats doubling from $1 to $2 dollars; ringside seats cost $11. Slattery stood to make at least $6,000 based on an agreed percentage of gate receipts, later estimated to have been around $27,000.

The crowd was on edge as 9:00 P.M. drew near and the bout was set to begin. Slats-Stribling wasn't technically the main event that night. It was billed, rather, as the front half of a "double wind-up," capped off with local hero Frankie Schoell versus Frankie Vanchell of Scranton. Murray wanted to make sure the many important Gotham visitors, who had all come for Slats-Stribling, would be able to catch 10:00 P.M. trains.

Pa Stribling and the boy came down the aisle first. One *Buffalo Times* account of the evening's events placed five city cops by their side. They were met by a scattered shower of boos, but not the feared hailstorm of negativity. Stribling climbed through the ropes and walked around the ring, gazing out into the rows of onlookers until he spotted her. Climbing back down out of the ring, the Georgian shuffled over to where his mother was seated and warmly greeted her with a hug and a kiss, a gesture which drew cheers of approval. Slattery came down the lane next, smiling away as a multitude of outstretched hands pawed at his shoulders and backside. Everyone he passed wished him good luck. There's one hilarious, if dubious, account of Slattery's entrance in which he purportedly pulled a clever stunt, stopping off to give his own mother a kiss, as if mocking his opponent while the crowd went wild. But if this even happened, Slats must have planted one on a relative or family friend—Mary Slattery never attended her son's fights. She couldn't bear the sight.

Nearing the steps leading up into the ring, Slats got a rowdy reception from the St. Stephen's gang, all sitting together, just feet away from Slattery's corner. Skitsy and Joe, meanwhile, in matching green cardigans, were arranging their accoutrements—stool, water bucket, sponges, towels. Inside the pockets of Skitsy's sweater were the usual trainer's trinkets—a pair of scissors, swabs, butterfly stitches, a jar of Vaseline. Slats scurried up three short steps and slid through the ropes as the cheering in the Aud grew louder. He stood in his corner, the smile never leaving his face. Immune to the reception being given to Slattery, Stribling stood confidently in his corner; he looked so confident, in fact, that it had the effect of making Slattery supporters apprehensive. The two youths were summoned by Purdy to the center of the ring for instructions. Now the Aud was really hopping; the long-awaited moment was almost here.

Pa never left his son's side, leaning in to hear every word Purdy was barking above the crescendo of crowd noise. The combatants clasped gloves in the customary appropriation of a handshake, each staring down at the other's gloves, their eyes never meeting. The ring announcer, Billy Kelly, introduced Stribling to random cat calls mixed with spurts of applause, a surprisingly hospitable reception, all things considered. The crowd simmered then came back to a boil when Kelly turned and waved his hand in the direction of the local hero. His bellowed introduction went unheard. Acknowledging the deafening reception, Slats waved his gloves over his head. The weights were read: Stribling, at 164 pounds, was a full-fledged light heavyweight; Slattery, at 159, had remained a middleweight with a few ounces to spare.

The crowd quieted to a murmur. Waiting out these final few seconds in his corner, Stribling broke into a spastic shadow boxing/calisthenics routine, as if expelling some excess nervous energy. Over in the opposite corner, Slats, looking greyhound-sleek, still smiling, clung to the ropes and stretched his legs, his back to Stribling. Almost time.

An abrupt whistle signaled an imminent clang. Fans held their breath. In those two seconds, the Aud fell silent. Timekeeper Marve Smith brought his index finger to rest on the starting lever of his trusty old stopwatch . . . and then sounded the gong.

The two nineteen-year-olds sped toward the middle of the ring like wildcats freed from traps. Right away, Stribling unleashed kill shots. Slats slipped away, leaving the Southerner swiping at air. Puzzled, Stribling kept up his barrage. Slats, circling backwards, bouncing on his toes, couldn't be touched. Stribling tossed haymakers that Slats ducked. Then Slats began to dictate the pace, which surprised and delighted the crowd. But toward the last one-third of the round, Stribling took over, landing long-range jabs to Slattery's body. Slats absorbed the blows with nary a grimace. Stribling showed off his superior defense. When Slats bore in, Stribling gracefully gave ground or covered up. When they knotted arms, Stribling, as expected, broke the clinch on his terms, tossing Slattery aside as if he were a child's plaything. Red was afraid of this. Skitsy and Joe traded disturbed looks. Slats had started off so sparklingly, but as the first round came to a close it was Stribling who appeared to have the edge.

In round two, Stribling kept up his wrestling-swinging and continued to connect to the body. Slats seemed to absorb the punches gamely. One of them, however, plainly hurt, causing Slats to tremble. His fans were sick with dread—and after such a hopeful beginning. But the battle was turning again, subtly, barely noticeable. In fact, only two people noticed. Skitsy and Joe had been watching their pal scrap since they were kids, and they knew when Slats was off, and they could tell when he was *on*. With the second round winding to a halt, Slats, brazenly—bizarrely—began to employ his opponent's own wrestling tactic against him. And much to Stribling's consternation, Slats outmuscled him. He held Stribling's arms firmly in place, which made the Macon boy snort with anger, and it was right then that a wave of relief fell over Slattery's corner. Skitsy and Joe were laughing and hugging, while the rest of the house sat hushed.

Infuriated at having the tables turned, Stribling set to deliver a death blow, cocking his right, and making no effort to cover up—an error. Slats caught him with a crushing right uppercut that snapped Stribling's head back between his shoulder blades. Until now, the Georgian had fought a wild-swinging, caution-be-damned fight. But Stribling tensed up for the remainder of the second round.

In Slattery's corner, lively banter cascaded into unbridled jubilation as the bout wore on. The tide, indeed, had turned. Slats forced the action, jabbing and waltzing in the face of Stribling's safety-first plodding. In the fourth, Slats tagged Stribling to the side of the head. In the fifth, he caught him with a hard right to the jaw. Stribling teetered back on his heels, scowled and lunged forward. Slattery danced out of reach. With one round remaining, Slats had the momentum.

Nevertheless, from the perspective of the sporting scribes, the judges and most fans—the fight, overall, looked even up to this point. Stribling had won early rounds, Slattery, later ones. Slattery landed more punches. They had stunned Stribling, dotted him with red welts, but not injured him. Stribling landed fewer punches, but some of his body blows carried authentic force. And yet Slattery seemed to have shaken them off.

At the start of the sixth and final round, it was anybody's fight. The two teenagers once again charged toward the center of the ring, where they traded a whirlwind of punches. Slats got the better of the exchange, landing two solid hooks to Stribling's jaw. The southerner seemed to lose interest after that. Slowing down, covering up, Stribling moved economically, which only served to accentuate the fleet footwork of Slattery, who kept shooting in and out, landing punches and disappearing. In the waning moments of the fight, Slattery dashed in close with a sudden, explosive assault to Stribling's body. All the Georgian could do was lock arms and hang on for dear life. That's how the fight ended.

At the bell, the enthusiasm level of the local fans had finally caught up with the gaiety that had overrun Slattery's corner much earlier. Slattery's attack in the sixth had been both an unrelenting fury and a thing of beauty, but the decision was still up in the air, officially. Red wasn't so overtly confident and glared at Skitsy as if to say "don't jinx it." But Skitsy couldn't contain himself.

Billy Kelly made it official. He raised Slattery's arm high into the air, uttering the words that would transform the Aud into a lunatic asylum: "Jimmy Slattery wins!"

Fans jumped and hugged. They stood on chairs, and looked around at each other in ecstasy. Many weren't sure how to react. They threw hats into the air, then their coats, too. In Slattery's corner, the verdict sent Skitsy and Joe and the St. Stephen's gang into a foot-stomping, arms-waving free-for-all. Above them, the rafters shuddered. In the ring, Slattery danced an elated jig. He took a quick second in the thick of the tumult to go shake hands, telling Stribling, "good fight." Stribling didn't say a word. Fans rushed toward the ring, looking to carry Slattery off. The decibel level was astounding. "I never heard anything like it," Red would later say of this jubilance. "The whole First Ward went crazy."

Five minutes elapsed before the delirium even partially subsided. It was easy to forget there was actually one more fight scheduled that evening. The two combatants, Schoell and Vanchell, were unable to get anywhere near the ring. Pa Stribling, visibly upset, led his son through the densely clogged walkway back to the dressing room. They were on their own. The police guard, as well as a line of firemen, now assembled near Slattery, as the mob pressed forward. For a time they were all trapped in the ring. Newspaper reporters were firing questions. At first, Red handled them. "Are you surprised at the outcome?" shouted one writer. "No," Red replied. "I believed Slats could win or I wouldn't have made the match."

Press flocked to the Stribling dressing room, determined to find out what went wrong. Pa had nothing to say. Not so, Ma.

"Our boy won the fight!" she hollered. "This was a hometown decision!"

Shielded by a cordon of civil servants, Slats pressed through the crowd and back to the dressing room area. Fans crammed the hallway trying to peek inside. A crush of reporters surrounded Slats, who took questions shot in rapid succession. Slattery's responses, like his left jab, were quick.

"What do you think of Stribling?"

"Oh, he's a nice kid."

"Can he hit?"

"Pretty fair."

"Did he sting you with those body punches?"

"Naw, not one."

"Not once?"

"Well, once he shook me up."

"Were you nervous?"

"Not after the first minute of fighting. Then I knew he was a cinch."

"Did he ever say anything to you inside the ring?"

"Naw, never opened his yap."

"Would you like to fight him again?"

"Every night of the week."

"Do you want to fight McTigue?"

"Bring him on by express."

"Were you thrilled when they gave you the decision?"

"I would have been if they didn't."

In the calm refuge of the Aud box office, Murray sat with Ma and Pa, trying to console them. Ma was sobbing and kept insisting that in any other setting her boy "could lick a dozen Jimmy Slatterys!" Pa was more philosophical. "I never should have made a short distance match with such a speedster," he sighed.

Right then, Sloak Slattery bolted into the office. His one good eye glimmered with satisfaction. Almost as if in his own vaudeville comedy act and semi-pretending the Georgians weren't present, Sloak grabbed the candlestick telephone receiver on the desk. "Central," he blurted into the transmitter. "I need to make a call." Sloak asked to be connected to his Fulton Street home. "That you, Ma? Listen, Ma, this is Pa Slattery. Our Jimmy just kicked the hell out of Ma and Pa Stribling's boy. So long, Ma!"

★★★★★

Slattery had summoned exceptional strength but he'd won with speed. Stribling still could have pulled out a victory in the sixth but he ended meekly, with Slats forcing the action. Watching the lively Buffalo lad dart and dance around the slower Stribling like some otherworldly woodland sprite, the pack of stupefied boxing beat writers, some of them ancient creatures themselves, were heard in the press rows mumbling an old and unusual, but apt, sports cliché: *will-o'-the-wisp*. As in, as the *Buffalo Times* would write, "Slattery was like a will-o'-the-wisp."

The term stemmed from Irish folklore, a reference to a phantasmal flicker seen out over the peat bogs, a flash that happened so instantaneously the farmers would question whether they'd seen anything at all, and at the same time never forget it. Such a split-second glow was some naturally occurring phosphorous reaction—but the bog people didn't know that. Going back decades, sportswriters had always latched on to the enchanting descriptor when confronted by bewildering speed, whether observing boxers or racehorses or halfbacks. One of the cleverest defensive boxers in history, Australian featherweight Young Griffo, was dubbed a will-o'-the-wisp during the 1890s. The phrase, however, would not become Slattery's sobriquet, just as "Buffalo Phantom" or "Buffalo Flash" never rang permanently. Other boxers after Slats would be called will-o'-the-wisps, the best-known being the unhittable Willie Pep.

Yet this enchanting Irish phrase would be associated enough with Slattery, on that momentous night he licked Young Stribling and thereafter, in print and in conversation, so that it might linger for two generations, such that a man—someone who had never seen Slattery fight—might merely blurt out "will-o'-the-wisp!" while describing Slats to a boy who knew little of boxing or the 1920s—and still somehow sufficiently convey much of what needed to be said.

The Irish down in the old First Ward went to bed dreaming of a St. Patrick's Day title match between their beloved son and light heavyweight champion Mike McTigue. But it was not to be. The Stribling narrative was too powerful. *The Ring Magazine* informed readers that the worst Stribling deserved from the judges against Slattery was a draw. Pa Stribling joined his wife in proclaiming that his boy was the victim of an unfair decision. Pressed on the matter, Pa whimsically, if disingenuously, put it this way: "My boy hit him with everything but popular approval and at the finish his adversary was dazed, hardly able to raise a hand—so the hometown ref raised it for him!" The Newark promoter, Culnan, so sure that demand for Stribling would wane following his loss in Buffalo, got a pleasant shock when just the opposite happened. Stribling's loss to Slats was discarded as a fluke. The Greater New York fans still craved the curious Southerner. Culnan could have doubled prices.

So Stribling got the shot at McTigue's crown, 12 rounds, in the Newark Armory, on the last day of March, 1924. The champion showed poorly, merely going through the motions trying not to get knocked out. He succeeded in hanging on to his title. Stribling took the newspaper decisions. Boxing publications dubbed him the "uncrowned champion." Slattery faded from the picture.

Though futile and mere formality, Red dropped off papers with the Boxing Commission officially challenging McTigue for the light heavyweight title. One vital role of the Commission, ostensibly, was to sanction bouts in a way so that the cream of the crop, not bums, received title shots, if just to maintain a veneer of integrity surrounding the boxing conducted in New York State. The Commission recognized rightful challengers. Any titleholder who refused to fight a formally recognized challenger could have his license stripped. But while New York was starting to succeed in monopolizing the topmost echelon of the sport, there were jurisdictional limits to their powers of facilitation. Moreover, the Commission sometimes seemed to pick its battles arbitrarily. Just ask awesome Harry Wills, the black heavyweight champion who was growing old waiting for authorities to force Dempsey to accept his challenge; or Gene Tunney, who, like Slattery, felt deserving of a crack at McTigue, and wasn't getting one.

World champion of the 175-pound division for one full year, McTigue gripped his crown ever more tightly—and had the perpetually injured hands to show for it, particularly whenever he needed to duck Tunney, who was considered the American light heavyweight champion. Even when the Commission threatened to take away his license if he didn't face Tunney, McTigue, at least financially speaking, knew he was better off engaging in soft, meaningless—but still lucrative—fights in New Jersey.

The heavyweight division was in a terrible slump for exactly the same reason—Dempsey was incredibly protective of his primary asset, the heavyweight crown. This caused much despair and nonstop speculation over whom he might fight next and when. That spring, Dempsey signed a $1 million deal with Universal Pictures to star in a series of matinee serials. The champ had not fought in six months. Prior to that, he'd fought only twice in two years. No one knew if Dempsey would ever climb into a ring again. No opponent ever made sense. Looming potential title fights proved to be mirages.

But the sun wasn't quite setting on the golden age of boxing. The economy was booming and the wheels of prizefighting—the nonstop schemes of moneymen, matchmakers, fighters, handlers, gamblers, racketeers and politicos alike—kept right on spinning with the onset of another outdoor season.

By this time, McTigue had split from Joe Jacobs in a financial dispute. McTigue bought out his contract for $10,000 and signed a new management deal with fellow Irishman Paddy Mullins.

A long-time Bowery bar owner who grew up staging backroom fights— men, bull terriers, roosters—Mullins was a beloved figure in New York's Irish-American community. Old-country loyal, a man of few words, Mullins always looked after the downtrodden, whether finding someone employment or paying their overdue rent. When a stray mongrel showed up at his door, Mullins took it in.

By 1924, he was running a prosperous stable of boxers based out of the Long Island City section of Queens, N.Y. In addition to McTigue, Mullins also handled Harry Wills. Wills, an ex–New Orleans dockworker, was down on his luck when he'd heard about Mullins' capacity for charity and had sought out his guidance. Their persistence in challenging Dempsey had helped sway public opinion in favor of a black boxer's right to fight for the heavyweight championship. More fans and sportswriters wanted to see Wills get his shot, while turning sour on the champ, increasingly seen as soft. The latest rumor (which would turn out to be true) was that Dempsey had had plastic surgery performed on his mashed-in nose.

Conferring with promoters in Queens, Mullins devised a route that might finally put Wills in line for that title shot. Plans were laid for a series of summertime bouts in which Wills would destroy a few heavies of note, fortifying his claim as the rightful challenger to Dempsey. This would pave the way, in theory, for a late summer championship showdown. At least that was the idea Mullins had in mind. Getting a Dempsey-Wills bout to come off would be a huge payday for all involved.

As for his other top fighter, McTigue, Mullins wasn't completely averse to matching him with Slattery. But he wanted to see the child star for himself.

In mid-April 1924, Mullins brought with him to Buffalo the second-string light heavy in his stable, Pat Walsh, 25, an Irish-American brawler from Cincinnati. At a minimum, Mullins could do a little scouting of one of McTigue's next potential opponents. Alternatively, and ideally, Walsh would beat the Buffalo boy who had beaten Young Stribling, and in the process jump a few rungs on the ladder.

Things did not work out that way. Slats knocked Walsh out in the second round.

"My God, he's fast," Mullins said after the fight. "That boy ought to be shown in the Big Town."

Back in the Metropolis, promoter Simon Flaherty, owner of the Queensboro Athletic Club, prepared for what looked to be his most successful outdoor season ever. Flaherty, known as "Si," was a part-time gambling parlor operator who had staged all varietals of fighting contests back in the days when Long Island City was relatively untamed wilderness beyond the ferry dock. In collaboration with his lifelong friend Mullins, Flaherty was angling to put on a Dempsey-Wills championship fight. In a bold move, Flaherty commissioned, at a cost of around $50,000, the construction of a large stadium bowl at the foot of the Queensboro Bridge. His club was expanding on a 5,000-seat arena already there. The new facility, built entirely of wooden boards and modeled after Boyle's 30 Acres in Jersey City, would seat up to 20,000. It would be ready in time for the first match in the Wills' worthiness campaign set to begin on the second Tuesday in May 1924.

The selected opponent for Wills would be Bartley Madden, an Irish heavyweight from the West Side of Manhattan. Giving away 30 pounds, Madden was given no chance to win. But Flaherty and Mullins knew Madden could take a pounding and that the local Irish would show up to cheer like mad for him. How badly would Wills trounce Madden and would it be enough to bolster Wills' claim as rightful challenger to Dempsey? This was pretty much the only storyline generating interest, albeit modest interest at best. Still, the location of the stadium was perfect. West Side Irish could get on a subway train in Times Square, ride ten minutes, get off at Bridge Plaza station and walk right to the new arena.

Boxing in Buffalo may have shut down for the summer, but in New York City the outdoor season was the peak time, a phenomenon unto itself.

Across Greater New York, in all boroughs, promoters, like wildcatters in an oil rush, jostled for turf and the talent to produce the most superior outdoor shows. No one was sitting back and allowing Tex Rickard to control the game. The Boxing Commission issued various clubs special permits for a specific night of the week. So, for example, Flaherty's club in Queens would have regular Tuesday night fights, while Coney Island promoters might have dibs on Friday night shows. The Nostrand Athletic Club in Brooklyn staged regular bouts at Henderson's Bowl, an open-air boxing arena capable of holding 10,000. There was outdoor boxing in Rockaway, Bayonne, N.J., and in Staten Island. Baseball parks—Ebbets Field, the Polo Grounds and Yankee Stadium—were all used for boxing events, including a regular set of annual charity fundraisers.

Few, if any of these endeavors, ever made money. Only Rickard had pulled off the mammoth scores, and that was because he had Dempsey to show in the ring. Rickard had promoted Dempsey's last fight, September 14, 1923, against Luis Angel Firpo, a beastly hombre who may have even had a touch of gigantism and who was known as the "Wild Bull of the Pampas." A stirring affair that saw Dempsey knocked clear out of the ring— only to climb back in and slay the mighty Argentine—the fight drew some 80,000 fans to the Polo Grounds. For Dempsey and Rickard, as well as a controversial syndicate of silent partners backing Firpo, it yielded enough cash to buy up half of Patagonia.

Simon Flaherty might expect 10,000 West Side Irishmen to come see Bartley Madden get his clock cleaned by a black man. But if he wanted to fill that new stadium of his, as Mullins saw it, he should put Jimmy Slattery of Buffalo on the undercard. The Irish would love him, Mullins promised.

So that's exactly what Flaherty did. He telephoned Red Carr with an offer: a $2,500 guarantee for Slats to appear in a six-round, semi-final bout leading up to Wills-Madden. Flaherty had just the opponent in mind, too.

Rugged Jack Lynch had arrived from out West several months earlier. Sometimes fighting as "Sergeant Jack," Lynch was originally from Prescott, Arizona, near Fort Whipple, and did most of his fighting in an open-air venue on the historic army base and in Phoenix. He was just breaking into the Metropolis, having been recruited east to join the Mullins stable the prior autumn. Lynch figured he was going places and that Slattery was just some chump from upstate. Red had never heard of Lynch. But Red was convinced there wasn't a fighter alive who could beat his boy in six rounds. He accepted the offer. Slattery was heading for the Big Town.

★★★★★

Buffalo was agog, but Slats played it blasé. "What's all this about a New York debut?" he'd chide the local boxing writers who kept banging on with that slant. "Why, I've fought in New York—and at Madison Square Garden no less."

It was classic Slats: sort of bashful, at the same time brash, and it was true; he had, of course, fought as an amateur in the A.A.U. tournament held at the Garden in January of 1921. All kidding aside, Slattery knew the stakes and desperately wanted to be at his best.

Red set up training quarters for Slats at a farmhouse on Grand Island, a short ferry ride from Tonawanda, N.Y., north of Buffalo. Little boxing was in store. Instead, Red pointed to a section of trees and told Jimmy to clear them. Swinging an axe several hours each day, Slats chopped them down, cut the limbs, sectioned the trunks and reduced the grove into neat stacks of cordwood. When he wasn't lumberjacking, Slats did his road-work, jogging in the morning, taking long, vigorous strolls after supper. His automobile, along with his large gang of buddies, remained in Buffalo. In addition to the creative physical routine, Red invented an effective psychological tool with which to cudgel his charge: "You'd better stay out of trouble, Jimmy," Red would tease. "Or I'll go get that little old man from Boston to come back here and teach you a lesson!"

As the fight drew closer, Charlie Murray was busy making arrangements with Western Union and the Associated Press so that telegraph wires could, effectively, connect the ringside of the Broadway Auditorium with the ringside in Queens, allowing for minute-by-minute updates of Slattery's performance to be read aloud to Buffalo fans. Radio broadcasts of fights weren't yet common; promoters saw radio as a threat.

Forty-eight hours before the fight, Slats, accompanied by Red Carr and his seconds, headed for the Lackawanna Railroad passenger terminal at the foot of Main Street. A spontaneous bon voyage party formed as word got around that Slats was heading out on a 10:00 P.M. train. It was a mix of roughly 100 people, family, close pals, members of the football team, along with assorted other city figures—Elk Street merchants, clergy, fellow athletes, newsboys and neighbors, brothers, fathers and sons—the people who knew and who loved Slats best. They brought growlers of beer and jugs of homemade wine. Some even brought fireworks. As dusk settled, the farewell brigade set off rockets and stormed the station's cavernous waiting room like a band of Fenian raiders. A few kids made their way into the concrete train shed just as Slats was climbing aboard his Lackawanna Limited sleeper car. Some of the boys boarded the train, whether they had tickets or not. Others were making plans to travel to New York by automobile. Around 100 Buffalo fans were expected to attend the fight.

Red kept Slats on a short leash. The next day, when they arrived in Long Island City, Red met with promoters and took Slats on an impromptu tour of the stadium, the enormous wooden structure incongruously sandwiched between some elevated train tracks and a high school. This section of Greater Astoria was in the midst of a building boom—factories, warehouses, industrial sites—and would have reminded Slats of his own neighborhood. In a cold rain, Red and Slats strolled the empty bowl. "This place is a gem," Red said. They were excited. But what they didn't know was that the Queensboro club still had not satisfied a requisite fire code inspection, and that without that passing grade, they could not obtain a permit from the Boxing Commission to hold their event. Without that permit, there would be no fight. Flaherty had already sold $35,000 worth of tickets.

The stadium was drenched. More rain lay in the forecast. And there was that not-so-insignificant matter of the fire code inspection. Flaherty announced that the fight would be postponed for two days, to Friday, due to the weather. He was buying time.

A large group of Buffalo pals aimed to stick around and whoop it up all week in the city. Red put himself and his fighter on a homeward-bound train. They planned to return in a few days.

"I don't trust the hotel food," Slats would later jest. He also said he didn't particularly care for New York City.

When their train rolled back into Buffalo, Billy Kelly of the *Courier* was at the station to break the bad news: Authorities had deemed the Queensboro stadium a fire trap—too much wood, too few exits and too close in proximity to residential housing tenements. The stadium was condemned. The fight was off.

Then the fight was back on. And then it was off, indefinitely. Tex Rickard and New Jersey promoters vowed to step in, but then they didn't. Perhaps it was all political double-crossing playing out in a tangle. But, as May gave way to June, the on-again, off-again event appeared to be exactly as fire deputies labeled it—doomed.

Slattery was crestfallen, retreating to Crystal Beach to ride out his limbo. Red fielded offers from promoters around the country, searching for other opportunities. Everyone kept telling Slats that he was on the verge of breaking out, that it was only a matter of time before his name would be written in electric lights. New thresholds of success always appeared to be around the corner, but then failed to materialize. It would have been easy for Slats to start believing his moment would never arrive. But just like that, in the early part of June, Red received an urgent telegram from Lew Raymond, a former burlesque comedian who served as Si Flaherty's matchmaker. The Queensboro club had sorted out matters with New York City Fire Chief John Kenlon, who ordered more exits and designated watch zones. The permit would be obtained. Red confirmed with the Boxing Commission what he'd been told. The fight indeed was a go. Slattery's moment had come. And did he ever make the most of it.

The evening of Monday, June 9, 1924, was cool and clear. The local Queens denizens arrived first, as soon as the doors opened, excited to see their new boxing venue. These were proud boxing fans. Wrestler-turned-boxer Paul Berlenbach, an Astoria resident, was the game's fastest-rising star right then. Flaherty and Mullins, beaming with pride, were first to arrive. Outside the main entrance, along Jackson Avenue, vendors peddled sandwiches while enterprising neighborhood kids accosted motorists with offers of one-dollar parking accommodations. Brazen children climbed up the elevated train trestle and jostled for unobstructed views. Others hopped on board the trains just to ride back and forth across the bridge, catching fleeting bursts of action when they passed by the stadium. Because of the roar of the crowd, local residents would have found it impossible to turn in early.

Slats stepped into the ring as darkness descended and with many of the 16,500 paying customers only just settling into their seats on wooden boards painted pine green. Stars multiplied above, the sky gently shading violet to pitch black. A blazing beacon owned the night horizon—it was a sign that read "Eveready," high atop the radio battery maker's headquarters a few blocks away. The just-installed banner was specially designed by an inventive Long Island City display maker—the Claude Neon Company.

In the center of the bowl, high-watt lamps were affixed to tall poles set behind each of the four ring pillars, illuminating the canvas and the faces (and oval-brimmed hats) of the men at ringside.

Right at the opening bell, Lynch, stocky, his head shaved down, rushed at Slats in a spurt aimed at stealing momentum. He failed. Slats nonchalantly brushed him aside, then proceeded to carry every round, looking as graceful as ever. Slats sealed his victory in the sixth, pinning Lynch along the ropes with a battery of rights and lefts to the chin. A few accounts of the six-round bout give Lynch his due, crediting him for crowding Slattery all the way and even landing a near knock-down in the third.

Compounding his lead with each progressive round, Slattery had saved enough gas in the tank to deliver a spectacular finale. Normally when he had a man licked, Slats eased up. But with about one minute remaining in the fight, Slats flew into an unrestrained rampage that ended with Lynch down on all fours. The referee was counting "three" when the final gong clanged. A newspaper photograph captured this precise moment— the excited ref's outstretched arm signaling his count, the beleaguered Westerner on bended knee, and the grinning Slattery, whirling around back toward his corner, his job complete. They say the crowd stood and applauded, including the hardboiled veterans in the press seats.

Most depictions of the fight ooze accolades for the wonder of Slattery. His ability, his style—the New York fans apparently had never witnessed anything like it before. Damon Runyon labeled him a sensation. One writer, whose name, perhaps mercifully, is lost to history, but whose wildly effusive eyewitness review was included in a magazine article four decades later, was supposedly so taken with Slattery that he cried at ringside. "Slattery was," the writer gushed, "that beautiful to watch."

Moving pictures of the Slattery-Lynch fight wound up being exhibited in New York City theatres as early as the following afternoon. One theatre manager, despite also having a reel of Wills-Madden—Wills had won, but had failed to do so impressively—chose instead to feature the Slattery film. High on the marquee, at B.S. Moss' Broadway Theater, on Broadway and 41rst Street, a mere 14 hours after his magnificent debut, there it was—the name "Jimmy Slattery" spelled in electric light bulbs. That next day, Slats and Red went down to the luxurious theatre, once home to extravagant productions, but now converted to a silent movie house. Slats grew up going to the little brick Masque Theater on Elk Street. He never imagined seeing himself on the silver screen. The first, third and final rounds were shown. What had floored Lynch right before the final bell was a right hook to the jaw. Now it hit Slats. "Golly, I had that lad licked!" he blurted aloud upon seeing his feat.

Rave reviews kept pouring in. New Yorkers had come out that night to see how badly Wills would beat Madden and left convinced they'd caught a glimpse of pugilism's brightest emerging star.

Everyone was talking about Slattery.

"He hits from all angles just like Dempsey," said Jimmy Walker, the nightlife-devouring, powerful state senator who was responsible for the re-legalization of boxing and rumored to be gearing up to run for Mayor of New York City.

"That kid showed me something I have not seen in a long time," said Kid McPartland, a lightweight legend of a generation earlier, and who was then a boxing referee.

"Slattery is all that we've heard he is," said James Sinott, boxing writer for the *New York Morning Telegraph*.

"He is as close to perfection as any man can be," said the unnamed reporter who wept.

A less emotional, rather clinical, description of Slattery in action in Long Island City that starry evening came from Thomas Rice of the *Brooklyn Daily Eagle:*

> Slattery has reduced to a science the trick of dancing back just far enough to make his opponent miss, then stepping forward and countering ... he steps back with his body upright, his opponent misses and Slattery steps in, leading with perfectly straight lefts and rights. As his opponent is badly off balance after a futile lead, those straight lefts and rights land almost at will ... Slattery is one of those rarities and his style should carry him far.

No less a respected voice than the *New York Evening Sun's* Wilbur Wood concurred: "Slattery will rise to the heights."

In a sport in which publicity is paramount, Slats had broken into the Big Town with what a Broadway producer of the era would term a "howling success."

He'd reached an entirely new threshold. Those who followed boxing commonly spoke of aspirants in terms of the rungs they occupied on some great ladder. For a while, it looked as if Slattery would either slip down or become stuck. Concerning his trajectory, debate now ceased. Further upward, surely, Slats was going to climb.

Nobody could have guessed how high.

The Slattery clan circa 1914; left to right: Sloak is holding his baby daughter, Helen; Joe and Jim are on the pony, that's Slats in the rear; Mary, the older daughter, is in the front with eldest son John just behind her. [Credit: *Buffalo Times*]

RED
CARR
A VETERAN OF THE
FIGHT GAME

IN HIS YOUNGER DAYS WAS A
CRACK HANDBALL PLAYER AT
Y.M.C.A., AND A FLASHY
FIELDING THIRD BASEMAN.

Red Carr, Slattery's manager in the 1930s, by newspaper cartoonist Leo Joseph Roche. [Credit: Tom Carr's collection]

One of the first publicity photos of Slats after he turned professional in 1921. [Credit: Author's collection]

Charlie Murray, promoter and matchmaker, Queensberry Athletic Club, Buffalo, N.Y., promoted many of Slattery's fights. [Credit: Author's collection]

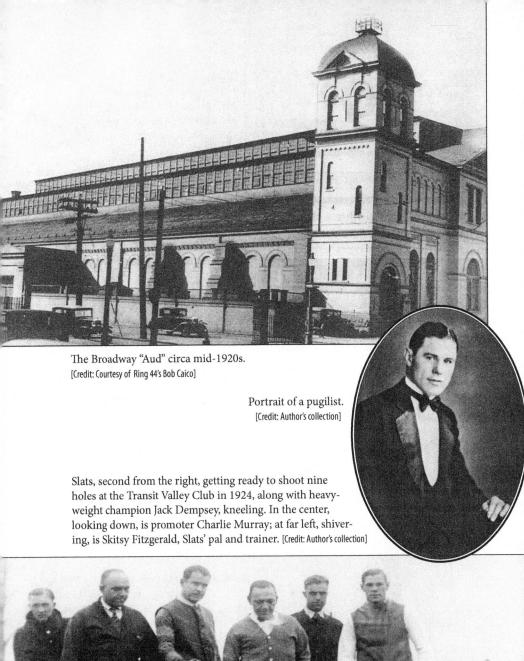

The Broadway "Aud" circa mid-1920s.
[Credit: Courtesy of Ring 44's Bob Caico]

Portrait of a pugilist.
[Credit: Author's collection]

Slats, second from the right, getting ready to shoot nine holes at the Transit Valley Club in 1924, along with heavyweight champion Jack Dempsey, kneeling. In the center, looking down, is promoter Charlie Murray; at far left, shivering, is Skitsy Fitzgerald, Slats' pal and trainer. [Credit: Author's collection]

Slats at Newsboys' Gym in February of 1925, age 20.
[Credit: *Buffalo Courier*]

The guest lodge at the Husson camp in Indian Lake in the Adirondacks, where Slattery trained in the summer of 1925. Slats is not in the photo. That's Red Carr, far left, on the front porch. The fellow in the center, leaning on the rail, is Joe Hickey, next to Skitsy, whose back is to the camera. A group of Big Town newspapermen look on. [Credit: W.H. Porterfield/*Buffalo Courier*]

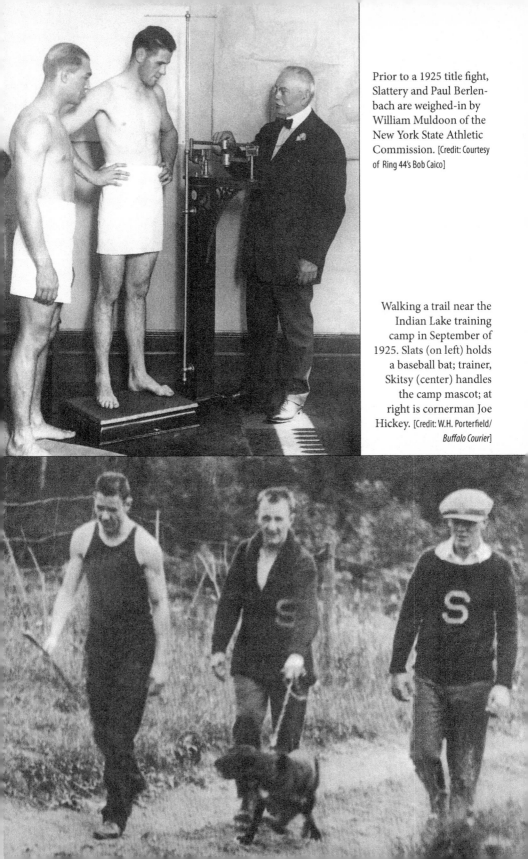

Prior to a 1925 title fight, Slattery and Paul Berlenbach are weighed-in by William Muldoon of the New York State Athletic Commission. [Credit: Courtesy of Ring 44's Bob Caico]

Walking a trail near the Indian Lake training camp in September of 1925. Slats (on left) holds a baseball bat; trainer, Skitsy (center) handles the camp mascot; at right is cornerman Joe Hickey. [Credit: W.H. Porterfield/ Buffalo Courier]

Slats (center) after winning the light heavyweight championship in late August of 1927, flanked by manager Red Carr (left) and trainer Skitsy Fitzgerald (right); photo taken at Lehigh Valley Terminal. [Credit: Cornelius Kennedy/*Buffalo News*]

Slats doing some old-school conditioning in Lake Placid, N.Y., in January of 1930. [Credit: AP Photo]

Lou Scozza has Slats on the ropes in the thrilling 13th round of their championship fight in February 1930. [Credit: *Courier-Express*, courtesy of Ring 44's Bob Caico]

Slats with his week-old son, Jimmy, Jr., in February 1931. [Credit: Author's collection]

Maxie Rosenbloom, hardly slapping, lands a left to Slats' jaw during a title bout at Ebbets Field in 1931. [Credit: *The Ring Magazine*]

Slats' favorite Chippewa haunt.
[Credit: Frank Luterek]

Slats, age 44, in Tucson,
Arizona, December 1948.
[Credit: Courtesy Patricia Kline]

SIX

THE MOST TALKED-ABOUT BOXER ON THE PLANET

LOUD, STRANGE NOISES WERE COMING from the Slattery residence. Neighbors on Abbott Road had grown accustomed to commotion since he'd bought the place earlier that summer. No one ever minded. No. 153 was a source of pride, not a nuisance.

But on this rainy August evening the whole block must have been wondering: *What was that noise?* Maybe the screech of a freight train grinding to a halt, or groans of animals being slaughtered? No, the Ward was alive with the sound of music. Wielding a saxophone and tapping his feet, Jimmy Slattery had installed himself as the leader of a hastily created jazz ensemble. With the most important fight of his life only days away, Slats, out of the blue, had formed a band. He selected tunes, furnished instruments and injected the energy and enthusiasm to keep practicing at night, regardless of how poorly they played. Bandmates included Skitsy Fitzgerald on drums and Joe Hickey on piano. Sam Mordeno, the neighborhood barber, was assigned the banjo. A fellow named Feeley butchered a fiddle.

Slattery's musical side has been documented. He would have liked to become a radio crooner, said admirer/writer Sammy "Newsboy" Brindis, who spent extensive time with his idol to pen his indispensible 1940 essay-pamphlet, *The Saga of Jimmy Slattery*. Counted among the people Slattery admired most was the piano tickler at the Big House. The same summer that he'd purchased the house on Abbott, Slats had picked up his first Victrola phonograph. Giving it a crank, he'd put on a recording of a symphony and telephoned a local paper claiming to have hired a real orchestra to perform in his front yard—and that he was the conductor. Slats was constantly humming a tune. "He can sing if he wants to," Sammy the Barber once said in a letter. Slattery's tastes ranged from Irish rebel songs to Italian love ballads, and included, of course, the rhythmic, up-tempo jazz coming to define his decidedly unserious generation.

A young Westbrook Pegler called these times "the era of wonderful nonsense." That line, describing the Twenties, came from a character in a Pegler short story written in the Thirties. Pegler later became more serious, and widely known, as a conservative political pundit. But back in the summer of '24, he was a New York-based wire service boxing correspondent hanging around the Garden and Broadway alongside the likes of Damon Runyon and Hype Igoe. At the time, those two were both nationally acclaimed sportswriters and close pals working together at Hearst on Park Row. What must have seemed nonsensical to all of these big-time boxing writers was the story breaking upstate in August of 1924—the out-of-the-blue matching of wonder boy Jimmy Slattery against Harry Greb, middleweight champion of the world and possibly the toughest dude who ever lived.

Forged by the Iron City, singularly indefatigable, Greb was a machine capable of churning out perpetual violence. Placing the relatively inexperienced Slattery, coming off a long layoff, in the roped square with the master mauler—surely this notion must have struck manager Red Carr as risky. Slats, for his part, didn't seem worried. Preoccupied with his jazz group, he had only one apparent concern, and that was the rainy weather.

If he was feeling apprehensive, it would have been understandable. The Human Windmill had claimed—chopped up—many well-known victims. Greb's horrific bludgeoning of Gene Tunney a couple of years earlier remained the benchmark for ring bloodbaths.

The national boxing press was certainly curious about the meeting between Slattery, still something of a mystery, and Greb, respected but not well liked. Murray needed to pull off a big outdoor show. He had spent the summer scheming in vain to stage his most extraordinary production yet: Slattery versus Georges Carpentier, the still-popular Frenchman and former light heavyweight champion. Murray saw fruit to be harvested before Tex Rickard and the other New York City promoters pulled Slattery away. It was already happening. Slats nearly got a coveted slot on an all-star boxing show in late June of 1924 at Yankee Stadium. Rickard offered Slattery a rematch with Young Stribling. But Red nixed it. He didn't think Slats, off vacationing, was ready for a fight.

Another summer hiatus had begun. Slattery, still a teenager for two more months, took it as a license for carefree living. He and Frankie

Schoell and some other Buffalo prizefighters rented a place in Crystal Beach. Ontario was hopping. The province had gone dry even before the U.S. did—but its four-year head start on the failed experiment only served to heighten anti-Prohibition revelry. Many breweries remained open to export beer to American scofflaws. A Labatt beer would have been vastly more preferable to bathtub gin.

"All summer long, [Slats] enjoyed himself at the beach and because of his popularity was a big figure there," wrote Billy Kelly in September of '24, responding to rumors concerning Slattery's high living across the border. "But there is no record of anything in his stay but clean, wholesome fun, some of it strenuous, but nothing to be ashamed of."

"The flower of [Slattery's] youth is at its height," wrote Murray around the same time. "His sheer love for boyish adventure has at times led him to violate the strict rules of athletic life."

"It only took one drink for Slattery to get drunk," said Red Carr's son, the late Paul Jr., repeating something his father had told him.

One of the most memorable highlights of that summer surely must have left Slats intoxicated. Buffalo native Winfield "Winnie" Sheehan, an ex-newspaperman and longtime assistant to theater-chain owner William Fox, had risen to become production chief for Fox's then booming, bi-coastal motion picture studio. Exhibitors across the country craved a steadier flow of new material to be shown on their screens—lengthy dramatic features, comedic shorts and news segments, particularly sporting news. Oversee-ing Fox's weekly newsreels, Sheehan arranged for a segment to be filmed in his hometown. The subject was Slattery, presented as the answer to society's most vexing question: who will be the next champion? The shoot took place at Murray's house on Starin Avenue in North Buffalo. A crew of technicians filled the backyard. Bulky cameras clicked and whirred.

Almost certainly discarded and/or disintegrated, the film was described by Murray in one of his columns, so we can at least imagine how the reel played: Slats skipping rope; Slats sparring with Luke Carr; a close up of Slats and Red smiling for the camera; a cutaway to Slats and Skitsy passing the medicine ball; and finally a closing shot, with the camera panning over a tremendous group of people—Slats surrounded by his gang of friends and the mob of neighbors who ran over as soon as they saw Murray's back-yard being transformed into a Hollywood studio lot.

For all of his frivolity, Slattery had shown sense buying the house on

Abbott Road. He gave it to his mother on her birthday. Spacious, abundantly windowed, adorned with a stone foundation and handsomely railed-off double porches, the two-floor (plus-an-attic) home stood that much taller after the famous family moved in. Part of him wished to buy his mother the finest home he could find in North Buffalo, the city's most splendid section. But his mother and father would never entertain leaving the old neighborhood. So Slats bought the grandest house he could find in proximity to St. Stephen's Parish. Total cost: $12,000. Slats put down a hefty down payment, several thousand dollars earned the night he fought Stribling. The Buffalo teen had turned those proceeds directly over to his mother, who went straight up to the bank. Slats took out the mortgage, but he named his parents on the deed. He bought all new furniture that his mom picked out. Mary Slattery was in heaven. She held an open house, inviting all the neighbors over for a tour and a full spread of food. The Slatterys were living comfortably but not ostentatiously. That would have been taboo in the First Ward.

A lot more money would be coming in the door if Murray could succeed in his quest to bring Georges Carpentier to Buffalo in August of '24. At the tail end of a fabulous career, the gallant French war hero still drew surprisingly well. The fame Carpentier attained fighting Jack Dempsey in 1921 had not diminished, even if his skills had. Carpentier versus Tunney at the Polo Grounds that July had been the most talked about fight of the summer. The Frenchman was knocked out in the 15th and final round. Slats had been offered a spot on the undercard. Red turned that one down, too.

Right before Carpentier lost to Tunney, there was growing talk of the Frenchman coming to Buffalo. So desperate to pull it off, Murray concocted a financial scenario in which he pulled down a $100,000 gate, allowing him to offer Carpentier an outrageous guarantee of $30,000. To make his math work, Murray would need to triple ticket prices. And he'd need a bigger arena; much bigger. Finally, at last, he had one.

Originally constructed of second-hand lumber in 1889, the Buffalo Baseball Park was long-time home to the minor league Bisons. It had since become a dilapidated disgrace. Starting in 1923, the club's primary owner, Frank J. Offermann, a local printing magnate, along with Sam Robertson, club president, as well as other fellow shareholders, came up with $250,000 to build an enormous new stadium of concrete and steel in the heart of the city's densely populated East Side. Spring of '24 brought the opening of the impressive new Bison Stadium and one awfully cruel season. Leading off, the club's chief financial executive died mysteriously. Opening day was rained and/or snowed out—five times. Nearly half of the home games were rained out. Manager George Wiltse, often asleep in the dugout, lost the confidence of his players. The Bisons couldn't fill the stadium, which held up to 20,000 people. Maybe Slattery could.

In late July, Murray got Carpentier's manager, Francois Deschamps, to agree to terms. A date was set for the middle of August. But Carpentier would not agree to hold a training camp in Buffalo for ten days prior to the fight, a revenue stream on which Murray insisted. Carpentier, dispirited by his loss to Tunney, returned home to France. Murray moved on. He quickly got Greb to agree to come fight Slattery in Buffalo. The shrewd promoter may have had him on a side burner all along.

Greb was game, as he was setting up a busy fall/winter campaign. He had a big rematch with Tunney set for late September in Cleveland. Murray expected Greb-Slattery to attract the biggest crowd in the history of Buffalo boxing. For Slattery, the fight would be his biggest yet. For Greb, it was merely a tune-up for Tunney.

Greb agreed to meet Slattery at 165 pounds, above the middleweight limit. Thus, the champion's crown would not be at stake. Neither Greb's fearlessness, nor his ability to make weight in a hurry, could be questioned. Greb weighed 168, having beefed up in preparation for Tunney, a light heavyweight transitioning to heavyweight. At the same time, Greb didn't want to risk losing his title on a foul or to a hometown decision.

Financial terms were a non-issue. Greb never quibbled over money. He usually bet his end on himself. Plus, he loved to fight.

Never was Greb more blissfully serene than when he was being smashed about the face; the harder the shot, the better. When he got really tagged, *hurt*, Greb would smile in ecstasy, and then the smile would turn maniacal in the fleeting seconds before he charged in for the kill. Slattery, had he truly been blessed with musical talent, probably would have ditched boxing. Slats didn't love the game, not the way Greb did. Greb lived for it. That he got paid to fight was an afterthought.

Likewise, Charlie Murray, in pursuing ever more ambitious sports promotions, wasn't really doing it for the money. Sure, he enjoyed making a buck. But his overriding motive was more about promoting Buffalo as a first-class sporting city. That goal prompted him to keep angling for

Slattery-Carpentier and for a Jack Dempsey title fight to be held in Buffalo—possibly against Greb. It was why that same summer Murray persuaded tennis superstar Bill Tilden to come compete in the "Great Lakes Championships." And it helps explain why Murray so aggressively pushed Red to match Slats with Greb outdoors in the new Bison Stadium.

As the event drew closer, Buffalo was soaked by rainy weather. An oasis of calm outwardly, Murray was communicating nonstop with the National Weather Service. Slats crammed in his training. He hadn't fought in three months. The old warhorse Willie K.O. Brennan, retired local middleweight favorite, offered to help Slats get ready.

Brennan, a rugged, two-fisted brawler, had fought Greb four times. After the retired veteran read in the newspaper about the coming Greb-Slattery match, he unpacked his boxing gear, untouched in two years, and sped over to Newsboys' Gym.

"I can help," Brennan told Red.

Slats had just finished his workout.

"We're all done for today," Red said. "But come back tomorrow."

Brennan did. He schooled the youngster on the various rough tactics he might expect to encounter. Greb's repertoire featured any and every conceivable method of administering punishment: butting; thumbing; kicking; slapping; cuffing; wrestling; clubbing; kneeing; elbowing; and, if he saw an opportunity, raking the laces of his gloves across an old cut. Some referees, especially in New York City, refused to tolerate his backalley ways. Other refs were afraid of catching an accidental elbow to the ribs.

If Greb did fight fair, his opponent often seized the occasion to beat him to the punch—to the groin. An alley cat sometimes must improvise in the heat of a whirling free-for-all. The incomparable punching style of Harry Greb came to include overhand and backhand blows, coming and going, up, down and sideways, combinations and flurries as damaging as they were odd, arriving, impossibly, all at once, and at a seemingly unsustainable pace. Greb defied the outermost limits of human stamina. A former corner man of Greb's once attempted to describe the cyclonic attack which came, the trainer said, with "such accelerated velocity that you could not see the punches being thrown."

Greb's five fights with New York heavyweight Bill Brennan are better remembered—a noteworthy series of examples of how capably Greb punched above his weight—but the significance of his fights with Buffalo's

K.O. Brennan can't be overlooked, either. The first two proved to be a turning point in Greb's career.

By the fall of 1916, Greb had defeated all of his rivals in his hometown of Pittsburgh. Manager Red Mason realized his fighter was ready to conquer foreign fields. Mason made a match in Erie, Pa., versus K.O. Brennan, then a nationally prominent middleweight contender and the top drawing card in Buffalo. Greb defeated Brennan and baffled fans with his rollicking display of speed and power. The bout generated headlines around the East. Right away, the Q.A.C. jumped at the chance to stage a rematch, which was held about a week later in Buffalo. This second meeting proved another terrific contest. Hometown fans gave the visitor a loud ovation. Greb's crazy style won them over. The *Courier*'s Kelly made references thereafter to the "slashing, smashing, crashing Harry Greb."

Greb had ascended to the upper rungs of the middleweight ladder. The climb had been long and difficult.

Born in Pittsburgh, Greb was a naturally gifted athlete. His German father, Pius, worshipped Pirate shortstop Honus Wagner. Pius convinced himself that his son would grow up to be a great ballplayer. Greb preferred boxing. He built a ring in the cellar. He competed locally as a teen amateur. Arriving home one day to boast of his achievements—he'd been named amateur welterweight champion of Pittsburgh—Greb was met by an irate Pius, ready to toss the boy out of the house for disobediently pursuing the forbidden pastime. Greb ran off, fighting in local clubs, eventually turning pro in 1913 at the age of eighteen. At that time, boxing was still treated as dirty business conducted in the shadows and subject to public scorn, rightly so if stories about Greb's encounters in the Pittsburgh area fight clubs are to be believed. His formative fighting years were a gauntlet of painful lessons, punctuated by fractures and teeth marks. And even though Greb rose to become the unofficial middleweight champion of the Iron City, in all that time his father never once came out to watch—which hurt Greb worse than anything he'd endured on the smoker circuit.

In 1917, Greb enlisted in the Navy. The outbreak of the war in Europe led him to set aside his career just as it was about to flourish. He would compete in inter-allied exhibitions, becoming the pride of the Atlantic Fleet. Following his brief hitch in the service, Greb picked up right where he had left off. Only 5'8", no more than 160 pounds, Greb met anyone and everyone—middleweights, light heavies, heavies, it didn't matter. Greb liked it best of all when he went nose to chest with a larger foe; the greater the mismatch, the more enjoyable it was for him to administer a thrashing. He often gave away twenty or more pounds. He fought constantly. In 1919 alone, Greb fought 45 times, including one 16-day stretch of 54 rounds against five opponents. That year, Greb faced Clay Turner in a Buffalo ring, went back to his hotel, then came back the next night to fight him again. "Bring 'em on," Greb would say when accepting a bout on short notice. "All I need is a haircut and a shave."

Just what fuelled his abnormal capacity for endurance remains a medical mystery. Daddy issues may have turned him into a boiling cauldron. Here's what Greb once said about himself: "I just pour on the speed. I put all I have into the attack. My plan is to start an offensive rush from the first session and from then on keep both gloves as busy as my arms can drive 'em, wang-bang, hammer and tongs."

One of Greb's most explosive, and best known, barrages came in September of 1920 while sparring with Jack Dempsey prior to the champ's bout with Billy Miske in Benton Harbor, Michigan. Dempsey was renowned for shredding his training mates. Doc Kearns specifically told trainer Teddy Hayes to spread the word that he wanted tough, speedy battlers to come help Dempsey prepare. When Greb got the invite he relished the chance to mix it up with the heavyweight champion of the world. Clad in his Navy sweatshirt, Greb arrived for his appointment twenty-five pounds lighter than the champ and four inches shorter. Over the course of two vigorous sessions, Greb smothered Dempsey, leaving him cut, red-faced and exasperated. Allegedly, Kearns ordered Greb to leave, although there are accounts of a third, more subdued sparring match. Grantland Rice, at the time among the most widely syndicated sports columnists in the business, watched the sessions and wrote: "Greb swarmed all over Dempsey and hit him more times than he had ever been hit before." A few years later, when Dempsey was considering Murray's proposal to have him defend his title versus Greb in Buffalo, Kearns shouted the idea down. Kearns knew Greb was dangerous. Moreover, though, the upside of the heavyweight champion fighting a much smaller man was negligible—too little to gain, too much to lose. Still, Greb continuously called Dempsey out, even as he hid a secret that would have caused most boxers to hang up the gloves. Greb was going blind.

The original injury is believed to have happened in August of 1921 in a bout versus Kid Norfolk. Greb suffered a detached retina in his right eye, resulting in the onset of partial blindness. Despite the worsening handicap, Greb continued to perform superbly, relentlessly, often against the same adversaries, ones who could at least give him a decent fight. He fought Bill Brennan five times. He had grudge sagas with Soldier Bartfield (five fights), Captain Bob Roper (six fights), Clay Turner (seven) and Fay Keiser (nine), to name a few of Greb's recycled victims. None of these rivals, however, were gamer—or more capable of stoking Greb's competitive furnace—than Tunney. It was their first meeting that produced the bloodiest fight in ring history.

Famous as the "Fighting Marine" after the war, Tunney was almost forced out of the game because of brittle hands. But by May of 1922, he'd become the American Light Heavyweight Champion. (He never could get the World's Light Heavyweight Champion, Mike McTigue, to meet him for that higher honor.) Tunney, a native of New York City's Greenwich Village, met Greb at Rickard's Garden in front of a large, partisan crowd, an eclectic intermingling of Bowery thugs and uptown dandies, not to mention a surprising number of ladies in elegant outfits—fodder for society pages. The Garden faithful didn't love Tunney. They disliked Greb.

From the first moment of the opening round, the hometown favorite was in trouble. Greb broke Tunney's nose one minute into the fight. Blood gushed, some accounts insist, as if from a hose. By the eighth round, both of Tunney's eyebrows had been sliced open. The cuts were several inches deep. Despite every trick tried by Tunney's veteran handler, Doc Bagley, the wounds would not close. Blood was everywhere—all over Tunney's face and chest, on Greb's gloves, on the canvas, the ropes, on the brims of the reporters' hats, on the white shirt of referee Kid McPartland, who refused to stop the brutality even when Greb begged him. Sickened by his own gore, and with a disgusting, liquid-chloride coagulant agent running from his nostrils down into his throat, Tunney was uncontrollably gagging and coughing as he stumbled through the late rounds. Greb's arms were completely exhausted from the volume of punches thrown. That would indicate a wild amount. After 15 terrifying rounds and an estimated two quarts emptied from his veins, Tunney was somehow still standing, his face a gruesome mockery of his handsome features. On the way back to his dressing room, following the declaration of Greb's victory, Tunney collapsed. Remaining conscious, lying flat on a rubdown table, Tunney, remarkably composed, chatted at length with newspaper-men. In a clinical speaking manner, Tunney recalled his horror while insisting that he had actually figured out, midway through the fight but by then unable to execute any plan, a way to beat Greb. Next time, he would stay away from the maelstrom and shoot punches from a distance. *Next time?* The newsmen figured Tunney was delirious. That he would ever consider climbing back into the ring with Greb after such an unholy beating would have seemed preposterous. About a day or so later, Tun-ney turned up at the Broadway offices of the State Boxing Commission to collect his fight check and post a $2,500 challenger's bond. Tunney, who had never lost a fight before, was formally seeking a rematch to reclaim his American Light Heavyweight Champion laurels. The title, not unlike Tunney's battered face, was largely unrecognized. Commissioner Mul-doon, who'd witnessed the massacre, urged Tunney to reconsider. "Forget Greb," Muldoon advised. "He's not a normal fighter."

But Tunney wanted Greb. And he got him, twice in 1923. Tunney won both, but they were close fights. Even Tunney was surprised when he took the judge's decision in the first of those two return matches in '23.

In that bout, Greb lost, to Tunney, his light heavyweight honors. But later in that year, he won the more widely recognized New York State version of the World's Middleweight Championship, defeating Johnny Wilson at the Polo Grounds. Slowly going blind, suffering in silence, Greb still managed to reach the pinnacle of his profession. He became a notorious night owl. Contemporary writers spun lurid tales of outrageous womanizing. A more recent biography depicts Greb as a sober and devoted husband to his wife Mildred, who died in March of '23. Amidst gossip of pre-fight romps in his dressing room and boozy late nights—Greb sometimes pretended to be drunk to fool a prospective opponent or move the betting line—there came exciting rumors that Greb was going to get his crack at Dempsey's heavy-weight title. But Murray's pipe dream to promote that bout was never to be.

What Greb really wanted was another crack at Tunney. Their fourth meeting was set for September 17, 1924, at the outdoor Olympic Arena in Cleveland, Ohio. Greb had recently reunited with Red Mason following a temporary fling with another manager. To prepare his man for Tunney, Mason scheduled two pro fights and an exhibition match ahead of the Cleveland date. The first of the two real fights was to take place in Buf-falo against Slattery. Mason and Greb had both heard some, but not too much, about the flashy local middleweight champion—certainly nothing to indicate that they should steer clear of him before an important fight with arch rival Tunney.

From Slattery's perspective, a date with Greb was the biggest thing that had ever happened to him, a chance to make a name for himself against the world's middleweight champion. Murray got what he wanted. Buffalo's profile as a top fight town would be raised.

On Tuesday, September 2, the eve of the scheduled bout, Murray telephoned the Slattery home bearing the latest weather update obtained straight from Chief Forecaster David Cuthbertson in the Buffalo branch of the National Weather Service. Originally from Scotland, Cuthbertson had headed the weather service in Buffalo going back to the days before Slattery's parents were born. The rain had passed, he'd said. No more precipitation was anticipated for the rest of the week. The fight was a go. Slats relayed the news to a house filled with friends. They all let out a cheer, prompting Slats to break into an impromptu address, concluding with, "All I can say is that I'll do my best." The gathering suddenly felt like a farewell for a young man about to march off to war. He was.

As the last days of summer gave way to the crisp start of fall, electrifying waves of anticipation swept across Western New York. Slattery versus Greb, outdoors at the new Bison Stadium—nothing more glorious could have helped usher in a new season. At every intersection along Main Street, the cries of the newsboys were louder than usual. On Elk Street, at the Mordeno Brothers barber shop, customers lingered that much longer to burn off nervous energy and perhaps convince each other that Slats stood a chance. At Newsboys' Gym, on the day before the fight, Red told Slats no more boxing, only light calisthenics. Sloak came by the gym to collect his son and take him straight home.

Greb arrived at the Hotel Statler on the afternoon of the fight, along with a herd of Pittsburgh sportswriters. Milling about the lobby and in nearby restaurants, the visiting scribes soaked up local chatter concerning Slattery's playboy living over at Crystal Beach. Inside the immense ballpark, workmen built bleachers in a semi-circle behind first and second base, having erected the ring over the pitcher's mound. Back at No. 153 Abbott, Mary Slattery, caught up in the excitement, had suddenly mustered the nerve to finally attend one of her son's fights. She busied herself cleaning and preparing a post-fight reception. The weather forecast turned out correct. Skies were clear. The air was cool, brisk. When the stadium gates were thrown open around 6:00 P.M., a growing multitude of boys unable to scrounge up a buck started staking out the perimeter, searching for a way to sneak in. Some would pose as newsboys assigned to peddle papers in the foyer; another trick—sidle up to a fighter right as he was making his way inside and offer to carry his equipment bag.

By 7:00 P.M., many fans were heading into the stadium. Those with the best seats usually waited until just before the start of the main event. Many of the fans had arrived on trains from numerous departure points: Pittsburgh, Erie, Bradford, Jamestown, Olean, Rochester, Syracuse, Toronto and New York City. More than one thousand automobiles had invaded the surrounding streets. Just as she was leaving the house to make her way over, Slattery's mom was overcome by anxiety. She gave away her ticket to her youngest daughter, Helen, who had pleaded all day to go. Older sister Mary would take her.

Greb got to the ballpark by 7:30 P.M. He was in a joyful mood. "Here kid," he said, flinging his gym bag over to one of the young boys hanging around the fighter's entrance. "Come along with me." Greb walked the boy, Joe Redmond, inside and even arranged for him to sit ringside as his guest.

The middleweight champion's bag contained fighting gear—shoes, trunks—and also some personal grooming items, including hair grease, which Greb used generously, and face powder, applied vainly to soften scars and dents. Although it was a movie-star look for which he was going, Greb, with his pale, ashen scowl, appeared frightening under the harsh glare of the lamps.

In his corner, before the bell, Greb stared over at the smiling, slender youngster in the opposite corner and wondered how in the world this guy could possibly be a fighter. An ovation for Greb as he was being introduced was drowned out by the one for Slattery. The crowd, restless and rowdier than usual during the preliminaries, continued to whoop it up as the referee, Ed Purdy, gave instructions. Purdy had been clear—he would not tolerate rough play. Under a sparkling moon, the whooping reached its crescendo, primal rejoice that the fight was finally about to start.

Anywhere, except for Buffalo, the odds of a youthful comer defeating an experienced champion would have been at least 5 to 1. But hometown pride held the betting line close to even money. Gamblers traded theories of how a draw could be in the rigging. On paper, the Greb-Slattery pairing was tailored for classic fan debates about street fighters and boxers, savagery versus science. What became evident to observers after the opening bell was the distinct possibility that no two faster foes had ever met in the ring before.

Keeping the champion at bay with crackling one-twos, Slats twirled around Greb, who moved about the ring in his own predatory orbit. Upright, arms dangling, Slattery set a furious pace. Greb threw a wild left. Slattery stepped out of reach and countered with a lightning-quick jab that clipped Greb on the chin and lifted the crowd to its feet. Greb swung wildly again and missed. Four times, he swiped air, stoking the fan frenzy with each miss. Backpedaling, Slats stopped, set his feet and launched a right uppercut that sent Greb into the ropes. Not even one minute had elapsed and the champ was stunned. *This kid has to be put down, immediately,* Greb resolved. But Slattery ripped him again, this time with a straight right, textbook, fired from the shoulder. It jolted Greb down to his shoes and put him back against the ropes. With the champion looking sloppy, Slattery flickering like a firefly and the contest starting off better than any of Slats' fans could have expected, there came a deafening roar that traveled up from the ringside boxes to the dollar bleachers in right field. The fans hadn't seen anything yet.

Slattery and Greb exploded into a frenetic toe-to-toe volley. It was an astounding sight, as if two funnel clouds had become one violent twister. The punches came so torrentially that the noisy throng, unable to react, fell quiet. Local writers would make reference to the fastest battle ever waged, featuring more gloves flying through the air than anyone could remember. "It would be an impossibility to describe the blows struck, attempted and landed," wrote the *Courier.*

In that opening round, three of Slattery's rights had pasted Greb. Afterward, Greb would tell Damon Runyon that the first round against Slattery was the toughest of his career. Slats caught Greb with two more rights at the start of the second round. Greb couldn't believe what was happening. Maybe it was out of embarrassment or anger at the unrestrained jubilance of the Buffalo crowd, but whatever it was, by the middle of the third round Greb was smiling. As outpointed as he'd been, the Pittsburgh Windmill knew what was coming next.

Greb played some possum during the second half of the second round and again in the first half of the third, allowing Slattery to burn fuel. Then Greb made his move. He attacked the body, landing two jarring hooks to the lower stomach. One blow landed a little low. Slattery gasped, slowing down. The instant he did, Greb pounced with vigor to spare. The assault was violent and methodical, almost comical—such was the outlandish number of punches Greb reeled off. Sapped of his strength, Slats could not escape the fury. Near the end of the third round, blood trickled from above his right eye. He'd never been cut before. The blood flow increased to a stream. Perhaps unnerved, Slats broke from form briefly to wipe blood away. Greb seized the moment, unleashing one of the windmill attacks for which he had become famous. Slattery staggered and tried to clinch. It had been a stunning reversal of momentum.

Round four was all Greb. Devoid of any steam, surrendering strength as Greb gained it, Slats slid helplessly into the teeth of the buzz-saw. He covered and held, and waited for the thrashing, which seemed as if it were coming from an octopus, to run its course. But respite never came. One fresh flurry of punches segued into the next, until the salvation of the bell finally came. Before the fifth, Skitsy worked feverishly in the corner to stanch the bleeding. Swabs coated in petroleum jelly weren't working. Skitsy really had no experience as a cut man. Blood was pouring down Slattery's face and chest. He seemed bothered by the mess. But he kept fighting. During those last two rounds, Slats endured more punishment than he had over the course of his three-year professional career. He bled all the way through. Greb laughed.

When they met in the center of the ring to customarily touch gloves to start the final round, the champion, brooding when he entered the ring, was grinning like a child at a carnival. Slattery, the smiling lad at the start, now wore the grim face. The round began. Slats staggered about with little stamina left in him. Greb, drawing on his inexhaustible reservoir of energy, proceeded to pour it on—his intent: registering a knockout or at least solidifying his latter round dominance. Slats, meanwhile, completely fell off a cliff, stumbling and teetering but nevertheless still bravely standing up to the onslaught. Greb clobbered him with five successive shots, including a vicious uppercut to the chin. All Slats could do was lurch forward and try to grab on to Greb. But Slattery's arms were so weak he could not hold them up. Greb was in top form. He battered Slattery's body, then shifted to the head, then back to the body, a non-stop, demonic barrage. Greb stayed continuously right on top of his prey. Slats would suddenly rally but just as quickly his arms would fall limp and Greb would overtake him. Not all of Greb's punches landed solidly. But plenty did. Slattery's legs, sturdy and nimble in the early going, now behaved as if laden down with man-hole covers. In the final thirty seconds of the fight, Slats slipped and fell. Greb helped him up. The crowd clapped with appreciation. And then the slaughter continued. Slats tried to jab Greb away, but the champ once again rushed in with both hands flailing, delivering three more crushing body shots. Slats tried to clinch. He could not take any more. Greb pushed him away, giggling like a mischievous child, but at last he was content to ease up to a light, sparring pace to close out the final seconds. At the bell, Greb put his arm on Slattery's shoulder, hugged him and said into his ear, "You're a great fighter, kid, and I'm not joking."

Seconds later, the referee pointed to Greb and declared him the winner. The verdict drew a boisterous, approving ovation. The crowd cheered for Greb, for the show he had put on. And they cheered for Slattery who, in defeat, had shown courage and the ability, for a few rounds anyway, to hang with the best in the business. Dejected, weary, Slats limped out of the ring, "a sorry, blood-spattered spectacle," according to Ray Coll of the *Pittsburgh Gazette-Times*. Coll added, in his unvarnished out-of-towner's assessment, "where Slattery ever gained the reputation he has is hard to see."

Late that night, Slattery's baby sister, Helen, came to his aching side. She was crying. "I'll never go to one of your fights again," the eleven-year-old whimpered. "I'm a jinx!"

★★★★★

Slattery's strategy of trying to outpace the master of perpetual motion had proven disastrous. Lack of conditioning nearly got him killed. Angry with himself, Slats later admitted, "I guess I just wasn't up to a fight."

He had trained for eight days after a three-month layoff—what Slats tried was, really, a stunt perhaps only Greb could have pulled off. No one was more complimentary to Slats than Greb. He said some incredibly nice things after the fight, perhaps being gracious to the Buffalo promoters. Not only had Greb told Runyon the first round had been the toughest he'd ever been through, but he also told Billy Kelly that Slattery was the best fighter he'd met since becoming middleweight champion. Save for one semi-low blow, Greb didn't do anything questionable. But, as Slats would say many years later, "Greb knew all the tricks."

One possible clue as to how the fight turned out the way it did has come echoing through the decades—from that lucky lad, Joe Redmond, who, from his choice seat, spotted Greb continuously pummeling Slattery's arms. What Redmond saw—"Greb kept hitting his arms, Slattery couldn't lift his arms"—he would repeat over the years to his son, Danny, a retired Buffalo detective.

Coverage in New York, Buffalo and the Pittsburgh papers made no mention of any limb bashing. That Slattery could not summon his artillery was widely attributed to his stamina splurge in the first two rounds. Greb had shrewdly exploited that—and may not have shared his plan to play possum in the second and third rounds with his manager. Red Mason's expletive-laced histrionics brought laughter from the ringsiders near Greb's corner. Mason confessed after the fight that he never should have scheduled it in the first place.

The Buffalo papers lapped up the laudatory remarks handed out by Greb and his manager. As Twenties' sportswriters tended to lean toward hyperbole, they ran with assertions such as: "No one ever gave Greb the fight Slattery did." As New York writers added their own flourish, the story became not that Greb had mowed Slattery down, but that Slattery "had Greb bewildered and almost out."

By the middle of September 1924, the word of the amazing Buffalo prospect who gave Greb his toughest fight had reached the community of artists and writers living abroad in France. They would read in the Paris edition of the *New York Herald* a column written by Sparrow Robertson, a famous boxing trainer. In it, Robertson relayed to his fellow ex-pats the existence of "Young Slattery," who was being looked upon as "the most likely successor to Jack Dempsey."

That he was receiving so much praise helped ease his pain. But Slats was hurting, feeling as if he'd blown his shot. Murray had always told him if he couldn't take the bitter with the sweet then he should get out of the game; but it was a painful period. There was physical pain, but it paled in comparison to his emotional state. Slats hated to let people down. But he had good reason to look on the bright side. Baby sister Helen had it wrong—there was no jinx. Her brother was lucky. Lucky to escape with the beating he got, and nothing worse. A huge break, meanwhile, was about to come his way.

While the future of Madison Square Garden may have been unclear that autumn of '24, Tex Rickard had a distinct vision for a spectacular series of main events worthy of capping off what looked to be the final indoor season at the venerated sports emporium. The property's owner, The New York Life Insurance Company, had notified the promoter a few months prior that his lease would only be extended one more year. It seemed the insurer was set on tearing down the iconic building—center of the boxing universe, beating heart of the city—to make way for a new headquarters. Not only fight fans, but New Yorkers everywhere, were broken-hearted but hopeful that a new Garden might rise (although where it would go and how it would be financed remained unsettled matters). Rickard's career had veered from one risky adventure to the next. He'd been a professional gambler, a silver prospector and a cattle rancher. Since coming East, Rickard had made The Garden the place to be on Friday night. Boxing became a social event for the Manhattan elite. Playing on the bittersweet vibe in the air, Rickard set about to craft a 1924–25 schedule to remember. Depleted of drama, the heavyweight class offered few storylines. In terms of talent, it was the leanest division. The next two weight classes down, however, were a completely different story. The middleweight and light heavyweight ranks were stuffed with young contenders. Mixing and matching the cream of the "little big men," such as New York City rivals Paul Berlenbach and Jack Delaney, as well as the Southern sensations Young Stribling and Tiger Flowers, Rickard was going to make sure the Friday Night Fights mattered. His true gift as a showman was an innate sense of what the public craved. The fans wanted a fresh face—a fighter capable of seriously challenging Jack Dempsey. Rickard would give them one.

Disappointed in his latest performance, Slats swore off the high life and hit the gym. Red said at the time that he never saw Slats so intensely focused. He was up early each morning for longer-than-usual jog-hikes, accompanied by his trainers and sometimes Luke Carr. Slattery's daily (except Sundays) sparring sessions wowed fans who packed every available inch of Newsboys' Gym. Female admission-seekers were turned away. Some of the sessions between Slats and Benny Ross—two skillful counterpunchers performing a pugilistic ballet—were better than most professional matches, it's been said. That September, Slattery's ring feats could be seen on Main

Street in Buffalo, where Shea's Hippodrome showed the moving pictures of his fight the previous June against Jack Lynch in Long Island City. Local fans were getting ready to pack the Aud to see Lynch in person—the Q.A.C. had arranged a rematch for Monday, September 22.

Meanwhile, Tex Rickard had instructed his matchmaker, Frank Flournoy, to pay close attention to the outcome of the Slattery-Lynch bout; if Lynch were to defeat Slattery, the husky Arizonan would, overnight, become another fresh face to add to the light heavyweight cavalcade.

Slats, as he had in their first encounter in Queens, won a convincing decision over Lynch. Except this time he changed tactics, interspersing full-acceleration rushes with slower-paced offensives, an energy-conservation approach that did not go over well at the Aud. Slats had Lynch woozy but neglected to finish him, at which point the crowd jeered. After the fight, a local sportswriter, Horace Lerch, kidded Slats about how fan hostility was actually a good sign. "They never boo a comer," Lerch told him. "It means you've made it."

The first reports of Slattery's six-round decision came over the wires around 11:00 P.M. that Monday night. Just before midnight, Frank Flournoy, head matchmaker for Madison Square Garden, placed a long distance telephone call to the home of Red Carr. Flournoy described the Garden's upcoming series of banner events, the first of which was to be held on the first Friday in October. Red was interested but asked to sleep on it. Flournoy agreed to phone him back the next day. By the end of that following Tuesday, the two men had hammered out an agreement. Jimmy Slattery had indeed arrived—he was about to appear in the world's most famous boxing ring.

At first, Red hesitated to put Slats against Rickard's handpicked ace, Jack Delaney, a top-rated New York-based middleweight moving toward light heavyweight. When Buffalo boxing mavens heard the news they collectively frowned. "Everyone said I was crazy to make the Delaney match," Red would say later. The dope from the experts: Delaney, a sharpshooter in possession of the ring's hardest right hand, spelled calamity for an arms-down, stand-up fighter like Slattery. His career, maybe even his life, would be imperiled.

Discussing the match, Red struck a grave note of caution. "You need to be ready, Jimmy," Red stressed. "If this guy hits you, you won't get up."

"He'll have to find me," Slats replied. "Let him try."

Jack Delaney shot to overnight stardom by virtue of his stunning stoppage of Astoria's Paul Berlenbach. At the time, Berlenbach was considered the game's deadliest knockout artist. Laying out Berlenbach at the height of his reign was the equivalent of landing a house on the scariest character in the Land of Oz. Delaney instantly became the darling of the Garden crowd, which comprised a rich stew of writers, press agents, gamblers, politicians, fight managers, ex-fighters, Wall Street stock operators, nightclub owners, gangsters, socialites and theater people, all of whom normally congregated in Midtown. New York boxing fans loved their knockouts. Just as Babe Ruth, with his prolific homerun hitting, transformed what fans loved most about baseball, Paul Berlenbach had helped to change boxing. Fans now came to see the big blow. The greatest thrill was to see one man counted out completely.

When Delaney fought around his former home base of Bridgeport, Connecticut, he was known as "Bright Eyes." It was a nod to his good looks and natural magnetism, which drew large numbers of female fans. Gotham wordsmiths rechristened Delaney (real name: Ovila Chapdelaine) "The Rapier of the North," a marksman with precision to match his power. Tall tales were circulating about Delaney's background as a French-Canadian lumberjack who grew up in a wilderness area playing cowboys and Indians with real Indians. Inside the ring, he was hardly a wild man. He was, rather, a calculating warrior who took his time until an opening presented itself. And when he fired his right, an opponent, as one writer put it, "was felled like a poled ox."

Not that he needed any, but Slats received some extra motivation when it was reported that Delaney had agreed to another important match, following Slattery, in November, at Rickard's boxing Mecca, versus Stribling. As Flournoy had explained it to Red, the Garden series was going to start with Slattery versus Delaney, and then the winner would meet Stribling. "I guess Tex Rickard believes Delaney will beat you," Red taunted.

New York boxing fans didn't think the upstate "kid fighter" stood much of a chance. Ticket sales were a major disappointment. True, what was to be the opener in The Garden farewell series had to compete with the opening game of the World Series between the New York Giants and the Washington Senators. Nevertheless, that only around 6,500 people—half capacity—ended up attending the Slattery-Delaney bout probably owed more to the lack of intrigue, mooted by the prevailing wisdom concerning the likelihood that the fast, accurate Delaney was apt to eviscerate Slattery's wide-open stance, dubbed the "weeping willow defense."

Slattery left for New York on the Thursday night before the fight, departing on a 10:35 P.M. train. His entourage included Red, Skitsy, Joe, Charlie Murray, fellow fighter Frankie Schoell, Bison president Sam Robertson and numerous other friends. More than 100 Buffalo boys, including about twenty from the First Ward, would make the trip by train and by automobile. They would encounter a feverish, wide-open gambling scene in front of the arena and across the street in Madison Square Park, as well as inside the venue, in the famously smoke-filled lobby. To the New York bookmakers, the upstate rubes were there to be picked clean; getting as much as 6-to-1 odds on their boy to win—and wagering large piles—the Buffalo boys thought the exact same thing with regard to the natives.

On the train ride, Slats slept while the gang played cards. Red had a long talk with him before they left Buffalo. "You have to be right," Red cautioned.

Slats gave him his word.

"Okay," Red said. "Otherwise, I'll have to get that old fella from Boston to come kick your ass."

Looking back on the career of Jimmy Slattery, it is hard to overstate just how huge and unusual of a shot the twenty-year-old was getting. Not only had Rickard reluctantly gone along with staging a "sprinter's distance" main event of only six rounds due to the age limit issue, but the keeper of the sport's biggest showcase was opening it up to an outsider who had only one single prior appearance in the Big Town under his belt—and that was in a preliminary match at a Queens club. Still, Slattery was a curiosity—the boy who licked Stribling, and who fought with hands down, and so fast that you might swear he was a ghost; a folk hero from the hinterlands, someone who very few people had actually seen in person. Many boxing aficionados were eager to get a look at him. But most of the regulars were there to see Delaney take Slattery's head off.

By 6:00 P.M., the scene out front was in full swing—bookies, scalpers, vendors, hustlers, arriving fans—a spectacle all itself. Some of the "wise boys" taking action were quoting even money on the proposition that Delaney would knock Slattery out. The First Ward was all over that action. At around 7:00 P.M., Slattery was in a sitting room in his suite at the Hotel Astor, near the venue, surrounded by well-wishers, pals and various expert advisers, all of whom were filling his head with the same notion: Delaney was dangerous and Slats needed to be careful. *Don't take chances*, they echoed. *Stay out of his range.* Slattery heard the story of how Delaney had slaughtered the Astoria Ox.

It happened back in the spring when everyone in New York City was talking about Paul Berlenbach. The former wrestler had recorded ten consecutive knockouts, even more than that going back to his amateur days. Rickard turned Berlenbach into his star attraction. Meanwhile, the state Boxing Commission was insisting Berlenbach needed to meet better opponents. Along came Delaney, who'd been on a roll, defeating the formidable Philadelphian Tommy Loughran, as well as Jimmy Darcy, a longtime sparring mate of Dempsey's. The Garden crowd had come to expect Berlenbach to deliver the kayo. They viewed him as invincible. From the opening bell against Delaney, Berlenbach came charging as if trying to administer the annihilation in record time. Delaney scurried out of harm's way, slipping to the canvas and looking nauseous. But Delaney kept his head, content to merely protect and observe for a couple of rounds. The German-American was a bludgeoner who hurled cumbersome blows that left himself exposed. Delaney averted them with foot speed. By the start of the third, Delaney, fighting in the Garden for the first time and starting to feel confident, decided he would take his shot. When he connected, the Garden throng went into shock. The suddenness of it all: Berlenbach stampeding forward one second, crashing to the canvas the next. Delaney had uncorked a short, perfect right hook. Berlenbach hit the floor so hard and so lifelessly that his head bounced in a ghastly way. Saved by the bell, Berlenbach came out for the fourth, barely able to stand. The fans yelled for the finishing blow. Delaney knocked Berlenbach down twice more before the referee stopped it.

Slattery could have used some quick slumber. Instead of catching a one-hour nap before heading over to the Garden—as he planned to do—Slats found himself besieged in his hotel room by a widening circle of well-meaning gadflies eager to talk strategy. All of the nattering ("watch out for the right") stressed Slattery out. He was due at the venue by 8:00 P.M. At 10:00 P.M. the main event began. Although the Garden was only half full that night, those fans in attendance made their spirit known, handing their pet Delaney an enthusiastic welcome, while dismissing the still relatively unproven upstate kid not so much with disdain as with indifference. Slattery surprised them. He opened strong. For two beautiful rounds, the pair *boxed*, fast, clean and proficiently. These were two artisans having a whirl that harkened back to another time. Purists were thrilled to behold such a rare display. Newly indoctrinated fans were witnessing the sport as age-old boxing instructors intended it, although many had mainly just come to see Delaney rudely penetrate the weeping willow defense. That did not happen—at least not for the better part of the first two rounds.

For one thing, according to multiple accounts, Slats fought with his hands *up*, a stylistic tweak that reflected his cautious fight plan. Slats did more prancing than punching, drifting out of range, mixing gamely but not necessarily all that aggressively. Then near the close of the second round, Delaney tagged Slats, solidly. Dazed, back on his heels, Slats began to struggle, not completely lost at sea but looking perilously adrift.

In the third round, Delaney was the clear aggressor. Retreating, covering, Slats eventually succumbed to the unrelenting attack of The Rapier. Two rock-solid rights struck his head. Next came over two lefts and then a right and then more of the same. To escape the steady stream of punches, Slats clinched. But Delaney continued to stifle him, determined to inflict as much damage as possible. Most fighters didn't want to mess around with the speed boy over a short distance, but Delaney was acting as if three rounds were all he was going to need. Delaney switched to the body. He roiled Slats with three sizzling jabs to the body. Slats shuddered, gasping, off kilter and completely vulnerable to Delaney's deadly right hand smash. When it came, it landed flush on the jaw, having flashed with all of the explosiveness of the blow that floored Berlenbach, the last time Delaney felt such a murderous rush and heard an arena gone mad. Delaney's right had been the hardest blow of the night. The Buffalo faithful had feared it; the Garden crowd had paid to see it. Slats staggered along the ropes. Delaney was going to end this quick.

The rakish French-Canadian flashed a smile and gestured to a friend ringside that the kayo was coming. Sitting in the press row, Charlie Murray braced for the worst. He looked directly into Slattery's eyes in that pivotal moment and saw a terrified boy. "His face was white," Murray later wrote. "His jaw, set, trembling . . . with his very life at stake."

Delaney lunged. The First Ward boys, who had come all this way, slumped down in their seats. It had been one hell of a run. But then an unexpected thing happened: Delaney missed, and by a wide margin. Instead of putting helpless prey out of its misery, he'd swiped at a mirage—Slats seemed to disappear from Delaney's path, fading, according to Murray, "like some weird shadow."

For roughly the next minute, Slats transformed from nervous wreck to the cleverest, most masterful boxer anyone had ever seen. Shooting the left—jab, jab, jab—and occasionally the right—horizontal lightning—Slats fought picture perfect, dashing, ducking, blocking, countering, and always beating Delaney to the punch. Slattery had started uncharacteristically cautious. Now he was standing in close, letting loose. No one who saw the rally would soon forget it. But would it be enough?

Delaney, too, was at his best, nearly as fast as Slats. The spectacle of two sharpshooters fully engaged had the crowd roaring. Moments earlier, the fans had been shrieking in anticipation of a kill. Now they were seeing a brilliant firestorm, which caused them to scream even louder. Though the crowd on hand was small, the decibel level was like that of a sold-out arena, or so the sportswriters claimed.

The see-saw battle spun toward conclusion. By the middle of the fourth, Delaney was back in command. He'd built a seemingly insurmountable lead on points with the contest slightly more than half over. Slats would either need to knock him out or pull off a frantic, next-to-impossible comeback. And that's exactly what he did. Flashing speed that surprised even his most fervent followers, Slats battered his dangerous, more experienced foe from one end of the ring to the other. At the bell to end the fourth, Delaney stood alone in the middle of the ring, huffing and puffing, watery-eyed and perplexed. Blood flowed from his nose and mouth. Slattery skipped play-fully back to his corner as the Garden throng, moved by the gutsy rally and pure artistry, rose in unison for a mid-contest standing ovation.

Slats didn't just win the fifth round. He destroyed Delaney, who grew increasingly desperate. Revered as a cool, deliberate ring general, Delaney turned into a crude bar brawler. His free-swinging attack kept growing cra-zier; Slats remained unflappable. He stood right up to it, a marvel of writh-ing fluidity. "It was then one got an inkling of what an exceptionally fast puncher Slattery is," recounted Andy Griffin, a veteran referee and noted boxing expert who was sitting ringside that night. "Possibly, Slattery is the fastest we have ever seen."

The instantaneousness of Slattery's counterpunches negated even Del-aney's crispest shots—the gifted marksman, outdrawn. Recognizing late in the sixth and final round that his once-commanding lead had slipped away, Delaney lost it, and not in a pitiful-meltdown sort of way; more like a trapped animal. Delaney fought hysterically fast but Slats—never losing his wits—fought *even faster*. Just before the final bell, Slats, fully turning the tables, crossed over a hard right of his own—a weapon about which no one apparently warned Delaney. The punch landed square on Delaney's jaw, a perfunctory capper for the Buffalo boy's incredible comeback. Delaney almost keeled over but stayed on his feet. His seconds helped him to his corner. On Delaney's bloody face hung a look of shock and despair. The same look was worn by some of Delaney's newly staked financial backers sitting nearby.

With a small speck of blood on his left ear but otherwise uninjured, Slattery did a happy dance in his corner as the New York fans gave him another standing ovation, followed by the official declaration of his victory. He'd edged a decision. Some Broadway wise boys lost stacks of money to the First Ward. Taverns were opened on the windfalls collected that night. "Another Corbett," many older fans would say in amazement afterward. Leaning over in the press row, Murray tapped the shoulder of the *New York World's* Hype Igoe, and said, "You fellows are looking at the next middle-weight champion."

It's written that ten policemen were needed to hold back the mob around Slats. Along with his manager, the young Buffalo fighter stayed over an extra night at the Astor on Rickard's dime. On the Saturday after the fight, Slats and Red met with the promoter to discuss future appearances at the Garden. Maybe a rematch with Greb, Rickard proposed, this time for the title. Red had been up early harvesting New York City sports page clippings. His boy was a star. It'd happened overnight. Praise for the bout itself and Slats, specifically, was abundant, effusive and prominently displayed. "The battle was as fast and clean-cut as any in these parts," wrote Jack Kofoed of the *New York Evening Post*. "'Twill be a long time before two big fellows get around the ring at the Garden or anywhere else, as prettily as that pair of speed merchants did," echoed Wilbur Wood of the *New York Sun*. "Slattery fooled the wise boys," taunted the *Brooklyn Daily Eagle*. Lathering it on heavy, Murray's friend Hype Igoe would later write in a nationally syndicated story, "The young master's technique was as sleek and as smooth as oil running down a mirror."

Igoe had smelled an exclusive. He'd dropped by the hotel early Sunday morning hoping to interview and sketch cartoons of the Buffalo boy. Slattery was up, dressed and about to check out. Sprawled out in a large, comfortable easy chair, the boxing world literally at his feet, Slattery ruminated humbly aloud, "Oh what can I say that would interest anyone?"

Igoe surrounded his signature charcoal drawings with colorful prose. Herbert "Hype" Igoe always told people his unusual nickname had been earned as a needle-thin cub reporter. An old black elevator operator at a paper he worked on supposedly always used to greet him, "Hypo!" Over the years, some people came to think the name was short for hyperbole. For a short time during his early days, Igoe helped manage the career of the great Stanley Ketchel. Ketchel's exploits inside and outside the ring, as chronicled by Igoe, read like the stories of Paul Bunyan and Pecos Bill. Ketchel was shot to death in 1910 at age 24. Igoe never got over it. In his story on Slattery, "Darling of the Boxing Gods," Igoe likened him to such bygone icons as Jim Corbett and Young Griffo, an early idol of Nat Fleischer. Both Corbett and Griffo, incidentally, were Garden regulars who could very well have been at the Slattery-Delaney fight, although we don't know for sure. Gentleman Jim followed Slattery's rise from its earliest beginnings. He used to arrive at his ringside seat dressed in a suit and top hat. Griffo, an indigent alcoholic who sheltered in a 42nd Street doorway, usually loitered in the back of the arena, having come through the doors gratis on the arm of an idolizer. Corbett and Griffo actually had a bar fight once. Griffo called Corbett a "Fancy Dan" in a hotel bar near the Garden. Corbett socked him. Griffo fell down, seemingly out cold. A moment later, from the floor, Griffo kicked the former heavyweight champion right in the worst possible spot.

Back in Buffalo, Sunday evening, October 5th, an overflowing throng of friends and fans gathered at the train station to celebrate Slattery's triumphant return. Even more than ever before, people from all over the city and region wanted to shake his hand, invite him to go places, see people, do things, invest, endorse—and the sob stories, did they ever start to come with greater frequency: a sick child or mother; an empty coal bin. Slats had a hard time saying no.

The buzz surrounding the new wonder of fisticuffs continued well into October. When the Boxing Commission convened for a regular meeting that month, the subject of Slattery came up. Andy Griffin, boxing referee and a highly regarded sage of the sport, told the governing body that they should watch the young Buffalo boy closely. "He will be a very serious bidder for the light heavyweight championship within a few months of his 21rst birthday," Griffin said. "His work in the last two rounds versus Delaney was a boxing revelation."

A new fall/winter season was only just starting up and already Slattery was being sought by promoters in every major city in the Northeast and Midwest. He could fight twice a week if Red were so inclined. Boston promoters offered $7,500 for a return match with Delaney. Rickard spoke of possible matches with Greb and Stribling. The word around Buffalo: Slats had hit the big time. Media attention continued to intensify.

One of the best-known sportswriters of the Golden Age of Sports, and of all time, was Paul Gallico, who became more famous later on as author of "The Poseidon Adventure." While still in his early twenties, Gallico had famously sparred with Dempsey during one of his Saratoga Springs training camps. Tall and athletic, Gallico had politely asked to get in the ring for a session on a dare from Igoe, and Dempsey obliged. The champion kayoed the young reporter and Gallico floored his competitors by writing about the experience for the *New York Daily News*. Legend sometimes holds that Gallico leapfrogged to sports editor on the back of that stunt, but in the fall of 1924, Gallico was still just a junior boxing writer at the *Daily News*. He'd watched, transfixed, Slattery-Delaney from the press row. Gallico's boss and mentor, Harry Newman, one of the most respected boxing critics in the game, had also seen the fight. So struck was Newman that soon after he hopped a train to Buffalo and tracked down Slattery at Newsboys' Gym. Red was all in favor of the article, which Newman proposed as a multi-part series, "Meet Boxing's Newest Sensation;" Slats was not as keen on the idea.

"So, Jimmy, why don't you tell me a yarn about your fighting career?" Newman asked.

Slats glared icily at the big city editor.

"Make me," he countered, his face turning flush.

"What a boy!" Newman chuckled, looking for backup from Red.

"Try and do it," Slats said.

Who knows how the brash Gallico would have fared in that situation—perhaps he might have ended up sparring with Slattery—but the seasoned Newman, with help from Red, eventually got Slats to lighten up. Before long, the bashful boy was speaking freely and enjoying Newman's company.

The informative, glowing series ran in mid-October. Asked that day what had been his hardest fight ever, Slats told Newman it had taken place back in his amateur days, against a tough bird named Colpoys. No one outside the Ward hit harder.

As a teenager, Jack Dempsey counted himself among the tens of thousands of nomadic American "tramps" roaming the countryside inside, on top of, underneath and in between freight trains. Snagging a free ride was hardly ever as simple as plopping into an unlocked, completely empty box car. The railroads employed "bulls," ruthless watchmen, to patrol the yards. Furthermore, what might appear to be an open car, ideal quarters, could instead turn out to be a sordid den of unfriendly, or worse, sexually deviant career hobos. A more common, extremely treacherous, means of ridership involved placing a wooden board across the rods connected to the undercarriage, sliding in horizontally and holding on tight. Presently when Dempsey rode on a train it was in a lavish private car. Nearing thirty, heavyweight champion for five years, Dempsey had it all. He was world famous. He lived in a Hollywood mansion. He dated movie stars and hosted celebrity-filled dinner parties. He'd be on an elk-hunting expedition in the mountains of New Mexico one week and off to the White House for lunch the next. That President Coolidge had requested Dempsey's company not only underscored how far the boxer had come since his days riding the rods, but also how high up boxing itself had been elevated in just the past decade.

The champ's favorite city was neither L.A. nor D.C. His family's roots were in West Virginia. He'd been raised in Colorado, fought his way west to Salt Lake City and Oakland, and spent time in Europe, but there was only one city that Dempsey considered home: New York. He loved strolling Fifth Avenue, visiting the finest tailors, or hanging around Broadway with his manager Doc Kearns and all the assorted characters who convened at their favorite nightclub, The Silver Slipper Cabaret. Dempsey didn't drink, nor did he smoke or even gamble much. He did enjoy the company of pretty showgirls and the simple camaraderie of sitting around with the boys, playing pinochle for nickels and having a gabfest. Some of the Big Town writers had soured on Dempsey during his stretch of ring inactivity, which by the fall of '24 was going on more than one year. Dempsey wanted to fight, but he now only trusted one man, Tex Rickard, to promote his next big one. Rickard had informed him that at the earliest it wouldn't be until the following warm-weather season, at least six months off.

Finished filming his serials in Hollywood, Dempsey had come back East to judge a beauty contest and discuss his future with Rickard. With nothing on the horizon, dreading boredom and needing a paycheck to support his lifestyle, Dempsey authorized Kearns to field some business propositions and pick one that made sense. Kearns, who had helped Dempsey acquire property in L.A. and a copper mine in Utah, came across a deal too sweet to pass up. Marcus Loew, owner of a chain of vaudeville houses, was desperate to attract customers. Loew offered Dempsey a ten-week gig touring his East Coast venues at $10,000 per week. Dempsey would be the highest-paid act ever to appear in vaudeville. First stop on the tour: Buffalo, N.Y.

On Sunday, October 19, 1924, the world's heavyweight champion arrived at the New York Central depot in downtown Buffalo. Dempsey, along with a small entourage, including some fellow troupe members, a showgirl, some theater executives, his manager and a few other pals, had climbed aboard the Midnight Express leaving Grand Central. The train rolled into Buffalo around 10:00 A.M. All night, passengers were abuzz, having learned from talkative porters and conductors that yes, indeed, the most famous man in the world was on board in a Pullman stateroom. No one outside his party would get to see him. Dempsey had gone to sleep before the train left New York. His close traveling companions had stayed up late playing cards. These men included Kearns, trainer Jerry 'The Greek" Luvadis, writers Damon Runyon and W.B. Seabrook, as well as Walter "Good Time Charlie" Friedman, a partly legitimate businessman and longtime associate of Arnold Rothstein, bankroller to bootleggers and Broadway producers alike. As Dempsey exited the train, he was spotted by the crowd lined up all along the platform. They yelled his name and converged upon the champ, who pushed through the mob with the assistance of a phalanx of policemen who cleared a path to an awaiting limousine. Four cops on motorcycles revved their motors and escorted the limo to the Hotel Statler, fans shouting, horns honking. In the lobby of the Statler, Dempsey's arrival caused a stir, with heads turning and necks craning. Gathered there to meet him were a few of his best Buffalo friends, Murray, Kelly and some other local boxing figures, Bert Finch and referee Dick Nugent. Also on hand to greet Dempsey was a delegation of Junior League girls seeking a photograph and somehow hoping to convince the champ to attend their charity dance. A short time later, up in his room, The Royal Suite, Dempsey started unpacking his wardrobe trunks and ordered some breakfast. Or rather, Jerry the Greek, a dwarfish man who doubled as a valet, ordered it for him. The breakfast of the champion: orange juice, a small pot of coffee and two slices of lightly buttered toast. In his fancifully furnished drawing room, huge windows offered a panoramic vista of Lake Erie. Out of the trunks came: silk-lined dinner jackets and double-breasted suits; leather pump shoes and Parisian neckties; a golf outfit and toiletries: face creams, even rouge and an eyebrow pencil, these latter items staples of any vaude-villian's makeup kit. This wasn't Dempsey's first tour.

Waiting for his food, Dempsey rifled through a small slice of a larger stack of invites sent to the hotel. Among those seeking an audience were a society ladies' club, a banker, the owner of a popular speakeasy and the Bishop of Buffalo. Also in the pile were business propositions and love letters. Although Dempsey had been playing coy about rumors of his engagement to movie actress Estelle Taylor, he secretly was moving ahead with plans to marry her. Doc Kearns was going to be sick over it. He'd always predicted that when the champ settled down it would spell his demise.

Late in the afternoon, Dempsey and Kearns were chauffeured over to Loew's State Theater on the corner of Main and Mohawk for rehearsals. They were booked for a week solid, Monday through Sunday, three shows a day, running continuously from the noon matinee (25 cents) straight through to the latter part of the evening, with Dempsey's 45-minute appearances coming at 3:00 P.M., 6:00 P.M. and 9:00 P.M. Leading up to it was a lineup of singing acts—a local girl, Evelyn Cunningham was slated to perform—dancing acts, assorted skits, a motion picture short and "Alvin and Kenny," who billed themselves as "comedy aerialists." Kearns joined Dempsey on stage for the first part of the act. The pair would not necessarily just be riffing off the cuff. Cleverly prepared lines—witty, fast-paced dialogue—had been penned just for them so that the tales of Dempsey's rise to the title could be spun with the proper rhythms while also dotted with ample, well-placed laugh-lines. After their scripted banter, Kearns was to exit the stage while Dempsey, having changed into his boxing attire, reenacted some of his greatest punches. To conclude,

Dempsey would spar one round apiece with some local fighters, hand-picked by Bert Finch. Frankie Schoell's younger brother, Anthony, would be one of the boys picked to go one round with the champ. Other promising youngsters, Bobby Tracey and Lou Scozza, would get the chance as well. The expectations for Dempsey's weeklong run were running high—the theater banked on packed houses. But a slew of other theatrical features were vying for audiences at the same time. A Spanish dance review played at Shea's Theater. The Gayety burlesque house reprised *Runnin' Wild*, the show that spawned the Charleston dance craze. A dramatic play was being put on at The Majestic, a musical comedy at The Teck, and at Shea's Hippodrome, which had fully converted to a state-of-the-art motion picture house, they were showing a silent adventure film, *The Alaskan*, starring a fresh-faced starlet—Estelle Taylor, Dempsey's flame.

The World's Greatest Champion, Jack Dempsey, In Person and In Action, opened to a sell-out crowd. With his powdered face and put-on rosy cheeks, Dempsey demonstrated a knack for public speaking, in spite of his strangely incongruous high-pitched voice. Kearns stole the show, displaying the silver tongue that talked Charlie Murray into matching Dempsey with giant Carl Morris at the Broadway Auditorium back in 1918. "I'm always glad to get back to Buffalo," Dempsey had told Billy Kelly when he arrived at the Statler. "When I finished with Morris, I was made."

Dempsey wasn't kidding about his fondness for Buffalo. Murray and Kelly had helped put him on the road to the championship. Buffalo's fondness for the champion was fully evident when Dempsey exited the stage door after finishing his first performance. A mob of people were waiting outside. Attempting to walk not even one hundred feet to a chophouse diagonal from the theater, Dempsey inched slowly through the throng, shaking as many hands as he could. An old woman lifted a little crippled boy into the air and cried out for Dempsey to come over. The child caught Dempsey's eye. What happened could have been a scene half-embellished by Billy Kelly invoking some harmless poetic license, but supposedly Dempsey took the boy into his arms, chatted with him awhile and, later, presumably having jotted down the boy's address, sent him some sort of toy. There's an even better story from that afternoon.

As Dempsey sat down in the chophouse for a late lunch, he looked up to see a crush of newsboys peering in through the windows, noses pressed to the plate glass. One of the newsboys, Red Mahoney, the son of a coal shoveler, on a dare, walked in and sat down at a nearby table. The place was empty except for Dempsey and his friends. When the proprietor tried to hustle him out, Mahoney fished a nickel from his pocket, slammed it on the table and ordered a coffee, adding, according to W.B. Seabrook, "This here's a restaurant aint it?" Dempsey, cracking up, invited the audacious lad to pull up a seat. Dempsey ordered him some pie. "When the boy went back out a half hour later," Seabrook would later write, "he was almost as big a hero as the champion himself."

More large crowds flocked to the two evening shows. Dempsey's boxing looked impressive, if only for the restrained but effective way he defended the aggressive attack of an understandably overenthusiastic Bobby Tracey, and all without injuring the boy. Between shows, Dempsey played pinochle in his dressing room and took visitors. Mayor Schwab came by to say hello. The pinochle and the gabbing spilled over to his hotel suite later that night. It was Dempsey telling stories to a rapt group that included Kearns, Runyon, Murray and Kelly. Someone had asked the champ to name his toughest battle. Dempsey normally preferred to talk about any number of subjects other than boxing, and at times he never talked shop, but he was not averse to sharing a few stories in the right setting. "My older brother Bernie was a fighter," Dempsey began. "He was supposed to fight some fellow named George Copelin in a town called Cripple Creek." As it happened, Dempsey continued, brother Bernie got sick. Seeing as how Dempsey looked like his older brother—and since there was one hundred bucks at stake—it was decided that he would make the trip instead. "The fans looked at me and the odds went up to 10 to 1," Dempsey recalled with a laugh. "I was a sight, but as the saying goes, you should have seen the other guy."

Jerry the Greek tapped Dempsey on the shoulder. It was time for bed. Dempsey played out his hand and did as he was told. He was rising early for a golf outing. Dempsey was playing a brand new course about which he'd heard rave reviews. Plus, his group was to include a prominent local figure, someone the champ was eager to meet.

★★★★★

Jimmy Slattery raced down the driveway leading to the Transit Valley Country Club in a Ford touring car traveling as fast as it could go. "I wouldn't ride with him on a bet," Dempsey would remark. "If the cops don't get him, the undertaker will."

Since it was freezing out and the champ was limited on time, it was decided that they would only play the front nine. Located several miles north of the city in leafy East Amherst, N.Y., Transit Valley was only still coming together; the back nine had just recently been completed and a clubhouse was still to be built. Among the country club's most important supporters was Ganson Depew, the nephew of railroad tycoon and former state senator Chauncey Depew. Ray Weil, club president, welcomed Dempsey and walked him over to the area where the planned clubhouse was to be built. Murray was a member here as well. He and Weil were considered the club champions. Murray paired up with Seabrook. Upon seeing the Buffalo boxer rip a practice drive—a beauty—Dempsey exclaimed, "Slattery is my partner!" Seabrook, who made his name writing fantastic true tales of voodoo, cannibalism and the occult, was covering Dempsey on assignment for King Features. Seabrook also happened to be a scratch golfer. Goading Murray, Dempsey suggested that Seabrook bow out of their foursome. "He's way out of our class," Dempsey said, suggesting that Murray instead team up with Weil. Dempsey, it turned out, really just wanted to play the club champions, and to beat them. Murray had boasted of being able to shoot the front nine in under 50 strokes. Normally, Dempsey didn't like to gamble. But his palms had just been royally greased by Kearns, who in typical fashion had demanded Loew's pay their full first week's salary up front, in cash. He had handed Dempsey his share in five neat packets of bills, each containing $1,000, in fives, tens and twenties. Not needing to impress young Slattery but still showboating slightly, Dempsey suggested a $100 wager, which to him probably seemed small and friendly. Murray and Weil accepted, although Murray spent the final moments before tee time scrambling to find someone to whom he could lay off some of his portion of the bet.

Compared to the average hobbyist, Dempsey was an excellent golfer, a man who'd played some of the top courses in California and Scotland. But he didn't play regularly enough to come anywhere close to mastering the ancient game. Slattery had only recently picked up the golf sticks and, naturally, was good. The match began with Dempsey plunking his drive on to the precipice of a bunker. He grumbled, and contorted his face into an angry expression appropriate for a prize ring, but not a golf course. Slats couldn't help but snicker. Suddenly self-aware, Dempsey brought his intensity down a notch and began laughing too. "Don't worry," he vowed. "The rest of my shots will be perfect."

And indeed, if Murray's description of the match can be taken at face value, trace elements of hero worship notwithstanding, Dempsey played like he was Walter Hagen. Slats held his own as the foursome fought a nip and tuck battle. The wind whipping, the leafs swirling and crunching at their feet, Dempsey and Slattery spent the morning gleefully cheering each other's best shots and Murray's missed putts. Weil played the best of any of them. Things remained tight right up until the last ball dropped in the cup. Dempsey asked for the scores. The heavyweight champion of the world had shot a 50; so had the middleweight champion of Buffalo. The champions of Transit Valley had a combined score of 101.

"We win, Jimmy me lad," Dempsey said affectionately in a phony Irish brogue, slapping Slats on the back.

A grainy, black and white photograph of the epic golf outing, Tuesday, October 21, 1924, at Transit Valley, shows Dempsey kneeling, as if teeing up a ball. Slats is standing next to him, wearing a stylish outdoorsman's vest and looking a bit star struck. According to Murray, the two fighters became fast friends. Later that day, Slats took up Dempsey's invitation to drop by his dressing room at the theater. One week earlier, Slats had made his stage debut portraying a boxing referee in a dramatic play at The Teck. *Plain Jane* featured the story of a heroic underdog who takes on a bully in a climactic ring sequence. Slats earned some critical praise for his small part.

"Hey, why don't you referee my sparring rounds?" Dempsey suggested.

He insisted Slats stick around playing pinochle with the gang until it was time to step before the footlights. Later on stage, Kearns, introducing Slattery as referee, uttered something to get a rise out of the seats: "I believe this boy will one day be a contender for Dempsey's title." Slats took a bow. The audience gave him a warm hand. By the time Kearns' on-stage ad lib got recycled in the New York papers, the line had been misattributed to Dempsey himself, and had become: "There is the boy who will one day wear my crown."

The champ had indeed taken a liking to Slattery. Dempsey had popped into Newsboys' Gym a few times, tutoring Slats and talking with Red. He showed them a few tricks. Slattery was preparing to meet the burly Ohioan Norm Genet on the following Monday night. "Slattery is going to fill out,"

Dempsey assured Red. "And when he does, he'll make trouble for someone in the heavyweight division."

His close association with the champ made a deep impression. Being called Dempsey's heir may have been an exaggeration, but such praise from the champ could not have been more overwhelming. On the one hand, kids grew up fast back then. Slats had been making his way on his own since the age of 15. On the other hand, Slats was still only twenty, brimming with vigor and self confidence. It seemed as if the whole world was being handed to him. "He was just a kid," Tom Carr, Red's nephew, pointed out. "He couldn't handle it." Slattery for the first time was earning money faster than he could spend it. He could do no wrong. If he was pulled over for speeding, the officer (often a cheerful Irishman) would send him on his way with a warning and a smile. Slattery's automobile antics were becoming increasingly reckless. Numerous were the stories of Slats smashing through toll barriers at 80 miles per hour, or cutting railroad crossings hair-raisingly close. But some truly colossal gall would be on display near the end of Slattery's time with the champ.

Repeating the same glorious ritual of the prior few days, Slats jogged in the morning, worked out at Newsboys' in the afternoon, then sped over to the theater to pal around with Dempsey backstage. Through Murray, whom Dempsey considered among his dearest friends, Slats had gotten close to the champ, so close that Slats felt it was okay to prank him. Playing on Dempsey's weakness for the ladies, Slats came up with an idea for a hoax to finish off the memorable week. He shared his plan with Murray, who wanted in on the caper. Even Doc Kearns joined the conspiracy.

After the last show on one of the last nights in Buffalo, Dempsey and his entourage were, as usual, back in his adjoining suites. In one of them, at a table, a pinochle game broke out; in another, Murray and some Buffalo friends were rehashing old times. The telephone rang. Jerry the Greek answered: "Who? What? Who? You wait." He passed the phone to Dempsey.

It was Slattery on the line, apparently able to disguise his voice to sound feminine. Slats had pretended to be one of those Junior League girls ("they were some swell chickens," Dempsey had mentioned in passing) seeking a romantic rendezvous. Dempsey hung up and sat back down at the card table.

"Anything important, champ?" asked Kearns, keeping a straight face.

"It's nothing," Dempsey innocently replied. "Tomorrow, I've got to go see a man about a dog."

Murray left a short time later. He reported to Slats that the trap had been set for the next day, in between shows.

When Dempsey turned up to meet the mystery girl on the hotel mezzanine, Slats, Murray and the rest of the guys were going to pop out and razz the bejeezus out of him. Just before 5:00 P.M., the appointed hour, Dempsey showed up dressed to kill. According to Seabrook, Slattery and Murray were hiding nearby, creating a scene that, if it is to be believed, seems straight out of some vintage silent-era comedy—Murray camouflaged by a potted plant, Slats covering his red-from-giggling face with one of those Japanese folding screens. Around the corner, Kearns, Good Time Charlie Friedman, Runyon and some others waited for the signal . . . which never came. Dempsey had the last laugh.

The previous night, an actor pal of Dempsey's had been standing behind a curtain backstage and overheard Slattery discussing the plot in his Irish whisper. Tipped off, Dempsey arranged for an actual female to show up, and not just any pretty face, but actress Margaret Quimby. She had starred in the *Daredevil Jack* serials, and happened to be in town, happy to play along. And she was quite possibly the prettiest woman Slattery had ever seen before in his life.

"Oh, Mr. Dempsey," she said, playing the part of an amorous society girl and speaking her improvised lines loud enough to be heard across the room. "I'm just so thrilled to meet you. I haven't told anyone I was coming."

Dempsey spotted Slattery and rooted him out of hiding. "Hey, meet my friend Jimmy Slattery," Dempsey said, introducing his companion while Slats squirmed. Then Dempsey and Quimby marched out of the hotel, holding back smiles.

On the golf course, Dempsey and Slattery matched up exactly even. In a game of wits, Dempsey took the decision. How and whether the two might one day match up in a ring would soon be a question every sports writer in the country would be asking.

★★★★★

The night of his final vaudeville performance in Buffalo, Dempsey wasn't his usual high-strung, fidgety self. He played some cards and talked with friends, but the champ seemed lethargic. He looked tired. Norm Genet, the Ohio boxer whom Slattery was to face the next day, came by to pay his respects and ended up joining the champ on stage for the sparring portion of the afternoon show, a thrill Genet would talk about for the rest of his life. Later that night, Ike O'Neil, the Buffalo-born trainer who was chief second to former heavyweight champion Jess Willard, came by the theater to say hello to Dempsey. The two men had crossed paths five years earlier in Toledo, Ohio.

"Remember this fellow, champ?" Charlie Murray asked, escorting O'Neil into the dressing room. The Buffalo native had gained some weight, so at first Dempsey didn't recognize him. But he slowly made the connection. It was in Toledo that Dempsey became champion. In the first round of that fight, Dempsey had slaughtered the Kansas farmer, knocking Willard down seven times. Each time he did, according to Nat Fleischer, Dempsey stood over him "quivering and snorting like a wild animal." The pounding Dempsey gave Willard was incomprehensible; most of Willard's face, from forehead to chin, was shattered. Ringsiders had screamed at Willard's corner to stop the carnage.

"Aren't you the fellow who worked in Willard's corner that day?" Dempsey asked.

"Yeah, that's me," said O'Neil, laughing. "I'm the guy who threw in the towel."

A clear vision of the very moment he first became champion came into Dempsey's mind as he stared over at Willard's trainer. He flashed back and could still see Willard swaying on his stool in the corner. That was the last time Dempsey ever saw Willard. The champion began to wax philosophical.

"Jess stayed in the game too long," the champ said. "When I lose the title, I'm done. They're not going to make a punching bag out of Jack Dempsey."

Later, packing up and saying his goodbyes, Dempsey asked Murray to examine a pile of business-related paperwork, some of which he didn't understand. He and Kearns were growing apart. Dempsey loved Kearns, but he didn't always trust him. The various investments and deals into which he'd entered seemed entirely sound, Murray assessed. But the Buffalo promoter sensed the champ was out of sorts. He was visibly fatigued.

Dempsey admitted he was exhausted. It wasn't the actual activity undertaken in the three shows per day that was getting to him, but rather the utter monotony of it all. The tour was moving on to Boston. The end couldn't come soon enough. Murray would later write that Dempsey reminded him of "a lion chained up in a cellar." Somehow between Toledo in 1919 and Buffalo in 1924, Dempsey had gone from savage brute to foppish man about town. Dempsey didn't want to make movies or host dinner parties. He didn't want to own any hotels or coal mines. What he wanted, desperately, was to get back in the ring.

On October 27, 1924, Slattery, riding high and rapidly approaching the threshold to a title shot, fought Norm Genet at the Aud. Only, it wasn't much of a fight. The Ohio Iron Man looked pretty slick sparring with Dempsey on stage at Loew's. Against Slattery, however, Genet seemed amateurish. Slats could no longer mess around with ordinary pugs. Red ordered more time off, three weeks, no boxing. For a few of those days, Slats clocked afternoon shifts at the shipyard cutting and driving rivets, earning a total of around $10 and impressing the foreman with his competency. He was playing football again, too. He'd formed a new team, the Euclids. Red was doing his best to keep the kid in check. But there were limits to what Red could realistically do. He had used his favorite verbal cudgel on Slats one too many times. "Well, I suppose I'll just have to go get that old fella Eagan to come take care of you," Red routinely said whenever he sensed Slats was slipping.

One day, toward the end of '24, Red used the line and Slats blew up. "Go get that guy!" he snarled. "*Get him!*"

So Red did. The very next day, Red arranged the match. It would be the main event of a New Year's Day Matinee—Buffalo's boxing feast day. Joe Eagan had just returned to New England for the holidays following a campaign out in California, which was in the process of fully legalizing boxing, opening the door to regulated ten-round bouts, ending San Francisco's famously fast and loose "four-round game." Eagan had shown well out west, even lost some weight. His manager, Solly Snyder, jumped at the chance to bring the newly slimmed-down veteran back to Buffalo. Eagan, the man who had handed Slattery his first professional defeat, lit a bonfire by predicting he would win again, and poured gasoline on it when he sent letters to the *Courier* insisting that he held "the Indian Sign" over Slattery. This was an ages-old reference to a form of unbreakable spell that gets cast whenever one fighter soundly licks another. Not one of Slattery's opponents had ever inspired hatred. The second Eagan fight was his first true grudge match. Referencing the pot of gold waiting for him at Rickard's Garden, Slats adopted a tongue-in-cheek battle cry: "I can't afford to lose this one." The night before, New Year's Eve, with the rest of the city ringing in 1925, it appears Slats spent a quiet evening with Red, who over the years would recall how Slats must have said to him at least ten times that night, "I must win, I must win . . ." as if seeking to harness the power of suggestion. All week leading up, Slats had put in extra hours of training. He doubled his roadwork, taking long hikes in heavy snow. Eagan continued to taunt him. His invocation of a throwback head game was ludicrous. Generally, boxing people considered the Indian Sign to be hokum. Eagan did look lean when he stepped into the ring, and he sprang out of his corner for some fast and heated milling at the opening bell. But he never had a prayer.

Less than thirty seconds into the first round, Slats caught him with a dynamite right cross. Eagan turned his head right into its path, multiplying the force of the punch, which landed square on the temple. The Boston journeyman crumpled as if he'd been sliced in two. At the count of five, he rose to one knee, clasping the ropes. Finding his legs paralyzed, Eagan fell over, senses vacant. Referee Dick Nugent and timekeeper Marve Smith counted out the final seconds in unison. Smith clicked his stopwatch. It read thirty-seven seconds. Slats took a look at out-cold Eagan and hopped back toward his corner. Red, all smiles, met him midway. "It's a good thing the louse stayed down *or I'd a killed him!*" Slats exclaimed, only partially kidding. Skitsy, Joe and the rest of the gang mobbed their pal and carried him back to his dressing room. News of the swift, spectacular knockout spread around Western New York. For hours after the fight, folks from all over the area deluged the switchboards of city newspapers, trying to find out what had happened. In the quiet of his dressing room, Eagan, his vision blurred and feeling as if he'd been hit with a cannon ball at close range, sat chatting with Charlie Murray who couldn't help but notice that the entourage with which Eagan had come to town had now disappeared. Not even his manager had stuck around. On Eagan's brow, a swollen lump, large enough so as to prevent his hat from going on. Just then, someone knocked softly at the door. "Come in," Eagan yelled.

In stepped a sheepish Slattery. All of his buddies were crowded behind him still patting his shoulders.

"No hard feelings, Joe," Slats said, extending his hand and shifting his feet.

"Don't be foolish," Eagan replied. "I'm getting too old, I guess."

"You know I wanted to win," Slats added, apologetically.

At least that's the way Murray told it. He liked portraying Slattery as a bashful boy.

After that, Slats and his pals went back to his house to celebrate. Eagan never fought again.

The year had certainly started off with a bang. Buffalo pride was on the upswing. The city saw a limitless future. Many Americans felt that way. It was the mid-point of the 1920s and like many U.S. cities, Buffalo was booming. New buildings were going up all over town. Construction of the city's tallest skyscraper, the Liberty Bank building, was well underway. Crowned with two small-scale replicas of Lady Liberty, the banking headquarters rose up 23 floors, double the size of Buffalo's famous Electric Tower. Developers had in the prior year sunk nearly $100 million into projects aimed at transforming the Queen City of the Lakes into an internationally known urban template—new residential sections, parkways and public spaces. Sewer lines and traffic signals were installed. Street lamps were placed along Delaware Avenue at a steep cost—rows upon rows of pretty Elm trees were cut down. The Hotel Statler had emerged as one of the grandest in the East. The Buffalo Athletic Club had built a new headquarters. Buffalo had gone mad for sports. Damon Runyon published a story in January 1925 naming Buffalo as one of the top three sports cities in the country, citing "variety and points of interest," while singling out champion oarsman Algie McGuire and, of course, Jimmy Slattery, with whom Runyon had become well acquainted during his visit back when Dempsey was in town. In Buffalo, across professional, college and amateur levels, one could find: baseball, basketball, bicycling, bowling, billiards, boxing, football, golf, handball, hockey, horse racing, indoor track, rowing, speed skating, swimming, tennis, trapshooting and wrestling. Calling Slattery one of the best boxers in the country, Runyon predicted the local hero's greatest battle over the coming years "would be with himself."

Buffalo ascended to its own kind of sports heaven when, in late January, articles were signed finalizing a bout for which fans had long been clamoring: Jimmy Slattery and Frankie Schoell. It wasn't a match Slattery wanted. He'd always looked up to Schoell. In the past year, they'd become good friends. Red wasn't particularly crazy about the idea, either. "We're just settling a long standing ghost, that's all," Red said before the fight, set for February 2.

Boys from Buffalo's East Side and the First Ward would now finally get to settle all arguments about whose fighter was superior, as would rival managers/gym operators Red Carr and Bert Finch. Slattery was risking a great deal for neighborhood bragging rights. Schoell, still in his prime at 24, had more to gain. A welterweight, Schoell would fight about eight pounds lighter than Slats, who, when in the pink of condition, now tipped the scales at 161. Red instructed Slats to stay at that weight. He nixed boxing workouts; instead, Red wanted Slats to stick to roadwork and other outdoor activity. Red did plan two days of light sparring, then two days of rest leading up to the fight. During his time away from the gym, Slats made arrangements to spend a few hours with the city work crew tasked with cutting down trees on Delaware Avenue. Axe in hand, Slats did battle with a massive section of a felled trunk that needed to be chopped into smaller pieces. He had such a lengthy, strenuous go of it that a crowd eventually formed and a photographer turned up, which was Slattery's cue to ditch down a side street. When he returned to Newsboys' Gym, the place was packed with people on hand to watch him train. Gawkers, kiddies, and newspaper reporters surrounded him as he sat on a stool toweling off. It was late in the afternoon of Saturday, January 31. Someone cried out, "Jimmy, will you beat Schoell?"

Slats raised his eyebrows. A smiling twinkle appeared in his darting eyes. The exact instant was captured in a photograph that would turn out to be one of the most recognizable, iconic images of the First Ward legend. A small towel is draped around his neck. His hair is bushy, tousled. His lips seem to just be cracking the slightest trace of an oncoming smirk. The image of the ripening idol still hangs on the wall of several First Ward taverns, including the Swannie House, as old as the river. Former Buffalo pugilist Tony "Kid" Sisti, who fought to earn money for art lessons, would sketch Slats, working (fairly obviously) from that photo, and this picture, it is said, was displayed for many years on the wall of The Big House until it closed. The omnipresent image of Slattery smiled back at patrons much the way a framed photo of *River*-era Bruce Springsteen stared down Buffalo revelers for years from the wall in the middle section of Mulligan's Brick Bar.

Slats went into the ring against Schoell "seemingly determined to carry Frankie Schoell along for six rounds," Willis Wilber would write in *The*

Buffalo Times. "But the fans got restive and began to boo." It was painfully noticeable to the crowd that Slattery's punches lacked the usual zip. "Come on, what's the matter Slats?!" one fan shouted. Even Schoell wanted to know why his foe was behaving so lethargically.

Boxing historian Angelo Prospero tells the story of a not-widely-known exchange of words between the two local combatants right around the start of the third round, when the fans began to get restless. "Schoell tried to get Slats to do something," Prospero said. "So he says, 'Come on you dirty mick, give me your best shot.' And then Slats says to him, 'okay you Kraut sonofabitch, here it comes!'"

It's been said the blow that followed hurt Slats more than it did Schoell, although that's unlikely. The Irishman delivered not one but three consecutive right hand punches. The first one rendered the German-American incoherent and in a haphazard sitting position on the middle rope. Slats could tell his pal was out just not down. He looked at referee Ed Purdy who motioned for Slattery to keep fighting. Slats paused, and then hammered Schoell twice more. The pride of the East Side slid to the canvas, eyes shut, his head propped against the ring post. Bending down to pick Schoell up, Slats quietly said (more to himself), "Sorry Frank, but I had to do it." The Aud rained coats and hats and canes. Slats carried Schoell to his corner and stayed with him until he came around. "You're a great boy, Jimmy," Schoell muttered.

Slattery felt remorseful for a couple of days. "I didn't want to strike again," he lamented. "Purdy made me."

That February, confirmation of Slattery's startling altitude came in the pages of *Ring*, which published Tex Rickard's inaugural list of the top ten boxers in nine weight categories. Setting off a thousand debates, Slattery placed third among middleweights, behind Tiger Flowers and champion Harry Greb. "Rickard's Rankings" lifted an idea set forth decades earlier by pigskin pioneer Walter Camp, former Yale coach and assigner of the "All-American" label to the nation's most outstanding college football players. Release of Rickard's selections set the stage for his cleverly planned carnival of middleweight bouts. The promoter was purposely playing up a division which most likely contained, many experts reckoned, the eventual successor to Dempsey. The continuing series of top-ranked pairings would unfold at the soon-to-close Garden throughout its final winter season while Rickard and his backers broke ground on a new sports facility on Eighth Avenue in the Broadway district. Despite the inclusion of a sub-floor piping system to make ice for hockey and skating events, the "New Garden" was being designed with boxing foremost in mind.

Among the primary boxers in Rickard's mind was Slats. But the Garden's matchmaker, Frank Flournoy, could not find anyone willing to meet Slats in six rounds. Greb, Stribling and Berlenbach all supposedly said no thanks. Berlenbach's manager, Dan Hickey, boxing instructor at the New York Athletic Club and a former sparring partner of Bob Fitzsimmons, was candid about it. "Why make a match you can't win? In six rounds, Slattery is too fast." When Slats reached voting age, Hickey insisted, there would be a match. When Berlenbach hurt his hand and had to bail out of a bout with Tony Marullo of New Orleans, Rickard tried to slip Slattery in as a substitution. Marullo said no way, get someone else. Still clinging to his self-proclaimed American Light Heavyweight Championship crown which he'd reclaimed from Greb, Gene Tunney dismissed Slats, according to Billy Kelly, by saying, "What, and risk my title, are you crazy?"

Boxing had a problem: Its titleholders were reluctant to defend. McTigue's refusal to fight Tunney for the New York State version of the World's Light Heavyweight title had led to a suspension. A similar situation was happening in the welterweight class where champion Mickey Walker refused to fight rightful challenger Dave Shade, the lantern-jawed San Franciscan and youngest of the "Three Fighting Shade Brothers." As far as most people were concerned, Dempsey was retired and would likely never fight again. Contender Harry Wills and his manager Paddy Mullins had just about given up hope at ever getting their shot. Even the great Benny Leonard was being cautious with his lightweight laurels. Leonard had not defended his crown in more than one year.

Media-shy most of the time, Slats started his own campaign to make noise about his frustrating predicament—on the cusp of being able to fight for big purses in the Garden and yet finding no one willing to get in the ring with him. Slats enlisted Runyon and Igoe, both of whom were annoyed by the business-first mentality at the topmost rungs of boxing, and thus hugely sympathetic to the boy's plight. "Isn't it a strange turn of affairs when a lanky twenty-year-old can wear a fright wig for three of the best?" Igoe asked in one of his columns. The only fighters who were worth paying money to see, Runyon argued, were the ones who *did not hold titles*. Grantland Rice also chastised the current crop of champions for their unwillingness to stick out their necks, and pointed to Slattery as one of the few boxers in the game willing to meet anyone.

But there was one top-ranked middleweight anxious to get a crack at Slats: the still-seething Rapier of the North, Jack Delaney.

Earlier that winter, Delaney, delivering the cleanest, most decisive knockout punch that Garden fans had ever witnessed, had sent Tiger Flowers to the canvas and shook up Rickard's middleweight order before *Ring* hit newsstands. Flowers, a church deacon who prayed in the ring, had been on an unholy tear, beating everyone he met. So when Delaney stopped Flowers, the New York Mythmaking Establishment was once again ready to tout the French-Canadian whose romantic narrative was the usual recipe of falsehoods, half-truths and incredible true things. Delaney was no woodsman; he'd worked as a machinist in a factory. His burly father, Pierre, was a seasonal lumberjack in Saint-Francois-du-Lac (St. Francis of the Lake), Quebec, where the family lived until Delaney was nine. As a boy, he likely did pal around with Indians—but bear in mind the Abenaki of the region were Catholic converts and some of the most fully assimilated indigenous peoples in North America. As for Delaney's superhuman right hand, yes, indeed, it was extra special. As a husky, unpolished preliminary boy coming up at the Acorn Athletic Club in Bridgeport, Delaney kept busting his hand. Tired of paying his medical bills, manager Al Jennings sold Delaney's contract to Pete Reilly, who took his newly acquired prospect to a doctor specializing in setting bones. The surgeon inserted an artificial cap over the shattered knuckle of Delaney's right middle finger. Delaney never broke his hand again after that. Berlenbach got the first taste. Delaney shot to top-draw status. Reilly sold a portion of Delaney to Scotty Monteith, an up-and-coming boxing manager who ran a stable in the Woodside section of Queens. Delaney then promptly lost the first short-distance bout to Slattery. Delaney's burst of fame was spoiled as fast as it had occurred.

Insisting that he'd merely had an off night, and intent on wiping the blot clean, Delaney sought a rematch with Slattery. A student of the game, Delaney convinced himself he was only a few strategic adjustments away from solving the "Buffalo Flash" (a sobriquet some writers were using, but which never took hold). Rickard, in mid-January of 1925, matched Delaney with Flowers (Rickard's No. 2-ranked middleweight); Flowers, in the midst of a lengthy and much publicized winning streak, had just destroyed

Johnny Wilson, former middleweight champion. Against Flowers, Delaney would throw a punch that would reverberate throughout the boxing world. It came in the second round and didn't look like much, a half-cocked, short right hook that left Flowers so dead to the world that his manager, Walk Miller, immediately, vociferously, announced his suspicion that Delaney's gloves were loaded. No one could hit that hard, Miller charged. But upon examination, nothing visible was discovered.

One week later, Rickard announced his upcoming winter schedule, a lineup that included the re-scheduled Berlenbach-Marullo match and, to the delight of New York fans, the rematch between Delaney and Slattery, February 13, 1925.

Right before the bout, the Commission revealed it was investigating a claim that Slattery was being untruthful about his age, that he had already turned 21 the prior August, meaning that the rematch with Delaney could go longer than six rounds. Someone had uncovered a publicly filed license application from 1921 listing Slattery's date of birth as August 25, 1903. On some level, Slattery, Tex Rickard, sports writers and fans alike all wanted, and were unanimously happy to learn, the Commission was now open-ing the door to Slats fighting bouts longer than six rounds. But Red Carr, not wishing to do anything below board, set everyone straight. He recalled how he had told Slattery to write down 1903 on the application instead of 1904, because the lad was only 17 at the time and needed to be 18 to get his license. So Red provided proof of Slattery's birthday: a photograph of his birth certificate on file with the Buffalo Health Department's Bureau of Vital Statistics. The age discrepancy rumpus fizzled out, prompting Igoe to write in the New York World: "I'm disappointed. You sit there and are just coming to worship Slattery's brilliant execution when the last bell rings. Six rounds slip by before you know it."

Recognizing how deadly Delaney could be with even a single well-placed punch, Slats, for his own safety, trained methodically, doing exactly what Red told him to do as far as sleeping, eating and exercising—nothing too strenuous. In fact, Red, like a chef determined not to over-season a dish, prescribed long *walks* and only two days of light sparring. "Just right," Red noted quietly while weighing Slats two days before the fight: 162½.

When it was time to leave for New York City, Red came down with a terrible case of the flu. Barely able to stand, he telephoned Bert Finch and asked him to work Slattery's corner. Putting aside past rivalries, Finch agreed. Known for his fat belly and keen eye for talent, Finch was among those Buffalo boxing people who scoffed at Slats when he was coming along as an awkward amateur. Finch sometimes agonized about it; there was Jimmy Slattery, all those afternoons watching Schoell train, right there in his gym, under his nose.

An estimated 500 Buffalo fans traveled to New York City for the bout. Most took overnight trains leaving the night of Thursday, Feb. 12. The Q.A.C. had secured a block of about 50 ringside seats that were instantly snatched up by leading city businessmen, bankers and commercial real estate developers. The V.I.P. delegation was headed up by Buffalo Mayor Frank Schwab, who not only was a major booster, but who also counted the First Ward boxer as a personal friend. An influx of Buffalo bettors pushed Slattery to a 2-to-1 favorite. In the end Red Carr made the trip, a risky move as this was a time when influenza was still associated with death. He and Finch worked the corner together. The Garden was close to a sellout. At about 9:50 P.M., Slats climbed through the ropes wearing a green silk robe and matching trunks. Delaney was welcomed by a bevy of hatcheck girls, who screamed for him throughout the bout—which, from gong to gong, was another scorcher. Smiling all the way through, both hands dangling by his sides, Slattery became an inviting but unreachable target, an apparition. He fought the best fight of his life, which was unfortunate for Delaney, who was also turning in the greatest work of his career. Across six blazing sessions, Slattery "outboxed, outgeneraled, outslugged and completely overwhelmed Delaney," reported the New York Times. Delaney kept missing. He couldn't catch Slats. Slattery, meanwhile, gaining confidence as the contest wore on, kept pressing, pelting Delaney so much so that the Rapier's face was covered with red marks. If Delaney tried to duck a left jab, he got plastered with an uppercut. Beguiled ring scribes later referred to Slats as a "dancing sprite" and a "phantom." Slattery proved his first victory was no fluke. Years later, Ring would deem this second bout a replica of the first, with the exception that Slats "whirled about with even greater speed and finesse than he did the first time." Fans were mesmerized, as if watching spectacular fireworks. A large contingent of New York City Irish went crazy when Slats was declared the winner. The demonstration Slattery and Delaney gave fans would reverberate after that night ended, and long after the old building was demolished later that summer. In his 1938 retrospective on his sports writing career, A Farewell *to Sport,* Paul Gallico referred to the pair of Slattery-Delaney bouts as "the most brilliant and graceful prizefights two men ever boxed." Two decades after Gallico's observation, *Ring* wrote: "To this day, old-timers will tell you that the two meetings were classics in ring artistry. Delaney couldn't quite match the pace set by his youthful rival."

Taken together the two fights were revered as one conjoined display of pugilistic perfection, with scribes trying to outdo each other with descriptions of the sheer delightfulness. No one could out-hype Igoe: "It took one's breath away . . . it was boxing at its prettiest, boxing at its best . . . boxing that a President could bring into the Blue Room at the White House for afternoon tea."

By some accounts, the return match could have been called a draw, as Delaney had staged a furious comeback in the sixth round. But the roar of the crowd after the decision was announced suggested the judges had it right. Delaney trudged back to his dressing room with a somber look on his blood-smeared, welt-speckled face. Slattery was unharmed and over the moon. His playful smile, which remained partially planted on his lips for the entire fight, grew ear to ear as his triumph was declared. As sick as he was, Red jumped into the ring and hugged and kissed his fighter—he then stayed in bed for a week.

Sitting ringside at the Garden that night was Jack Dempsey. "This lad has everything," Dempsey said. "He's a coming world champion."

The gang from Buffalo mobbed their idol, showering him with backslaps all the way to his dressing room. "New York was his that night," Sammy "Newsboy" Brindis would later write. Wild tales about that evening in the Big Town spread and expanded over the years. According to one account, Slats was paid $24,000 for his Friday night's work—and blew it all in a single weekend. A closer look at total attendance for the fight, around 9,500, suggests ticket receipts were approximately $40,000, of which Slats got paid 25 percent. But it's not like Tex Rickard handed the 20-year-old ten large in cash back in the dressing room. Fighters normally picked up their checks, minus a state tax, the following Saturday at the Commission's office in the Flatiron Building located a few blocks from the Garden. Red's cut likely was at least 20 percent, although no one knew for sure. Skitsy and Joe got paid as seconds. Travel and training expenses had to be paid, as well. It all added up. All of which is not to say that Slats didn't have a hefty wad of cash burning a hole in his bell-bottom trousers. His hangers on, who now included men of means and expensive tastes, were all flush with cash too, as were many of his pals who won their wagers. It's highly probable that Slats strolled into the Silver Slipper with Dempsey and Kearns not far behind. Few things gave Slats more pleasure than walking into an establishment and shouting, "Drinks for everybody!" One admirer, Quentin Reynolds, writing in Collier's magazine in 1934, recalled how "those bucks rolled in . . . Jimmy used to laugh gaily and say with mock annoyance that he couldn't spend the money as fast as he made it."

With its festive, glamorous vibe, live band, dancing beauties and famous clientele, the Silver Slipper was, next to the Cotton Club uptown, among the hottest spots in the city. The club's manager, "Big Bill" Duffy, still had a hand managing boxers. He'd spent a few years in prison and was aligned with gangster-bootlegger Dutch Schultz, whose illegal booze—whiskey, beer and champagne—flowed freely. In his fedora and round spectacles, Damon Runyon, who stopped drinking several years earlier, was a regular at the Slipper and several other Broadway establishments, such as Lindy's Restaurant, which was basically just a Jewish deli serving enormous combination sandwiches, but nevertheless, a place to be seen. Lindy's was a favorite hangout of Rothstein's and a place where ordinary New Yorkers mixed with writers, singers, comics, musicians and prizefighters. Whenever some famous Broadway producer came in, there was usually a clatter of aspiring showgirls or songwriters who jumped up from their tables to make a pushy impression. In Runyon's stories, Lindy's became Mindy's. These places, such as the Slipper and Lindy's and Billy LaHiff's Tavern, served up a buffet of characters recognizable from Guys & Dolls. LaHiff's, located on West 48th near Broadway, was known for its beefsteak and its colorful employees, such as the insult-hurling head waiter, Jack Spooner, and friendly doorman, Toots Shor. Politicians, showmen, gangsters, as well as Runyon and his writer friends, all hung out there together. At the heart of the whole Broadway scene was a nonstop parade of gorgeous gals. That fall, at the New Amsterdam Theater on West 42nd & Broadway, Florenz Ziegfeld was putting on the eighteenth version of what was billed as the National Institution Glorifying the American Girl, better known as the "Ziegfeld Follies." Rival productions featuring scantily clad beauties opened to packed houses. Young women from all over the country came to New York with dreams of joining a chorus line. By early 1925, the Charleston craze had ceded the floor to an even more infectious, and provocative, dance, the "Black Bottom Stomp," which carried instructions to "hop down front, doodle back." People who inhabited this wonderful world—the Great White Way—talked fast and used slang phrases such as "doggone it," "let's scram," "she's the cat's meow" and "making whoopee." The hugely popular jazz number right then was George Gershwin's "Rhapsody in Blue," a rambling fusion of smaller numbers jumbled together—a sullen clarinet solo, some jaunty piano and that soaring crescendo many modern television viewers would later come to associate with United Airlines. Supper clubs all over Midtown hired jazz combos to play endlessly requested Gershwin tunes. Speakeasies were everywhere. Impeccably dressed gangsters with oversized fedoras and brightly colored hatbands shared highballs and cramped dance quarters with respectable citizens, some of whom had turned criminal aiding and abetting the flow of liquor that sloshed into Manhattan from large boats miles offshore to smaller crafts navigating every conceivable cove, bay, inlet and waterway that connected to the East and Hudson rivers. There were literally thousands of secret watering holes popping up, shutting down and changing locations. Just in Midtown, on one stretch of 52nd Street, there were more than one hundred brownstone-housed nightspots. Among the best known speakeasies: the Stork Club, Hotsy Totsy and 21. The Peacock Club, on West 48th, was run by Abe Attell, ex featherweight. Former boxer and jockey Bill Hardy ran a "speak." Usually the last stop of the night, well after dawn in most cases, was Texas Guinan's movable party, wherever she had it set up. Guinan, a foul-mouthed former movie cowgirl, operated her bordello with gangsters backing her. "Give me plenty of laughs and you can take all the rest," she was fond of saying. Last call never came at her places (the El Fey and later the 300) which featured sultry, procurable vixens, Moet champagne and a narrow square space where people could dance packed together on top of the band. When the bill came, many times patrons' eyes would bug out— that extra bucket of ice or a quick phone call was marked up ten-fold. It would have been effortless to rack up a tab of $100 ($1,200 in today's dollars) in just a few hours. If you were carrying along a large group of pals and paying for everything, it would not be inconceivable to flat-out hemorrhage money. It's not known what Slats did that Friday night after his win, where he went or how much he spent. But when the weekend was over, supposedly, according to the legend, Slats heard a knock at his hotel room door. A sizable group of his pals were broke, and had no way to get home. As the story goes, Slats picked up the telephone and, at his own expense, made arrangements for one dozen or so lads to ride back in their very own Pullman sleepers. As an aside, there was one small item in the paper (Erie County Independent) concerning a rowdy bunch of guys riding the New York Central home to Buffalo after Slattery-Delaney II. They trashed some private cars and beat up a Pullman porter.

Slattery rode a special train home. Huge lettering—SLATTERY—marked the sides of the car carrying him and his party. First Ward residents, despite the cold weather, scrambled to their roofs and back porches to view the train, The Lackawanna, as it came through the neighborhood. They waved and cheered. Many Southside kiddies climbed viaducts and stood in frozen fields in a line along the tracks, which ran straight through their backyards. When the train reached the foot of Main Street, the adjacent harbor erupted. Tugboats and freighters drew up steam and all at once sounded their whistles, producing such a loud clamor that some unaware city residents panicked and called the Bell Telephone Co. to find out if there was an emergency.

After beating Delaney again, Slats was made. "The world lies bright ahead," a newspaper in Rome said of Slattery (Rome, N.Y., that is). The Boxing Blade of Feb. 14 featured Slats on the cover. "Those who have followed Jimmy's career closely say that he has by no means reached the maximum of his physical development," said Wilbur Wood in the New York Sun. "They believe that he will be a heavyweight in two or three years, and that before he is through he will mount the heavyweight throne."

Nobody followed Slattery as closely as Red Carr. For all of the energy he exerted trying to keep Slats from going off the rails—it was, said Red, like "sitting on an active volcano"—there was a firm belief on the part of the manager that Slats really could live a madcap existence and still get it done, because he was that talented. Red idolized Slats just like everybody else. He wasn't only in charge of Slats, he was in awe of him as well. "For three years, I've watched Slats day in, day out," Red wrote in a letter to Igoe. "And I'll pledge you my word that I honestly don't know how good he really is."

Obviously, this would not be the first time a boxing manager puffed up one of his fighters to a newspaperman. But consider that by this time, Slats was already the talk of New York and a top gate attraction. What's more, the original point of Red's letter to Igoe was to shed clarity on the whole age-discrepancy kerfuffle. "Not a day goes by that he doesn't show me something new," Red concluded in his communiqué. The former newsboy himself, it needs to be pointed out, had reached a personal level of fame and professional prestige that he never imagined possible back when he was peddling papers on a street corner. Red's handling of Slats drew praise. Once he'd been portrayed as mere figurehead-pawn in Murray's scheme to concoct a paper champion. Now the press credited Red with patiently bringing the gifted boy along.

But the least-restrained fawning was reserved for Slattery himself. Every generation, sportswriters attach sentiment to the heroes of their own era, and this so-called Golden Age seemed to allow for roomier license to inject personal perspective (adoration) and to be descriptive (exaggerate), and so it was that the scribes lovingly arranged phrasal bouquets such as these: "His feet twinkled over the canvas like careless sunbeams;" "he was a wraith in the ring, a delicate fantasy."

"This youthful Buffalo boy has startled the fistic multitude," proclaimed the *Syracuse Journal* of Feb. 21, 1925, in an article titled, "Slattery Gets into Calcium Glare by Sensation Defeat of Delaney." Next to it, a brand new photo of the ever-grinning Slattery, his eyebrows lilting, hair perfect and looking more mature. In communities where there were large numbers of Irish, newspapers knew it paid to showcase Slats. The *Long Island Daily Press*, taking that same photo and rendering it as a charcoal sketch in which Slats is made to look slightly more boyish—he'd turned 20 but editors coyly clung to the idea he was 19—declared Slattery to be the next champion.

Most people in boxing thought Slats inevitably was going to be champ. It became increasingly apparent to people in New York circles that Rickard, realizing he needed a colorful, compelling attraction to draw customers to his new million-dollar Temple of Sport, was grooming Slattery to be the next Jack Dempsey. In the lobby of the Garden, Rickard had unabashedly told friends and colleagues that, in his opinion, Slattery was "the finest boxer he'd ever seen, better than Corbett," according to Billy Kelly. That March, Rickard announced he'd reached a one-year deal with Colonel Jacob Ruppert, owner of the Yankees, securing the lease-rights to stage spring/summer boxing shows at the American League ballpark. The first such promotion, already being planned for May, would be the annual all-star Hearst Milk Fund show, and there was no question Slats would figure prominently. After boxers were paid, Rickard took half of net proceeds and pledged the rest to buy milk for the poor babies of New York. The event had been a springtime rite for the past two years since Yankee Stadium opened. Rickard also was thinking about the rest of the warm weather season to come—and planning a late-summer title fight for Slattery when he turned 21 and could finally box longer bouts. For the moment, though, Rickard kept that card close to his vest (and, like many men of the day, he usually did wear a vest). Additionally, with ground broken on the New Garden, expected to open at the end of the year, Rickard began to plan ahead for the first-ever Friday Night Fight to be held at his new Temple of Sport. He envisioned a New Year's Day extravaganza— the two prodigies, Slattery versus Stribling, who, as Rickard well knew, turned 21 on the day after Christmas.

Some boxers journeyed from all over the world to come to New York just to find a manager who had connections to Tex Rickard. Slats and Red had Rickard coming to them. And they would not bow down. "Stop trying to kid me because I'm from the small town and call me when you can believe that all the smartness isn't in New York," Red once barked at Rickard during a long-distance negotiation, just prior to hanging up on him. Red had wanted 25 percent of gate; Rickard had offered five.

Living in Buffalo, on a break until his spring matches were squared away, Slats found it difficult to evade the spotlight, which he was beginning to tire of—but which he still naturally gravitated toward. Slats would turn up ringside at Frankie Schoell's fights and wave to the fans; he'd get involved with (and contribute heavily to) Mayor Schwab's Shoe Fund; he'd anchor the dais at charity dinners and benefits. The Buffalo Athletic Club's first-annual "Sports Night," honoring top athletes with Buffalo ties, was held that spring at the Elmwood Music Hall. Slattery, of course, was the guest of honor. He shined brightly, exuded vigor and made everyone feel a part of his gravity-defying orbit. There was, however, no hiding the fact that Slats was racing around in his Roadster pursuing a hedonistic playboy life, or what the *Courier*'s Kelly dubbed "the pastures of dalliance." Red tolerated, and even encouraged, liberties. His old-school thesis held that an over-trained athlete went stale. Plus, Red wanted Slats to add pounds. The plan was to take him up a division ("Red knew there were too many great middleweights fighting right then," explained First Ward boxing legend Jackie Donnelly) to light heavyweight.

One morning in early March of 1925, Slats played in a Knights of

Columbus handball tournament, and then hopped on an afternoon DL&W train to Wilkes-Barre in the coal region of Pennsylvania. In a freezing-cold Armory shed, Slats knocked out a once-promising Greenwich Village Irishman, Mike Burke, with such expediency that it caused fans to wonder aloud as they filed outside whether they had just witnessed a dive. More likely, it appears, Slattery, who spent the moments before the bout shivering in his robe and clinging to a radiator, wanted to end matters quickly so he could get back into some warmer clothes.

With no upcoming bouts on his schedule, and with Red's blessing, Slats went into vacation mode. He didn't take off into the north woods on his skis. He stayed in Buffalo. Down in the First Ward it was the most beloved time of the year, St. Patrick's Day, a stupendous feast commemorated with corned-beef luncheons, music-filled parties and a giant parade. Toward the end of March, Slats returned to the gym to prepare for a return to the ring. He weighed 178. Red pulled an offer from his stack. To hell with New York, Red decided. They were going to Boston.

Arriving at South Street Station, Slattery was met by representatives of Boston's Commercial Athletic Club, local reporters and a small but impressive fan club, which included a brass section. Delighting reporters, Slats used the six hours before his fight with Augie Ratner to take himself on a whirlwind tour of historic places, including Paul Revere's home and the North Church. He also visited the Harvard campus. Ratner, though not a top-ranked middleweight, was by no means a patsy. Harlem-bred, a product of Doc Bagley's stable, Ratner was known for his convincing kayo of Delaney several years earlier and for his ability to withstand a beating. He got one. Slattery's assault came so quick Ratner could do nothing in the first round except cover up. Boston was a city of boxing lovers. Fight followers here were as smart and as rabid as they came. "The Hub" knew about Slattery, his speed, his grace and his Corbett-like fundamentals. But nothing prepared them for this. Early in the second round, Slats drove the bald-headed veteran into a corner and bathed the helpless foe in a stunning collection of blows—"a hurricane of lefts and rights," according to one eyewitness, a "tattoo of punches that not even a chronometer could register," said another. Ratner let down his guard for a split-second. In that tiny instant, Slats nailed him on the chin. He toppled, his head coming to rest on the middle rope. Before the referee began to count, Ratner's seconds threw in the towel. Slattery's custom of carrying his stricken opponents back to their corners was both an authentic act of sportsmanship and, to some extent, showmanship, as he knew the crowds ate it up. Not only did Slats carry the stupefied Ratner across the ring to his stool, but the Buffalo fighter in the green velvet trunks even is said to have helped administer smelling salts (although it is not explained how Slats could have done so while wearing boxing gloves); regardless, Slattery stayed with Ratner until he regained his senses. The Mechanics Building rang with the surprised and delighted shrieks of the Boston Irish. Local sportswriters hailed Slattery as a coming champion. The *Herald*'s George Hamilton called Slats the "fastest fighting machine I ever saw." Lawrence Sweeney of the *Boston Daily Globe* said: "There have been great fighters. Corbett was one of them. Fitzsimmons was another . . . but for all-around fighting ability, no boxer who ever appeared in Boston created the universally favorable opinion that Slattery did last night."

A tidal wave of consensus all pointed toward one unmistakable conclusion: Slattery could not be stopped. His inner confidence broke all barriers, feeding off his ring achievements and subsequent accolades in an increasingly amplified feedback loop that continued to play out all spring. One place Slattery certainly suffered no boundaries was in his automobile. He would race it at top speed knowing that one of three things was going happen: the police, many of them First Ward friends, would look the other way; or wave him along with a warning; or give him a citation which Slattery would happily pay—or not.

Offers kept rolling in. New York promoters were scrambling to sign Slats for open-air appearances against anyone they could find. Not only was Rickard planning the Milk Fund show, but some upstart rival promoter was putting together an all-star card to be held at the Polo Grounds, across the Harlem River from Yankee Stadium, to raise money for the Italian Hospital Fund. Boston wanted Slattery to come back. Promoters in Philadelphia, Pittsburgh, Minneapolis-St. Paul, Detroit and Cleveland all made offers. Red's stack of letters and telegrams turned into a mountain. Rumors flew that Billy Gibson, now Gene Tunney's manager (Tunney had bagged Doc Bagley), had offered Red $100,000 for Slattery's contract. Promoters in Indianapolis were planning a boxing show to be held on the eve of the city's world-famous 500-mile automobile race. They promised Slats a $12,000 guarantee to appear. But Red declined it. With a busy outdoor season approaching, he ordered more rest. Sometimes, the Slattery narrative, as told in old news clippings and ancient neighborhood lore, suggests Red tried to keep Slats out of trouble by keeping him to a breakneck schedule of ring appearances, but this was not exactly the case. Red was still keeping to the usual pace of no more than two fights per month, and sometimes longer interim rest periods. Coming up were the most important months of Slats' life, a chance to cement his stardom.

With tens of thousands of dollars in summer-season purses coming down the pipeline and widespread belief around the country that he would soon be champion, Slattery must have felt like he was on top of the world. One afternoon in early May, on the kind of energizing spring day that makes a young man behave impulsively, Slattery talked a steelworker pal into taking him and Skitsy up to the top of the new Liberty Bank building, the highest point in Buffalo. The lads got the thrill of a lifetime when they were swung out over Main Street on a boom. Slats gulped down the exhilaration. Skitsy crossed his arms, determined not to seem frightened.

A couple of days later, Slats pulled another daring stunt, climbing into the ring with a heavyweight, Jack McDonald, described as a Montana miner. Slats drilled him, knocking him out in three rounds.

Gliding ever higher, Slats caught a powerful gust when he emerged as the most sensational combatant on Rickard's otherwise not-so-entertaining Milk Fund bouts. In front of the 40,000 people gathered at Babe Ruth's House, on a night that also saw the world's light heavyweight title change hands (from McTigue to Berlenbach, in what was panned as a dreadfully dull match), Slattery, as one writer put it, "saved the show." Firing a double-right, as if a sniper getting off two cruelly efficient rifle blasts, Slattery sent opponent Jack "Bulldog" Burke sailing heels up across the ring and crashing shoulder blades-first to the canvas. The sight of Burke airborne jolted Yankee Stadium like a sudden crack of lightning. Hoarse-voiced New Yorkers rehashed it for days. Their refrain: "Slattery alone was worth the price of admission."

The New York press went into full-throated exultation: "The deft manner in which Jimmy Slattery put Jack Burke out of the way is still the talk of New York," wrote the anonymous columnist known as "Fairplay." That was on June 1, 1925, two days after the show. "It ended like a flash of light," wrote the World's Igoe. "Seldom have New York fans been treated to a more thorough job than Slattery performed," wrote the Sun's Wood. And there was this from Henry Luce's fledgling weekly news capsule, Time:

"The beauty of Slattery's bright merciless speed made grizzled gentlemen at ringside mutter of Corbett." *Time*, which was priding itself on succinct, punchy prose in order to pack a week's worth of international happenings into a breezy periodical, managed to find the space to say this: "Slattery, so fast that he never lifted his hands from his sides to parry, struck with his wrist slack and whippy until the moment of impact."

Films of the Milk Fund bouts were rushed to Buffalo by airplane and shown the next day to a packed Olympic Theater. (Also playing, *White Fang*, the silver screen adaptation of Jack London's best-seller starring Strongheart the wonder dog.) Surprising everyone there, Slats turned up at an early screening. It had been presumed Slattery was going to stay over in New York an extra night. But after the fight, back in his room at the Claridge Hotel, Slattery was so inundated with callers, promoters, newspapermen, pitchmen, friends, admirers and charity cases—he was completely overwhelmed. At the same time, Slats had wanted to make some stops and pay some visits without his large gang tagging along. Slats told Skitsy to go secure some berths on a midnight train and when the time was right, Slats and Red slipped out of town.

A quick double-right smash had, in one moment, flipped over an upright man and solidified Slattery's national reputation as the top light heavyweight, even though Berlenbach owned the title. Jack Delaney was also on the Milk Fund card. He beat Tony Marullo. But no one seemed to care much. All that New York fans wanted to know: when would they get to see Slats again?

On Wednesday, June 10, 1925, a network of some 2,000 wholesalers, retailers and suppliers descended on Grotto Park in Elmira, N.Y. for their annual picnic. An idyllic "Any Town U.S.A.," Elmira was a small but important regional commercial hub. Its wholesalers distributed goods—beef, poultry, dairy, fruits, vegetables, confectionaries, baked goods, dry goods, sporting goods, sundries, clothes, shoes, oil, gas, cigars and cigarettes—to merchants and shop owners up and down the spine of the Alleghenies in such small Pennsylvania towns as Sayre, Athens, Canton, Troy, Towanda, Tioga, Millerton, Mansfield, Wellsboro and Lawrenceville. The weather all morning had been cloudy, but today was Elmira's time to shine. Main Street was festooned with "Welcome" signs and American flags. A delegation from

Canton turned up first and in style—a slow-moving parade of automobiles trailing behind the Canton High School marching band. Awaiting all invitees was a smorgasbord of barbecues, baseball, musical performances, races and, best of all, an amateur boxing tournament to be officiated by a special guest of honor, former heavyweight champion James Corbett, who was also slated to give a keynote address later that evening at the gala banquet. And what a fete that was to be—organizers were bringing in a motherlode of western meats slaughtered in Chicago and shipped by rail in "fireless cookers." The ambitious main course reflected the upbeat spirit in prosperous Elmira and throughout the entire land. Unbridled speculation in the stock market—much of it on margin—spurred on more of the same behavior, with the spread of anecdotal evidence of people getting rich quick. The situation was worrisome enough for some politicians to speak out. Everybody else reinforced a shared mindset: these good times were meant to last awhile. Since the summer of '22, the Dow Jones Industrial Average had steadily climbed higher on the backs of the automobile and communication sectors. Unemployment had dropped below 5 percent. Productivity was up, which by definition raised living standards. The work week was shortened. Saturdays were suddenly born. Farmers who struggled for years with low commodity prices, economic recessions and mini-depressions and who had somehow managed to hold on to their land were rewarded for their resilience. By 1925, the Dow hit 150, up from 67 in 1921. Financial euphoria was in the air.

Also in the air: nonstop chatter concerning the Buffalo boy, Jimmy Slattery, and his unbelievable knockout of Bulldog Burke, hardly a stranger in these parts. Burke was a product of the Allegheny foothills; folks here could remember a few years earlier when Burke fought Gene Tunney in Tex Rickard's Garden, and how he had been invited to join Dempsey's training camp. Burke was said to have knocked Dempsey down back in that summer of '23. Everywhere in Grotto Park, men in straw hats discussed the weather, turning sunny, and Slattery. Conclusions were drawn, connecting what Burke once did to Dempsey with what Slattery had done to Burke. By the time the raspy-voiced, round-spectacled, three-piece-suit-wearing ex-champion Corbett delivered his lecture ("Memories of an Active Life & How to Keep Young"), it was 10:00 P.M. A singing group led by Arthur McLeod, chairman, wholesaler division, Elmira Association of Commerce, finally concluded the long day of festivities with a stirring rendition of "Auld Lang Syne."

As he left the banquet, Corbett found himself being followed by some reporters looking for easy copy. For many years, Corbett had been a go-to commentator on the fight game. His opinions were widely disseminated in his own King Features column and via a steady dose of quotes in newspaper stories. Strangely, and conspicuously, Corbett had amassed an abysmal track record of fight prognostications, almost to the point of being a running joke in the boxing world. A Corbett endorsement still meant something to the multitudes. But in certain circles, it was the kiss of death.

"Within a few months, Slattery should develop into a logical contender," Corbett told a wire reporter who had asked for an opinion on the next heavyweight champion. What came next was fashioned into a brief story, "*Slats the Boy, Says Corbett*," that was picked up by sports pages around the country.

"Slattery is scientific, has plenty of speed and he can punch," Corbett said. "A combination of these three qualities makes a champion. It would not surprise me if Slattery succeeded Dempsey as ruler of the heavyweight division."

It wasn't just Corbett making such predictions. The most respected boxing critics of the day, including the most hard-boiled newspapermen alive, were all unanimously singing odes to Slattery.

The term "hard-boiled" owes to Tad Dorgan, a groundbreaking, phrase-coining sports page cartoonist. He first used it to describe the old codgers who sat with him ringside smoking cigars and who were not easily impressed. Dorgan's brother, Ike, was chief of publicity for the Garden and had helped Nat Fleischer start *The Ring*. Another Dorgan brother, Dick, became a cartoonist and a Slattery admirer. In one spread of drawings, accompanied by some verbiage, Dick Dorgan pronounced Slattery "in a class by himself" and ranked him as "the greatest six-round man since Philadelphia Jack O'Brien."

Joe Villa was the Dean of boxing critique with three decades under his belt. His "Setting the Pace" column in the *New York Sun* was considered Gospel. "Slattery, who has been hailed in some quarters as the coming heavyweight champion of the world, not only is a wonderful boxer," Villa wrote, "but he also has unusual hitting power."

Otto Floto was a former Rocky Mountain dog-and-pony showman, a contemporary of Bat Masterson and Buffalo Bill, a boxing promoter, and, later, sports editor at the *Denver Post*. Floto had been a mentor to Runyon (who got his start as a newspaper man in Colorado) and knew Jack Dempsey when the hobo youth was working the Cripple Creek district. Floto was considered the Dean of the Western boxing critics. When he spoke, people paid attention. "So here we go and we want folks to remember this," wrote Floto, who was credited as being one of the first to predict Dempsey's rise. "It looks right now as if Jimmy Slattery will someday be heavyweight champion of the world. He has all the essential qualifications."

Syndicated sports columnist Bob Edgren made his name in the late 1890s covering Corbett's big fights for the *San Francisco Examiner*; straightforward reliability was his trademark. He rated Slattery as one of the boxing game's most sensational figures. "If Jimmy Slattery isn't light heavyweight champion within the next couple of years it will be because he has graduated into the heavyweight class."

The list of respected boxing authorities didn't end. Neither did the Slattery coronation ceremony. Ed Curley, sportswriter for the *New York American*, theorized that "if Slattery packs on more weight, which he should, no man in the ring will be able to beat him." Sid Mercer, *New York Journal*: "Slattery—not Berlenbach—emerges as featured gladiator." From the *Brooklyn Daily Eagle's* Ed Hughes: "Can you imagine a comparatively old and slowed up Dempsey attempting to fathom the speed and magic skill of this amazing Buffalo youth?" The *New York World's* George Daley: "Slattery has everything. If he goes to the heavyweight class I venture to say he'll wear the crown." James J. Wood in the *Brooklyn Times*: "James Patrick Slattery of Buffalo is the crown prince of pugilism." The *Boston Globe's* Lawrence Sweeney: "Slattery has set the boxing world in a furor . . . he is the most-talked-of boxer in the world today."

Probably the singularly most obsequious paean came at the height of that heady spring in the form of a three-part series by Sid Sutherland of the *Chicago Tribune*.

Jimmy Slattery Called Athletic Phenomenon
BUFFALO BOXER IS VERSATILE

Combines Traits of Famous Fighters in History;
Speed, Power and Ring Brains;
Rising like a Meteor

Sutherland was a versatile writer who enjoyed his own stardom. Spinning true adventure tales of the Mexican revolt and the hunt for Pancho Villa, Sutherland attained prestige as a magazine writer while still in his twenties before turning his sights to politics and unsolved mysteries, becoming obsessively fascinated with the unsolved Wall Street bombing of 1920. By the mid-1920s—peak ballyhoo era—Sutherland was doing lengthy feature stories for the *Tribune,* which syndicated them around the world. In June of 1925, Sutherland was dispatched to Buffalo's First Ward to profile the sporting marvel of the moment. Utilizing prose as florid and exceedingly effusive as anything produced by the ragtime-era idol makers in New York, Sutherland let loose: "*Occasionally an individual stands colorfully forth from the drab monotony of the nameless herd, seemingly endowed with all of the attributes mankind admires and yearns to emulate . . .*"

Painting Slats as a sensible, pleasant lad who liked a beer with pals now and again, Sutherland conceded that Slattery had his vices—those being, his automobile (too big, too fast) and his fashion tastes (too loud).

"Jimmy's a good boy, a good boy, sir," Slattery's mom kept softly reiterating during the writer's visit to the Slattery home.

Sutherland's big reveal: "So far as can be gleaned, the lad has no bad habits."

Starkly contrasting reports were winnowing their way downstate prior to Slattery's early July meeting with the lantern-jawed San Franciscan, Dave Shade. The "smart money"—investigative hoodlums and full-time gamblers with an ear to the ground—knew of the Buffalo boxer's appallingly besotted state leading up to the fight. Rumors of out-of-control revelry eventually reached the 23-year-old Shade and even his wife, Irene. Upon hearing the tip, the young stay-at-home mom wanted to tap her private $300 nest egg to place a bet, but her husband forbade her. Shade knew Slattery was among the best in the game. But Shade was confident. So was his manager, Leo Flynn, who had spent weeks trying to get the match made.

Apart from Shade's inner circle and the dialed-in Broadway denizens, few others gave the Californian so much as a prayer or a puncher's chance. For starters, Shade was known as a light hitter. The match was actually kind of absurd, a catchweight affair; it almost seemed like more of an exhibition, what, with Slattery, hailed as coming light heavyweight champion, weighing around 164, ten pounds heavier than Shade, a welterweight. But the perception of a mismatch didn't bother the public. Fans merely wanted to catch a glimpse of Slattery. They would pay their money to see him flash his magnificence, and hope that he might show some mercy.

Shade, for his part, was unworried.

Growing up in Vallejo, California, near San Francisco, Dave Shade and his two brothers were prodded into the ring by their dad, an ex-fighter who bought his sons boxing gloves for Christmas. The boys were each born two years apart. George, the oldest, grew into a strapping coming heavyweight. Middle brother Billy had speed. Chief attribute of the runt, Dave, had been his survival skills. At 19, George was an experienced professional and Billy had been in the game for about a year. Instead of practicing on one another, the two older brothers made their baby sibling lace up so they could tee off on him. Their ring was a small room off the back of the house. It offered nowhere to hide. Dave Shade did the only thing he could do. He ducked down, really low.

George was discovered by Frank Tabor, who had toiled briefly in the Bay Area four-round game before deciding he was better off as a manager and trainer. Soon George was off to Australia, where boxing was legal and thriving. Billy followed. He did even better Down Under than George, winning titles. Tabor agreed to evaluate the youngest of the brood. With his short legs, long torso, enlarged forehead and protruding chin, Dave Shade had a slightly unusual, almost Leprechaunesque quality about him. Tabor took one look and advised the 16-year-old to give up boxing. "You'll never make it as a fighter," Tabor told him.

Sticking with his oddly low crouch out of habit, Shade competed as a featherweight at the tin-roofed Association Club on 16th Street in the Mission District. The older brothers came back from Australia as nationally known figures. Billy in particular had cleaned up. With New York City poised to become boxing's richest hub, the Shades looked east. Their dad traveled ahead of them. One afternoon in 1921, Charlie Shade burst into the office of Leo Flynn. At that time, Flynn was part-time matchmaker for the Garden and a fight manager with about two dozen prospects in his stable and dozens more on whom he was keeping tabs. Flynn used the Garden as his headquarters. McLevy's Gym occupied the space near the corner-entrance of the building on Madison Avenue & 26th Street, diagonal from

Madison Square Park. Canny, elegant and extremely knowledgeable about the sport, Flynn was classic, a top-hat wearing relic of little old horse-drawn Gotham.

The elder Shade had come a long way. He articulated his rehearsed message. "I'm Billy Shade's father. Seems everybody wants to manage Billy. You seem like the best, what with your connections to Tex Rickard and the Garden. You could do more for him than anybody else. So you can have Billy."

Flynn could hardly believe his luck. He sure had wanted Billy Shade.

"But there's one condition."

"What is it?" Flynn asked.

"Well," continued Mr. Shade. "His brothers are fighters, too. If you want Billy, you have to take the other two. I want them together."

So Flynn acquiesced and the novelty of three boxing brothers sat well with Garden matchmakers. It seemed the world was about to hear much more about the Fighting Shades. But Billy, bitten by the gabling bug, flamed out. Hard-punching George, who had always struggled with an alcohol problem, also faded from contention. To everyone's surprise, it was the youngest Shade, Dave who turned out to have the most talent.

At 19, Shade made his Garden debut against Georgie Ward, darling of Elizabeth, N.J., and on the verge of national acclaim as a star welter. Bobbing up and down into the most exaggerated crouch anyone had ever seen—one writer described Shade's long chin as being closer to the ground than his shins—Shade startled the fans by giving Ward a sound licking. Few could figure Shade out. He held legendary Jack Britton to a draw. When Englishman "Bermondsey Billy" Wells was making waves in the U.S., Shade beat him in the Garden. In three bouts with Frankie Schoell held in 1923-24, Shade took two. He was a true journeyman. During one stretch in '24, Shade fought in Boston, Chicago, St. Paul, Omaha and Oakland, where in September of that year he defeated Oakland Jimmy Duffy (not to be confused with Lockport Jimmy Duffy).

Shade, settled down with a wife and young son by age 20, raked in purse money and came to define, along with the likes of Dempsey and Benny Leonard, a new breed of fiscally responsible pugilist. One sad look at the once brilliant Young Griffo, now middle-aged and living in a 42nd Street doorway, was an ever-present reminder to all in the game of how too many fighters ended up indigent. Shade bought a house on the Grand Concourse in Bronx, N.Y., and a hunting camp in the Berkshires.

Rickard ranked him the second-best welterweight behind champion Walker. Shade was knocking on the door of national fame. But the New York sportswriters weren't buying in. Shade wasn't interesting. Critics dismissed him as a soft puncher in an era when fans increasingly desired knockouts. Shade had no Garden appearances in 1925. His last fight there had been in '23. Meanwhile, Walker refused to meet him for the title. This was a source of consternation for the men who regulated boxing in New York State. And the situation was growing thornier.

A heavily publicized all-star boxing card was about to be held in June 1925 at the Polo Grounds. In its main event, Walker, moving up a weight division, was challenging Harry Greb, middleweight champion. Shade's crafty manager, Leo Flynn, keen to get his fighter in the mix, spotted an opening.

The Italian Hospital fund show, brainchild of a neophyte promoter with whom fight fans were only just getting acquainted, was, nevertheless, the most anticipated sporting event of the summer. Fans craved spectacle. Jack Dempsey was dormant. Babe Ruth was having a lousy year. Humbert Fugazy had never put on a boxing show before, but he was kick-starting his foray with a real corker—not only was there the Greb-Walker championship fight, but also Harry Wills, the top-ranked heavyweight (behind Dempsey), meeting fourth-ranked Charley Weinert of Newark, N.J.

Fugazy, a bookish financial adviser and theater owner, had recently turned forty. The Brooklynite had done some fighting as a young man. Fugazy's father had presented him with a choice: come work in his private bank and live comfortably, or make it on his own as a fighter. Fugazy gave up boxing. To get his promotion off the ground, Fugazy pledged *100 percent* of net proceeds to fund a hospital for poor Italian immigrants. He drew the support of the Boxing Commission, hardly averse to a new player on the scene to challenge Tex Rickard's corner on big-money shows. Fugazy enlisted newspapermen who—and this wasn't considered particularly shocking at the time—could be bought, and so publicity was abundant. But to truly make his show a howling success, Fugazy needed one more splashy name.

He had recruited the Queensboro A.C.'s matchmaker, Lew Raymond, to help arrange the card. Raymond, a former burlesque show comic, knew Jimmy Slattery and Red Carr from one year earlier when Slats helped christen the new "Queensboro Bowl." Getting Slattery into the mix proved to be tricky. He was still two months shy of his 21st birthday, and still limited to six rounds. And so it went. Nobody wanted to take on the speed boy in a sprint. Raymond persisted. Fugazy leaned on him. Make it happen, Fugazy told him, get Slattery. "Any opponent would do, so long as Slattery appeared," *The Ring's* Ted Carroll later explained. "So intense was public interest in Slattery, fans practically demanded that he be included on the card."

In suggesting Shade as a possible opponent for Slattery, Flynn was ridiculed. Yet he was certain he was tugging on exactly the right strings, for the manager knew Fugazy was desperate to add the Dancing Master from Buffalo (that one didn't catch on, either) to the Italian Hospital show lineup. Included in Flynn's machinations was the presumption that Slats could easily be led into the temptation of a soft match with a light-hitting welterweight. In this respect, Flynn miscalculated. "Shade was a hard man to fight, which is why Slats protested when Shade was picked as his opponent," wrote Grantland Rice. Fugazy and his matchmaker lobbied Red incessantly. Exhausted, Red at one point asked Fugazy, "Why don't *you* fight Shade?"

Over the ensuing years, Fugazy would put on many more boxing shows, so many of which were rained out that his nickname became "Hard Luck Humbert." On June 19, 1925, the night of his first big show, inclement weather forced postponement. Fugazy pushed it back two weeks. Ticket sales had been strong but Fugazy needed a sell-out. Wily Leo Flynn needed Shade on that program. He had one more play. In sanctioning the show's main event (Greb-Walker), the Boxing Commission forced Walker to agree to fight Shade thereafter. With Walker refusing to sign papers sealing a meeting with Shade, Flynn *had a legal claim to have Walker suspended*, which would ruin what was shaping up to be one of boxing's biggest nights. To placate Flynn, the Commissioners, Billy Muldoon, James Farley and George Brower, took the unusual step of calling Slattery into the body's Flatiron Building offices so that they might personally convince him to accept the Shade bout. The *New York Sun's* Wilbur Wood describes a conference during which Slattery, who never, ever, ducked anybody (maybe Tiger Flowers, once, supposedly) and who knew full well how frustrating it was to be ducked, refused to budge on the matter, despite the cajoling, pleading and strong-arming of powerful elders. Wood describes a curious scene: Slattery then huddling up closely with the commissioners, at which time "he was made to see the light."

Rumors flew that Slattery would be guaranteed $17,000. When the news broke about a week before the fight that he was being added to the card, rescheduled for July 2, New York City boxing fans were ecstatic. The impact was immediate. Fugazy printed up a new batch of tickets for remaining lower grandstand seats originally priced at $5. After Slats was added to the program, the price for the same seats went up to $15. In the eyes of the public, the match was an exhibition. Slattery was a heavy favorite, a meteoric, hugely popular future champion going up against a powder-puff giving away ten pounds—it may as well have been Sir Lancelot jousting with the village idiot. What's more, the discerning New York fans, extremely intolerant of uninteresting matches, still were enthusiastic. They just wanted to see Slattery in action. Fugazy had delivered.

In actuality, the gap separating the two boxers was not as wide as most people thought. In the pink of condition, Slats weighed 163, which made him more of a heavy middleweight than an authentic light heavyweight. Shade, by the same token, was always considered an elastic welter who was due to make the jump to middleweight. Fight fans had heard so much ballyhoo about Slattery as the next Dempsey that many presumed Slattery already *was* a heavyweight, especially when he manhandled Bulldog Burke, a heavyweight (175). In street clothes, Slats, with his broad shoulders and muscular arms, looked like he was the same size as Dempsey (185). But Slats was narrow of waist and his legs, though sturdy, were on the scrawny side. For all the talk that he still had room on his lanky frame, Slattery was hardly barreling toward heavyweight. A pairing between Slattery and Shade earlier in the year would not have been considered absurd. Boston promoters had floated just such a possibility and no one at that time, only months earlier, deemed such a match as particularly lopsided. What very few knew was that Slats and Shade *had already boxed* before.

According to Red, a never-publicized, impromptu sparring session between Slattery and Shade took place at Newsboys' Gym in early March of '25 when Shade was preparing to fight in nearby Rochester. But Shade, too, produced a memory of sparring with Slats, and in his version, the session occurred in 1921 when Slats was just turning professional and Shade was in Buffalo to fight Jack Perry. One thing was clear. Slattery, then 17, did not impress the then-nineteen-year-old Californian.

Reacting to the recent May-June monsoon of Slattery accolades, Shade was amazed. "I couldn't believe they were talking about the same kid," he said.

Preparing to fight Slats for real, Shade was confident, and not because of those reports coming out of Buffalo. His manager was instilling in him a belief that he would not only win, but that he would knock Slattery out. Flynn was a student of technique. He based his prediction on the dynamics of a toe-bouncing, standup fighter like Slattery pitted against Shade's low crouch, his bobbing and weaving. Shade did not believe he was capable of stopping Slattery, but he was feeling optimistic about his chances of winning a decision.

Amplifying the excitement was Fugazy's decision to allow the event to be described live over a radio broadcast—a not-yet-common technological tie-in that never would have been on the table if this were a Tex Rickard production. But for true fight fans, particularly the Slattery faithful, nothing could have diverted them from the Polo Grounds, a gigantic concrete-and-steel horseshoe situated along 155th and 157th streets at the base of a rock outcropping known as Coogan's Bluff. Spectator Bill McCormick grew up despising Jack Dempsey and by then was smitten with Slattery. McCormick, who would go on to cover boxing for the *Washington Post*, had come and bet all the money he had, around $3, on Slattery, and without thinking twice. For every $5 bet on Slats, only $1 was bet on Shade. Casual fans, latecomers to the sport, were on hand to get a glimpse of the marvel everyone was talking about. Slattery fever was burning. The summer sun was at its near-highest point. A dozen or more determined First Ward kids made a difficult, risky trip riding the rods to Harlem. To this day, people from the South Buffalo environs can relate scenes that had once been described to them, a mob of brazen youths running along the sides of the New York-bound trains, jumping and falling dangerously about. More than a few of them made it, as there are accounts of the bellhops at Slattery's hotel chasing away a sizable throng of grimy street urchins.

In the first preliminary bout, "Little Jackie" Sharkey defeated Joe Lynch. Slattery entered the ring as darkness descended. The sky was clear and filling up with stars. By several accounts, Slats looked tall, lean and handsome with his dark hair greased and perfectly combed. He was accompanied by his 31-year-old, red-headed manager. The shorter, blonde-haired Shade arrived with his grey-bearded manager. Many fans—a full house of 55,000 was anticipated—were still streaming through the gates, creating a bottleneck. Most did not expect the fight to last very long, so they sped to their seats.

Red Carr insisted for years that Slats did not show up at the Polo Grounds intoxicated. Everyone else seemed to have heard the opposite. "Slattery went into the ring drunk," said Batavia-born boxing historian Angelo Prospero, explaining how handlers Skitsy Fitzgerald and Joe Hickey had to prop Slats up. Regardless, Slats hurried toward Shade at the bell, as if seeking to make short work of him. Slats wore a devilish grin. The crowd, presuming Slats was about to cut Shade to pieces, winced, some turning away. Slats threw a right, but Shade, bobbing down into his crouch, ducked under. Both fighters tumbled into the ropes but instantly resumed the fray. If Slats was impaired, it was not evident. Several ringside reports depict Slattery as boxing artistically, but just not effectively. Shade used his hip as a wall and kept his tantalizingly pronounced chin tucked out of range. Taking his time, Slats kept firing, and missing. He found Shade a locked box, the crouch even more annoying than he anticipated. Slats displayed no defensive inclinations whatsoever. Shade even landed a few decent shots. Runyon gave the first two rounds to Shade. A large swath of fans had only just sat down when the bell rang to start the third.

Slats danced out of his corner. Shade came out somehow crouching even lower. Slats stood intently before his prey, strategizing anew, on the fly, seemingly on the cusp of cracking the riddle. Shade trained his eyes on Slattery's chest. Shade knew what was coming. About one minute of the third round had elapsed.

Slats stabbed downward with a left. The Californian shifted to his right, easily avoiding it, and countered with an overhand right. The gaudy punch originated near Shade's ankles, looped a twirling 180 degrees and collided with the flushest portion of the Irishman's chin. Slats never saw it coming. His feet froze in place. Shade jumped up and hit him again. Slattery's knees buckled. Then he fell backwards to the floor like an unfilled burlap bag, his head striking the canvas with an awful thump, his skinny legs flying up in the air. An unsettling cascade of gasps and groans spread throughout the immense ballpark. At ringside, the zealous timekeeper used his gong mallet to hammer out the count, each second bringing a bang to the ring floor—not far from where Slattery lay sprawled—and in perfect time with the referee's motioning arm. By the count of five, Slats was sitting up along the ropes frowning and staring nervously at referee Ed Purdy as if pleading with the official to agree to pretend that the whole thing had never happened. Slats hopped to his feet. Shade was all over him with a leaping left hook. Slats went down again. He struggled back up right before the count of ten, groggy and reeling into the ropes. Shade put him down a third time. Slats, functioning on instinct alone, somehow got up again. Red tossed a towel into the ring.

Disbelief gripped the stadium. Slattery momentarily, pitifully, objected, thinking he could wave off surrender, but it dawned on whatever semblance of mental faculties to which he still had access that the only thing to do now was walk over and congratulate Dave Shade, who was speaking into a microphone and telling a radio audience it was the most thrilling moment of his life. Nearby, Leo Flynn danced a jolly jig. The fight had lasted two and a half rounds. The sheer completeness and unexpectedness of the rout was, in every sense of the word, unbelievable.

"Talk about a surprise," Runyon said after.

Calling the fight's outcome the "most startling upset in years," Runyon's coverage was distributed across the land by Universal Service. Weeks later, Rice wrote, "Outside of the [Dempsey-Firpo] fight there has been no contest in recent years that caused so much discussion . . . they are still wondering how it happened." Months later, *Ring* would declare Shade-Slattery, "Upset of the Year." And decades later, the magazine's Ted Carroll added: "No one can convince me that it was not the greatest surprise in boxing history."

Slattery was the most talked-about boxer on the planet, but for reasons heartbroken Buffalo fans never could have imagined. Across Western New York, indeed, across the sporting world, incomprehension reigned: *What caused Slattery's collapse?*

SEVEN

Hunter's Rest

"**W**HAT THE HECK HAPPENED?"

A nervy pal made the mistake of asking Slats at a New York City bar following the Dave Shade debacle. So goes a tale told for generations in the Irish section of Buffalo. The story concludes with Slats beating up every single guy in proximity. How many he cut down depends on the teller of the story. Not included in the South Buffalo oral tradition is another fairly incredible anecdote said to have occurred in the immediate aftermath of Slattery's shocking defeat.

Inside one of the dressing rooms at the Polo Grounds, Harry Greb was waiting to appear in his main-event bout with Mickey Walker. The Harry Wills–Charlie Weinert heavyweight match was underway. Greb could hear sobbing. He glanced over and saw the anguished Buffalo fighter slumped over on a rubdown table, quivering and bawling uncontrollably.

"How could this happen?" Slats implored of his manager, Red Carr.

Red had no answers. Greb, who epitomized tough, came over and gently placed his hand on Slattery's shoulder. "Take it easy, Jim," Greb said. "It happens to everybody."

This account comes, in part, from an article written by John Lardner (son of Ring Lardner, master of short fiction) and was published in *True* magazine in February of 1950. According to the article, Greb instantly made it his business to cheer Slats up. "Hey, after I win my fight, we'll go hit the town," he supposedly told Slats.

Greb won his fight, keeping his middleweight title and his promise. Afterward, Greb found the kid, still a wreck, hiding out in his dressing room. The champ ordered Slats to get cleaned up then physically led the Buffalo boy by the arm out of the Bronx ballpark and into a waiting car. Slats confided in Greb that he was afraid to face his friends.

"Forget about it," Greb replied. "The bastards can go —— themselves."

A 1936 article in *Esquire* included the same account. In it, Greb biographer James Fair asserts the two prizefighters went to the Silver Slipper together and that Greb made it a point to keep checking on his bereft young friend in between dances. A post-fight column by Charlie Murray also puts Greb and Slats at a Broadway restaurant (one with a dance floor), although the name of the establishment is not given.

As it turns out, one of the most fantastic stories from boxing's golden era involves Greb and Walker bumping into each other that very night at the Slipper, exchanging words (pertaining to a mutually admired female) before picking up their scrape where they'd left off hours earlier at the Polo Grounds. Greb always denied this encounter ever really happened, as did his manager, Red Mason, as did Pittsburgh sports editors who hung around the Human Windmill. Still, Walker repeated versions of the story numerous times over the years. It does appear Greb was at the glitzy nightspot for some portion of the evening and that he may have even crossed paths with Walker. But it seems more likely that Greb was preoccupied with Slattery's well being than anything else (besides a blonde with whom the widower purportedly planned to rendezvous).

Charlie Murray was seated at a table with Greb and some Pittsburgh writers. Murray described another poignant scene.

As the band took five, Greb was urged by patrons to deliver a victory speech. He rose from his seat, still riding the high of defeating Walker, and waved the room to a hushed murmur. Eyes searching the crowd, Greb spotted Slats sulking at a corner table. Everyone in the restaurant trained their eyes on Greb as he walked over to where Slats was sitting. The room fell quiet as Greb lifted Slats out of his chair by the lapels, and dragged him squirming into the center of the now empty dance floor. Many people recognized Slattery and a friendly hurrah rose with him.

"Brace up," Greb whispered, supposedly. Perhaps it was an Irish whisper (because, really, how else would Murray have heard?). Slattery was raw with emotion. The shouted applause brought more tears.

"I've been in the dumps myself," Greb said to Slats. "It will *make you.*"

Then, according to Murray, Greb turned to his fellow Broadway denizens and announced to the crowd: "Ladies and gentleman, here stands one of the greatest who ever walked into a ring. And he's just a kid. I want to make a statement . . . I consider him the best man I ever met. Keep your eye on Slats."

As the middleweight champ bellowed out his words to the room, Slats shifted back and forth on his feet. Murray thought he saw a trace of a smile emerge.

"I wish I was just starting out," Greb said, extending his hand. "Put it there."

Everyone let out a cheer and the party resumed. The crestfallen boxer was choked up.

"Thanks," was all Slats could say.

That same Thursday night, back in Buffalo, reporters brought the dreadful news to the doorstep of No. 153 Abbott Road. Asked for a comment about her son's misfortune, Mary Slattery sighed: "Well, he can't win them all, can he?"

A few hundred dedicated fans had stood for hours in the street outside the *Courier*'s headquarters downtown, at the intersection of Swan and Seneca, waiting for results. A megaphone-toting announcer read telegraphed fight returns every few minutes. When it was revealed that Shade had won, no one believed it. The crowd refused to disperse, so utterly convinced were Slattery's fans that the wire reports were somehow wrong. The paper's switchboard was deluged. Callers had heard but wanted to know—was there some mistake? Told the bad news was indeed true, many city residents hung up, then called back moments later just to check one more time.

The next day, Slats went to Yankee Stadium to see the American League club play the Athletics. It's said that Tex Rickard introduced Slats to the entire Yankee team and that even the thrill of meeting Babe Ruth was no tonic for the brokenhearted warrior. The next day, Slats returned to Buffalo by train. A sizable contingent of First Ward supporters was waiting at the station. "We're with you, Jimmy!" one of them shouted when Slats emerged on the top step. Tearing up, he covered his face. "Thank them for me, will you?" Slats told Red and then jumped into a friend's car. He needed to go home.

Loyal pals Skitsy and Joe had not left his side. But now it was time they bid him adieu.

Slats sat with his parents and re-lived his nightmare. The family was feeling devastated yet determined not to appear that way, at least not publicly. A neighbor had come to the door to wish everyone well and to see if anything was needed, as if a death had occurred. Old Sloak sent the well-wisher on his way, saying: "One reverse doesn't turn the world around—there will be another time."

"This might be the best thing that could have happened," Red would say. "Maybe now Slats will stop fooling around and take his training seriously."

Red's plan was to give the lad, a few weeks shy of 21, another long summer off. Red believed young men developed fast and naturally in warm months. One more restful growing season, as the manager figured it, would bulk up Slattery's frame.

Red took him to a cottage in Crystal Beach for a few days. Slats remained downcast. He eventually showed his face in public, attending outdoor fights at Bison Stadium. Fans met him warmly. Some small newspapers continued to publish flattering cartoons with captions cruelly predicting Slattery to someday succeed Dempsey—syndicated feature bits furnished pre-Shade and run in ill-timed manner by clueless editors. Many writers, meanwhile, turned their backs on Slats, as he'd made them look foolish. "Unless Jimmy learns how to park his chin in a safe place," wrote one Big Town boxing critic, "the jig is up."

Buffalo fans mourned for one solid week. A fan wrote to the *Buffalo News* in verse, a take on Ernest Thayer's 1888 baseball ode, "Casey at the Bat."

The parody's opening stanza:

> *"In Buffalo, joy doesn't loom*
> *The bugs are feeling sure*
> *Since Slattery succumbed to Shade with whom*
> *They thought he'd wipe the floor."*

At Newsboys' Gym, Slats worked out with Vic St. Onge, Red's feisty little flyweight from Genesee County. Barely 100 pounds, "Kid Vick" earned Slattery's admiration for the heart he showed. St. Onge liked to swing the wooden Indian clubs, old-school. The two sparred together and spoke of one day taking a deer hunting trip. St. Onge had frequent adventures outdoors. One of his relatives helped run an Adirondack lumber camp, which in the summer doubled as a hunting and fishing lodge. Red heard about the place and decided it would make a perfect getaway for Slats.

So the manager arranged for his fighter to go stay at the remote property, deep in the woods, at an elevation of 2,000 feet, near the village of Indian Lake, N.Y. Sending his fighter off to an authentic lumber camp was, on some level, a posture Red took to assuage fight game people who questioned Slattery's toughness. But it was a great idea. Of course, Slats would be accompanied on this recuperative expedition by his two closest companions. The three pals would spend two weeks breathing clean, thin air and adopting a lumberjack's lifestyle.

Before leaving Buffalo early that July, Slats stopped by Mordeno Brothers Barber Shop and got himself a brush cut. Head cleanly buzzed, inspired to turn over a new leaf, Slats, leaving his automobile behind, lit out for the north woods by rail. In Saratoga the boys changed trains, switching from the New York Central line to the Delaware & Hudson, which had absorbed the Adirondack Railroad. The closest they could get to Indian Lake was a depot in North Creek, some 22 miles away. The North Creek station had played a bit part in American history. A quarter-century earlier, Theodore Roosevelt stood there waiting to board a Buffalo-bound train that would take him to be sworn in as President following McKinley's assassination. Roosevelt was initially informed that McKinley was going to survive the shooting. An avid outdoorsman, the Vice President disappeared into the Adirondacks on an impromptu hiking trip; when McKinley took a turn for the worse, a federal search party scrambled to retrieve Teddy.

From the North Creek station, Slats, Skitsy and Joe were collected in a motor truck arranged for them. Their trip took them past the tiny town of Indian Lake—consisting of a post office, a restaurant, a hotel, a church, plus a few houses—and up along a winding, rock-and-dirt road leading from the main mountain route into the heart of the dense forest. The camp was situated seven miles off the main road, in a grassy clearing alongside a spectacular, boulder-strewn bend in the Hudson River. Mountains loomed in the distance. It was a loud, turbulent stretch of the Hudson, nor far from its point of origination and near where it crossed the Indian River. The adjoining property was vast and unsettled. Several miles to the north stood the farm and seasonal lumber camp looked after by Lucy St. Onge and her husband, Carl. A completely separate camp farther south was where Slattery would lodge. This part of the camp was run by 51-year-old Frank Husson, with the help of his son, Earl, and Earl's wife, Dora. They were simple, good-natured people who lived off the land (although Frank did own a home in the village) and they all immediately took a liking to Slattery. Earl and Dora, in their mid-twenties, were busy feeding the lumber workers as well as looking after their two tiny tots.

They called the place "Hunter's Rest," but it was also known as "Hunter's Home," and more often than not, people simply referred to it as "the Husson

Camp." Frank leased the land from the Finch, Pruyn & Co. paper company, which operated its mill down-river in Glens Falls. In the winter, Husson turned the place over to the lumber workers who cut down trees and stacked the logs in a long row to be skidded off the bank and into the river come springtime. Earl Husson would join in these sometimes treacherous "river drives" which included log-jam breaking missions conducted in fast-moving rapids using skiffs, poles and dynamite. The Hussons occupied a large, cedar-built dwelling. Rustic and cozy, the ground floor of the main house contained a big kitchen and a sitting area with a fireplace. Slats and his friends stayed at the guest lodge, a short distance away, across a field, atop a hill overlooking the riverbank. It was a smaller version of the main house and featured an elongated front and side porch overlooking a postcard-perfect scene—roaring river, tall timber, high peaks, endless greenery and sky. Nearby, perched on the river, was a windowless ice house for the storage of massive blocks carved out of ponds in wintertime and eventually shipped all over the state by refrigerated railroad cars. Skyrocketing demand for ice was a natural byproduct of the Prohibition-era drinking surge (as was the proliferation of speakeasies, brandy-prescribing drug stores and dead bootleggers).

Frank kept the boys busy. He took them fishing for brown trout and hunting for fox. Slats wore an enormously wide-brimmed mountain man's hat and strapped on an Adirondack pack basket—hand-woven forerunner to the modern backpack, filled with food, water, extra clothes and ammunition—while Frank led their march up into steep, rough terrain. Slats learned to shoot, rifles, shotguns and pistols. He rode horses each day. He took long hikes on his own, or with Skitsy and Joe tagging along. Slats joined the lumber workers who were still working in the area, cutting up firewood. He ate breakfast with them and wore the customary flannel, suspenders and high boots. He even grew a beard. Skitsy joked that he looked like "some Russian grand duke." Slats, however, did more than just look the part. Though instructed to avoid strenuous exercise—the idea was to slow down and gain weight—Slats was swinging a woodsman's axe at least a few hours each morning, hardening his hands and bolstering his forearms. He learned to work in tandem on one end of a giant cross-cut saw. If it rained, the pals sat on the porch and played cards. Slats brought a ukulele, and they all took turns trying to play it.

Curious villagers came by to visit, having heard about the prizefighter holed up at the Husson camp. They all took to Slats, adopted him as one of their own. Slats and Skitsy joined the Indian Lake baseball team. But, as it was bound to do, the memorable summer trip slipped away. Not one of them could imagine leaving their wilderness heaven. But Red summoned them.

The manager changed plans and booked a fight for Slats in Coney Island in early August. He required his fighter back at Newsboys' for boxing work-outs. Arriving back in Buffalo, Slats told writers camped out at the station that he had gotten himself right and that he was ready to return to the ring. His buzz-cut was starting to come back in one-inch bristles. He'd only just shaved off his growth of beard, right before leaving the camp. Slats lived like a hermit, Joe Hickey assured one local writer. "We woke with the birds singing," Joe insisted. "At night we sat and watched the deer come down to the river and drink." But Joe left out some other details.

Part of Slattery's rejuvenation process led to the youth feeling so fresh and full of energy that it became impossible for him to sit on the porch and just listen to the owls hoot—he needed to join in, for there was nightlife *somewhere*, and if anyone was going to find it, it was Slats and his buddies. Earl Husson's son, Gerald, though not yet born in 1925, would later hear all about that memorable summer of Slats. "My father told me Slats and his friends went to the bars every night," recalled Gerald, a longtime resident of Indian Lake, speaking in 2013. Several miles up that dirt road—the trio must have walked or arranged for a ride—in the heart of the village there was a popular, rocking spot called Farrell's. Here, lumberjacks and tourists alike mingled in an inconspicuous back bar behind a dancehall. Plenty of liquor flowed through the region, which became a convenient stopover for bootlegger convoys heading downstate from Canada. Very often, accord-ing to Indian Lake historian Bill Zullo, gangs would stash liquid cargo in a local barn for secret pick up later on. Explains Gerald Husson: "My father liked to drink. He and Slattery got along great."

Sensing Slattery wasn't right, and fearful that a once promising ring career was in jeopardy, Red became desperate. In a narrative spun by the *Buffalo Times*' Willis Wilber, Red at one point that summer got down on his hands and knees and literally begged Slats to clean up his act. Why, just look at what proper living and training can accomplish, Red told his young prospect. He pointed to the shining example that was fellow Newsboys' stable member Jimmy Goodrich. While Slats was off in the woods, Buffalo had welcomed Goodrich home as a most unexpected boxing champion. Goodrich had been included in an elimination tournament organized by the New York State Boxing Commission, which was seeking to anoint a successor to retiring lightweight champion Benny Leonard. No one thought Goodrich would win. But he reached the finals, held at the Queensboro Bowl in Long Island City. Knocking out Chilean Stan Loayza, Goodrich took home the crown. Red had cultivated a champion named Jimmy after all. This turn of events was a slap in Slattery's face. But he did look up to Goodrich, who visited the camp that August.

Adding salt to the wound, Tex Rickard announced he was putting on a major fight—his long-envisioned, late-summer Light Heavyweight Championship extravaganza. It was an event that originally was supposed to include Slats. The fight would be held at Yankee Stadium. Champion Paul Berlenbach would meet Jack Delaney, whom Slats had twice defeated. It was always Rickard's intention to showcase Slattery in a long-distance title bout as soon as he reached age 21. That would happen on August 25th. In a bittersweet twist, Slattery was offered a spot on the undercard of the title fight. Rickard at first sought to match Slattery against fellow Irishman Mike McTigue, off whose head Berlenbach had lifted the light heavy crown. McTigue wasn't thrilled. Insulted, and still insisting on a rematch with Berlenbach, McTigue demanded $10,000 to fight Slattery. Rickard instead recruited Philadelphia's Tommy Loughran to meet Slats in one of the preliminaries. With the New Garden under construction and set to open in late autumn, Rickard needed to cash in dividends from his year-long campaign to generate interest in the light heavyweight class.

Fans didn't know it, but Rickard had heavyweight champion Jack Dempsey completely on ice. As usual, there was speculative talk of an impending title fight between Dempsey and Harry Wills. But that meeting was never, ever, going to come off. Plus, and Rickard knew this, Dempsey was not entering any prize ring until his profit-sharing contract with Doc Kearns expired—which would not happen until the summer of 1926. Rickard, as the scribes put it, needed to "keep the kettle boiling."

Capturing the country's attention during that whole scorching summer was a battle of words happening down south, where two lawyers argued scripture versus evolution in connection with a schoolteacher's decision to teach Darwin. Mixed with newsreel highlights of the "Scopes Monkey Trial" were obligatory moving pictures of the heavyweight champion—in street clothes. At some New York City movie houses, fans hissed when they saw the image of the long dormant Dempsey, according to Roger Kahn's *A Flame of Pure Fire*. In the span of seven years Dempsey had gone from nobody to world-famous Manassa Mauler to slacker. Though it's hard to imagine today, Jack Dempsey was widely disliked in '25.

In bruiser Paul Berlenbach, Rickard had a well-known attraction. But outside Astoria, Berlenbach was not a widely popular champion. The German-American was viewed as slow and clumsy. Post-war anti-German sentiment did not help. A seemingly innocuous but often-used slur at the time was "Dutchman." Remember that night back in May when Berlenbach beat McTigue to claim the light heavyweight title? The newly crowned champ got heckled and all anyone could talk about was Slattery. Weeks later, Berlenbach, in his first title defense, was tossed out of the ring for stalling. He claimed he'd hurt his hand. Challenger Tony Marullo of New Orleans was disqualified as well. A storm of boos showered both light heavyweights when the fight was halted. Such treatment stung Berlenbach more than anyone could have known.

As for Slats, fans still wanted to see him, but debate simmered over a timeless hazard of boxing—what kind of fighter would the previously never-knocked-out Slattery become after being socked right on the button and stripped of his self-confidence? What made Slats such a curiosity was this question coupled with the fact that weeks earlier he had been hailed as the future of boxing. Now what?

For a while there that summer Slats' future did not look bright. His match in Coney Island versus Harlem's Maxie Rosenbloom had to be called off. Slats informed promoter Johnny Leon that he was sick. It's entirely possible that Red instigated the postponement to allow Slats more time to return to form. Either way, it didn't fly with Leon. His boxing amphitheater, built right off the famed seaside boardwalk, had struggled to turn a profit since it opened around Memorial Day. The fans wanted to see Slats. The promoter complained to the Boxing Commission, which was in the midst of cracking down on fighters who suspiciously begged off scheduled bouts with unexpected ailments.

Slattery pulling out only fuelled stories of his demise. Some tales were downright lurid. Rumors spread in early August that Slattery was finished with boxing forever, in part based on a report that Slats had turned down a $10,000 offer to fight Berlenbach for the championship. The wolf pack of sportswriters stuck pins into the bubble of their creation. *Slats had a glass jaw. He was a front runner—fine until faced with adversity. He was too frail. His style was unorthodox. He couldn't stand the gaffe.*

Red's plan that summer was to beef Slattery up, but it wasn't working the way he had hoped. Too much flesh accumulated around the fighter's middle, while his legs remained scrawny. If Slattery was to get into shape, he had to get out of Buffalo. Once again, he would return to the mountains.

The Coney Island fight with Rosenbloom, a tough but unusual twenty-year-old, was rescheduled for August 22. Red personally accompanied Slattery and his pal trainers to Indian Lake. They also took along with them two sparring partners: Benny Ross, a member of Red's stable; and Vic McLoughlin, a rising light heavy from New York City. With Frank Husson's blessing and assistance from lumber workers, Red oversaw the construction of an enclosed, 20' x 20' practice ring set on the hill off the back of the guest lodge. They also built an adjacent platform where a punching bag was installed. Everybody pitched in on the whole ambitious project. Earl Husson began busing in visitors from a nearby lakeside resort to watch sunset sparring sessions thirty yards from the rushing river. It was fine boxing in the middle of nowhere. Plus, the Husson's made a few extra bucks.

Slattery wasn't exactly well-prepared for his fight against Rosenbloom. Competing in a ring just a stone's throw from the Atlantic Ocean, Slats was victorious—but he looked bad. He still sported an unsightly ring of flab around his middle. Throughout the fight—his last one in New York that would be limited to six rounds—he appeared fatigued, harried. And Rosenbloom had done nothing to ease Slattery back into the ring, not with his nonstop, smothering style. Slats won the decision, but it took everything he had. Some 10,000 fans had turned up for the Saturday night show, August 22, 1925. They were treated to an impressive main event featuring recently dethroned light heavyweight champion Mike McTigue versus top-ranked contender Tony Marullo. McTigue won in a bout some ringside scribes insisted was his best showing ever.

It was the height of one of the busiest summer seasons anyone could recall. On the following Monday, bouts were scheduled at the outdoor stadium in Queens. The prior Friday, open-air boxing shows were held in Rockaway and in Long Branch, New Jersey. Fans could attend boxing matches almost every night of the week. Some writers wondered whether so much boxing was overkill—not the worst problem for a city that employed at least fifty boxing writers. Every single one of them was eager to find out what effect the humiliation at the hands of Dave Shade had had on Slattery. Some, including veteran Ed Hughes, warned readers not to write Slattery off.

Damon Runyon had come to Coney specifically to see Slats, and not McTigue-Marullo. Runyon left disappointed. Better thrills were found for a nickel on the Boardwalk. Slattery's humbling at the hands of Shade, the celebrity newsman deduced, had in fact caused irreparable damage to Slattery's psyche. After he left the ring, Slats either spent that night and the next day taking in the metropolis, or, alternatively, as some conflicting accounts hold, he drove straight back to Indian Lake to play in a baseball game with the village team. What is known for sure is that he was with his friends, and that he had his automobile.

Watching Slattery and other rivals perform that night in Coney was Paul Berlenbach. The 24-year-old was keenly aware of the criticism floating in the briny air. Berlenbach should have been beloved in New York City, a local boy crowned champion, and a knockout artist—exactly what the fans wanted most. But Berlenbach's reputation was taking a beating. That day, newspapers all over the city carried stories about the champ's appointment, one day earlier, with a Boxing Commission physician who examined his hurt hand and declared nothing wrong with it. Berlenbach's upcoming title defense against Delaney would go on, but not in one week as scheduled. Turning sympathetic in spite of the doctor's report, the Commission decided to give "Punch 'Em Paul" a few extra weeks to train. They ruled that Tex Rickard could stage the fight in mid-September. Headlines blared "Berlenbach's Hand is Just Fine," which made him seem like a malingerer. Here he was, already unpopular with the Irish fans, many of whom viewed him as crude and clumsy. Now Berlenbach was losing credibility with the sportswriters.

Following McTigue-Marullo, Berlenbach, accompanied by his manager, Dan Hickey, got into an automobile and motored to Southampton on the eastern end of Long Island, where they would set up training quarters at Captain Billy Jones' seaside casino. Also making the trip was Berlenbach's prized Great Dane, "Shorty." The Pride of Astoria vowed to put in the hardest work of his life, heeding Hickey's every instruction to the letter. That kind of dedication was why Berlenbach had come as far as he had in such a short period of time.

Only three years earlier, Berlenbach had been driving a taxi. Right before that, though, he'd been a nationally ranked amateur wrestler who had competed in the 1920 Olympics in Antwerp. Upon returning to New York, Berlenbach assumed he'd turn professional. In sports-obsessed America, professional wrestling was thriving. Heavyweights like Strangler Lewis and Doctor Roller drew large, enthusiastic crowds. Though muscular, Berlenbach was nevertheless still too small for main events. Heavyweights completely monopolized the sport. Even after winning an A.A.U. national title and reaching the pinnacle of international success, Berlenbach couldn't find representation. Not one of the managers who hung around George Bothner's 42nd Street gym, headquarters for the pro wrestlers who performed at the Garden, wanted to take a flyer on the German-American kid. Finally, one manager did make Berlenbach an offer to go wrestle in Albany for a whopping $25. To collect, all he had to do was "take a flop."

Ditching his wrestling aspirations, Berlenbach made a living the best way he could. Thus, the taxi. He worked a stand on Central Park South across from the Plaza Hotel, down the block from the New York Athletic Club. The N.Y.A.C. had sponsored Berlenbach during his amateur wrestling rise and he still held on to his membership. He'd work out during slow afternoons, fooling around in the boxing room, a lefty with some raw ability and a hunger to learn. In those days, being a hack was tough work. One had to be handy with their fists. Scuffles with other drivers or a surly customer were routine. Berlenbach could fight. He had to, growing up in the German tenements on the Upper East Side. At some point hanging around the N.Y.A.C., Berlenbach caught the attention of Dan Hickey, then the club's boxing instructor.

A former prizefighter who decades earlier had trained and toured with Bob Fitzsimmons during his reign as heavyweight champion, Hickey had sworn off the fight game and was comfortable in his job schooling middle-aged businessmen and their sons in the manly arts. But everyone in and around the sport of boxing seemed to have the same dream: finding the next great champion. Hickey sensed, watching the burly wrestler lurch around, that he had just that specimen. Legend has it that the two sparred and when Berlenbach caught him with a wicked shot, that's when Hickey made up his mind to take him under his wing. Regardless of whether that encounter ever happened, it is true that at some point Hickey became convinced he could mold Berlenbach into a champion.

"I'll turn you into a boxer," Hickey told him. "But you have to do everything I tell you, no questions asked."

Berlenbach agreed. He boxed as an amateur, knocking out almost everyone he faced. In his first ten professional fights, Berlenbach won them all by knockouts. Going back to his amateur days, he had recorded a string of two dozen straight K.O.s, an unprecedented streak of "slumber dealing," to use a vintage ring phrase.

In May of 1925, at Rickard's Milk Fund show, Berlenbach fulfilled the destiny Hickey foresaw—winning the title from McTigue, who, ironically, was once the boxing instructor at the N.Y.A.C. prior to Hickey taking the position. But fans, as it has been noted, were soured by the sheer dullness of the fight. McTigue was the type content to stay out of harm's way until opportunity knocked. Berlenbach was not pretty to watch. His bulk and crudeness—a converted southpaw, he had no right punch to speak of, just a left hook, albeit a deadly one—made him appear plodding, cumbersome. "Just wait until that ham n' egger meets Slattery," the Irish fans would say after Berlenbach became champion. "Slattery will box circles around that big ox!"

Winning the crown wasn't supposed to bring about such hurtful criticism. No one realized how sensitive Berlenbach was. He looked every bit the brawler. Though cherubic-faced as a youngster, Berlenbach now looked like a Cro-Magnon, as his knack for taking multiple punches in order to throw one had left him with a build-up of scar tissue over his eyes and a flattened nose. Ultimately, for Berlenbach, the fight game was a way to make excellent money. But he always wanted to be liked. And he definitely had something to prove in his upcoming title fight with Jack Delaney, the only person ever to beat him.

As Berlenbach and his manager motored through Queens, out toward Southampton, a significant development was unfolding across the Long Island Sound in Bridgeport, Connecticut. Delaney had come down with a throat ailment. It was so bad, in fact, that he had to be scratched from a scheduled bout in Detroit. Within a few days, there would be rampant speculation that Rickard's big, end-of-summer light heavyweight championship event not only had hit another roadblock—it might have to be called off.

Between radio broadcasts and long-distance telephone service, the 1920s stretched real-time connectivity to previously unimaginable levels. Ubiquitous utility poles and overhead lines did not just forever alter the landscape of the country; the ever-expanding communication loop changed the rhythm and rituals of everyday life. The act of information gathering and dissemination, in and of itself, had undergone a dramatic transformation. In newspaper offices, large, loud contraptions—teletypewriters—automatically spat out printed dispatches transmitted by telegraphic code from an army of writers and editors at the wire services, the two largest being the Associated Press, which had existed since the days of the Pony Express, and its more recently launched rival, United Press.

The AP and UP leased use of the wires from Western Union, which shared an infrastructure with telephone companies (at one time there had been one behemoth, American Telegraph & Telephone, but by 1925 that had been busted apart) along with some other telecommunication providers likewise feeding off this nationally scaled operating system. Such businesses included stock price quotation services, which piped rivers of data into brokerage houses via tickertape machines. Speculators of another variety, meanwhile, were served up timely information in gambling establishments that were connected to horse racing tracks around the country. This linkage was made possible by Mont Tennes' General News Bureau, better known as the "race wire."

Tennes was a stone-cold Chicago gangster, so on some level his involvement in this enterprise would have almost been akin to, say, John Gotti owning ESPN in the late 1980s. Every city in America had off-track betting parlors, Buffalo included. Italian mobster Joe "The Wolf" Di Carlo ran one on the north end of the city. Paddy Lavin ran one on the south side. After Lavin's mysterious death at the start of the Prohibition Era, his nephew, Roggie, also a boxer, would carry on the tradition at his place, which served beef and ale downstairs and simulated live horse race calls—picture the movie *The Sting*—upstairs.

On Sunday, August 23, 1925, all of Buffalo was buzzing with a startling rumor, sparked by an unconfirmed report said to have flashed over the race wire: Jimmy Slattery was dead.

Actually, the initial report was that Slattery had been hurt in an automobile accident in Brooklyn. That rumor had spread fast. By nightfall, the story had taken a turn for the absolute worst—Slats had gone off the road near Albany and had been killed.

The telephone at the Slattery residence rang continuously throughout the evening. *Was it true? Had anyone heard from Slats?*

The notion of speed-obsessed Slats in a car crash was all too plausible. People around town had been predicting this moment for years. All Red could say was that Slats and his friends had departed by automobile after the fight in Coney Island. Slattery's family members were frantic, although Billy Kelly at the *Courier* had spent hours working the phones, checking with AP and UP staffers in Albany, and could find no confirmation whatsoever of any auto mishap in the vicinity. If Kelly wasn't making calls he was receiving them from worried city residents.

By Monday afternoon, anxiety was at its peak. The Slattery home had filled with nervous friends and neighbors, all of whom were soon to gather anyway for Slats' birthday party, set for the following night (and the reason he was coming back to Buffalo in the first place). What began spontaneously as a somber vigil suddenly erupted into a jubilant celebration around 6:00 P.M., when Slattery's big touring car came barreling down Abbott Road. He was perfectly fine—there'd been no accident. Sighs of relief gave way to euphoric weeping as Mary and Sloak and Slats' brothers and sisters rushed to give him the warmest embrace of his life. Everybody hugged and laughed as the party got underway. On the one hand, Slats found the whole thing humorous, but when he realized just how traumatized his mother had been, he became angry. "I'd like to find the fellow who spread that false story," he would say later. The source was never discovered.

That next day, calls and messages came pouring into the Slattery home, all wishing Jimmy a happy 21rst birthday. Charlie Murray, vacationing in Saratoga Springs, sent over a telegram. Tex Rickard sent congratulatory words from New York. Tex had been waiting a long time for this day.

The birthday party was held, as planned, on Tuesday night, August 25, 1925. Mary Slattery baked a fancy cake decked out with 21 candles. Sharply dressed neighborhood guys filed in with their wives or sweethearts in tow. Neighbors came by for cake, some slipping souvenir birthday candles into their pockets. The atmosphere was as if Slats had won a championship, even though in truth, his career had pretty much hit the skids. Festivities went late into the night. And at least one guest partook in a little too much merrymaking.

The boxer's older brother, John, in the early hours of Wednesday morning, took off in another guest's automobile (without permission) and raced downtown to the cabaret district, only to crash into a police car. John Slattery's head went straight through the windshield and he suffered a serious gash. He was taken first to the hospital to get stitched up and then to the police station on Franklin Street, across from Newsboys' Gym. He was charged with driving while intoxicated, reckless driving and grand larceny. By the time he appeared in front of a city court judge that Wednesday afternoon all but one of the charges had been dropped. John Slattery ultimately pleaded guilty to operating a motor vehicle without a license and was fined $10. Slattery's brother's stunt made the local papers—and got picked up by the wires.

Slattery was going back to Indian Lake. His automobile was staying in Buffalo. He and his party took an overnight N.Y. Central train bound for Saratoga. There, he, Red, Skitsy and Joe would switch to the D&H line. Slattery's train pulled into the famous spa town before sunrise on the morning of Friday, August 28. All was quiet except for the hiss of exiting locomotive steam and chirping birds. About the only souls around were a few yawning railroad employees, a milkman starting his deliveries, and Gene Tunney.

Tunney had jogged to the station from his training quarters five miles away at Tom Luther's White Sulphur Spring Hotel on the east end of Saratoga Lake. Slats stepped off the train and broke into a smile when he saw the New York fighter standing on the platform.

"Are you going north?" Slats asked, shaking Tunney's hand.

Tunney wasn't necessarily the best-loved American boxer, but within the game he was quite well respected. He'd graduated to heavyweight and that summer was finally getting some deserved attention as someone who might possibly challenge Dempsey someday. Tunney's campaign as a heavyweight contender under the guidance of manager Billy Gibson had received a boost with his knockout, a few weeks prior, of Tom Gibbons, whose name was constantly (along with Harry Wills) being bandied about as a worthy foe for Dempsey. Slattery's name began to slip from such conversations. Slats and Tunney had crossed paths at the Garden and at the Boxing Commission's offices in the Flatiron Building. Slats didn't know it, but Tunney was among his most ardent admirers.

"I heard you were coming into town," Tunney said. "So I decided to get in some early road work and see if I couldn't get you to come to my camp and train with me."

Slats was shocked Tunney would have any interest in him.

"Come on, get your luggage," Tunney pressed.

It must be noted here that this exchange shows up in a "C.J. Murray's Comment on Boxing" column, and that Murray almost assuredly had been the one to inform Tunney of Slattery's pre-dawn arrival. The night before, Murray had dropped by Luther's place to speak to Tunney about a possible Buffalo engagement. Standing on the platform, the sports editor/fight promoter may have been just as surprised as Slattery to see Tunney show up—or, who knows, perhaps it was Murray who arranged the whole encounter.

"Sorry Gene," Slats said. "All my fighting togs are at Indian Lake and I've got sparring partners waiting for me."

Maybe, Slats suggested, he could come back in one week.

"I wish you would," Tunney replied. "You'll like it out where I am. We'll box together every day."

A conductor cried "all aboard!" and the two gladiators shook hands goodbye. Turning to Murray, Tunney remarked, "Do you know what a week of boxing with Slattery would do for me?"

★★★★★

Slats would not have merely changed trains in Saratoga if it were left up to Charlie Murray. He would have preferred to see the Buffalo boxer change training camps, as well. Even a few days with the brainy, straight-edged ex-Marine would have benefited Slattery, Murray reckoned. "If Slattery had half of Tunney's determination and willingness to work he would outclass the world," Murray told a fellow boxing writer.

Not far away, meanwhile, on that same Friday, Mike McTigue was working out at Father Dan Hogan's boxing camp in Ballston Lake. The former light heavyweight champ received some interesting news: Jack Delaney was having surgery in Bridgeport. Doctors had located a pus-filled abscess on his throat and feared septic poisoning. Delaney would not be able to fight Berlenbach. Now, instead, McTigue was going to get his shot to win back the title. Rickard simply refused to be thwarted in his quest to stage a big-money championship battle at Yankee Stadium. The Boxing Commission, then led by Chairman James Farley, sanctioned

McTigue as the new challenger. But neither Farley nor Rickard really wanted this match up. Public interest dimmed.

Boxing promoters had been trying for years to keep fans interested in weight classes other than heavyweight. Efforts to make light heavyweight seem compelling had been ongoing ever since the division was created more than two decades earlier.

The first-ever fight for the designation of World's Light Heavyweight Champion occurred in 1903 in Fort Erie, Ontario, near Crystal Beach. The title was cooked up on a ferry-boat ride across the river from Buffalo. Lou Housman, a Chicago newspaperman and the manager of aging middleweight Jack Root, started brainstorming with promoters about how to stir interest in Root's upcoming match with Irishman George Gardner. Famed promoter Jack Curley suggested inventing a brand new title for middleweights such as Root and Gardner—both of whom were around 170 pounds, too large for middleweight, but too small to meet 200-pound heavyweights such as Jack Johnson. It was Curley's idea to declare the battle as being for the "Light Heavyweight" title; Housman agreed to pay for a fanciful winner's belt, keeping with an old boxing tradition. Gardner, born on St. Patrick's Day in the small County Clare town of Lisdoonvarna, knocked Root out to become the inaugural champion in the newly concocted weight class. As it turned out, in something of a "Forrest Gump" moment, there had been a teenage newspaper reporter sitting on the deck of the ferry listening to Curley and Housman make history. That cub reporter was Charlie Murray.

Gardner later lost the crown to lanky Cornishman Bob Fitzsimmons, who, well past the age when he should have been retired from boxing, became the first man to hold three titles, having previously earned middleweight and heavyweight laurels.

Fitzsimmons lost the light heavy crown to Philadelphia Jack O'Brien, who eventually lost it to the oft-overlooked French-Canadian Tommy Burns, who paid it no mind while he pursued the heavyweight division during the period when boxing was big in Australia. The title was vacant, and largely irrelevant, for several years, until Jack Dillon claimed it during the period when newspapers handed out decisions. Eventually, Battling Levinsky won a newspaper decision after a few close contests with Dillon. But it wasn't until Levinsky lost the title to the gallant French war hero Georges Carpentier that the division, like boxing itself, fully flourished.

In defeat at the hands of Dempsey, Carpentier grew in popularity, having helped put boxing on the map, with his role in the "Million-Dollar Gate." The light heavyweight division was then seen as a breeding ground for future heavyweights and an intriguing division in its own right. A ringside seat at one of the Frenchman's fights was said to have fetched more than $100, which at the time was believed to be the highest price ever paid to see a boxing match.

Carpentier eventually lost the title to Louis Phal, also of France, by way of Senegal. The new light heavyweight champion was better known by his ring name, Battling Siki.

Siki would lose the title to Mike McTigue in an epic contest held on St. Patrick's Day in Dublin amidst Ireland's civil war following its liberation from British rule. McTigue had lived in New York since he was a youngster. But prior to that, he'd grown up in the low, desolate pastures of Kilnamona, a speck of a village on Ireland's southwest coast. A sprinter as a lad, McTigue, like many his age in County Clare, left his home for America. He found a job in a meatpacking plant, entered the ring where he toiled in relative anonymity during pugilism's formative years. Slowing down, McTigue landed a position as boxing instructor at the N.Y.A.C. Ordinary looking, well-mannered, McTigue ran a bar and continued to fight on the side, scoring a few impressive victories now and then. Through the club, McTigue met Wall Street millionaires, influential politicians, writers and sportsmen. He was more than content with his lot. Becoming a world champion never would have crossed his mind, until the day he was crossing the Atlantic Ocean on a visit back home (which not many Irishmen got to do in those days) and word reached the ship that Battling Siki had lifted the light heavyweight crown from Carpentier in Paris. A wealthy Dublin racehorse trainer, Lad Ray, heard McTigue was en route and despite having never promoted a boxing match before, made up his mind that an Irishman—McTigue—should have the opportunity to wrest the title—from a black man—on the Feast Day of Ireland's patron saint during one of the most fragile times in the nation's history. That spring of '23, Free State supporters were clashing with supporters of the Republic, led by the uncompromising Eamon de Valera, who tried to have the fight shut down. About 3,000 fans turned up at an O'Connell Street theater next door to the Post Office, which had been an iconic battle site during the Easter Rising of 1916. Literally, right before the bell to begin the fight, a bomb went off nearby, shattering theater windows and ratcheting up the tension. At the opening bell, Siki himself exploded.

According to Robert Cantwell's 1979 *Sports Illustrated* article, pegged to the discovery of a lost film of the fight some fifty-odd years later, Siki chased McTigue around the ring, pummeling him all the way. McTigue put honor aside, ran from Siki, took his medicine, saved some energy, won some late rounds and somehow (it was Dublin on St. Patrick's Day) won the decision. He was declared the new World's Light Heavyweight Champion. That night, celebratory bonfires blazed all across the lonesome County Clare countryside. The rural area had produced the first light heavyweight champion, George Gardner. Now it had produced another.

McTigue went back to New York an overnight sensation. He bought himself new clothes and hit all the Broadway hot spots, soaking up every last drop of his stardom. He would become even more well-known after the Dixieland fiasco that was his first bout versus Young Stribling. McTigue's gamesmanship outside the ring mirrored the way he fought—patiently biding his time until he saw an opening. He certainly wasn't Rickard's first choice to meet Berlenbach. The pair's championship fight in May was widely panned as a snore fest. Still, when Delaney was a scratch, the Boxing Commission opened the door to McTigue to take his spot. At least, it looked that way as the summer wound down.

On September 2, 1925, more major boxing news broke in Saratoga. A pimple on McTigue's arm got infected. The limb became swollen. Just Rickard's luck: another curious case of blood poisoning. McTigue was out.

★ ★ ★ ★ ★

Seventy miles north of Saratoga, Slats was sparring away in the idyllic outdoor ring. During a pause in the action, he could hear his manager shouting something to him from the back porch of the guest lodge. Slats removed his protective headgear so he could make it out.

"Do you want to fight Berlenbach on the eleventh?" Red hollered again. "McTigue has an infected arm and won't be able to fight."

"What?" Slattery said. "Are you kidding?

Red repeated the news once more. Tex Rickard had sent word to the village by long-distance telephone. He was offering Slattery a shot at the title.

★ ★ ★ ★ ★

On Friday, September 4, Rickard announced he had signed Jimmy Slattery to substitute for McTigue, who'd been a substitute for Delaney, in a 15-round title match with Paul Berlenbach, the world's light heavyweight champion. Rickard joked with reporters how, should something happen to Slattery, no one need worry—the promoter would get into the ring at Yankee Stadium and take on Berlenbach himself.

That same Friday, Slats was back in Buffalo getting ready to fight Frank Carpenter, a light heavy from Rockaway. The bout, scheduled for 10 rounds (now that Slats was 21) would take place Friday night at Bison Stadium. Some people swear Slattery spent time at a bar beforehand. With so much at stake this seems outlandish, but then no one could really ever understand a lot of the choices Slattery made. Former *Buffalo News* writer Anthony Cardinale has penned feature articles and a play about Slattery. Cardinale heard the tale from the late Jimmy Griffin, former mayor of Buffalo and a product of the First Ward: "Slats hopped off his bar stool, went and knocked out Carpenter, and made it back to the bar within an hour." Murray, however, made a point to note in his coverage of the Carpenter bout that Slattery left the ring and immediately boarded a 10:30 P.M. train headed north. Slats had indeed scored a swift, fourth-round technical knockout.

Most managers, Red included, recommend up to two months of intensive training prior to a championship fight. Slattery had roughly one week.

★★★★★

Up at the Husson camp, on the morning of Sunday, September 6th, Earl's wife Dora fixed Slattery a hearty woodsman's breakfast—four eggs, stewed prunes, toast and orange juice. Slats had been up since 6:00 A.M., hiking a 3.5-mile mountain trail and then jogging back. Slats and Red then borrowed Frank's truck and drove into town to attend mass at a little country church. After breakfast, Slats sat around the lodge, reading a newspaper and strumming his ukulele. Later, around 2:30 P.M., Slats shed his flannel shirt, put on his boxing togs and limbered up for an ambitious session. Red instructed the training team to press Slats as hard as they possibly could. A third sparring partner, Buddy Ahearn, a Buffalo preliminary boy, had by this time joined the camp. Meanwhile, an inspector from the Boxing Commission and a slew of big city writers were said to be en route. *Courier* reporter Seb Naples was there shadowing Slats (and getting on his nerves). An estimated 100 spectators turned up for that Sunday afternoon sparring session. The visitors, disproportionately female, spread out atop the grassy slope, looking down on the raised-up boxing ring which, with its high, slanted roof, resembled a quaint, center-of-town gazebo.

Red looked awesome that summer. He sported what essentially was a Mohawk haircut, shorn on the sides, high and thick on top. His daily outfit was a white button-down with the sleeves rolled up and his necktie tucked into his shirt at chest-level like a bartender might. Earlier, after church, he had notified Slats he would be trying something for the first time. He was going 15 rounds; three with McLoughlin, four with Ahearn and the last seven with Ross, who did his best Berlenbach impression, crowding in close and spraying left hooks, which Slats instinctively ducked. As the rounds with Ross flew by, Slats, to everyone's surprise, was *gaining stamina* as he galloped along, oblivious to what round it was, having lost count. At the end of the last round with Ross, Red called out, "Okay, that's all for today."

Slats seemed surprised.

"I thought I was going 15 today," he protested.

Replied Red: "You just did."

★★★★★

Slats appeared to take his training seriously, although the camp was often a scene of lively play. As soon as Ahearn arrived, Slats subjected him to an initiation ritual, a hair-raising ride down a steep hill in a rickety wagon. When Slats wanted to—and this is not uncommon for alcoholics—he could stick to prolonged dry spells. With Red in camp, it's possible Slats really was content to watch the deer drink at night. He enjoyed his early morning hikes and swinging the axe, building up absurdly powerful fore-arms. "He's as busy as any of the lumberjacks," Red wrote in a letter home.

Even in the rain, Earl's charter bus filled up. Many locals trekked through the forest to meet the boxer. One delegation of citizens came bearing a gift: a pair of brand new boxing gloves. Indian Lake couldn't have been more proud.

On Monday, the New York writers arrived. They included Sam Hall of *Universal Service* and Murray Lewin of the *New York Daily Mirror*—both of whom had predicted Berlenbach to win, in part, based on Slattery's having never gone 15 rounds before. They couldn't get over how hard it had been to find the place and would later insinuate that their expedition involved days traversing uncharted wilderness by pack mule, when in actuality the dirt road to the Husson camp ran directly off the main mountain road. The Slattery they found, went exaggerated tales, could be seen outrunning deer and uprooting trees with his bare hands, a wild warrior living in the woods, hardened and bronzed.

The atmosphere around camp was jovial. Some guys played cards on the porch, tossed a baseball or threw a line in the river. Some writers sat at their typewriters, just gabbed or picked up Slattery's ukulele. Slats, in turn, borrowed Seb Naples' typewriter and pecked out a letter to his mom. The friendly group bonded, for the most part. They really couldn't have asked for a more breathtaking setting. Frank Husson owned the lodge and his son Earl ran the place; Red Carr and the lumber men had transformed it. But Hunter's Rest was Slattery's. His moods and whims prevailed. He set the tone.

Training camps had long been synonymous with screwball hijinks and practical jokes. The late great Stanley Ketchel had his famous midnight snipe hunts, which involved tricking an unsuspecting stooge (the most irritating person in camp or maybe just the freshest face) into standing alone in the dark woods holding an empty bag while Ketchel and friends ditched out. At Slattery's camp, the pranks were just as delicious.

At some point, the writers got bored hanging around. They heard about Farrell's bar in the village, and so as night fell they set off on foot to wet their whistles while Slats and his friends stayed back. Later, stumbling back to camp by lantern and the light of the moon, the pack of city slickers were startled by a masked figure who stepped out of the trees, shouting: "Stick 'em up!"

Aiming his pistol in the air, the shadowy highwayman started firing, which spooked the newsmen so terrifically that they all went scurrying into the woods, their screams echoing for miles, the clamor only exceeded in volume by the uproarious laughter of Slattery as he pulled the bandanna down off his face.

Another bout of hilarity came one evening when Earl Husson, one too many drinks in him, asked Slats if he could put on the gloves and box a round or two. Sure, said the Buffalo boy, and the two climbed into the ring. The next thing Earl knew, he was flat on the dewy grass, seeing double. Slats had knocked him clear out of the ring.

Early on the morning of Wednesday, September 9th, the last day before they broke camp, Red took the truck and drove to the train station to collect Charlie Murray, who was coming for a brief visit on his way to New York ahead of the Berlenbach fight on Friday night. Even with all the many guests pouring in, Slats kept asking, when was Murray coming? In the middle of that night, yet another visitor had arrived. John Hodges, a Boxing Commission inspector, journeyed from Albany, apparently after hiring a driver, who got completely lost in the woods for hours, only to eventually find the camp dark, shuttered and everyone asleep. Slats greeted poor, bleary-eyed Hodges at 6:00 A.M. as the fighter set off on his morning hike. The Commission had ordered the inspector to ascertain first-hand that Slats was healthy. After a quick examination to which Slats gladly subjected himself, the inspector went on his way back to Albany, exhausted, but with his assignment accomplished.

When Murray reached camp, everyone let out a cheer and led him over to the steep hill where the old rickety wagon awaited; the Buffalo promoter, as a new arrival in camp, had no choice but to take the customary plunge. That day marked the last sparring session before the actual bout. A day earlier, an eye-popping session saw Slats knife through his practice partners one after the other over 15 fast rounds; all of the writers were astonished at Slattery's stellar form. Red changed the script, calling for eight low-intensity rounds. He then halted all further boxing activities.

As the sun set, Charlie Murray declared he had to be in New York by morning, and that he had arranged for a taxi to take him from Indian Lake to Albany. The *Mirror*'s Murray Lewin was going with him. Red loaded the departing guests into Frank's truck and they all set off down the dirt road. As the bumpy ride got underway, Red started to explain what had been happening in these parts of late. "The Indians are getting real mean," Red said. "They've been robbing travelers in this vicinity."

It was getting darker. About a half mile up the road, someone lurked in the trees. A menacing masked figure steadied a rifle and ordered the truck to stop. "Uh oh," Red said, hitting the brakes.

"Hands up!" shouted the rifle-toting bandit. Blood racing, Murray threw up one hand and drew the other to his mouth, cramming his finger between his teeth in a desperate attempt to gnaw free the gemstone from his ring. Buck shot went off in the trees behind the roadside bandit— which turned out to be old Frank Husson getting in on the fun. Murray was convinced it was a real stickup until he heard Slattery's familiar cackle coming from his hiding place.

"I'll fix you!" Murray yelled. Out came Slats, laughing his head off. For many years, Red and Slats would recreate the sight of Murray putting his prized diamond ring into his mouth in a panic—and it never got old.

Continuing to New York by train together, Murray and Lewin were still absorbing the phony truck-jacking and chuckling about it. Lewin was still reeling about what he witnessed in the sparring ring.

"I saw Slats versus Rosenbloom in Coney Island," Lewin told his traveling companion. "That's why I picked Berlenbach. I didn't believe it was possible Slattery was anywhere near proper condition."

"And now what do you think?" Murray inquired.

Replied Lewin: "I'm switching my opinion."

The next day, the Slattery party broke camp. Slats did some light road work and sat with Sam Hall, who wanted to ask an uncomfortable question. Hall was just as impressed as Lewin. But no amount of training could toughen Slattery's chin. Wasn't he worried Berlenbach might blast him?

"Well, Jack Delaney hit me a couple of times on the chin with his right duke and I stood up," Slats said, reminding Hall that Delaney had knocked out Berlenbach. "If I have a bad chin it looks like there will be two of them in this fight."

It bothered Slats how Hall and the other writers were so preoccupied with whether he could hold up in a fight lasting more than six rounds. The notion that he had never fought more than six rounds was simply incorrect. While he had not looked sharp doing it, Slats had gone ten rounds in Boston with Johnny Gill; two years prior to that, Slats went eight of ten scheduled rounds in Toronto against Jack McFarland. Slattery didn't have to worry about poor coverage from Hall, though. The influential wire correspondent returned to New York and boasted to all of the boxing writers hanging out at Billy LaHiff's joint that he had visited Slattery's mountain hideout. Hall, like Lewin, was changing his prediction.

Right as Slats was about to leave, writes Seb Naples, there was a touching scene at the camp. As the truck was being loaded with suitcases, the Husson men slapped the boxer on the back and said their farewells. "Don't forget to come back here when you're champion," Frank Husson said, his voice cracking.

"I'll pray for you, Jimmy," piped in Dora, wiping away an errant tear with the corner of her apron.

At 2:45 P.M., Slats and cohorts boarded a train at the North Creek station heading for Albany, where they would catch a 7:30 P.M. train bound for Grand Central Terminal. On board the train, Naples wrote up his account of life at the Indian Lake training camp while Slats sang songs and kidded around with Skitsy Fitzgerald. In New York, a large faction of Buffalo fans set up home base at the Vanderbilt Hotel on 34th and Park Avenue. Tex Rickard had sent over a stack of tickets. His new Garden was under construction, but he had already opened up a special box office at 821 Eighth Avenue. Sales for his championship fight were decent—not a sell-out—but a solid throng of 30,000 was expected. West Manhattan dockworkers would be out in force to root for their fellow Irishman. Interest in the fight had definitely ticked up after Slattery was substituted. Rickard sold it as science versus strength.

One morning paper carried a photo illustration depicting Berlenbach as a tortoise and Slattery as a hare, with Rickard (who sort of resembled actor Jeff Daniels) between the two holding a starter's pistol. Months earlier, Slats had told Hype Igoe that "Berlenbach couldn't hit me with a pan of green peas." Igoe, not the most skilled artist, but capable, sketched a skinny-legged, long-armed cartoon boxer showering a faceless foe with what we must presume to be a tub of peas.

As mentioned, New York City must have had fifty boxing writers . . . and not one of them could agree. Many picked Berlenbach, but when Hall and Lewin came back with tall tales from the mountains it caused second guessing. Coverage was intense. Slattery, said the AP, had an opportunity "to vault from the abyss to the throne." Thomas Holmes of the *Brooklyn Daily Eagle* pointed out that there was exceptional interest surrounding the battle because of the many differences of opinion. "It's a great fight to talk about because there are dozens of angles to it." And each one got explored in debates that took place all week at newsstands and shoeshine stands and inside taxis and speakeasies and haberdasheries—and no airtight case could be made. Slats had speed and he could punch. Berlenbach had zero speed but a much harder wallop. Slats owned the advantage in both height and reach. Berlenbach had a ten pound weight advantage. Sam

Hall's printed verdict had shown up in evening papers all over the country on that day before the fight: "Slattery," Hall wrote, "is unquestionably in the finest shape of his career."

In addition to sending their own reporters, some Buffalo papers secured the exclusive services of America's best-known sportswriters. The *Courier* contracted the *New York American's* Runyon to cover the bout. The *Morning Express* enlisted Harry Newman of the *New York Daily News*. A pack of writers were gathered in the lobby of the Vanderbilt waiting for Slattery to arrive, which he did shortly after 11:00 P.M. on Thursday night. As his taxi pulled up, four teenagers approached.

"Jimmy!" one of them shouted. "We had to see you win the championship!"

A couple of Park Avenue patrolmen were keeping watch, too, and they in turn pounced on the boys. Slats waved the cops off.

The boys explained how they rode the rails as far as Syracuse and then walked twenty miles before hitching a series of automobile rides.

"Had anything to eat?" Slats asked them.

"Nah," one of them replied. "But we could use some tickets."

Slats slipped them a ten-spot and told Red to get the boys some tickets. Then Slats marched the four into the hotel dining room and instructed the waiter to serve them anything they wanted, and to put it on his room. Murray, who'd been among the reporters waiting in the lobby of the hotel, reported on the encounter with the Buffalo teens. Murray insists Slats then went straight up to his room and was asleep by midnight.

The morning of the fight, Friday, September 11th, began with gray skies and thick fog. The clouds and mist lifted as the sun popped out. Unbearable humidity lingered. Slats hung around the hotel and took a brief stroll. He liked to read the tabloid, the *Daily News*, which usually had a sensational story concerning a scandalous murder or an heiress committing suicide or some such. At 2:00 P.M., Slats went to the weigh-in at the Boxing Commission's offices, not far from where a work crew was demolishing the old Garden. Slattery came in at 161 pounds, ten pounds lighter than his opponent. When Commissioner Billy Muldoon saw Slats with several days' growth of beard he ordered him to shave. Some boxers, Dempsey among them, liked to go into the ring with heavy stubble with which to soften blows and scrape against an opponent's forehead in clinches. Muldoon was not joking. The weigh-in was completed. Photos were taken. Slats promised he would be clean-shaven for the fight. Muldoon informed him that he had better be. It was the first time anyone could remember a boxer being ordered to shave before a bout.

Making its way to New York right about then was a bus loaded with Indian Lake villagers. Frank and Earl Husson had organized the trip and about 30 of their friends and neighbors were coming to see Slattery at Yankee Stadium. Many of them had never been to the big city. Their hunter-trapper ancestors had settled in the Adirondacks one century ago and, embracing the isolation, had created a self-reliant, separate world of their own. They would have been awed by the hectic pace at which the city dwellers walked, talked and existed, crammed in on top of each other. And obviously, in return, the slick cosmopolitans would have been equally taken aback by the mountain people in their tall boots and broad-brimmed, Civil War-style slouch hats.

As the night drew closer, the huge contingent of Buffalo fans made its way to the Bronx. Some were confident, while others could not shake the nagging feeling of apprehension. Finally, their long dreamed-of chance at a world title had come. But could Slattery pull it off? The betting line had at first tilted heavily toward Berlenbach. The line then shifted to where Berlenbach (after Sam Hall's story) was merely a slight favorite. By the time the Buffalo money got to town, the line was even.

"Slattery is one of the greatest pugilistic prospects in the world," wrote Runyon on the morning of the fight in a story that went out over international wires. "He has been showered with many gifts by nature. A little sincere application and he can become the Prince Charming of boxing—dashing, spectacular."

Slattery entered the ring first. The welcome he received was near riotous. His Buffalo followers—upwards of 300 people, many of them at ringside—were having the time of their lives. Word was spreading that Slattery would next fight Harry Greb for the middleweight crown. Polo Grounds promoter Jimmy Johnston was putting on a program to benefit the Jewish Maternity Ward fund. Wild fantasies were indulged; in two weeks, Slats could conceivably rule two divisions with only Dempsey's crown to go. Beaming faces in the crowd were captured in split-second intervals by a distant searchlight panning back and forth over the throng, movie premiere style, which heightened the sense of the happening. Some newspapermen claimed Col. Jacob Ruppert had installed the powerful fixture on the roof of a nearby hotel he owned so that the wealthy owner of the Yankees could watch over his star player, Babe Ruth, who had just slipped into his seat at ringside right as Berlenbach was climbing through the ropes.

The light heavyweight champion was met with a cold reception—booing, and a litany of hurtful comments. Berlenbach didn't hear too well. He *could* read lips. Because for a long time growing up—he couldn't hear at all.

As a three-year-old, Paulie Berlenbach was stricken with scarlet fever in an epidemic that swept through his family's crowded tenement on East 88th Street near Second Avenue. The illness took a heavy toll—the child emerged deaf and unable to utter so much as a squawk of toddler gibberish. Doctors labeled him dumb. His mother refused to let him play sports with the other children, not that the boys on the block would have allowed him, anyway. The kids used a cruel phrase whenever Berlenbach came around. He read it on their lips: "dummy." At around age seven, Berlenbach was sent away to the St. Joseph's home for deaf boys, a church-run institution in Throgs Neck at the eastern tip of The Bronx. Essentially, it functioned as a for-profit printing press and boys were schooled in that trade. Even at St. Joseph's, rival factions formed. But Berlenbach kept to himself. He was an introverted, sullen child. All he ever wanted was to be accepted by the regular kids. One spring day, around Easter, while on a break from the deaf home, Berlenbach made his way back to the old neighborhood. He wore the best clothes he owned. In his Sunday suit, walking along 86th Street near First Avenue, he was accosted by a dozen or so older boys from a neighborhood gang. They rammed him with their shoulders and razzed him, and wouldn't stop. For the first time in his life, little Paulie felt an urge, a feeling so overwhelming that he plowed into the pack, spitting mad, fists flying, even though he knew the large group might kill him. After that, he simply refused to be an outcast. He'd play in the street even if he was mocked. To impress his tormenters, Berlenbach pulled crazy stunts. On one subsequent Easter break, Berlenbach shimmied up a telegraph pole and accidentally touched a live wire. The forty-foot fall could have been fatal. But he got off lucky with a broken arm and some bruises. And something truly crazy did happen—the electric shock restored his hearing. At first, the thunderstruck lad thought it was all happening inside his head, but a scary situation turned into a dream come true. Eventually, he started to move his lips and formulate words. His ability to speak came slow, but he was part of the world again. Berlenbach switched to a regular school. He played sports. He talked to girls. Slurred words and wrong-sounding intonations invited ridicule, sure. But Berlenbach was never happier. He started lifting weights at the Y.M.C.A. and took up wrestling. Some big shots at the N.Y.A.C. gave him an athletic membership and put him on the path to amateur competition. Coaches could see in the youth a specific quality that had first manifested itself when those kids were razzing him on 86th Street. Berlenbach would come to learn the exact phrase for what he possessed: killer instinct.

The fight was only moments away. Thousand-watt arc lights blazed yellow on all sides of the ring. Night baseball was still more than a decade off, but artificially illuminated boxing was the hottest trend in sports. Lit up, Berlenbach's muscular physique was all the more impressive. Though shorter, he appeared to have more than ten pounds worth of extra bulk. Across the ring, the taller, leaner Slattery looked every bit the part of an antelope tossed into a pen with a bull.

Joe Humphries, the Garden's beloved, booming-voiced announcer momentarily ceded his role to a special guest in the center of the ring: light heavyweight contender Jack Delaney, who was charged with introducing a few additional surprise guests making their way into the ring. Delaney doing some guest ring announcements was a particularly bizarre twist to the program, considering he was supposed to have just undergone throat surgery. In a time before microphones were in use, Humphries was sufficiently stout of lung to be heard, even without the aid of a megaphone (which at the time were in use). First, Delaney welcomed Harry Greb, who came into the ring wearing an eye patch. Simultaneously, another world-famous fighter climbed through the ropes to take a bow: Dave Shade. The Cinderella welterweight couldn't help but gaze over at Prince Charming. Slats' trademark smile suddenly went missing.

Across the ring, an expressionless Berlenbach muttered a few words of hello to Delaney, who was ready to turn the announcer's responsibility back to Humphries as the opening gong drew closer.

At that moment, about 400 miles northwest in Buffalo, some 8,000 fans assembled downtown, awaiting live wire reports to be read aloud (by megaphone) in front of the *Courier's* offices on Seneca and Swan. Traces of a gathering began after supper. By 8:00 P.M., mounted police were sent in to clear the streets so automobile traffic could pass. By 9:00 P.M. it had started to rain, *hard*—monsoon-like sheets accompanied by thunder and lightning. Anyone watching the scene would have automatically expected to see a scampering mass of humanity when the storm hit. But apart from the fortunate few able to squeeze themselves into doorways, the crowd stayed put, drenched, stoic and impervious, waiting patiently for the first results to trickle in.

At Yankee Stadium, thousands of fans were likewise soaking wet, but not from rain. Sweltering humidity had been building all day and was intensified at field level, where spectators were packed in tight. During the preliminaries, men kept their hats and suit coats on; this was a dignified occasion, and no one wanted to look a rube. But by the time Slattery and Berlenbach were set to touch gloves, all such outerwear had been shed in a chain of heat-induced capitulation, which had the effect of altering the view from the upper deck, with a solid sea of dark-toned jackets giving way to a tide of white shirts. Uninvited guests, tiny insects, swarmed everywhere, getting into eyes that were already squinty from beads of perspiration. By now, Humphries was clearing his throat. A couple of hours earlier, he strode into the ring adorned in a high, stiff collar. It had since collapsed, low and floppy.

Referee Patsy Haley, resembling an eccentric science teacher with his bushy white hair, instructed each corner to thoroughly towel fighters between rounds. "Send 'em out dry," Haley shouted. But this was an impossible task, such was the heat.

The boxing stars started to take their seats along with the rest of the famous faces of the worlds of sports, entertainment and high society. Not far from Babe Ruth sat John McGraw, the venerated, irascible manager of the city's National League club, the Giants, winners of ten pennants in two decades. Also close by was Columbia University's new football coach, Charlie Crowley. A war hero, Crowley had been a player at Notre Dame. He brought several players for purposes of team-building and to expose them to elite athletes. Billy Gibson had the exact same notion. Best-known as Gene Tunney's manager, Gibson had started out as a Bronx boxing promoter and now also dabbled in football. He'd just installed himself as acting manager of a brand new expansion team he'd helped bring to town, although the purchase (total cost $500) was actually made by a bookmaker pal of Gibson's. Sitting next to Gibson (and several members of the New York *football* Giants) was Maxey Blumenthal. He ran boxing at the St. Nicholas Arena. For many years, "St. Nick's," on West 66th and Columbus, rivaled the old Garden. Taking seats near the sportsmen were Broadway royalty Flo Ziegfeld and George M. Cohan, as well as movie producer Robert T. Kane and wealthy songwriter Gene Buck, whose lavish lifestyle in Great Neck, Long Island, helped inspire a new novel written by one of his neighbors. Also at ringside were prominent society women, most notably Margaret Baker, formerly known as Mrs. A.G. Vanderbilt, as in Alfred Gwynne Vanderbilt I, great grandson of railroad titan Cornelius Vanderbilt. Alfred had died several years earlier on board the sunken *Lusitania*. She remarried into money, so to speak—Raymond Baker was a former Director of the U.S. Mint. Slattery woke up that morning in a hotel built by Margaret Baker's late first husband.

The boxers in street clothes exited the ring—Shade last. Slats' eyes followed him until the haunting vision disappeared under the ropes. Humphries began. "Ladies and gentleman ... in this *cor-nah* ..." When Slattery's name rang out, the stadium burst into applause, a wild demonstration, said one writer. Slats and Berlenbach posed for a few quick photographs, got their instructions, touched gloves and returned to their corners for a few token seconds. Then the gong sounded.

Slowly, Berlenbach trudged toward the center of the ring, his eyes fixed on his own two gloves, as if reaffirming their existence. Slats met him in the middle, having glided there, bouncing on his toes. The two men circled about. Slattery's snicker let everyone know he was neither impressed by Berlenbach's muscles nor concerned about his wallop. The German American fired a telegraphed one-two; Slats danced out of the way. Berlenbach was much faster than anyone would ever give him credit for, though not nearly as fast as Slattery, making it hard to notice. They traded a few punches and clinched. The champion rocked Slattery with a shot to the stomach. Slats volleyed right back, thumping Berlenbach with a picturesque combo—uppercut, straight right, left jab—forcing Berlenbach to the ropes. They prowled around one another, Berlenbach expressionless, Slattery smiling. That's how the first round concluded. At the stadium, Buffalo fans reacted as if Slats had won the round. Moreover, Slats had weathered an early storm and come out fine. He'd used his speed to box at long range. Back in Buffalo, the mob was ready to celebrate any inkling of positive news over the wires. The *Courier* announcer declared Slats had won the round. Screams were intense. Hoarse-voiced baritones were offset by the shrill, high-pitched cries of the many women in the mob.

Berlenbach waded in close to Slattery to begin the second. His head was down, his greased-up hair out of place and in his eyes, not that it mattered. Berlenbach's strategy was to bore in and conduct savage in-close combat, even if it meant taking a few shots to deliver one crusher. He smashed away with the expectation that something would eventually land. Slats hung tough, ducking and shifting, fluid, perfect, as if with extra-sensory perception. He threw a right that landed, but caught a hard right in return. Both of their gloves were sweat-logged and heavy. The punch hurt Slats. His eyes went glassy. The crowd let out a tense mumble, wrote ringside eyewitness Jim Tully, a former boxer who'd become an unlikely literary sensation for his gritty portrayals of America's have-nots.

Slattery's bid to become champion was disintegrating, and it was just midway through the second round. Berlenbach's storm of left hooks to the body had Slats groggy. Slats dodged and writhed, as only he could, while trapped in a corner. Somehow, Slats survived the barrage, head up, still smiling. He forced a clinch as the round ended. Slattery's cocky smile was now more of an anxious defense mechanism.

During the break, Runyon laughed and shouted a *howyadoin'* to Slattery's corner, which could have been affectionate jab or outright taunt. Someone else nearby murmured, "Slattery is as sick as a lonely Mick in London."

In the third round, Slattery got into worse trouble. Trapped again along the ropes, Slattery's only chance to ride out the hurricane was to keep moving, bouncing and sliding away; for some reason he paused and stood toe to toe with the Astoria Assassin. The beating was awful. Berlenbach hit with debilitating force. Even the punches Slats blocked hurt. Glancing blows deadened nerve endings. Punches that struck clean damaged bone and tissue. Slattery was once again trapped in a corner. Sapped of strength, helpless, Slattery held out his chin defiantly. But Berlenbach was unable to execute a kill shot. Slattery slipped out of the corner. Berlenbach chased him around the ring, said Runyon, like "a clumsy butcher trying to knock a nimble calf on the head."

The Buffalo fans at ringside got quiet, despondent. "It can't go far," said someone in the press row.

When Slats sat down on the stool in his corner after the gong sounded to end the third, his supporters could see he was struggling. Sucking on a lemon, Slats seemed completely drained. His eyes mourned vanished strength. But he wasn't finished.

Slats came out for the fourth round buoyed by the support of the crowd. "Slattery's pluck captured every heart in the stadium," Murray wrote.

The thunderous applause inspired Slats and annoyed Berlenbach, still swinging wildly in an effort to go home. He caught Slats, who reeled into the ropes but bounced back strong, dancing away and out of range. The lull in the Berlenbach assault seemed to break the tension, giving the audience a moment to catch its breath.

In the fifth round, surprisingly, it was Slattery who became the aggressor. Spitting blood, lips raw and red, Slats started jabbing, like a fencer with his foil. He had fended off a strange move by Berlenbach. The former wrestler had attempted to bend Slats into a doubled-over knot—Haley either didn't notice or didn't care—but the move failed. Slats jabbed Berlenbach all over the ring and the crowd grew louder with each shot, the turning of the tide causing grown men to start jumping up and down like children. Hype Igoe sprang from his seat at the end of the round and started dancing in the press section, an unabashed Slattery supporter. "I shouldn't have bet on a Dutchman anyhow," one scribe, sitting close by, had grumbled.

Sensing a great comeback, awed by the rally, fans let loose with evidence of their zeal in a display the boxing people swore they had never seen before or since. By the hundreds they came, sailing through the air from all directions—straw hats—flung in jubilation. One was launched all the way from the upper-tier of the grandstand and eventually floated into the center of the ring. "They looked like huge moths under the arc lights," Jim Tully wrote. The start of the sixth was delayed so the ring could be cleared of hats.

In the sixth, Slats nearly dropped Berlenbach. At that moment, the screaming at Yankee Stadium turned primitive. Each time Slattery hit Berlenbach, the stocky brute exhaled steam through his nostrils and shook his head side to side, a mastodon shooing tiny bugs.

Fears about Slattery's inability to travel a long route were subsiding as the fight wore on. Slats had his way during the seventh, eighth and ninth rounds, by all accounts. A film of the fight—the only footage of Slattery in existence—shows a pale, flickering form, lightly bouncing on his toes, the jerky motion accentuated by the glow and sputtering frames of early moving pictures. The film clearly shows Slattery's hands-low parrying style, and the uncanny way he could snap cobra-like punches from hip level, jab-jab jabbing, crisp and fluid. Writing in *Boxing International* in 1969, Bob Waters described getting his hands on the film. Today, portions of the film are on YouTube, but back then it was as if Waters had discovered a magic portal to another world. "Take it from a man who saw Jimmy Slattery fight," Waters wrote of his personal screening. "Slats was the finest boxer who ever lived."

"Under the spell of wild acclaim and frantic fandom at ringside, Slattery drove Berlenbach with a wonderful assortment of punches, a boxing lesson," the AP wrote. "The early silent throng was transformed into a howling pack that made the great stadium echo," said Richards Vidmer of the *New York Times*. Of the Slats-dominated middle rounds, Charlie Murray pronounced: "Jimmy made Berlenbach appear as if he had never worn boxing gloves before."

At times, Slats had Berlenbach dazed and stumbling around the ring. But if there was one thing at which Berlenbach excelled, it was withstanding punishment. His lips bled and puffed and his body was painted with raspberry welts. But the bull kept rushing forward.

Slats socked Berlenbach on the chin to commence the ninth. The German was losing more ground. Slattery seemed to grow timid. He absorbed a shot to the body but gave one back, right to the champion's heart. Slats charged and clinched, repeatedly, as if trying to run out the clock. Berlenbach, sputtering, welcomed the window of respite.

The blank expression on Berlenbach's face still remained when he came out for the tenth. Slattery's up-tempo toe-hopping faded to a feeble shuffle, his punches sapped of power. As long as Slats kept moving, he had an advantage. But the Irishman switched strategies. Instead of stalking his quarry from long range, Slattery stood in and slugged with the champion.

"For just an instant, Slattery stopped," Waters said, viewing the 1925 film (back in 1969). "He hadn't slipped. For some inexplicable reason the wraith came to a dead halt."

Slattery did so straight into the path of a Berlenbach onslaught. Berlenbach had been throwing desperate left hooks all night long, hoping one would land. In the last minute of the tenth, one did, hard, to Slattery's solar plexus. All of his wind evaporated. The tide turned once again. The crowd braced itself. In the aisles, policemen knelt, "their faces tense," wrote Tully, "as if battling gunmen."

Berlenbach tore at Slats looking to finish him. Three times, he hit Slats in the head. A left turned the challenger completely around, knees wilting.

With juvenile abandon, Berlenbach reverted to a wrestling hold, arm locking Slattery by the back of the neck and slamming him to the floor. Any air Slats had recaptured was instantaneously jarred out of him. Slats stood up and huffed angrily at referee Patsy Haley, who took no issue with Berlenbach's aggressive tactics. Once again, Berlenbach body slammed his opponent. Again, Slattery got up but did not bother to complain. He could not catch his breath, which left him at the mercy of the champion. Berlenbach leapt in, knocking Slattery to the canvas for the third time in the round. Slats sat gasping against the ropes. At the count of four, the bell rang, saving him. Grateful, he smiled. But a fog set in. Slats staggered to his corner. Before Skitsy could get the stool in place, Slats collapsed. He'd returned to his corner so physically exhausted and befuddled that a full minute of frenzied revival efforts—Skitsy and Joe poured water over him, stuffed smelling salts up his nose, fired questions (*"What day is it? Where are you?"*), slapped and shook him—nothing could bring Slats back to his senses. With a few seconds to go before the bell to start the eleventh, the Buffalo boxer was still in no condition to fight. Skitsy frantically took a razor and cut the back of Slattery's trunks below the waistband in a desperate ploy. Maybe, Skitsy figured, Haley would see the trunks in disrepair and call for time.

Subsiding on superhuman will, or just raw instinct, Slats wobbled out. Haley never noticed the slit trunks. Only Red could prevent what was about to occur. And for some reason, he did not.

Berlenbach had a free shot. He smashed Slats in the face with a savage right that carried the impact of a dropped crowbar. Slats went down. Haley stood above him, stooping down to holler out the count directly into his ear. At nine, Slats rose. Berlenbach immediately nailed him again, this time with a left. Slats dropped to the canvas for the fifth time. Yet he refused to be counted out. At nine, he rose once more to endure the bludgeoning without end. He became sandwiched between the middle and bottom ropes, his left mitt clinging to the topmost strand. Reduced to a human punching bag, out but not down, his trunks in tatters, bum showing, mouth agape, Berlenbach wailing away, Slattery was beyond beaten. Then, at last, Haley mercifully waved Berlenbach to his corner, stopping the fight.

In Yankee stadium, the Buffalo contingent—which only moments earlier could almost taste the championship—swallowed down their grief, crippled by it. Meanwhile, the rain-soaked crowd of 8,000 Buffalo fans in front of the *Courier* building heard one final return called out from a mega-phone: "Jimmy Slattery loses and the fight is over."

The fight ended at 1:28 of the eleventh round, about 10:45 P.M. The Slattery devotees in downtown Buffalo dispersed in silence. "The men simply pulled their wet coat collars tighter 'round their necks," said one witness, "and, with shoulders slouching and hands in pockets, moved up the street."

Semi-conscious in his corner, Slats sat on his stool and cried. Skitsy and Joe did not console him. They cried, too.

When Berlenbach left the ring, the scene was observed by the *Courier*'s Seb Naples, who'd spent weeks with Slattery in the mountains and had been helping to file the round-by-round updates heard back home. "The champion was booed and catcalled," Naples reported.

No one loves a loser, or so it's been said. But leaving the ring that night, Slattery received a tremendous ovation. In the age of hype, some writers hung their fedoras on reliability. One boxing critic regarded as exceptionally trustworthy was James P. Dawson of the *Times*. Here is what Dawson had to say afterward: "Referee Patsy Haley stopped the fight, retaining for Berlenbach the championship, and for Slattery, the consolation of one of the greatest, most spectacular ring stands a boxer ever has made ... Slattery went down like the true fighting man he is and gave the crowd in Yankee Stadium one of the most thrilling battles any member of it ever has seen."

The ring deserted, true-grit chronicler Jim Tully lingered a while to process what he had witnessed. "Moths fly under the strong lights where but a few minutes before a gallant lad went down with a broken dream of a championship," Tully would write. "*Alas for dreams.*"

The next day, a brutal series of International Newsreel photographs splashed across the front pages of newspapers around the world. In them, Slats is shown in every conceivable position of repose—laid out prostrate, down on all fours, Indian style, fetal—and at least one shot showed his rear-end hanging out of his shredded trunks. He's depicted flying through the air and crashing to the ground, crawling and cowering. And to think 1925 had started so promising for Jimmy Slattery ...

Some say that after the Berlenbach defeat, Slattery went on an unbelievable bender. His check for the fight, cut by Rickard at the end of September, totaled $11,000, more than enough to replace the automobile Slattery destroyed a few weeks after the fight in a scary 3:00 A.M. mishap at a railroad crossing at Tifft Street and the lakeside turnpike road leading out to the steel plants. Slats, driving Joe Hickey and two female passengers, crashed his auto into the side of a string of boxcars. Luckily, the foursome escaped with only some cuts and bruises. Slattery's drinking was so out of hand during this period, some insist, that it hastened the aging process, as the once youthful-looking sprite surrendered any last traces of boyishness.

Plans to fight Greb were scrapped. A fight, instead, was booked in Syracuse for early November. Slats was still a draw. Berlenbach-Slattery Fight Pictures had packed in audiences at ten-cent movie houses across Western New York. And Rickard still had plans to enlist Slats to help unveil the New Garden, possibly in a rematch with Shade.

Slats trained at Newsboys' and in Indian Lake with his spirited flyweight friend, Vic St. Onge. The two sparred in biting cold and took that shooting trip they had always talked about now that Slats knew how to handle a firearm.

Slats came back to Buffalo from the Adirondacks on Sunday, October 25, to play for the Euclids, the semi-pro football team he'd formed a season earlier along with pals Chuck Colern and Husky Dognan. "Slattery's 11" trounced the New York Haberdashers that day, 24 to 0, in a game waged in shin-high mud.

On Slattery's instruction, St. Onge carted the fine buck they bagged over to Forton's butcher shop on Elk Street. Slats delivered steaks and roasts to a dozen First Ward families, as he'd promised he would.

Around the same time, Slats was trying to break a promise made to Syracuse promoter Charlie Huck, none too pleased to be informed that the Buffalo superstar was trying to wriggle out of his contract with a claim of illness.

On the first Friday of November 1925, Huck hauled Slats in front of the Boxing Commission.

Chairman Brower was a Slattery fan. So was Billy Muldoon. Glaring disapprovingly, Muldoon listened to Slattery's request to be excused from the Syracuse match scheduled for that following Sunday.

The Commission granted Slattery his wish. "Take sixty days rest to recover," Muldoon said.

And with that went Rickard's plan to have Slats appear in one of the first matches at his new temple of sport. So much for being seen as the future of boxing—Slattery was now on hiatus.

EIGHT

CHAMPIONSHIP GLORY

A FEW DAYS BEFORE CHRISTMAS, Tex Rickard put on a special holiday boxing show at New Madison Square Garden. His temple of sport had just opened. Some critics griped about poor ventilation and obstructed sight lines. Most people were impressed. Crowds filled it regularly. Ice hockey, basketball, bike races, dances and, of course, plenty of boxing were all on the menu. Although the long rectangular box wasn't much to look at from the outside, the Eighth Avenue building immediately became the place to be for New York's society crowd.

Meanwhile, about 350 miles away in Warren, Pennsylvania, a small town on the banks of the Allegheny River in the northwest corner of the state, Jimmy Slattery was enjoying a bowl of soup. In a few hours, he would be fighting a little-known opponent at the Warren Knights of Columbus. Sitting in Pete's Restaurant on a Saturday night, Slats was in high spirits. Later on, during the first round, Slats placed his glove over his face to hide a chuckle. His foe, "Indian" Joe Burke of Detroit, had crumpled after only a few shots. Before the opening round was halfway finished, Burke sunk to the canvas. Slats stood over him, inspecting him as would a referee. "Get up you tramp," Slats commanded.

Burke continued on but lasted only another two rounds. That night, the AP wire carried five lines on the fight: *Jimmy Slattery of Buffalo knocked out Joe Burke in the third round of a scheduled ten-round bout. Slattery weighed 172 and Burke 169.*

Relegated to boxing's backwater—only one-half inch of column space in the morning paper. It wasn't supposed to be this way. Rickard's new matchmaker, Jess McMahon, originally wanted the Christmas show to feature Slattery in a rematch with Dave Shade. To smooth the way, Rickard sent the Buffalo fighter down to the marbled corridors of the Boxing Commission to make an act of contrition, so that the ruling fathers would consider shortening his unwanted sixty-day furlough. Nattily dressed, eyes clear, Slats went before Muldoon, who was still remarkably fit for eighty. Nothing offended him more than watching a healthy young man self-dissipate.

"Son, you are one of the finest boxers to come along in my lifetime," Muldoon told Slats. "*And I trained the great John L. Sullivan.*"

Whipping a washed-out Sullivan into shape more than three decades earlier was Muldoon's claim to fame; that and inventing the medicine ball. Sullivan, a notorious imbiber of spirits, retreated to Muldoon's Belfast, N.Y. farm to train for his 1889 title fight—the last to be waged without gloves—against Jake Kilrain. Fifty pounds overweight and sickly from alcoholism, Sullivan was turned over to Muldoon by alarmed management. An ex-wrestler turned physical fitness pioneer, Muldoon told the champion's backers that if Sullivan lost the Kilrain fight, there would be no need for any compensation. However, if Sullivan won, Muldoon would be paid $1,000. The regimen consisted, in part, of Muldoon wielding a club and chasing Sullivan out of the village tavern, back to the barn from which he had escaped. Sullivan won the fight, one of the first sporting events to attract national interest.

Though he was no longer chair of the Boxing Commission, Muldoon still loomed large as a patriarchal leader. Denying Slattery's request for reinstatement, the white-haired elder also dispensed a solemn lecture. "You still have a bright future ahead," he told Slats. "Take care of yourself."

In a busy boxing year filled with numerous highs and lows, twists and turns—the opening of the New Garden, the legalization of the sport in California, the completely unexpected crowning of Buffalo's Rocky Kansas as the new lightweight champion, the untimely deaths of Battling Siki and Pancho Villa—perhaps no single ring story of 1925 was more stunning than the downfall of Jimmy Slattery. Rickard, a bit remorseful about how Slattery had been handled, wanted to help get him back on top. "Slattery undertook too much too soon," the showman told sportswriters back in the fall during one of many gab sessions aimed to publicize his new arena during its construction phase.

Built in less than nine months at a cost of $5 million, the humongous sports emporium—200 feet wide, 350 feet long—could hold 20,000 people. The facility was designed with boxing foremost in mind, but every conceivable amusement would have a place so long as tickets could be sold. Seating and lighting were state of the art. The most modern feature of all: underground piping that could produce a one-inch thick ice sur-face in eight hours. A hockey game was played the same weekend that the first boxing match was held at the New Garden, December 11, 1925, with Berlenbach successfully defending his title against Delaney. Several weeks earlier, Rickard personally tried to put some finishing touches on the building. During an ill-fated publicity stunt to mark the completion of the framework, the promoter went to drive the final rivet into a girder, but was not able to handle the high-pressure steam drill. Teeth loosened, sweat pouring, Rickard averted a stroke by wisely turning the heavy-duty equipment over to an ironworker.

Though it lacked the splendor of its predecessor, the New Garden was drawing crowds. Millionaires mingled with gangsters. Mayor Jimmy Walker sat ringside next to gambling kingpin Arnold Rothstein. Nearly $1 mil-lion worth of tickets had been sold for Garden attractions since it opened its doors. To close out the first indoor season, Rickard staged a rematch between Slattery and Young Stribling—this time over a long distance.

Since their first meeting two years earlier, Slattery had soared to dizzy-ing heights before crashing back down to earth. Stribling had toured the country with his parents in a special bus that was really an early iteration of a mobile home. He fought in small towns against mediocre opponents. When no suitable challenger could be found, rumor held, Stribling boxed his driver. The young performer was raking in cash. He purchased a 640-acre farm in Thomasville, Georgia. He snatched up beachfront parcels in South Florida. He married his high school sweetheart, Clara Kinney, and supposedly planned to attend the University of Georgia. Stribling's wealthy father-in-law, W.O. Kinney, was nudging the boy to join his cot-ton brokerage.

Dropping by the New Garden for a visit in late December of 1925, Strib-ling introduced his new bride to Rickard. They had been married the day after Christmas, Stribling's birthday, and were en route to Niagara Falls for their honeymoon. Rickard was happy Stribling had finally turned 21.

"I see you're under new management," Rickard commented. "When do you expect to fight?"

"Why, Mr. Rickard," Clara interjected. "We don't ever expect to fight."

Rickard's associate, Matchmaker McMahon, joined in the conversa-tion. He was ready with some offers. Really, there was only one match he wished to pursue. Stribling, likewise, had one specific opponent in mind.

McMahon and Rickard were glad to find out they were all on the same page. Stribling wasn't going to college nor was he going to become a cotton broker.

"Get me anybody," the Georgian said. "Most of all, I'd like to fight Slattery."

This was welcome news for Slattery, who was slipping into the valley of pay-no-mind. Slats had kicked off 1926 with a ten-round bout in Buffalo against Maxie Rosenbloom, the tough, strangely frenetic Harlem kid whom Slats defeated in Coney Island back in August. At the time, Rosenbloom had been deemed a lout, someone inferior to help ease Slattery back into the game after his embarrassing loss to Shade. But the Rosenbloom whom Slats met by the sea was a whirlwind of a fighter who hadn't lost a single bout since turning pro. In a New Year's Day rematch at the Aud, Slattery and Rosenbloom boxed ten hectic rounds. Slats once again had his hands full. Just like Greb, Rosenbloom hurled punches nonstop from all angles, showing such speed and aggression that Buffalo fans were actually won over by his antics. "It was among the fastest exhibitions ever witnessed in these parts," one wire service reported. Slats took the decision, but this wasn't quite the comeback campaign launch he had envisioned.

The March 25, 1926, rematch against Stribling was Slattery's last best hope to get back on track. Stribling treated the fight as the most important of his career. In his mind, there was no margin for possibly losing. Slats promised everyone he would get into shape.

Some 18,000 fans would attend, making it one of the largest crowds ever to watch an indoor sporting event. During the weigh-in ceremony, overseen by Muldoon, Stribling reportedly turned to Slats and said, "Well, this will make the third time that you have been knocked out."

Entering the ring to a shower of boos (his alleged Klan ties still haunted him, as did tales of set-ups with his chauffeur), Stribling sneered at the crowd like the villain in a wrestling match, and then the stocky Southerner trained his stink-eye on Slats. With his new bride seated ringside, Stribling went to work, determined it would be a brawl, not a boxing match. Accounts suggest he went into a full roughhouse routine which included butting and wrestling, even some low blows. Such blatant fouls prompted one sharp-dressed dignitary at ringside to stand up on his chair and holler for a new referee. The ref, Jack Denning, an ex-boxer, did issue warnings—to both combatants—as Slats started throwing rabbit punches. In one early round, Stribling mocked Slats by doing a snide imitation of his bouncy-toe dance. Every chance he got, Stribling manhandled the Buffalo speedster. "Stribling looked like a Hercules against willowy Slattery," wrote *Variety*. Though the verdict was not popular with the fans, Stribling took a close decision. Corbett declared Slattery out of contention and predicted Stribling would one day take Dempsey's crown.

Prior to the bout, the press played up the notion that the two youths had animosity between them. Stribling's scowling demeanor seemed to underscore such subtext, at least on his part. One would think he was out for blood. Curiously, according to Tom "Luke" Carr, Red's nephew, Stribling went to Slattery's dressing room after the fight and offered to take him for a ride in his airplane. The anecdote does not turn up in either Stribling biography, although it is true he was a budding aviator.

For a third straight time, Slattery flopped on the big stage. His astounding exploits of the year before were roundly written off as a mere flash in the pan. Following some earlier ring failures, Slats healed his wounds by embarking on wilderness sabbaticals. *Go enjoy yourself,* advisors now told him. *Get away from the game.*

This time he would be traveling farther away than he had ever dreamed. Slattery was off to Europe.

★★★★★

He only had a few days to sort out his affairs, say his goodbyes—and somehow obtain a passport. Skitsy and Joe wouldn't be coming along on this adventure. Slats met up with his party at the Pennsylvania Hotel in New York City. The tour group included Buffalo Mayor Frank Schwab, Deputy Police Chief Frank Carr and a delegation of hotel owners, part of an even larger contingent, the American Hotelmen's Association, sponsoring the entire junket. On board the ocean liner, Slats did some light sparring with reluctant laymen whose ribs ultimately paid for accepting his offer. By the end of the journey, he (surprise) was crowned the ship's shuffleboard champion.

Mayor Schwab brought along a movie camera and a suitcase filled with film. He actually tried to claim the trip was at least in part official city business, in that he was researching the latest advancement in municipal buses and sewage disposal plants. Over the next three months, this enormous group of 300 wealthy Americans would visit France, England, Belgium,

Holland, Austria, Switzerland, Germany and Italy. Slats had the most glorious time of his entire life.

In London, the Buffalo party met up with actress Peggy O'Neil, a blue-eyed First Ward gal who had risen to become the toast of British theater. "Tot," as she was known to friends back in the old neighborhood, would be immortalized in a famous song: *"Peggy O'Neil was a girl who could steal/ any heart, anywhere, anytime . . ."*

When Tot learned that folks from Buffalo were visiting London, she threw a lavish reception, greeting Slats as if he were her long lost brother. In a way, she was kind of like a female version of Slats, that is, a neighborhood kid made good, unimaginably so. She'd struggled to make it in Hollywood, though eventually found her niche abroad. Success had not taken the First Ward out of the girl, at least going by the song's reference to her "rascality."

Slats showed his devilish streak in Venice, Italy. He disappeared one night, and when he failed to turn up by morning, his companions mulled whether to alert local authorities as to their suspicion that he may have wandered off and stumbled into one of the canals. But Slats was eventually located "drifting aimlessly in a stolen gondola," according to Sammy Brindis. Of course, Slats had a female friend drifting along with him.

Slattery's favorite city of all was Paris. "There's no other city quite like Paree," he would often remark later, repeatedly, drawing on a stockpile of fond memories. Before leaving for the trip, Slats stuffed his pockets with sheaves of American currency, and spent much of the vacation throwing five spots to every waiter, taxi driver or bellhop to cross his path. That spring, the franc plummeted in value as France struggled to repay a mountain of wartime debt. With the exchange rate at roughly 4 to 1, a greenback dollar went a long way. Slats couldn't be bothered to learn even a few token French phrases. "You don't have to know the language if you have this!" he'd once exclaimed, whipping out a thick bankroll. Slats naturally was smitten by the gorgeous, forward women and he laughed like hell when he saw the outdoor public urinals of Paris, where blasé Frenchmen relieved themselves in plain sight, waving to people who passed by. One day, the mayor, occupied by some business engagements, handed Slats his movie camera. "Take some nice footage of downtown," Schwab directed. Slats had a blast, strolling along the boulevards, shooting whatever caught his fancy.

Each night, the VIP tourists were feted by some local hoteliers. This itinerary replayed itself over and over, each new city, sightseeing, followed by a grandiose feast. Everything was paid for, even the rail fare, by European tourism officials. When the delegation arrived in Rome, they found a famous American hanging around the lobby of the Excelsior Hotel—cowboy humorist Will Rogers. Trekking across Europe and writing syndicated columns, Rogers made his signature folksy, common-sense observations. He called the hotelmen the "Barnum and Bailey circus of American tourists." Included in his priceless account of this run-in in Rome, Rogers mentions Slattery. "He is a great one," Rogers said. "And what a fine time he is having. Although, I'm not sure what hotel Jimmy represented, maybe one of Mr. Statler's."

One night, Rogers was asked to speak at a party thrown by the hotelmen of Rome for their guests. The one-time Wild West show star aimed his verbal lasso at the haughty Americans.

"You fellows have eaten enough free food to feed Europe through two more wars," Rogers told the audience, stiffening, and grateful that the Italians couldn't understand any of it. "Why, if you had to pay American prices for what you drank up over here, Europe could pay its debts!"

At some point during the talk, one of the hotelmen got up and tipped the band leader to cut in with music.

When the Buffalo delegation arrived back in New York harbor in early June, an official city-dispatched welcome committee rolled up to meet them by chartered yacht. Once back on land, Slats immediately raced to a telephone and called home. He spoke to each member of his family, and even had a long-distance telephone reunion with Skitsy and Joe. Schwab had plenty of funny Slattery stories, some from the slow ride home. Apparently, Slats became obsessed with doing laundry on board the ship. Like a lot of men at that time, Slats was keen on personal grooming (what one might call a "dandy") and he spent so much time in the laundry room that someone hung a sign on his cabin door which read "Laundry, Neatly Done, Delivered Same Day if Dropped Off by 7:00 A.M."—which Slats did not find amusing in the least. A much more hilarious story concerning the trip abroad unfolded days later back in Buffalo.

The mayor had invited a group of fellow travelers and other guests to his home to watch the movies he had taken during the trip. At one point, the viewers gasped. Up on the screen flashed candid shots—of Frenchmen pissing! Slats had secretly filmed them and never told Schwab. The mayor turned red and tried to explain. Eventually, the shock gave way to uncontrollable laughter. Slats, the auteur, had brought down the house.

Returning to the ring, however, Slats bombed. His victory in late July over Bob Sage of Detroit might as well have been a loss. Cautious, ineffective and uncharacteristically slow, Slats was booed by a miniscule Garden crowd (less than 4,000) and ripped by the press. "He was a shadow of the Slattery who a year ago was hailed as another Jim Corbett," one writer said. Added the *Times*' James Dawson, "Slattery no longer warrants consideration as a contender."

Even if Slats had knocked Sage out of the ring, no one would have cared. The sporting world moved on to more important matters: Jack Dempsey was coming back. Rickard signed him to fight Gene Tunney later that summer. Although the 28-year-old Tunney was neither colorful, nor widely known, he would more than suffice for a public that was starving for a heavyweight title fight. That Dempsey would finally defend his crown after a three-year absence was enough to grab the attention of the entire world.

Most Big Town scribes had respect for Tunney. They had watched the lanky ex-Marine mature into an excellent boxer. But not one of them gave Tunney a chance to win. For Rickard, Tunney—very good, but not viewed as dangerous—was the perfect low-risk foe to present to Dempsey, who had some rust to work off. Tunney, meanwhile, was certain he would win. He had prepared long and arduously for this moment. As a full-fledged heavyweight of 189 pounds, Tunney had scored some impressive victories in 1925, including a win over the highly touted Johnny Risko of Cleveland. Tunney had envisioned fighting Dempsey for the heavyweight crown as early as 1919, when he was participating in inter-allied boxing tournaments in France, and Dempsey had just won the title. With a straight face, Tunney predicted to a fellow Marine, Bill Osborne, that one day he would beat Dempsey and become champion. Osborne, who helped out in Tunney's corner during the AEF matches, took his friend seriously. Thinking of his family's hotel spread back home in the Adirondack Mountains, Osborne gave Tunney something to think about. "Gene, if you really want a winning place to train, I can tell you where," Osborne said. "You come up to my family's place at Lake Pleasant. Roam the mountains, live in that invigorating air." Sounds perfect, Tunney replied, promising Osborne he would take him up on the offer some day.

Now, seven years later, Tunney really did need someplace to train for the biggest fight of his life. He set his sights first on Tom Luther's hotel in Saratoga. The clean-living contender couldn't imagine a better spot. But Luther broke the news that Dempsey's people had already booked it. Dempsey had trained there in '23, prior to his famous fight with Firpo. Tunney understood. With Dempsey at his place for the summer, Luther would make a fortune charging admission to sparring sessions. Tunney knew what to do. "We'll train at Lake Pleasant," he flatly told his manager, Billy Gibson. Then Tunney wired a telegram to his buddy Bill Osborne. "Make room for me," the telegram read. "Here I come to make good on my promise."

Osborne was ecstatic. He and his brother, Bob, along with some fellow hotel and restaurant owners, were in the midst of trying to boost tourism. One year earlier, the cadre of business leaders formally changed the name of their sleepy little lakeside enclave, borrowing from the nearest mountain. They called their resort haven *Speculator.* Having only just been legally incorporated, the Village of Speculator was not yet on the map. That was about to change.

★★★★★

To Slattery's dismay, and Red's delight, the state motor vehicle bureau revoked the boxer's driving license. Five months earlier, in February of '26, Slats had his license temporarily suspended following an early morning smash-up on Genesee Street. Slats initially tried to claim his car had been stolen and that he knew nothing of the crash, but then later admitted he was driving it when the accident occurred. After a few more mishaps—and having been busted trying to falsify an application for a new license—Slats received a one-year suspension.

By early August, he was in Indian Lake getting ready to fight in Albany for the local Lion's Club. Tunney invited Slats to come visit the Osborne Inn, which was only 24 miles away. Osborne and some fellow townspeople built an outdoor training ring similar to the one made for Slattery at Husson's hunting camp. Similarly, it was built up on a platform, like a porch with no walls, so people could see in, but with a slanted roof to protect it from the sun and rain. The structure was positioned adjacent to the shoreline of the calm, shimmering, postcard-perfect Lake Pleasant. Newspapermen, locals and large crowds of affluent day-trippers descended on Speculator to watch Tunney prepare for his championship bout. Earl Husson went to visit one day and, according to his son Gerald, had a conversation with Tunney during which Tunney declared Slattery to be the best fighter he had ever seen, adding that he would be champion one day if he ever took his training seriously.

Jay Tunney, Gene Tunney's son, spent years researching his father's life for his book, *The Prizefighter and the Playwright*, which told the story of Tunney's lasting friendship with George Bernard Shaw. "I'm sure my dad had many conversations with Slattery and saw what a natural fighter he was," Jay Tunney said in 2012. "But I found no mention of it. He may well have advised Slattery against too many women and too much booze, as dad was that type. He believed in total dedication. To chase his dream to become champion he really embraced a Spartan existence."

Tunney selected lighter, faster sparring partners to prepare for Dempsey, Slattery chief among them. Several writers have claimed that Slats knocked Tunney around the practice ring; but Slats' presence is not acknowledged at all in Jay Tunney's book, nor is he mentioned in Tunney's autobiography (*A Man Must Fight*), nor in Jack Cavanaugh's (*Tunney*). Various other accounts of Tunney's time in the mountains likewise make no mention of Slattery. But Slats definitely was in Speculator.

So too was the commissioner of motor vehicles, who came personally to arrange for the restoration of Slattery's license, according to Ted Aber and Stella King's *The History of Hamilton County*. Warned how even the slightest future violation—so much as a fender bender—would result in a severe penalty, Slattery acknowledged the condition and soon was back behind the wheel of his huge Lincoln limousine. One night, Aber and King wrote, Slattery took some friends to dinner at Doak's tavern in Wells, about seven miles south of Speculator. "On their return, the party met up with a lumber truck trailer with wood piled heavily at the front," the authors said. "The vehicle was bobbing and swaying all over the road. As Slattery's car passed, the trailer lurched sideways and knocked a headlight from the prizefighter's automobile. Lumber truck and Lincoln stopped. The two truck drivers proved to be burly bar room brawlers who did not recognize the other driver, but were nonetheless ready for a fight. Remembering the matter of the license, Slattery hesitated. Finally, the bullying got out of bounds. Slattery drew back his powerful fists and knocked both men over a fence and into the Sacandaga River."

It had only been one summer before that Lake Pleasant area tourists came by bus to watch Slattery spar in Indian Lake. Now Speculator was the main event. The Manhattan society crowd, daffy about boxing, arrived by rail, auto, even single-engine seaplanes which splash-landed on the lake. Each day throughout August, crowds flocked to the Osborne Inn, paying fifty cents to watch the late afternoon sparring sessions. Speculator became the place to be that summer. Department store mogul Bernard Gimbel, who owned property in the area, brought all of his wealthy friends. Newspaper columnists came to meet the demands of a public ravenous for the latest crumb of information about the championship fight.

Situated on the eastern shoreline of the lake, on its own small spit of peninsula, the Osborne Inn and surrounding vacation complex (the beachfront and adjoining cottages) became a zoo: gawkers clustered around the ring; autos clogged the main road leading into town; newspapermen, banging incessantly on their typewriters at all hours, took over the hotel restaurant; big shots crowded the lobby to use the telephone, obnoxiously barking buy and sell orders back to their brokers in New York City—the whole scene became too much for Tunney. Though he'd fallen in love with his mountain retreat (Tunney made Speculator his legal residence), the circus atmosphere was more than he chose to bear. He took his meals alone, hiding himself away in Bill Osborne's private office. When he wasn't ducking Slattery's sparring blows, Tunney was busy ducking intrusive reporters and female admirers. The training ring was built not far from a tap room that was always jammed with people; local sheriff Frank "Pants" Lawrence did not enforce Prohibition and, to the contrary, was a frequent patron of the Osborne bar. Lawrence and Tunney became great pals that summer; when Tunney wanted to get away, Lawrence, a legendary hunting guide, would take him on vigorous hikes deep into the woods. Eventually, the Osborne brothers set Tunney up with his own secluded cabin, away from the inn, near the lake, and hidden by pine trees. Tunney made it his personal meditation haven. Rest, an abundance of it, was all part of his routine. His training schedule included long stretches of designated down time during the middle of the day. It was during this time Tunney retreated to his minimalist quarters—the tool-shed-sized dwelling had room for a cot and a desk and little else—and quietly read. He devoured Shakespeare and Shaw and histories of civilization. Jay Tunney says that back around this time, his father had a love affair with nature and was reading the works of Thoreau and St. Francis. As for the rest of his schedule: Up at 5:00 A.M. for roadwork, at least 15 miles (five of them backwards), conducted on the town road leading to Wells and back. Midway through, Tunney would stop on a dime in the quiet of the mountains and practice a special secret punch he was developing for the start of the first round. He'd scamper, halt and unleash, always envisioning Dempsey in the middle of the desolate road. Actual sparring took place later in the afternoons. Tunney liked having Slats in camp. He invited other lighter, faster sparring partners, and wasted no time slugging with any heavies. Tunney punched bags and he swam. He'd row out into the middle of the lake in a canoe, another one of his favorite ways of escaping the masses. Tunney made it work. He felt his training site provided him a perfect means for building both body and mind.

Relaxing one afternoon in his tiny cabin, Tunney got a visit from an enterprising AP reporter, Brian Bell, who had sniffed out the secret location. Tunney invited him in and Bell noticed right away the prizefighter was reading Samuel Butler's *The Way of All Flesh*. Bell engaged him on the topic of literature, figuring he'd start a natural conversation (and that he had a nice angle for a feature story no one else had).

"It's one of my favorites," Tunney said. "Butler had a great influence on Shaw, you know."

Bell kept him talking about books. Tunney was quite content to discuss literature. What happened next changed only the dynamics of the fight, but how it and Tunney would forever be remembered. Bell filed a story that ran in newspapers around the world. In it, he portrayed Tunney as brainy and aloof. Millions of people now perceived him as some kind of dainty snob, not qualities typically associated with a heavyweight warrior. Not that anyone thought Tunney would beat Dempsey anyway, but after the AP story, the idea of a bookworm taking the crown from a man-eater like Dempsey seemed inconceivable. Cartoonist Rube Goldberg drew Tunney sparring with Macbeth. Al Capone called him a pansy.

Meanwhile, at Tom Luther's place in Saratoga, Dempsey was losing patience. He could find no relief from the mobs of fans and writers tracking his every step. He'd once lamented to Charlie Murray that "the next time I train, I'm going to hide in the hills where the crowds can't find me."

Dempsey finished his training in Atlantic City. The title fight would take place mid-September in Philadelphia. Rickard had wanted to stage it at Yankee Stadium. However, Boxing Commission politics complicated the issuance of a state license to Dempsey, so in the end, Rickard moved the fight to a massive, yet barely used, 150,000-seat stadium in the City of Brotherly Love.

Tunney concluded his training in early September in the Poconos. Each day he continued to practice running, stopping and shooting that surprise right-hand smash, and that's just how round one of the long-awaited Dempsey title defense began, with Tunney unleashing his secret weapon. The blow caught Dempsey on the cheek and rattled him. After landing that first punch, Tunney set the tone and proceeded to box circles around the champ. He shocked the world, won the decision and became the new heavyweight champion. The fight at Philadelphia's Sesqui-Centennial Stadium—built as the centerpiece of a summer-long exhibition marking America's 150th birthday—took place in a driving rainstorm. Billy Kelly of the *Buffalo Courier* was there at ringside, pecking at his typewriter while another spectator held a poncho over them.

At least one boxing expert called it right. Harry Greb had sparred with Dempsey, and had also waged war, several unforgettable times, with Tunney. Greb bet a bundle on his old rival to win. One month later, Greb was dead. His heart had stopped during a simple nose operation. Tunney served as a pallbearer at the funeral in Pittsburgh.

Asked around this time what it felt like to be champion, Tunney admitted that it wasn't quite as satisfying as he imagined it might be. "I much preferred the milestones along the way," he said.

For John "Sloak" Slattery, Tunney's victory brought a mixed reaction. Sloak had never stopped believing that one day his son would be champion. But at least now an authentic Irishman wore the heavyweight crown. Sloak had seen his fair share of heavyweight champions come and go. As a lad growing up at the water's edge, he heard the stories of John L. Sullivan. As a young boxer, Sloak admired James J. Corbett. When Sloak was starting his family, James J. Jeffries was champ. He lamented Jack Johnson, loathed Jess Willard. By the time Jack Dempsey came on the scene, Sloak was more interested in his own son's amateur bouts. Tunney would be the last heavyweight titleholder of Sloak's lifetime. He died November 18, 1926, at Our Lady of Victory Hospital. He'd suffered from multiple illnesses, including tuberculosis. The entire family was by his side at the end. Sloak would be missed in the First Ward. By some important measures—such as humor, toughness and genuine friendships—Sloak was a larger figure than even his son.

Slats vowed to sober up and to take his training seriously. The road to redemption approached a dangerous intersection when, in the early spring of '27, Red matched him with a top heavyweight, rough Johnny Risko. Red would say later that he was never more worried about his fighter than on the night Slats climbed into the ring with the hard hitting, much heavier

"Cleveland Baker Boy." A slugger weighing 190 pounds, Risko was near the top of his class. This was no anonymous chump in Albany or Jamestown. Risko's manager, Danny Dunn, had steered him into the national spotlight. Risko was in line to meet Jimmy Maloney or Jack Sharkey, both of whom were in line to fight Dempsey for the right to challenge Tunney. "Don't think for a minute that we're going to let a stripling like Slattery give us twenty pounds and stop us from a chance at a championship," Dunn told the *Courier's* Billy Kelly.

Holed up that winter in Lake Placid, though, Slats astounded everyone by getting into terrific shape—and the contest bordered on slapstick comedy. In a demonstration of speed and skill trumping brawn, Slats jabbed Risko goofy. Wrote Willis Wilber of the *Buffalo Times*: "As Slats' long left flickered in and out, Risko's head bobbed back and forth as if on springs . . . it seemed at times that Slats would poke the Clevelander's head loose from its mooring." Frustrated, Risko fouled, blatantly, and was disqualified midway through the ten-round fight.

Delighted to be relevant again, and flush with winnings, Slats resumed his old habits—parties, jazz clubs, and late hours. He bloated up and sprouted the unsightly paunch of a man twice his age, even as he agreed to an endorsement deal with Fleischmann's yeast cakes. "It's part of my daily diet, giving me pep and vitality," Slats attested in a print advertisement.

Barley and hops were also apparently among his daily staples. "Now 22, Slats showed he had no more sense than he had at 20," Wilber said.

Some people believe Slats became convinced the Grim Reaper was stalking him, and thus deliberately set out to have as much fun as he possibly could. The indignity of performing in tank towns or sharing top billing with former sparring partners didn't seem to bother him. It wouldn't have been thought possible nine months earlier, but even Benny Ross was on the verge of eclipsing Slattery in the light heavyweight rankings.

"Jimmy Slattery is trying to climb back again to a high place in the pugilistic realm," wrote John Kieran of the *New York Times* in April of '27. "Jimmy will be remembered as the brilliant light heavyweight from Buffalo who was so fast that he left his own future behind him."

★ ★ ★ ★ ★

For all of the effort trying to stoke interest in the lower weight classes, Tex Rickard knew the public craved heavyweight action. The whole world waited for the Tunney-Dempsey rematch, which Rickard planned for late summer. To capitalize on interest, a mini-elimination tournament was held that spring. Maloney would fight Sharkey and the winner would meet Dempsey. The winner of that (there was no way it wouldn't be Dempsey) would fight Tunney. The Sharkey-Maloney fight was held May 20, 1927 at Yankee Stadium. As dusk fell, heads bowed in unison as one minute of silent prayer was held for pilot Charles Lindbergh, who was flying solo over the open ocean in an attempt to be the first aviator to complete a transatlantic flight. Among those 23,000 people praying for Lindbergh's safety were Red and Slats who had both come down by train to witness the fight. The next day it was Red praying for his fighter's safe return. Slats had stepped out of their hotel, telling his manager he would only be gone a short while. "I'm just going out to buy a new straw hat," Slats had said.

Three days later, he had not yet returned. Red, distraught but trying to stay calm, feared Slats might have been kidnapped by mobsters or extortionists. He made an agonizing phone call to New York City Mayor Jimmy Walker, asking whether some of his detectives might discreetly make some inquiries. Slats eventually showed up back at the hotel, acting as if nothing out of the ordinary had happened.

"Where the hell were you?!" Red demanded to know. "You had me worried sick!" Slats shrugged him off with some vague answer. He never did explain where he had disappeared to, nor did he even produce a straw hat.

★★★★★

And so, according to several chronicled remembrances of those who knew him, Slats continued to repeat a predictable pattern: extensive benders followed by periods of remorse and sobriety. Why did he abuse alcohol? Why does anyone? Mickey Walker, former welterweight champ and a friend of Slattery's, was someone who battled the bottle. He once put it this way, reflecting on himself: "I drank because I wanted to have fun and there was more fun when I drank."

Fans and writers and boxing elders and people on the street all wanted to know how such a wonderful talent like Slattery could be wasted. Red was constantly on the defensive, covering for his fighter and insisting stories of excessive drinking and outlandish behavior were just that—stories.

Supporting Red's claim is an account provided in the mid-1970s by a former Elk Street tavern owner, Mike Dillon, who purchased his place in the spring of '25 with cash he had won betting on Slattery. "The whole gang used to hang around my saloon playing euchre, so I know," Dillon told Anthony Cardinale, writing a piece for *Buffalo Fan*. "Slats liked the girls, and he didn't like to train. But during his fighting days he never drank much in my saloon. I never saw him drunk during those days."

And then, just when it seemed Slats was going to be banished to boxing oblivion . . . fortune smiled upon him. Early in the summer of '27—with the world fixated on the prospect of a Tunney-Dempsey rematch—the light heavyweight division produced an intriguing series of developments. Berlenbach by then had lost the crown to Delaney, who was matched against McTigue (who considered by the New York Boxing Commission to be the No. 1 challenger). When Delaney abdicated the light heavy throne to compete as a heavyweight, the Boxing Commission announced that, by default, McTigue was champion, provided, that is, he fight the next contender in line—Philadelphia's Tommy Loughran. As soon as the Delaney-McTigue match was scrapped, things got testy. The National Boxing Association— rival sanctioning body to New York, comprising athletic commissions from two dozen states—decried the naming of McTigue as champion. Seizing an opportunity to undercut New York's monopoly on title fights, the N.B.A. announced that promoters in Hartford made a match between the two top-ranked light heavies not named McTigue or Loughran. The N.B.A.'s version of the crown would be contested by Jimmy Slattery and Maxie Rosenbloom. This would not be the first or last time the two organizations would clash. *The Ring*'s Nat Fleischer positioned his magazine as a settler of such disputes, awarding belts, and establishing hurdles to be met before it recognized a champion. Fleischer, in his record books, would put an asterisk next to the 1927 Slattery-Rosenbloom meeting (*advertised as a title bout*). Protective of their turf, New York writers downplayed the N.B.A., but knew the dual-sanctioning situation was a muddle. New England sportswriters, in turn, lambasted as ludicrous the idea that only New York could crown champions.

Regardless, Slats was going to get another crack at a title, at least one recognized in 24 American states, Canada, Mexico and Cuba. He permanently relocated his training headquarters to Speculator, taking up residence at the Osborne Inn. Unlike Tunney, Slats went all in for the commotion and the camaraderie, not to mention the omnipresent flocks of gorgeous ladies circling the premises. But like Tunney, Slats loved the simple charms of

Speculator and the friendly nature of its inhabitants. Tunney was happy to share his training camp and looked forward to sparring regularly with Slats when the time came. For the better part of July, Tunney—with the eyes of the world upon him—made it a point to do no strenuous exercise and only some light shadow boxing, if that. He was content to take long hikes, play tennis or just relax in his hideaway. His master plan was to steadily ramp up training in August so he would reach peak conditioning by mid-September, in time for his return engagement with Dempsey. A new-and-improved, larger ring-pavilion was built in a clearing across the road from the Inn so that the crowds wouldn't interfere with those beachgoers who weren't interested in boxing. Slats didn't mind helping his friend Gene train, but this was his camp now, too. Slattery had his own date with destiny.

Speculator will always be connected with the glamour that followed Tunney there during those glory years. Much fainter are the echoes of Slattery's time. But stories—wee snippets—did pass down from the Osborne brothers to their sons and grandsons and to Jim Pattatucci, who used to tend bar at the Inn before it burned down. In turn, Pattatucci passed a few things down to Neil McGovern, who still runs a hotel near the site. Stories scorched in time paint a picture of Slats bounding through the doors of the Inn with an armful of fancy suits. Or having a chat out in front of Charlie Downey's filling station, ogling the Indian Chief motorcycle owned by Charlie's son Hugh; and then there's the episode with Slats and the burlesque queen. Haven't heard this one? Slats lusted after one particularly irresistible dancing girl, call her Mary—the resort town was crawling with seductresses that summer—and he managed to convince her to join him for dinner. Sometime after dessert, she vanished. After everyone in the hotel was asleep, Slats did a room-to-room sweep, pounding on every door and calling "where's Mary?!" until an Osborne staffer whacked him over the head with a club. Slats denied the incident ever happened, but the tale turns up in Sammy Brindis' *The Saga of Jimmy Slattery*.

Brindis also recalls a sparring session between Slats and Tunney that summer of '27. By mid-August, the pace of Tunney's ring work was accelerating. He and Slats would go full on. "During one furious milling," Brindis wrote, "Slats sent Tunney sprawling through the ropes." Tunney supporters and newspapermen insisted that the champ merely slipped; friends of Slattery say he landed a clean punch. Local villagers took part in the sparring, too. A county worker, Jack Reynolds, went several rounds in the practice pavilion with Slattery. Years later, Reynolds, by that time a prominent area businessman, spoke about his brush with greatness. "Slattery could have been one of the greatest of all time had he taken better care of himself," Reynolds would tell a small Adirondack newspaper. Ludicrously, department store tycoon Bernard Gimbel liked to put on the gloves as well (and there are some who insist he held his own). Tunney did have a regular roster of young preliminary boys brought to camp for him to chew up. The younger sparring partners formed a clique. Slats wanted no part of them. They could see, and they craved, the respect Tunney gave Slattery. Everyone was drawn to Slattery. At times, it seemed, Slats got even more attention than Tunney. This didn't bother Tunney. But it did not sit particularly well with one of the young sparring mates, Billy Vidabeck.

"All the boys spar with one another," Vidabeck groused to his mentor one day. "But Slattery only spars with *you*."

"Well, you're a professional boxer," Tunney replied. "Perhaps you'll get a fight with him one day."

"Let me go with Slattery," Vidabeck pressed. "I don't think he's so hot. I'll show up that shine."

Tunney smiled and strongly advised the kid to watch his step. Slats heard about Vidabeck's beef and shrugged it off. "Don't know why he's so unfriendly."

As Tunney's rematch with Dempsey drew close, the crowds in Speculator grew larger. Some 5,000 people a day passed through. Many were trucked in from the train station in Fonda, N.Y. "Millionaires were so thick underfoot you had to fight your way through them," wrote columnist Bill Corum. Gimbel arranged for special trains that were packed with all of his affluent pals. Visitors came by limousine. Local pilot Clyde Elliott would tote rich guys in his single-engine pontoon craft. The rich had made prizefighting their primary passion. In lightly colored seersucker suits, they gathered around the sparring ring by day and partied in the well-stocked bar all night. And at all times, the hotel lobby crackled with the nonstop clatter of typewriter keys flying as columnists churned out whatever details they gleaned in camp, no matter how seemingly trivial, such was the unquenchable thirst for information related to the championship fight . . . "*Tunney stopped for a rest today and then boxed three more rounds before retiring to his quarters . . . Tunney got a vigorous rubdown . . . Tunney went on a nature hike with Pants Lawrence.*"

Though he had not entered an actual ring in one year, Tunney stayed in ideal shape. However, he was determined not to over-train. His idea of the perfect workout was a long walk through a mountain forest. Lawrence would show the prizefighter his favorite spots. They'd go out looking for an old Indian burial ground and cook a chicken out on an open flame for lunch. In the evenings, tucked among the pines, Tunney read and let the cool breezes and gentle lapping of the lakeshore lull him to sleep by no later than 9:00 P.M. Not Slattery. To him, Speculator was a nonstop carnival. His opponent, Maxie Rosenbloom, didn't seem to be taking their upcoming title match all too seriously, either.

Rosenbloom had a system of training which Slats could appreciate. It was as if the two of them were competing for the distinction of who could have the most fun. Perhaps no boxer in history maintained a more unorthodox, downright ridiculous—although apparently effective—fitness routine than Rosenbloom. The "Harlem Harlequin" would arrive at the Silver Slipper around midnight. He'd toss back a few soft drinks (never anything stronger than a sarsaparilla), scout out some honeys, strike up the band and then dance like a fiend until dawn, finishing off with an 80-block jog back uptown. Some guys boasted about how much weight they could lift; Rosenbloom took pride in the size of the women he could twirl in his arms. Asked how he could possibly get in shape this way, Rosenbloom quipped: "I don't drink, I don't smoke and I don't leave the dames alone."

Early in his career, Rosenbloom knew he wasn't going to be a conventional fighter. His decision to never train too seriously, he said, owed to a 1925 fight in Pittsburgh with Harry Greb. Rosenbloom found himself in a clinch with the veteran. "Take it easy," Greb told him. "I've got a hangover." The younger challenger, sensing a weakness, instead upped the pace, which angered Greb. The ensuing beating was severe. "I figured if this old guy did that to me—with a hangover—then what's the point of being in shape?" Rosenbloom would explain years later.

The rise of Maxie Rosenbloom in the mid-1920s occurred at a time when Jewish fighters dominated boxing. This proud prizefighting heritage traced back to the beginning of the sport. One of the earliest recognized bare knuckle champions in the late 18th century: Daniel Mendoza, a Sephardic Jew from Spain then living in England. He was considered one of the most elegant and scientific boxers in history, never weighing more than 160 pounds. He opened a famous boxing school. Decades later, the core curriculum got passed down to Irish-American Jim Corbett who beat John L. Sullivan by adhering to the finer points of the craft—countering, feinting, ducking, sidestepping, rolling with punches, contorting his body—all tricks invented by Mendoza.

Corbett earned his crack at Sullivan in part by beating Joe Choynski, who was known as one of the hardest punchers of all time. Joe Bernstein was another Jewish slugger. He was an early hero of the Old Garden. Bernstein's father, who sported an Old Testament–style beard, would sit in the corner yelling "hit him in the *kishkes!*" Decades later, all kinds of fans (Irish and Italian alike) at the New Garden were still yelling that phrase when they wanted their man to aim for the stomach. The list of Jewish greats was long. Among the notable names who came before, or during the same time as Rosenbloom, were: Abe Attell, Sid Terris, Lew Tendler, Kid Kaplan, Ruby Goldstein and, of course, Benny Leonard, to whom the saying "pound for pound the greatest fighter of all-time" was first applied.

Like many of these greats, Rosenbloom was a product of New York's impoverished, congested Lower East Side. His father, a cobbler from Russia, moved his family to Harlem, east of Lexington Avenue, where a smaller but no less congested Jewish ghetto had formed. Two writers—Ken Blady (*The Jewish Boxers Hall of Fame*) and Allen Bodner (*When Boxing Was a Jewish Sport*)—have fleshed out some details of Rosenbloom's formative years. Expelled for striking his fifth grade teacher, Maxie spent his early teens in the Hawthorne Reformatory. Rosenbloom could brawl. One day a few other kids in his gritty neighborhood figured they'd test him. After witnessing Rosenbloom fend off three or four other boys, another neighborhood kid, George Raft, joined in. "You should take up boxing," Raft (who would go on to be an actor) told Rosenbloom afterward. "Those fists of yours will get you out of here."

Rosenbloom tried his hand. He went to the Union Settlement Athletic Club where numerous other teenagers had the exact same notion. Hundreds of Jewish boxers earned a living in New York City around the start of the Twenties. As an amateur, Rosenbloom looked like he would not become one of them. He lost all of his early bouts. But a club member, Frank Bachmann, who had been an amateur boxer himself, took Rosenbloom under his wing, showed him a few things, and soon enough, Rosenbloom launched into unbeaten streak that continued well after he turned professional in 1923. Fighting in small Harlem clubs, Rosenbloom, the gifted street fighter, fancied himself a slugger in the mold of Joe Bernstein. That changed at the Pioneer Athletic Club in March of '25. Rosenbloom's opponent that night was a frighteningly powerful puncher from Boston named Joe "Hambone" Kelly. Trading blows at close range with this mauler proved disastrous. Rosenbloom looked like he might end up in a hospital before the night was through. Before heading out for the fourth round, Bachman gave Rosenbloom orders that would change his career: "Use your feet to dance out of range until this guy gets frustrated," the savvy manager instructed. "Wait for an opening. Take what he gives you." Rosenbloom obeyed and turned the tide. In fact, he not only won the decision, but he broke Hambone's nose and knocked out two of his teeth. Rosenbloom realized his true talent was clever boxing. He explained the tactical shift a bit differently. "I wanted to save my face for the *goils*."

In time, Rosenbloom would invent a style of his own, one that would have absolutely appalled Daniel Mendoza. Rosenbloom's wacky arsenal of bizarre techniques came to include an odd, spasmodic twisting motion designed to tie an opponent in knots, and, above all else, his endless tap-and-dodge routine—tap, dodge, tap, dodge, over and over—like a hyperactive child bent on frying the nerves of a younger sibling in the backseat of a car on a long ride. He could become a blur of groping and swiping and poking. He tweaked noses, messed up hair. It's not inconceivable that the Three Stooges copied him.

Rosenbloom developed an open-gloved slap delivered with a flick of his wrist. His objective was not to inflict damage but, instead, to pile up points. Watching Rosenbloom one night, Damon Runyon dubbed him "Slapsie Maxie."

"I always hated to hit hard," Rosenbloom would say. "I don't want to hurt anybody."

"Anyone who gets into the ring with Rosenbloom is slapped with great frequency and moderate vigor," said the *Times'* Kieran.

Make no mistake, though. Few fighters were as vexing in the ring as Rosenbloom. In 1926, he beat Dave Shade, twice. Rosenbloom won decisions that year against Tiger Flowers and Johnny Wilson, both of whom had worn the middleweight crown. The New York boxing establishment came to frown on Rosenbloom's clownish antics. But the N.B.A. recognized his accomplishments in the ring. And so they matched him against

Slattery, another out-of-favor light heavy. One of these two outcasts was going to be the next champion.

A fragment of a legend concerning a stunt Slattery allegedly pulled prior to his championship bout, coupled with a corroborating anecdote supplied in the 1960s by Dr. Louis Kaiser, underscore the *carpe diem* mentality of the fighter and his times. The story begins in Speculator, early one morning, believed to be Saturday, August 27, 1927, which would have been two days after Slats turned 23, and two days before his big fight with Rosenbloom in Hartford. Kaiser was an examining physician with the New York State Athletic Commission during the 1920s, and good friends with Charlie Murray. The two had journeyed to the Adirondacks to visit Slats. They were due to take a train home, but Slats informed them on this morning that he was driving to Buffalo, and invited them to ride along with him in his Lincoln. "But we have to hurry," Slats said. "I have a pressing engagement and can't be late."

In the days before thruways, the route from the Southern Adirondacks to Buffalo involved narrow, winding roads. Slats had the accelerator to the floor the entire time. Jostled and petrified, Murray and the doctor demanded to know what was so important to risk life and limb, but Slats wouldn't say. The harrowing trip left the two older men that much grayer. But they made it home safe. The pressing engagement? Slats needed to make the noon ferry bound for Crystal Beach. That night, at the Crystal Ballroom, a Charleston contest was taking place. Slats really wanted to win. As the story goes, he did.

★★★★★

"There's the boy who is to fight for the championship tonight." Onlookers in downtown Hartford pointed and stared at the tall, handsome young man out for a stroll in their city on the morning of Monday, August 29. Slats had taken a walk to the outdoor stadium, five minutes from downtown, near the banks of the Connecticut River. A large wooden bowl that could accommodate 15,000 people, it was originally built for motorcycle races. Seats were high and steep. Impressed, Slats was feeling confident he would bring a championship back to his city. He seemed to radiate that confidence. All eyes were upon him. The sky was blue. The sun was shining.

Back at the hotel, Red informed Slats there was suddenly talk that the fight would be canceled. The weather bureau was predicting a rainstorm to arrive by nightfall. Slats couldn't believe it. He and Red rushed over to speak with promoters, who informed them that indeed, they were notifying the afternoon newspapers that the fight would be postponed until the next evening.

The weigh-in ceremony went ahead nonetheless. Thomas Donahue, head of the N.B.A., presided. Slats and Rosenbloom were businesslike. It was their third fight together. No antics, no intimidation games.

"Hello Maxie," Slats said.

"How are you Jim?" Rosenbloom replied.

They shook hands and said nothing more to one another. Slats weighed in at 169 pounds, Rosenbloom 168. Gone was the paunch Slats had developed. His body was lean and contoured like a greyhound.

After the weigh-in, Slats went to a local gym and worked out his frustration. Rosenbloom went for lunch. They were both irritated and perplexed. So too were the fans many of whom were beginning to arrive from all over New York State and New England just in time to read the evening papers, explaining that the fight had been postponed. At 7:00 P.M., the rain came. It rained for about one minute. Then the clouds passed. It became clear and cool—a perfect night for boxing.

New York may have been the center of the boxing universe, but boxing was big everywhere. New Englanders were pigging out on ring action that August. On top of the title fight scheduled in Hartford, a pair of rival Boston fight clubs, the Suffolk and the Argonne, each staged multi-bout shows on that same Monday night, which might explain why the Velodrome promoters pushed the fight to Tuesday.

Word of the strange and unexpected delay rattled fans back in Buffalo. The fight was all anyone talked about. *Had something happened? Was something wrong with Slats?* The entire city was on edge. Hard-working folks knew Slattery might break their hearts, but held hope that he wouldn't. Buffalo had another day to find out.

★ ★ ★ ★ ★

With two ear-splitting blasts from her steam whistle, the *S.H. Robbins* eased up the Buffalo River toward a bustling, maze-like stretch of the waterfront known as Elevator Alley. A 500-foot-long freighter, the *Robbins* had come in from Chicago, her cargo hold groaning with 7,000 tons of grain. The three-day haul had started on Lake Michigan, took her up the Mackinac Straits to Lake Huron, then east to Lake Erie by way of the Detroit River. Slowly, she passed under the Michigan Avenue Jack-Knife Bridge. To the right stood the mills operated by Spencer Kellogg Sons & Co.; to the left, an enormous freight house owned by the Great Lakes Transportation fleet. All along Ohio Street were docks and freight sheds, a gauntlet of transshipment activity running from the mouth of the river to its first bend. Murky and shallow, the Buffalo River snaked a sideways W through the First Ward. Up and down the river, some two dozen concrete and steel grain elevators towered over the Ward like sentinels. The largest, Concrete Central, loomed over a U-turn in the river, where it cut back across the neighborhood. The low, straight deck of the *Robbins* was secured alongside. Descending diagonally from the seven-story monolith structure was a narrow chute that was inserted into the belly of the vessel, as if a tremendous metallic insect had lowered its proboscis to feast on an outstretched limb. Inside the chute were buckets fastened to a steam-fired conveyor belt. As the buckets dove down into hold, a gigantic stockpile of crushed wheat fell in on itself, the way beach sand fills in when sifted by cupped hands. When the pile diminished to the point at which automated unloading was rendered unfeasible, tall remnant piles in the corners had to be removed manually. Down into the stiflingly hot cargo hold climbed a crew of about a dozen or so coverall-clad men who used shovels and buckets to load the rest of the grain onto the conveyor belt. After the last dusting of grain had been transferred to the elevator (to be stored and ultimately dispensed into rail cars), the scoopers trudged back to the neighborhood, some stopping by the union hall on Louisiana Street to collect their pay or peruse an inbound freighter schedule. Most of them bee-lined it to one of the many secret and not-so-secret watering holes that dotted these closely clannish blocks. The post-shift ale binge was a regular part of the scooper's life, embedded by rote into the culture.

All but a few of the 100 or so saloons that once filled the waterfront had shuttered at the dawn of Prohibition seven years earlier. A few, such as Quinn's Tavern, stayed open, serving corned beef sandwiches and "near" beer. In place of the saloons there sprung up an equally ubiquitous number of speakeasies, sometimes only half hidden, in the back room of a boarded-up gin mill, or the rear section of a soda shop, or sometimes in a small, secret room in some otherwise ordinary-looking storefront business. Men sent their young sons up to the corner with pails and jugs—"growlers"—to be filled up with beer. In back rooms and front porches, scoopers and other waterfront workers were well on their way. Today was a day to savor.

Buffalo was cool and cloudy on Tuesday, August 30th. It had been the coldest summer on record. The mild temperatures made a scooper's life that much more bearable. The morning *Courier* indicated that Jimmy Slattery was healthy, confident and as puzzled as everybody else by the promoters' decision. The weather for that night looked favorable. Slattery's shot looked to be a go. Could an Irishman from the First Ward be champ by the time this day was over? Optimism was tempered by raw fear. Scoopers and dockworkers analyzed and dissected both the known and unknown variables. *Was Slattery right?* If he was, the thinking went, he'd be champ.

As these important matters were contemplated, the waterfront continued to clang and clatter with activity. Ore hauling ships chugged up the river toward foundries and iron works plants, accompanied by barges and tugs announcing themselves with noisy bells as they came around river bends. Grain—crushed wheat, rye, barley, corn—was loaded continuously into elevators, or emptied from elevators and loaded onto trains which rumbled in every direction. Locomotive horns blew like clockwork. The railroads connected to the grain elevators and coal docks via valuable waterfront tracks owned and operated by the small but mighty Buffalo Creek Railroad. Its line spanned a mere six-mile horseshoe around the inner harbor. The major railroads could not get in and out of their customers' mills without a Buffalo Creek escort. On Ohio Street, near the river, adjacent to seven lines of New York Central freight track, sat massive freight sheds where workers sorted "less-than-carload lots," smaller bundles heading to and from the Midwest. As many as 500 freight cars a day came through carrying crates, boxes, casks, parcels and sacks bound for motorized trucks en route to local businesses. Supplanting all of this commotion and industrial mayhem was the high-decibel clamor of children everywhere, running, skipping, leaping from idle ships and lift bridges into the river, fighting in lots or under viaducts. Baseball games at Lanigan Park lasted all day. Younger kiddies pitched pennies, shot marbles, skipped rope, tossed jacks, chalked out tic-tac-toe games and played hide-and-seek. Older boys shot dice or played cards on Elk Street's wood-planked sidewalks. Young mothers with toddlers chatted in front yards. Teenagers flocked to the silent picture houses. Shea's was showing *Hula*, starring Clara Bow whose adorable short bob hairstyle and sparkling eyes made her an American pet.

Summer's grand finale was unfolding, from the Erie County Fairgrounds to the lakeside beaches. Area residents enjoyed picnics, softball tournaments, auto races, dog shows, waltz contests and concerts. Being the last week before school started, this day marked one of the last fleeting opportunities for a family outing to Crystal Beach. Boats making the 12-mile trip left hourly. Large crowds gathered at the docks at the foot of Main Street. Penned in like cattle, the passengers stood in a sheltered waiting hall, anxious for the arrival of one of the Crystal Beach boats, twin steamers, the *Americana* and the *Canadiana*. Excited, eagle-eyed boys would cry out when one of the boats came into view. Dancing on board began soon after departure. Reaching the smooth waters out past the lighthouse was a cue for Jolly Jack Crawford to strike up his orchestra.

A fast trip to Canada by automobile was officially made possible three weeks earlier with the dedication of the International Peace Bridge, spanning the Niagara River, linking Buffalo with Fort Erie, Ontario. The ceremony, marking the first time automobile traffic would flow freely and directly between the U.S. and Canada, drew the focus of international radio broadcasts which framed the event as a landmark demonstration of two peace-loving nations cementing their alliance. Millions tuned in to hear speeches from British Prime Minister Stanley Baldwin, Canada's Prime Minister W.L. Mackenzie King, U.S. Vice President Charles Dawes and New York State Governor Al Smith. Making it a truly memorable occasion—the attendance of Prince Edward of Wales, heir to the throne, and his younger brother, Prince George, who eventually would become the King of England, but only after his brother abdicated the throne (and despite an acute stuttering problem).

One week prior to the opening of the Peace Bridge, Charles Lindbergh had lured a national radio audience to Buffalo. The world-famous aviator, in the midst of a tour celebrating his transatlantic flight, flew into the recently built Buffalo Airport, one of the first modern facilities of its kind. Lindbergh was met by thousands. A parade was followed by a banquet. Euphoria was the order of the day. Anything was possible. People were on the move. In the First Ward, Irish families pushed further south, to be closer to the steel plants—they could do so now that flooding along the Cazenovia Creek had been mitigated by civil engineers. A century's way of life was fading.

At the Dublin Restaurant on Elk Street, the dinner rush was in full swing. Every table chattered about the fight. The lights of Shea's theater began to twinkle. A brand new theater, The Erlanger, was readying for its grand opening. Special gold tickets were produced. George M. Cohan was set to attend the show, a new musical being polished up before a run on Broadway. On mansion-lined Delaware Avenue, affluent factory owners settled into private clubs for cigars and brandy, perfectly legal because the alcohol had been procured (in bulk and stashed away) prior to 1920. On the 18th floor of the spectacular new Rand Building, the Buffalo Broadcasting Company prepared for its evening programming. In just the past five years, the number of radio stations in the U.S. had increased from about 30 to more than 500. During the same period, the number of American homes to own a radio surged from 500,000 to *six million*. Actors, singers, announcers, technicians and producers took their places. One of the company's flagship stations, WGR, was airing a jazz performance live at the Statler. Anyone trying to find the Slattery-Rosenbloom fight would have been out of luck. It would not be broadcast. Results of the first round would be coming over the wires in a few hours. All across Buffalo, fans waited nervously to find out whether Slattery came through.

About 8,000 people showed up at the open-air arena in Hartford. It was not quite the crowd promoters had prophesized. Slattery, over ten blistering rounds, did not disappoint. He won every round. A haphazardly flailing Rosenbloom failed to land anything resembling so much as a tap.

As Charlie Murray put it, "Slattery did about everything to Rosenbloom that is permissible . . . he jabbed him and stabbed him and hooked him and slammed him until it seemed poor Maxie couldn't continue." So utterly whipped was Rosenbloom that he grumbled afterwards, "I've got a notion to quit this racket." In his dressing room, Slats was surrounded by friends. Red was on a cloud. Slats hopped into the shower, dancing a happy Irish jig, not a mark on his body.

The results came into Buffalo around 11:00 P.M. Newsboys cried it out: "Jimmy Slattery won!"

The First Ward went wild. People poured out of their homes and filled the streets, screaming for joy, laughing and hugging, basking in the shared triumph of one of their own. As the news spread that Slattery had won the championship, the jubilation cascaded into an impromptu parade. Fathers lifted sons on shoulders. Surly dock workers clicked their heels. This would be a night to remember forever. From the rowdy scoopers to the uptown elite, and all over the city of Buffalo, people could not contain their pride. Everyone shared in a taste of glory. Slats was champ.

The New York State Boxing Commission, of course, refused to recognize Slattery as champion. As far as the boxing establishment was concerned, Mike McTigue was the world's light heavyweight champ. Arriving back in Buffalo, Red, clutching some rolled up newspapers containing definitive accounts of Slattery's overwhelming victory, marched into the Boxing Commission's local office to post a bond and to file paperwork challenging McTigue. It was a spirited but entirely symbolic gesture. McTigue was set to meet Tommy Loughran. Slattery would have to get in line.

A few weeks after Slattery's win in Hartford, the attention of the world turned to Chicago. On September 22, 1927, heavyweight champion Gene Tunney and challenger Jack Dempsey met in what could be considered the single most unforgettable bout in the history of boxing. Well before the start of their rematch, both participants and their handlers were apprised of a rule that was known and accepted in New York but bore emphasis: In the event of a knockdown, the deliverer of the lethal blow would not be allowed to hover above his fallen opponent waiting to pounce. He would have to retreat to a neutral corner. If he did not, the referee would not start to count. The rule wasn't controversial, and no one in either camp objected.

That night, before more than 100,000 people jammed into Soldier Field, Tunney outboxed Dempsey for six rounds. But in the seventh, Dempsey knocked Tunney to the canvas. Either forgetting about, or deliberately ignoring, the neutral-corner rule, Dempsey stood over his fallen opponent exactly as he had been warned not to do. Referee Dave Barry refused to start the count. Finally, when Dempsey went to a corner, Barry began to count. Tunney arose at nine. Fight footage suggests he was down at least fourteen seconds. Tunney survived the round and dominated the rest of the fight. He claimed later he could have gotten up at nine even if Dempsey had gone straight to a neutral corner as instructed. Dempsey said afterwards that he was robbed of the championship. Fight fans have argued about it ever since. Not in dispute is the effect the infamous "Long Count" had on Dempsey's popularity, at the time and forevermore. His legend was made—in defeat.

★★★★★

In early October, McTigue met Loughran for New York State's version of the light heavyweight title. Loughran won.

Wrote the *Times*' Dawson: "Two champions for a single class, one with the support of the greatest boxing center in the world, and the other with the endorsement of an Association having jurisdiction over practically every other boxing center in the country, while novel, is not in the best interest of boxing."

Asserting its reach, the N.B.A. held its annual meeting that month in Toledo, Ohio, at which time it admitted the athletic commissions of four additional states—Montana, Arkansas, Colorado and Missouri—and the territory of Puerto Rico. Before adjourning, the body released its official roster of recognized champions, with Slattery topping the light heavies. Within days, the Pennsylvania State Athletic Commission, upon learning Philly's Loughran had been snubbed, promptly reneged on a decision to join the N.B.A. Undermining Slattery's claim to the throne, Big Town scribes denigrated that summer's "elimination tournament" as one to which "the only ones who showed up were Slattery and Rosenbloom." Paradoxically, the schism simultaneously cheapened and buttressed the light heavyweight division at a time when heavyweights were more interesting to more people. All would be sorted out soon enough.

Cognizant that his fighter was in line for a shot at a unified title, Red didn't take any chances. In early November, he matched Slats against Murray Gitlitz, the boxing instructor at Yale University. Slats beat him so severely the ref stopped the bout in the sixth. Three weeks later, Slattery and Loughran signed papers to meet in a 15-round bout at the Garden on December 12. Fans of pure, scientific boxing salivated at the prospect of seeing two master craftsmen match wits. Many writers, down on Slats, saw it differently, predicting that Slats would be knocked out. No one thought the hedonist playboy could go 15 rounds. He never had before. Conventional wisdom: the former boy marvel wasn't half the fighter he once was.

Slats desperately wanted to prove the experts wrong. He rose early for road work, spent afternoons at the gym and evenings at home.

Loughran was similar to Slats in numerous ways—height, weight, reach, technique—yet the two couldn't have been more opposite. Loughran was an altar boy by comparison. He didn't drink, didn't smoke. And he left the dames alone. Loughran's approach to training was meticulous. He wanted to be perfect.

Growing up in South Philadelphia, Loughran knew from an early age he wanted to be a prizefighter. The South Philly of the early 1900s wasn't a rough neighborhood. Most of Loughran's boyhood pals aspired to be policemen. Loughran's dad drove a trolley car. Loughran wasn't a fan of boxing. He couldn't even name a single boxer. Yet, standing in front of a full-length mirror in his basement, practicing his punches over and over until they were just right, Loughran just knew.

When he was 14, Loughran and some friends snuck into the back of a darkened parish hall. A bunch of young men were rehearsing an amateur vaudeville show. The only lights on were above the stage. The boys lurked about, giggling in the shadows. When the troupe's lead performer finished his song, Loughran let go with a loud raspberry. The performers, young men in their mid-20s, gave chase to the brazen interrupters; Loughran allowed himself to be caught. He ended up giving one of his captors a severe beating. The police came knocking on the door of the Loughrans' home on Ritner Street and searched Tommy's room for the brass knuckles they were certain he'd used. "Better watch that boy," one of the officers said to Mrs. Loughran. "He'll wind up in prison for killing somebody with those fists. Either that, or he'll be a boxing champion."

By 16, Loughran found a job working the bellows in a local blacksmith's shop. But he still had the itch. He hit a local fight club and asked to be put on a card. Told he needed a manager, Loughran knocked on the door of a friendly neighbor. Joe Smith had been a professional boxer and liked the boy, and could certainly see he had the determination. Soon, the two were training together in Loughran's basement. Smith would tie the boy's right behind his back so as to force him to rely on his left. "Forget you even have a right," Smith instructed.

Working in the blacksmith's shop by day and training in his basement

at night, Loughran turned pro in 1919. Fights came regularly in local Philadelphia clubs. The seventeen-year-old looked so promising that Smith
brought him to New York City. In '22, Loughran had a memorable bout
with Tunney, who took a razor-slim decision. Loughran would have a prolific series with Greb, losing a couple and winning a couple, too. In June of
'26, Loughran defeated the Frenchman, Georges Carpentier, and later that
summer, in Saratoga, he bloodied Dempsey's surgically altered nose during a public sparring session. Loughran licked a slew of top light heavies,
including Delaney. Later, when Delaney became champion (beating Berlenbach) it was Loughran who was first in line. When the Boxing Commission named McTigue its de facto champion, it had come with a stipulation.
McTigue had to agree to fight Loughran. Before lifting the crown from
McTigue, Loughran nearly was upset in Buffalo against Benny Ross, who
at that time was emerging from the shadow of Slattery and making his own
bid for contention. But Ross couldn't escape Loughran's slashing left, the
primary weapon of any fine boxer.

Ross was able to help Slattery prepare a defense for Loughran's left. Red,
curiously, had Slats on a *light* training regimen when all of the wise boxing folks were prescribing 10 miles and 10 rounds, every day, to get him
ready for a long distance match. Red's strategy was more like 5 miles and 5
rounds. "Jimmy is naturally high strung," Red explained. "Too much work
is the last thing I want to do with a kid like Slats."

Slats notched a few more victories, one in late November against burly
Pat McCarthy, and another laugher in Akron, Ohio, over Joe Lohman. That
night, the Elks Club of Akron held a party in Slattery's honor. Slats telephoned his regrets from his hotel and went to bed.

A few days before Slattery and Loughran met in the Garden, the boxing world mourned the passing of Young Griffo, the cleverest man ever
to climb inside a ring. He was 56. Griffo had spent the better part of the
past two decades living in that doorway on 42nd Street, existing on hand-
outs, often drunk. Griffo would have appreciated the Loughran-Slattery
championship fight.

In one for the ages, two defensive masters gave the Garden fans something special—the referee never once had to break a clinch or prod combatants to mill. Punches unfurled textbook straight; reactions were automatic.
Bodies, heads and hands moved with fluid precision. Spectators roared

with appreciation, not unlike the way baseball purists savor a classic pitcher's duel. Fans knew they were seeing boxing at its prettiest.

Slattery took the upper hand early on, dancing artfully away from Loughran's left, while using his own jab to color Loughran's cheek. Absorbing those jabs, along with the realization that the Buffalo phantom was every bit as fast as advertised, Loughran appeared nervous, and the shouting from his corner likewise suggested panic was setting in. Late in the third round, Slats abandoned his left, causing the ringsiders to suspect he was already arm weary. But what they didn't know was that Slats had badly bruised his left hand, and the pain was so intense each time it connected there was an unbearable burning sensation that raced up his arm and into his elbow.

Sitting in his corner, waiting to go out for the fourth round, Slats gave Red a jolt.

"The left's gone," Slats said matter-of-factly.

Red looked like he was about to have a heart attack. Slats stayed calm and upbeat.

"Don't worry Red," he told his manager before the bell to start the fourth. "I can play around with the right."

Essentially, Slats was saying he thought he could beat Loughran with one hand tied behind his back. And he almost did. By the 10th round, Slats looked to be well ahead on points and on his way to a decisive victory. To conserve energy for a furious finish, Slats coasted through rounds 11, 12 and 13—which proved to be a mistake. Loughran seized the opportunity to stage a comeback.

New York scribe Ed Hughes called the verdict "about the closest of close decisions" one could get. It went to the Philadelphian.

Slats took the news with a beleaguered smile and congratulated Loughran. The crowd jeered the verdict loud and long, according to newspaper accounts. Red, who thought an undisputed title was in the bag, was on the verge of a nervous breakdown.

Still, the fight had been an absolute classic. Days later, the heads of both sanctioning bodies wrote Slattery consolation letters, each offering the same dual message of encouragement: Firstly, well done; and second, *take care of yourself.*

Back in Buffalo, fans were devastated. For many it was one of the first times ever listening to a fight on the radio. Longtime Buffalo resident

Robert Noonan recalled standing in a Bailey Avenue radio store huddled with a group of fans. Noonan, nine at the time, had gone to the Varsity Theater with his father, who played piano there. While his dad was busy providing a live soundtrack to the silent picture, Noonan ducked out and ran next door. "I knew the store had the fight on," Noonan recalled at age 97. "We stood and listened to the outcome. People were upset. My father was a big boxing fan. I ran back to the theater and told him Slattery lost. I can still remember how heartbroken he was."

One of the most devoted Slattery fans in all of Buffalo was James Monohan, a loyal First Ward lad who went to great lengths to watch his idol perform. Monohan was among a group of four youths who hopped a freight car April 30, 1928, headed for the New York City area. Slattery was matched in Newark, N.J., against Tony Marullo. The unhittable will-o'-the-wisp was back with a vengeance on this night. Slats seemed to be a man on a mission in handing Marullo, once a top light heavy, a considerable pasting. Monohan was not there to see it.

Somewhere near Schenectady, N.Y., the train had passed under a low bridge which struck and killed the seventeen-year-old. Slats reacted to the upsetting news by promising to arrange for two dozen or so youngsters to attend his Madison Square Garden rematch with Loughran being planned for the end of June. New Yorkers were still talking about their first beautiful battle. With Dempsey officially retired, a Slattery-Loughran return engagement looked to be among the top drawing cards of the summer. Slats would have taken every kid in the neighborhood to the Garden if he could have figured out a way to pull it off. Not that he could have possibly been more popular in the First Ward, but Slattery's generosity made him all the more of an endearing personality. When he showed up at the barbershop, children came running. Even if 100 kiddies filed into an ice cream parlor when Slats was buying, he stood there for as long as it took until each and every one of them got a treat. He was always among the first and largest contributors to the Catholic Charities drive around Easter and Mayor Schwab's Shoe Fund around Christmas. People talk about Slats throwing wads of crumpled bills out of his car window as children ran alongside, but his giving could be much more subtle. If someone needed a medical bill paid, or a delivery of coal during the freezing cold winter, Slats handled it without asking questions. They say Slats was a sucker for a sob story. If a hard-luck gambler concocted a tale of a sickly child, Slats, regardless of whether he suspected the story to be untrue, would have helped the guy out. Because he liked to, and because he could.

Money did not matter to Roberto Duran, wrote biographer Christian Giudice in 2006. "People did." Slattery was the same way. He treated money as if he *disliked* it, trying to rid himself of it as quickly as he could. He spent to excess on himself as well. When he purchased a new automobile on a whim, he'd give away his old one to a neighbor whom he knew could use it.

The Loughran rematch was expected to bring a rich payday. Ten days before the bout, scheduled for June 28, Slats defeated Marullo once again, this time in Buffalo. In a sparring session preparing for Loughran, Slats threw his left and struck the top of his practice foe's head. Doctors said it wasn't broken, but Red scratched Slats. "We did that once," Red said of Slats fighting Loughran with a bum hand. "Not again." The rumor at the time was that Slats agreed to fake the injury so Rickard could push the fight off to later in the summer, thus allowing him to hold it at Yankee Stadium, and to draw a bigger gate. Red firmly denied this. They wanted the title shot. As decreed by the New York State boxing authorities, Loughran was contractually obligated to fight Slats for the title in New York on June 28, 1928; after that, there was nothing to force the light heavyweight champion to give Slats another shot. The rematch never happened. Slattery and Loughran would not fight again.

Although he would not step inside a ring for the rest of the summer, Slats still found a way to shine. Growing up, Slats pitched and played second base in the Lanigan playground league. Throughout his heady climb to the top of his profession, Slats played for the Snyder's cigar store team in the Buffalo Municipal Amateur Baseball Association, or for the Indian Lake team. In the spring of '28, a highly competitive South Buffalo softball league (run by the American Legion, Post No. 721) admitted a new team organized by Skitsy Fitzgerald and sponsored by Burns Brothers clothing store. Skitsy put together a crackerjack squad, anchored by his two best pals, Joe Hickey and Slats, who was by then converted to a power-hitting centerfielder. The team was built to make a run at a Rich Dairy squad that had dominated the league since its inception in 1923. As it turned out, Burns Brothers and Rich's won their respective divisions and thus met in a three-game championship series held in early September at Cazenovia Park.

Crown jewel of the burgeoning South Buffalo section, "Caz" had a splendid ballfield complex carved into a creekside meadow. On the back of two Skitsy Fitzgerald singles, Burns Brothers won a taut game one; Rich's took the second game on overwhelming pitching. The stage was now set.

Nearly 9,000 spectators formed a complete ring around the diamond on a gorgeous Indian summer evening. In the third inning, the game still scoreless, Slats strode to the plate. Two batters had been retired in order. The crowd roared for Slattery to lace into one. Slats swung violently at the first two pitches he saw, whiffing on both. A loud-mouth yelled something scornful. Slats turned red-faced and squared up for the next pitch. He swung with all of his might and smashed one over the leftfielder's head. The ball plopped down in the middle of the pulsating throng, and by the time it was retrieved, Slats was home with the game's first run. Later in the seventh, he crushed a grand slam to seal the championship. His most fervent admirers had cheered for him to do it. And sure enough, he had come through.

NINE

The Dame

ALTHOUGH SLATTERY WAS NO LONGER embraced by sportswriters as God's gift to boxing, he was still idolized in his hometown and remained in the conversation as far as top light heavyweights angling for a shot at the title. But new faces were bobbing up every week. The latest sensation was James J. Braddock, 23-year-old pride of North Bergen, New Jersey. Braddock's surprising second-round knockout of mighty Iowan Tuffy Griffiths caught the attention of New York fans and landed him on the cover of *The Ring Magazine* in early 1929.

Slattery was sinking. His final performance of 1928 was a disgrace. Instead of easily defeating Chicago's Jimmy Mahoney, Slats slogged through ten taxing rounds with his mouth wide open and lungs heaving. His blinding speed was gone. Now he dragged his feet around the ring as if they were chained to cinder blocks. His timing was off, too. The punches he landed were ineffective. When Slattery was declared the victor, the Aud reacted with a low, confused grumble; most spectators assumed he had lost.

Buffalo was awash with tales of Slattery's depravity—staggering from cafe to cabaret, socializing with notorious characters and lewd women, getting tossed out of the Big House by bouncers fed up with his belligerence. Slats didn't have much time to prepare when he found out late that snowy winter of '29 he would meet Braddock at the Garden. Only his boxing future was on the line, and yet the bout's importance barely seemed to register with him.

On March 4, 1929, Slats took on Len Darcy of Grand Rapids, Michigan; a six-round tune-up at the Aud to get him ready for the hard-hitting Braddock one week later. Slats took the decision. Most people figured he would head off to Speculator and lay low.

Braddock trained at Stillman's Gym on Eighth Avenue near the

Garden. Mornings began with road work in North Bergen. One morning, Braddock was jogging up a steep hill alongside a quarry. As he turned to start around a downward bend, he witnessed a frightening explosion. Some dynamite had accidentally been set off in a spot he had passed only moments before. Four workmen were killed in the blast.

Braddock's training was going perfectly, if for no other reason than the fact that he had not just been blown to smithereens. Slattery's preparation, on the other hand, was a disaster. Brindis, in his 1940 bio, places Slats on the roof of a New York City taxi, guzzling champagne, on the eve of the match. If true, that's not even the half of it. A hangover was one thing. Red had to tackle bigger problems. His fighter was missing.

One written account places Slattery at a South Buffalo house party a few days after the Darcy tune-up. Kay Griffin, then 24, recalls her brothers attending that bout, and being surprised to see Slats at the party, considering he had an important fight looming (according to author Thomas Murphy, Kay's son). As he tells it, Kay and her two friends, Jean and Marion, ascended the snow-covered front steps of a large red brick home on McKinley Parkway. The heavy oak door opened and there she found Jimmy Slattery, grinning, dark hair parted in the middle, his shirt and tie disheveled, a drink in each hand. As he stumbled boorishly across the living room, Slats steadied himself on the arm of one of the newly arrived guests—Kay's friend, Marion.

Several days later, Marion's anxious mother started asking around. Had anyone seen her daughter?

Meanwhile, Red had no idea where Slats had disappeared to. He eventually got a phone call from Mayor Schwab. The police chief in Elkhart, Indiana, had given Buffalo's mayor a courtesy call. "His men arrested Slats and some dame after a barroom brawl," Schwab reported, instructing Red that he needed to go there, pay Slats' fine and make whatever additional restitution might be required. Apparently, while in custody, Slats had proclaimed, "I'm the former light heavyweight champion of the world!" to a group of policemen who had been ready to trump up charges to include a violation of the Mann Act. At Schwab's imploring, the charges were limited to vagrancy and public intoxication. The city was soon buzzing with the rumor that Slats had been picked up in Elkhart, a railroad hub en route to Chicago. In some versions of the Midwest misadventure, Slats and his female friend were out riding the rods with a pack of hobos.

Red collected his fighter, unshaven and reeking of alcohol. Mayor Schwab dispatched a city detective to pick up the girl. When the girl's mother came to fully comprehend the shame that had been brought upon their cottage, she ordered her daughter be sent away to a convent. But before you picture the stone-cloistered hilltop retreat from *The Sound of Music*—here are a few words on the Home of the Good Shepherd: Run by Roman Catholic nuns, the facility took up an entire city block and was surrounded by ten-foot brick walls topped with barbed wire. Dozens of wayward girls were remanded here indefinitely, wards of the Diocese, doomed to a life stuck in a steam-belching laundry facility where every linen, vestment, cloth, sheet and towel from every church, hospital and orphanage in the Diocese was sent to be laundered. They toiled at large vats and long tables in sack cloth uniforms and were not permitted to talk, according to Ray Meegan, a Buffalo detective who had been tasked with dropping the girl off after her mortified mother signed the order. (Meegan's story was repeated over the years and included in Murphy's book.) If indeed a young woman had the misfortune of a chance run-in with free-spirited Jimmy Slattery, he was probably better off not knowing what had become of her.

Slattery's zeal for the nightlife seemed glamorous when he was on his way up. His attitude—conquer as many females as hours of the day permitted—was cheered. But his charm was wearing off.

"Reports from Buffalo state that Slattery is in fine shape and predict dire things for Braddock when they meet," one New York newspaper wrote a few days prior. Retired lightweight champion Benny Leonard was assigned to cover Slattery's comeback. In a syndicated column published on the day before the fight, Leonard predicted Slattery would defeat Braddock. Leonard, citing people close to Slattery, declared the Irishman to be in top condition. Odds makers had Slats as an 8-to-5 favorite. Indeed, for most of the fight, Slats held a slight advantage over Braddock. His famous speed and cunning, so lost of late, were on display for more than 12,000 Garden fans. One Braddock biographer described the fight as an "all-out war." Slats could not have been less prepared for a ten-round boxing match and yet, somehow, he managed to leave an impression on Braddock that lasted the rest of his life. Prior to the bout, Braddock's manager Joe Gould informed him that Slattery was a nifty boxer, but that he didn't hit too hard. After Slats tagged Braddock in the third round, the Jersey boy "thought the lights at the Garden had fallen on my head," he would say years later. Braddock would also recall failing to land many blows in the early rounds. "I was making foolish passes at a 'now you see it, now you don't' sort of wraith," he would admit.

Benny Leonard was sitting ringside, right off Slattery's corner. As the fight wore on, Leonard was barking out orders as if he were Slattery's chief second. "Step in and break his lead!" Leonard cried.

But then Braddock turned the whole fight on one punch that was delivered with one minute to go in the seventh round. The hard right smashed Slats under the heart, and it really hurt him. Though he cleverly defended himself during the eighth—Leonard screaming at him the whole time—Slats was clearly distressed.

Gasping in his corner before coming out for the ninth, Slats made an appeal to Red.

"Tell that sonofabitch Leonard to shut up," he huffed. "I'm trying to stay ten rounds with this guy."

One minute was not enough recovery time. Slats limped out for the ninth, his head clear but his body physically exhausted. Braddock pursued him. Slats kept away. Braddock's eyes nearly popped out of his head as he sensed victory was at hand. He chased Slats from one corner to another, and finally caught up with him. Hooks flew, perhaps two dozen in all, right, left, right, left. Slats bravely stood up to them, his arms crossed in front of his face, with just his battered forehead and bloodshot eyes peeking out. He finally dropped to the canvas, but was back up at the count of four. Referee Lou Magnolia stopped the fight, stepping between an incoming blow and helpless Slats.

"He sold his boxing birthright for a mess of good times," a wistful Ed Hughes, once a great admirer, wrote of Slats the next day.

As far as the boxing establishment was concerned, Slattery was washed up at 24.

The Braddock defeat was a turning point in how even the most devoted Slattery fans viewed their hero. A slow, deliberate plodder like Braddock should have been easy pickings for even an out-of-shape Slattery. After the bout, Tommy Loughran came by the dressing room at the Garden. Slats, beyond dejected, talked about quitting.

"Listen Jimmy," said the light heavyweight champion. "There are about

100 men right now that you can knock over and get an average of $3,000 each for doing it. Where are you going to get that money anywhere else?"

A small cadre of fans met Slats at the train station when he arrived back in Buffalo. His take from the Braddock fight was around $10,000. Slats had no other funds stashed away. It was disturbing enough, the trouble he found in Elkhart but even more so that Red had to pony up the dough to get him released.

These were some downcast days for the usually chipper lad. But he soon cheered up. As Sloak used to say, there would be other times.

★★★★★

Slats didn't fight all summer. He partied at Crystal Beach, the festivities ultimately interrupted by one particularly sad event: Almost one year to the day of the glorious Burns Brothers softball championship, the team was tragically reunited—to bury fellow player Joe "Bay" Hoffstetter, killed along with some other neighborhood youths in an automobile crash on a desolate Fort Erie road between the beach and the Peace Bridge.

At the end of September, Slats officially hit the comeback trail, again, vowing to take his profession seriously. First order of business: a tune-up at the Aud against Michigan whipping boy Len Darcy. Next up was Maxie Rosenbloom, for the fourth time, in Philly.

Slats didn't train properly. In a stunning metamorphosis, he went from finesse boxer to ugly barroom brawler. Few hometown fans had bothered to come down. No one would have believed it. Slats, on some level adapting to the challenge of fighting a walking maelstrom, wrestled and held, and threw cheap rabbit punches. This was Rosenbloom's type of fight. He grabbed Slattery's arm with one glove, and used the other to work over his ears the way a pizza maker kneads dough. Neither the referee nor the fans seemed to mind when Rosenbloom rough-housed. But when Slats played cheap it seemed almost doubly noticeable—Slats was called out by the ref and razzed by the crowd, as well.

Rosenbloom, who had lost the first three fights to Slattery, finally won a decision. The Harlem playboy was on his way to being considered first in line for a title shot.

The local Philadelphia papers were not kind to the Buffalo has-been.

The Evening Ledger: "Rosenbloom administered quite a trouncing."

The Enquirer: "Maxie won because he was the only one who made any real effort to punch."

The Public Ledger: "Trickster stuff, without sound physical conditioning to back it up, could not win for Slattery."

When Slats got back to Buffalo, there was no one waiting to greet him.

The light heavyweight division, indeed all of boxing, was in a transitional phase. Tex Rickard's sudden death at the start of '29 capped the golden era of boxing as definitively as Rickard's "Million-Dollar Gate" in '21 had kicked it off. Gate receipts for the summer season were abysmal. New taxes on tickets weren't helping matters, either. Charges of corrupt influences taking hold began to rise after Rickard's money man, Mike Jacobs, took control of the Garden. But Jacobs, as Rickard would have put it, "kept the kettle boiling."

Fans demanded fresh faces. The heavyweight class—that's where the action was. Many of Slattery's old light heavyweight rivals—such as Loughran and Stribling and now Braddock—had moved up. The division was wide open. New light heavies were coming up the ladder. New York State organized a tournament with the aim of finding someone to challenge Rosenbloom for supremacy. Slattery wasn't even in the mix. No one paid much attention. Americans had other things to worry about in October of 1929.

The Wall Street Crash struck like an economic tsunami. During the preceding build-up years, in the mad scramble for a piece of the boom—in autos and radios and other goods—shares listed on the New York Stock Exchange rose from 113 million in 1925 to more than 1 billion in 1929, a largely unsupervised speculative trading frenzy fuelled by greed, unchecked optimism and borrowed money. Omens that it would all fall apart—off-the-charts margin-loan levels, European banking woes, a bursting of the Florida real estate bubble, shoeshine boys giving out stock tips—led wealthy insiders to start cashing out, spurring a trickle that grew into a tidal wave that hit with full force on Thursday, October 24, 1929: "Black Thursday." The next day, a bank-led buying spree restored calm, but only momentarily. The panic selling resumed on October 29 ("Black Tuesday") when an estimated $10 billion in share value—or twice the value of all the money in circulation in the U.S.—sold off on the floor of the NYSE. By 5:00 P.M. that afternoon, millions of Americans were wiped out. Cataclysmic ripples—a grinding cascade of bank failures—would plunge the world into the financial abyss. Folks tightened their belts and prepared for tough times. They had no idea.

Considering the market crash and Slattery's plummeting stock, it would not have seemed possible that the Q.A.C. could match Slats at the Aud against Rosenbloom and attract more than maybe a few thousand people. Not only did the pair's fifth meeting draw well, it was a total sell-out; every single ticket for the late November event was purchased in advance. It was a first. Even some of Slattery's most monumental battles had not completely sold out. On the night of the match, some 2,000 fans assumed that, as usual, there would be some remaining tickets available at the door. Hundreds crowded around the box office window and were turned away. But now they could not leave. Hundreds more had crammed in behind them, creating a wall of bodies trapped inside the lobby.

All around the building, fans were scampering about, asking for tickets, casing out entrances and climbing the roof. A group of kids had the ingenious idea of sliding down a coal chute that led into the basement of the Aud. About a dozen had taken the plunge before it dawned on them that the door to the dank and dusty coal bin was locked.

Back in the lobby, fans were stuck. The crush of the mob became unbearable. Without warning, the people closest to the main doors were compressed so hard into an adjoining glass partition that it shattered into pieces, with a heap of bodies toppling through. A full stampede followed. Word quickly spread that the mob had broken down the doors, which sparked a mad scramble of emboldened gate crashers streaming toward side and back doors, muscling past police and Aud employees. Reserve police who rushed to the scene to quell the chaos didn't do much good, although they did end up rescuing the group of boys who had been trapped in the coal chute.

Although most people did not know, Slats had worked hard for this one. Red no longer demanded very much. "Just train for three weeks," he said. "Then you can do what you want."

Rosenbloom and his slamming, slapping, smothering style of an attack was no longer laughed at in the New York salons. The stamina he displayed in his swarm of relentlessness had to be respected. During the first two rounds, Rosenbloom showed why he was the top-ranked light heavy;

Slattery demonstrated why he hadn't been invited to the New York State tournament. Once again, Slats abandoned fundamentals and resorted to roughhouse tactics. For a few rounds it looked like a contest to see who could land the lowest blow. The feverish mob seemed to fancy an old-fashioned street fight and roared them on. All possible dirty ploys came out. Knees and elbows; head-butts; thumb gouging; Slats essentially became a pro wrestler. Repeated warnings from exasperated referee Lou Magnolia were ignored. Fed up, Magnolia stopped the fight for a moment, called the two together and amended his opening instructions. "Okay guys, have it your way," he said. "Foul all you want—I won't stop you."

Rosenbloom had the edge heading into the stretch. That's when the Slattery of old showed up. To the delight of fans, Slats had the legs working, the toes bouncing and the jab pumping. Over the final two rounds, Slats boxed the daylights out of Rosenbloom. He had turned in a swift, decisive rally to close out the proceedings. Slats won the decision. Rosenbloom was certain he carried more rounds, even with the final two clearly going to Slattery. He threw a tantrum and cried hometown bias although no one ever explained why he ever agreed to fight Slattery in Buffalo in the first place, a risky proposition with a New York-sanctioned light heavyweight title shot at his doorstep. Rosenbloom would claim afterwards that he was threatened at gunpoint by Buffalo thugs. Red blew his top at that outlandish charge. He countered that if anything, it seemed more likely that Rosenbloom came to Buffalo, placed a large wager—and took a flop. Either way, Rosenbloom's stock plunged.

Practically out of boxing just a few months prior, Slats suddenly was back in the limelight.

★★★★★

On the day after Christmas, some sorority girls from one of Buffalo's top performing arts academies held a formal dance at the Statler. A student orchestra was set to play starting at 10:00 P.M. Slats arrived early, decked out in a tuxedo, his hair slicked back. He was feeling on top of the world again.

Immediately, the prizefighter became fixated on a vivacious nineteen-year-old blonde. The aspiring young singer was Elizabeth Pendergast, daughter of a prominent Buffalo businessman. Her friends knew her as Betty. The young beauty knew nothing about boxing, but she and Slats shared a love of the popular songs of the day. Her favorite was "Has Anybody Seen My Gal? (*"Five foot two, eyes of blue . . ."*)

Drawn by her spark, Slattery could not peel himself away. Both would say later that it was love at first sight.

TEN
—
BATTLE OF THE CENTURY

FOLLOWING THE UNTIMELY DEATH of Tex Rickard, the responsibility of authoring *The Ring Magazine*'s annual rankings in January 1930 fell to Jack Dempsey. Dempsey's pick for the number one light heavyweight: Maxie Rosenbloom.

Despite the prestigious endorsement, Rosenbloom wasn't officially recognized as champion. As far as New York State was concerned, no titleholder existed. Tommy Loughran, the previous champion, had relinquished the crown to go compete in the heavyweight scramble in the wake of Gene Tunney's retirement. When the Boxing Commission went to loosely arrange a four-man elimination tournament, Rosenbloom's name was, naturally, at the top of the list.

Rounding out the other three slots were Yale Okun, George Courtney and Lou Scozza.

A handsome Italian Adonis from Buffalo's West Side, Scozza had bruised his way up the ladder, quietly toiling in the shadow of Jimmy Slattery. For Scozza to finally earn acclaim—to be firmly in the contenders' mix when Slats was left out—was nothing short of remarkable.

Okun fell by the wayside, losing in lopsided fashion to Rosenbloom.

Rosenbloom, as has been explained in the previous chapter, blew his tournament spot and upended the Boxing Commission's configuration by dropping that ten-round decision to Slats in Buffalo.

All of which meant that, at the dawn of a new decade, Slats wasn't washed up after all; he was going to get his fourth crack at a title. He would face the winner of the semi-final held at Olympia Stadium in Detroit between Scozza and Courtney. Strange, how that fight turned out.

Courtney, known as the Tulsa Cowboy, kept hitting below the belt. Each time, Scozza stoically fought on, while Courtney got off with a warning from the referee. In the fifth round of a fight Scozza was winning, Courtney flung a fourth low blow. Scozza, crippled with pain, could not continue. Courtney was disqualified and Scozza was declared the winner.

The light heavyweight championship landed squarely in Buffalo's lap. Slattery would meet Scozza at the Aud—two native sons vying for the title, an almost too-good-to-be-true turn of the wheel. And it was all about to fall apart unless some bitter, interconnected rivalries could be settled in a hurry.

Leading the way, Charlie Murray and Billy Kelly agreed their Queensberry Athletic Club would co-promote the bout with the Crescent Sports Club, a relative upstart run by Grant Quale and Hugh Shannon, which held the rights to promote Scozza's fights in Buffalo. Fifty percent of total gate receipts would be divided between the two clubs. The other half of the haul would go to the two fighters. Here's where things got tricky.

Red demanded 30 percent. Scozza's manager, Bert Finch, a longtime nemesis of Red's, insisted on nothing less than 25 percent. Negotiations dragged on through the holidays. James Farley, chairman of the Boxing Commission and state Democratic Party kingmaker, called for a sit-down at the Statler. Either sign the contracts, Farley told the managers, or he would pick another two boxers to fill the slots. Red refused to budge, arguing that Slattery was the greater draw. Finch, knowing that Slattery desperately wanted the fight, held his ground. Emotions ran high. Finally, Finch, under pressure from Farley, caved in and accepted 20 percent.

On January 3, 1930, the papers were signed and a date was chosen. The 15-round affair would be held on February 10th. The mighty Gotham scribes yawned and did what they could to downplay the absurd little upstate title bout that didn't have Maxie Rosenbloom in it. Buffalo dubbed the fight "The Battle of the Century."

The factions were neatly drawn: Queensberry Club against Crescent; the Irish First Ward versus the Italian West Side; Red Carr v. Bert Finch; Skitsy Fitzgerald and Joe Hickey v. Doo Doo Parisi and Joe Spero . . . well, okay, maybe there was no real rivalry between the sets of trainers. But the fight was still 30 days off. Certainly some animosity had boiled over during the contract finalization. Finch and Scozza came to resent the Slattery camp for ignoring them over the years. Slattery's indifference had stung during a time when Scozza was still trying to crack the upper echelon, and when a match with the superstar would have meant everything. Now that Scozza had made it to the top—and could provide Slats with a boost—the Irishman was overheard telling people, "I want Scozza."

During Slattery's rise over the decade, Scozza was often lurking nearby, like some seemingly insignificant yet ultimately pivotal character in a mystery novel. When Slats sold papers at Main and North Division, Scozza, one year younger, sold them up the block on Main and Tupper. When Slats was breaking into the game, Scozza was just being bitten by the bug, poring through boxing magazines and religiously taking his spot in the bleachers on Monday nights with the rest of the "dollar boys." When Dempsey came to Buffalo and pulled Slats on the Loew's stage to officiate his sparring exhibitions, Scozza was one of the boys who got to go a few rounds with the champ. On the night Slats knocked out Frankie Schoell, Scozza made his professional debut in the curtain raiser. On the day of Scozza's second pro fight, his path to the Aud crossed a parade going up Main Street—it was for Slats, just back from New York City after defeating Jack Delaney for the second time in five months.

Some similarities between Slats and Scozza existed. Both were idolized in their neighborhoods, and both stayed connected to their upbringing by having their best buddies work their corners. At the moment, both fighters also had girlfriends with the same name. Slattery was seeing Elizabeth "Betty" Pendergast. Scozza had just gotten engaged to Betty Trippi.

Some of the differences between the boxers were quite stark. Slattery was a purebred. Scozza had to be taught—not much came naturally. But while Slats disliked training, Scozza worked at his craft tirelessly. And he lived clean.

On Sunday, January 5, Slattery, determined to do some clean living himself, set off for the Adirondacks. He would spend a few weeks at the Lake Placid Club, getting plenty of rest and light outdoor exercise, sort of a limbering-up phase preceding the more rigorous boxing phase that would take place in Speculator—in the outdoor ring in the dead of winter. Jarring mountain air had been a beneficial tonic before. But now Slats would be training in sub-zero temperatures.

Scozza's camp was established at a farm 40 miles southeast of Buffalo in hilly, rural Delevan, N.Y. Frankie Schoell would be chief sparring partner and personal coach. Finch would commute back and forth. Schoell had been tutoring Scozza ever since the Italian lad first turned up at Finch's Gym. Not surprisingly, Scozza got right to work—early morning jogs, followed by wood chopping, and then afternoons sparring at a gym in Delevan which had a small boxing scene. Meanwhile, Slats was jogging around

Mirror Lake in the mornings and skiing all afternoon. He was having a ball, with downhill speed sufficing as his stimulant of choice. It was evident to the people close by—Red, Skitsy, some of the hotel guests, *Buffalo News* reporter Frank Wakefield—that Slats was hunkering down and taking his sobriety seriously. He spent his nights in the club's private bowling alley. But Red did notice at least one troubling development, something no manager ever really wanted to see: Slats was falling in love.

He spent hours writing letters, and Red knew they weren't all headed to his mother. Then one day, Slats disappeared—he'd hired a pilot at a flight school in Albany to shoot him over to Buffalo to visit Betty for an afternoon. She was thrilled. Her parents were not. James J. Pendergast, a senior executive at the Seneca Washed Gravel Corp., didn't want any men whatsoever calling on his daughter; that a notorious playboy prizefighter was taking interest was his worst nightmare. He wasn't in the most cheerful state of mind right then, either. Like many wealthy men, Pendergast had just become a lot less wealthy. The Crash had practically ruined him, and his company was struggling as orders and receivables came to a sudden halt. Slattery would not have appreciated being told by Mr. Pendergast to stay away from his daughter.

Considering his work ethic and adherence to the old book of boxing wisdom, it's unlikely Scozza was able to steal any time with his sweetheart during camp. But a special visitor did call on John Bowers' farm—Jack Dempsey himself showed up. He hung around for two hours, giving Scozza some pointers and posing for some pictures. The two fighters had become friendly a few summers earlier, when Scozza fought Dave Shade, crouching conqueror of Slattery. At the time, Shade was part of Dempsey's Saratoga training camp. Shade's manager, Leo Flynn, was handling Dempsey then. Watching Scozza give crafty Shade a tough fight, Dempsey had taken an immediate interest in the Italian's career, and the two had stayed in touch. It was a major confidence boost for Scozza, who grew up following the exploits of the champion. Just to spar one round with Dempsey as a youth was the thrill of a lifetime—but now Dempsey was throwing his support behind Scozza ahead of the big showdown. That meant everything to Scozza. He had been seeking respect for as long as he could remember. His quest stretched back to the days when fans at the Aud used to boo him, and before that, to when his father harassed him about his chosen profession, and even further back, to when fellow newsboys slighted him in the streets.

Louis Scozzaro was born on Trenton Avenue near the gritty Gas House tenements. His parents, Carmela and Phillipo, were poor Sicilian immigrants. Phillipo Scozzaro found work as a cement finisher. Lou went to public school and sold papers. He had a regular arrangement with his friend, meek Tony Lamonto. They partnered on a bundle and sold them on separate corners, splitting the proceeds at the end of the evening rush. One rainy night, Lou met his friend and noticed he was crying. Another newsie, Bobby Tracey, had punched him off his corner. Tracey was already a promising amateur boxer and also a friend of Lou's. But Lou called him out on the disrespectful treatment afforded his partner and it wasn't long before the two of them hopped to it behind the Gayety Theater. The pair battled for thirty ferocious minutes until Tracey declared he'd had enough.

"Hey Lou," Tracey beckoned. "You handle those fists pretty good. Why don't you become a fighter?"

That wasn't happening. Lou's dad would never allow it. He was pushing instead for Lou to get a full-time job so he could start pitching in even more with household expenses. Lou bounced around from one unpleasant gig to the next during his teenage years. He worked at a pants factory and at a mattress maker. Around this time, Lou got swept up in the boxing craze, and fancied following his pal Tracey into the game (but without his father catching wind of it). Enlisting his friends as trainers, Lou entered an amateur smoker thrown by the bed company. Lou ended up matched against a fellow employee. Normally the guy was mild mannered, but on the night of the smoker, he turned feral fighting under the name Tommy Gibbons. Lou held on to win a slam-bang match held at the 174th Regiment's drill shed on Niagara Street. Eventually, Lou found a better job making $22 a week driving a laundry wagon. One of his customers was a barber named Anthony Pianci, who knew Scozza was trying to break into the game. "Go see Bill Bauer at the Orioles Gym," Pianci advised the youngster. "Tell him I sent you."

Bauer was indeed the right man to see. He was the head boxing instructor at the gym. Scouting for talent was his forte. Bauer told Lou to jump some rope and to do some shadow boxing. After that, Lou never saw him again. For two weeks, Lou would show up but Bauer wouldn't be there. As it turned out, Bauer was in the throes of a rapidly escalating horse betting hobby and had ditched his role mentoring young hopefuls in order to dedicate more time to picking the ponies. Lou stopped going. He left all his gear behind, deciding he no longer needed it.

Some months later, suddenly feeling underappreciated by exactly $3 a week, Lou approached his boss at the Royal Linen Supply Company. How did $25 a week sound? Instead of the pay bump he had hoped for, Lou got berated. In a huff, without thinking, he quit. The boss handed him his final week's pay—$22—and told him to get lost.

Stunned and upset—he would have to tell his father—Lou stood on a curb pondering his future. Out of the blue, a good friend pulled up in a Ford coupe. It was Bobby Tracey, by now a professional welterweight.

"What's the matter, Lou?" Tracey asked. "Did you lose your best friend?"

"No worse," Lou replied. "I lost my job."

"That's nothing," Tracey said. "Jump in. We're going over to Bert Finch's gym."

As it happened, Finch wasn't around that day. But Tracey welcomed Lou right into the fraternity, which included the great Frankie Schoell. Tracey made Lou his chief sparring mate. Each day, Tracey baptized him by fire, cutting his friend to pieces, but always showing him the tricks of the trade, and the lessons started to sink in. Lou was soon giving just as wickedly as he got. Feeling confident he could actually make it in the ring, Lou came home one evening and broke the news to his father. Writing in the *Buffalo Times*, John Boccio relays a hilarious and heated exchange at the Scozzaro home (they had since moved to Whitney Place).

"I'm going to be a boxer," Lou blurted.

"Of what?" Phillipo asked, incredulously. "Oranges?"

What really lit Papa's fuse was finding out his son had spent $5 on boxing shoes.

Lou returned to the gym each day. A lucky break occurred one night when Finch was staging a charity boxing exhibition for a local hospital. Schoell's scheduled foe never showed. So he ended up going a few rounds with Tracey's Italian friend. Lou had only turned up to help Finch work in the corner. He ended up giving Schoell a real workout. Afterwards, Buffalo's star welterweight pulled Finch aside. "This boy is good, Bert," Schoell said. "You better keep an eye on him."

Finch decided to take the kid pro. To get Murray to put him on a Q.A.C. card, Finch invented a story that Lou was a high school boy boxing his way toward college savings—the old schoolboy angle never failed to win over promoters, for some reason. Making it slightly easier for Murray to add the kid to the program, Finch shaved a syllable off his name—and that's how

Lou Scozza ended up on the card the night Slattery knocked out Schoell in February of 1925.

Scozza's opponent that night was Stanley Smith, a veteran from the East Side. Scozza knocked him out in the closing seconds of a four-round preliminary, an impressive debut on a big night for Buffalo boxing. During the prior few weeks, Schoell had taken a personal interest in Scozza, giving him tips and drumming lessons into him over and over until he understood. Scozza gradually came up the curve but only after many patient hours spent practicing.

On the night of his debut, Scozza hung around to watch his teacher get knocked senseless. Finch was inconsolable that night. Scozza took it hard, too. Schoell, when he came to, shook it off. "It's all in the game," he said.

In the dim, empty arena, goes a Finch story, Scozza predicted that one day he would fight Slattery.

"I'll get your revenge," Scozza vowed.

Scozza won several of his early fights as a preliminary boy, although the crowd tended to give him a hard time. One night, Red rolled out a promising new Irish boy, Mike Carroll, and the First Ward gamblers went all in. Scozza ruined their night with an upset. Boos were less understandable the night Scozza earned a decision over Jack Pry, the Salamanca journeyman. Why the fans cheered Pry and booed Scozza for five full minutes may have had something to do with the virulent anti-Italian sentiment that prevailed at the time. Southern Italians were the new mongrels on America's doorstep, and were being demonized as anarchists and thugs.

One of Scozza's first featured bouts was against a rising star of Central New York, Binghamton's Johnny Haystack. Scozza knocked the stuffing out of him.

It was against Dave Shade, though, that Scozza made a name for himself. Though he only earned a draw, it was one of those moral victories. Shade (on orders from his manager) had spent the entire fight walled off in his protective turtle shell of a stance—and the crowd appreciated the spirit Scozza showed in relentlessly taking the fight to the clever, cowering Californian. That was the performance that caught Dempsey's eye.

By now, Finch was pestering Red to get Slats for Scozza, on the verge of breaking into the big-money game. But Red demurred. Slattery ruled Buffalo then. Scozza had simply come along at the wrong time. Oddly, in August of 1927—ten days before the Slattery-Rosenbloom title fight in

Hartford—Scozza defeated Rosenbloom in Buffalo. But from the standpoint of the national and Buffalo press, it was as if the fight had somehow never happened.

Slowly but surely, Scozza inched his way up, transforming from slugger to boxer. For a brief period in 1928, he became a sort of fighter-in-residence in the Wilkes-Barre, Pennsylvania coal region. Scozza seemed to fare better away from Buffalo. During one of his three Wilkes-Barre appearances, Scozza took an early shot on the chin from Tiger Thomas. For one of the few times in his career, he hit the canvas. Up at the count of nine, Scozza, unable to clear the cobwebs, gutted out the rest of the match on instinct. He didn't remember anything until near the end. Before the tenth round, Finch worked his fighter's head over with an ice pack. Suddenly, Scozza's faculties returned. He looked over across the ring at the grotesquely swollen jaw of his opponent.

"What's that guy doing with his mouth all puffed up?" he asked his manager.

"This is the last round," Finch said. "Go on out and puff it up some more."

Scozza went undefeated in 1929. He wasn't flashy, didn't ooze charm. But he beat some solid foes, including Del Fontaine and Osk Till. Additionally, Scozza delivered a heinous beating to Art Weigand. Fans stopped booing him. His father became his biggest fan—there were no more household expenses about which to fret. Phillipo was able to ditch the cement crew. The proud immigrant got terribly upset when the negotiations for the Slattery fight dragged out, according to Scozza's nephew, Jim Messina. He was adamant that his son's title shot should not be allowed slip away. "*My boy ainta' 'fraid ah no Irishman!*" Phillipo apparently shouted.

Hero to his West Side neighborhood, Scozza handled his stardom with class and humility, a perfect gentleman. He trained dutifully and stayed out of trouble. Scozza never trained so hard in his life as he did prior to his fight against Slattery. It's been said that he cut down three or four large trees just as a warm-up each morning—and the winds blew frigid in those Delevan hills. As his boxing activity increased, Scozza eased up on the axe work but added a new wrinkle to his routine by playing basketball with a local Delevan team. Nights were spent in the farmhouse playing pinochle.

Slattery was ready to begin the more strenuous phase of his training. They were moving the camp to Speculator. Upon learning that a snowstorm had made certain sections of mountain roads impassable, Slattery contacted his pilot friend, causing Red to have a nervous breakdown. Blessedly, for Red, the blizzard continued and the pilot nixed the trip. A drive that in normal conditions would have taken half a day somehow ended up lasting three days as Slattery and his companions traversed a circuitous route on treacherous roads. They repeatedly got stuck in the snow and moods turned as foul as the weather. But they finally made it.

One reporter at the time described the camp as being pitched on the fringe of the woods adjacent to the Osborne Inn. But with temperatures dropping to twenty below zero, it is a safe bet that much of the time was spent in the main house where a fireplace would have been roaring. Bill Osborne had his place adorned with so many photographs of Gene Tunney that it might have seemed like the retired champion was there in camp watching over Slats. He would need a guardian angel, as it turned out.

Slats substituted winter sports thrills for wild parties. Poor Red finally had his charge booze free but now had to contend with new horrors. Red could live with the sight of Slats shooting down a toboggan run in 19 seconds flat. But Slats decided to hook a toboggan to the rear bumper of an automobile which ended up swerving around a corner, flipping the sled on its side and tossing Slats like a rag doll into a snow bank. Later, Slats nearly wiped out going 70 miles per hour on a bobsled run. Suddenly, Red was thinking he had to get Slats back to Buffalo before he killed himself.

Boxing was not going well. It was too cold, and the sparring was slow and painful. Red left for a few days. He instructed Slats and sparring partner Eddie Connors, a bull-strong childhood pal, to put the gloves down for a few days. In Red's absence, Slats and Connors ended up boxing twice as much. With Red off in Buffalo for a few days, one might think that Slats would have been tempted to scare up some mischief, but it appears he was content to spend evenings by the Osborne fireplace catching up on the hometown papers. In addition to detailed accounts of the activities at both training camps, articles updated readers on seating arrangements being mapped out, the various dignitaries due to attend and the movement of the betting lines. The *Buffalo Times* published biographies of the combatants. A good deal of the Scozza backstory distilled in prior paragraphs came from the lengthy, multi-part series on him. Willis Wilber's famous "maze of crooked streets" line about the First Ward was used to kick off his series on Slattery.

Excitement grew with each passing day. The first tickets went on sale

Saturday, January 25 at 10:00 A.M. Seat prices ranged (tax included) from $2.10 bleacher seats to $19.50 ringside seats. Battle lines extended to cigar stores—Slattery fans bought tickets at Snyder's on Main Street; Scozza fans got theirs at Foster's, a couple of blocks away.

Rumors circulated as the fight loomed closer, adding to the buildup. No one was more tension-wracked than the managers. Finch's heart almost stopped when a reporter telephoned him to check out a rumor that Scozza had broken his arm. To Finch, it seemed all too plausible. Scozza, despite his ring success, still drove an old fashioned Model-T with an engine that had to be hand cranked, and the injury was said to have occurred while trying to start the auto. Finch immediately drove out to the Bowers' farm to definitively ascertain his fighter's condition. Scozza was not injured. The story was untrue. Finch found the Scozza camp buzzing with a story about how Slats had supposedly uttered the phrase "that bum Scozza." Everyone was fuming, except for Scozza, who didn't buy it.

On Thursday, February 6, promoters placed an additional block of $3 bleacher tickets on sale. Some two thousand of them sold out in about half an hour. That same day, up in Speculator, Slats and Red were getting hostile with one another. Slats had Bill Osborne arrange for a local pilot to fly them back to Buffalo. Slats knew full-well how Red felt about flying machines. It was knowledge that almost seemed to double the prizefighter's determination to get his manager up in the air. Slats, who loved flying in planes, got Red to at least look over the single-engine craft. Red wasn't sufficiently impressed, finding the contraption much too fragile-looking. Red persisted with his final veto. Slats got testy.

"Listen Jimmy," Red said through gritted teeth. "With the proper kind of encouragement I might start swinging."

After everything they had been through together, this argument over their mode of transportation was probably the closest the pair ever came to trading blows. But the situation diffused. Red had the final word. Pointing to the runway on the frozen lake and at Speculator Mountain towering in the distance, Red told Slats to take a nice long look from the ground. "Because you will not be seeing it from the air," Red concluded. "We're taking a road plane."

From Speculator, they drove to Utica, N.Y., and climbed aboard the Empire Express. The party arrived in Buffalo about 5:00 P.M. on the Friday before the Monday night fight. A busy time of the day and the week meant a fairly large and curious impromptu crowd of people gathered around Slats on the platform posing for pictures in his gaudy raccoon coat, reminiscent of one that might be worn by an Ivy League college football fan shouting the "Bula-Bula" fight song.

The next day, Red brought Slats to Newsboys' Gym for a locked-door session with their unflappable workhorse, Eddie Connors. Slow but game, Connors (reported the newspapermen whom Red allowed inside) withstood a breathtaking fusillade of lefts that would have leveled him but for the 16-ounce training gloves. When Slats shot the right it came with the eye-blinking speed of what, at the time, would have seemed like a lifetime ago. Over the years, Slattery's antics had brought Red to his knees in tears. In the past, when reporters had asked Red if Slattery was in shape, the question was difficult, even depressing, to have to answer. Now when they asked, Red just smiled.

Red called an end to the Saturday sparring. But Slats kept wailing away. He was still throwing punches when Skitsy started his rubdown.

Scozza returned to Buffalo on Sunday, the day before the fight. He visited with his parents and then, on Finch's orders, cordoned himself off at his manager's apartment for the rest of the evening. He was finally allowed to see his fiancée the next day—briefly, at her office job—prior to the weigh-in ceremony.

Slats woke up at his mother's house on the day of the fight and feasted on a home cooked breakfast of poached eggs, plums, orange juice, toast and coffee. After breakfast, he gave the victrola a crank and read some mail. He and Skitsy drove downtown for the weigh-in and then walked around the city soaking up the electricity. Scozza hit his barbershop for a haircut and a shave. One last batch of $2 tickets was placed on sale. An estimated 2,000 fans stood freezing in line for only about 500 available tickets. Most of the crowd remained in front, scanning their options, searching for scalpers. In an effort to thwart the black market, the box office put another 400 premium tickets, reserved but not claimed in time, on sale. All of those sold out immediately. Some members of the crowd, priced out or just plain unlucky, had stood shivering for hours on a frigid, blustery day only to come up empty handed. The tense mob of teeth-chattering, discouraged but undaunted fight fans congregated in front of the Aud. Inside, ticket-takers, ushers and police, all personally supervised by Chairman Farley, went over their battle plan: staggered entry times; strategically designated entrance points for upper and lower sections and a variety of security protocols. Farley called for a dry run and then finalized the selection of the referee and judges, which had been kept secret until just a few hours before the first bout. For days leading up, Scozza and his seconds badgered Bert Finch to make sure he requested at least one Italian judge to offset what was certain to be at least a few Irishmen. Finch made a point to do so, purely to placate his camp, who wouldn't let up about it. As it turned out, one of the judges assigned by Farley that night was a New Yorker named Joe Agnello. The second judge (Art Donovan) and referee (Jim Crowley) were indeed both Irish. Related fight night preparations, meanwhile, were happening all over town. Promoters had ruled out having a live radio broadcast—no microphone at ringside anyway—but a clever plan was being hatched by *The Buffalo Evening News* and WEBR in which the *News'* Frank Wakefield would bang out minute-by-minute descriptions that would be telephoned by a colleague to the radio station, where an announcer would read them over the air with minimal real-time delay; copies of Wakefield's mini-reports would also be relayed to the paper's Main Street headquarters, where a public address system and loudspeakers were set up. Some in the crowd figured this was their best bet. Soon, around 1,000 people were huddled in front of the paper waiting for the announcements to start rolling in as the winds picked up and temperatures plummeted. In the lobby, the betting scene was heating up—not a fever pitch, but more like a futures trading pit during a slow session with a few large orders moving the market. Some Italian-looking speculators were seen betting on Slattery, putting financial interests ahead of kinship. The word was that Slats was in the best shape of his life. Inside the building and out, rowdy packs of young Italians and Irish stared each other down and swapped taunts as zero hour grew near. Slattery-Scozza hysteria reached its zenith as dozens of daring kids made a run for the roof. Numerous eyewitness accounts preserved over the decades describe a chaotic scene of kids clambering up the slanted portion of the roof as high as they could go before encountering an icy patch that sent them hurtling into a terrifying, uncontrollable downward slide off the edge, dropping two stories to the ground below. One boy landed with a sickening crash on top of a parked car.

The first to climb into the ring that night was Scozza. He was met with a thunderous reception from the West Side contingent. Slattery came into the ring next and the First Ward made sure it equaled if not exceeded the decibel level. Slattery donned a slick leopard-skin robe.

Both he and Scozza waved to their fans, avoiding looking at one another. The room was fully electrified as the opening bell sounded and the battle commenced. The two hometown heroes went blow for blow in the early moments. Scozza landed one to the stomach, causing Slats to grimace. But Slats won the first round. He fed off the crowd's early intensity, flashing speed and craftsmanship, connecting from long range with his left. Slats also landed two hard rights. His aggression came in a roundabout way—backpedaling, a dancing retreat designed to draw Scozza in, only to be rocked by crisp, masterful combinations.

Scozza stormed back in the third round. His supporters livened up and flooded the hall with their roar. Slats freely backed into a corner, inviting a furious exchange. By the end of the third, Slats opened a gash under Scozza's eye. At the end of the fifth, both of Scozza's eyes seemed on the verge of closing up—somewhere in the milling, Slats stuck a thumb in.

Crowd energy waned slightly for it could not be sustained, nor did the action warrant the kind of feverish enthusiasm shown at the start. Slats danced out of reach, scoring as he backed away. Stretches of dullness marred the fifth and prompted fans to yell for action.

The sixth round was Slattery's best so far, and Scozza's worst. He lunged awkwardly but couldn't land. A maestro, Slats shot four clean, stinging lefts, and then crossed a savage right. Scozza, blinded, bleeding, and sporting a nauseating goose egg high on his cheek, barreled ahead, swatting at air. Though he flailed clumsily, he forced the action and refused to let up. Slats stayed in backpedaling mode. He was relying on his legs more than ever before.

Lively enough save for a few spots, the fight was nothing spectacular. As the final one-third of the contest approached, the ringside scribes had their storylines set. Slats was out in front and well on his way to becoming champion.

To trick his fighter into saving some gas in the tank, Red kept telling Slats that each round was one ahead. Slattery was definitely growing weary. Scozza, left for dead, was coming alive.

In the 12th, the Italian smacked the Irishman into the ropes, setting off tumult among the still hopeful West Siders. First Ward fans still were feeling confident they had this one wrapped up.

"It's the 14th coming up," Red informed Slats right before the bell sounded to start the 13th.

Some in the crowd may have figured the contest was winding down. All anyone expected was for Slattery to spend three minutes dancing out of range. But Scozza had other plans. If the fight wasn't living up to its billing as a once-in-one-hundred-years epic, that was about to change. No one who saw it would ever forget what happened next.

"With all of the suddenness and surprise of a mid-summer thunder-clap," wrote Frank Wakefield, "Scozza pounded Slattery into a state of near insensibility."

Scozza could barely see what he was doing. One eye was completely shut and the other gushed blood. He just went ballistic. On sheer instinct, Scozza unleashed a barrage of left hooks. One of his blows struck Slats on the Adam's apple, staggering him. Scozza followed with a frantic, overhand right hand club, whacking Slattery on the chin. He slumped over the ropes like a hastily discarded child's toy.

Slats was badly battered, stuck between the ropes, his body and head sticking halfway out as if trying to escape. Bent over, he clung to the middle strands with both arms. Scozza was hitting his back and shoulders. Eyes closed, Slats somehow reached back, clutching at his opponent. As his legs went limp and a fog descended over his brain, Slats could only do one thing, and that was to desperately grab a hold of his foe and hang on for dear life. Scozza was weak from throwing about a hundred punches. The pair toppled to the canvas together and rose up in tired tangle.

Wakefield: "Scozza savagely shook off the staggering Shamus and stalked him to the other side of the ring."

The Italian connected twice more, hard. Slattery, a glassy-eyed zombie, instinctively tried to clinch his way through the remainder of the round, with referee Crowley quick to separate the two and Scozza still hammering away. As the thrilling 13th drew to a close, Slattery's legs seemed on the verge of giving way. Scozza had him on the ropes once again. Slats slid down to a knee but hung on to the middle strand. Bedlam let loose in the arena. Scozza stood at the ready. The howling Italian faction knew what was about to happen. Everyone was screaming. Scozza set. Just when it looked like he was about to deliver the finisher—the bell sounded. Slats had been saved.

"Slattery had weathered the storm of leather like a staunchly caulked boat," Wakefield said.

Red darted across the ring to collect his fighter and guide him back to their corner. Skitsy waited with towels, ice packs, smelling salts—but he would need a miracle to revive his lifelong pal. And he would have one minute to find it.

The crowd was breathless and amazed. At this point, not one person inside the packed auditorium would have bet on Slattery to win the fight. Not at any odds. Not a nickel.

Skitsy worked Slats over like a champ. His old pal was regaining consciousness.

"It's the 14th coming up," Red told him.

"That's what you told me last round," Slats replied.

Red let out a deep breath. Slats was going to be okay.

Finch instructed Scozza to go out there and finish it. To the manager's dismay, Scozza, caught up in the frenzied excitement of becoming champion, suddenly forgot basic fundamentals. He abandoned his left. Right-handed death blows rained down, but Slats was able to just barely evade them and then force a clinch. His head was starting to clear. His strength returned. When Scozza threw a wild swing, Slats actually shot over a few punches of his own into the openings left for him. He continued to tie Scozza up, surviving the round. Finch was still mystified that Slats could even come out for the 14th round and now here he was suddenly looking as spry as a woodland faun.

Despite the stormy 13th, Slats had a narrow lead going into the 15th and final round. Astounding 11,000 Buffalo fight fans, the pride of the First Ward fought stronger and faster in the final round than he had at any point prior that night. Scozza, meanwhile, had exhausted himself throwing haymakers. The crowd rose to its feet. No one could believe what they were witnessing. Slattery was pummeling Scozza all over the ring. He'd saved his best for last.

After the final bell, it took only a few seconds for the verdict to be reached. Clasping three small slips of paper, referee Jim Crowley pointed at Slattery. The ring announcer could barely be heard, but he uttered the words Slats and his corner longed to hear. "*Winner and new light heavyweight champion of the world . . .*"

Deafening hurrahs from the First Ward boosters met the bellowing boos of the angry West Side throng. Most of the press corps gave Slattery the win. Crowley and one judge voted in favor of Slattery. The other judge had called it a draw.

Scozza had knocked Slattery down for at least a few seconds and Slats would have folded had the gong not sounded when it did. Scozza was devastated. Finch was furious.

In Slattery's dressing room there was a scene of unbridled jubilation with all of the old gang mobbing him and dancing around, and not so much as a single iota of pent-up emotion was held back. When the chaotic celebration died down, Red made his way over to the opposing dressing room to pay his respects. It indeed had been a fight for the ages. Scozza had pushed a living legend to the brink.

Inside Scozza's locker room, bitterness prevailed, with Finch telling every reporter within earshot that his fighter had been robbed of the title and that he intended to file a protest. Some of his frustration was reserved for his own man. If Scozza had simply shown some patience and delivered a measured finishing punch, he might be champion.

As Red approached, he heard his rival through the door. In a cruel twist, one of the two officials who had scored the fight for Slats turned out to be Agnello.

"Well," Finch exclaimed. "You wanted an Italian judge!"

★★★★★

Red sent Slats back to Speculator for some rest. The post-championship celebration had lasted straight through the rest of the winter and almost into St. Patrick's Day. As Red saw it, there was one remaining mountain to climb. Talks were underway for Slattery to meet Rosenbloom in April.

Despite Slattery's victory over Scozza—and the New York State–sanctioned designation that came with it—Rosenbloom was now being recognized as the National Boxing Association titleholder. Even in its updated rankings, *Ring* put Rosenbloom first and Slattery second.

On Tuesday, March 4, Slattery came back to Buffalo from Speculator to pursue Betty. "Don't come around," Mr. Pendergast had barked into the telephone when Slats rang the home on Prospect Street.

Slats was more determined to win Betty than universal title recognition. A defiant streak had always burned within him. As far as the 25-year-old was concerned, he had accomplished everything he had set out to do in the ring. Betty enjoyed all of his swooning. But she tried to end the affair. Not four months earlier, she'd never even seen Slattery. It was all happening too fast. Not only did her parents sternly object to the relationship, but the nineteen-year-old herself didn't think Slattery was ready to be a one-woman man. He was out to prove her wrong.

The following weekend, Betty packed some things and told her parents she was going to her aunt's home on Delaware Avenue, where a dinner party was planned for Saturday evening. Betty never arrived. Instead, she hopped into Slattery's Lincoln and the two motored toward Speculator. They stopped off along the way in Fonda, N.Y., a small rail hub on the banks of the Mohawk Barge Canal. Slats and Betty paid a visit to Father Joe O'Connor, pastor of St. Cecilia's Church.

Father Joe had been visiting Slattery's training camp for years and the two had become good friends. Slats informed him of their secret plan—they were there in Fonda to elope. The priest was happy to help them out, but he couldn't perform a wedding right on the spot; first, there were formalities. The most expedient thing for them to do would be to get a marriage license, wait the required 24-hours, then have a local Justice of the Peace officiate the union, making it legal. Records at the Fonda town clerk's office suggest that's exactly what Slats and Betty did. One charming detail gleaned from a copy of the marriage records in Fonda is what the couple listed as their occupations. Slats, naturally, wrote "*Boxer*." Betty put down "*Lady*."

Around dinner time on Sunday afternoon, Father Joe performed a solemnization ceremony in his residence adjoined to St. Cecilia's—Slattery could then tell his mother he was married in a church. St. Cecilia's was a quaint, red-brick structure that had been built about five years earlier, and was nestled among some pine trees just off Fonda's main drag. The next stop for the newlyweds was Speculator—but first Slattery had some long distance calls to make. His first was to Betty's parents. They were totally blindsided. Soon, reporters learned of the news and were calling all over for reaction quotes. No, Slattery had not been welcomed into their home, Mrs. Pendergast told the *Buffalo News*, but that was because they wanted Betty to focus on her musical studies and, moreover, she was too young. Red was deluged with calls right before he was set to take a train to New York to try to cement a match with Rosenbloom. Although he was surprised to learn that his fighter had dropped a decision to Cupid, Red also felt relieved. Maybe Slats was finally growing up.

Slattery's nuptials had created a bit of a stir in the sports world. His new boxing crown did not. It attracted a collective yawn. What crumbs of acknowledgment came his way were tossed left-handedly.

"Well, well, Jimmy Slattery finally won that light heavyweight title," wrote Lank Leonard, eager to note how Slats had won the title "long after passing the peak of form."

"The crowning of Slattery as champion is not entirely convincing," said *The Ring*. "Had Jimmy taken care of himself, trained earnestly and allowed ambition to blanket his desire for pleasure . . . he might have won the title a long time ago. Perhaps it is just as well he has been recognized."

Hugh Shannon's column in *The Ring* made no effort to conceal his view that Scozza should have been the winner. "Slattery is a most fortunate young man," the Crescent club matchmaker wrote in describing the fateful 13th round.

At least the boxing establishment was acknowledging Slats as the rightful titleholder. Such acceptance was not widespread when he won the N.B.A. title. Now that rival governing body refused to recognize Slattery. The N.B.A. named Rosenbloom its light heavyweight champion.

Slats had agreed to fight Rosenbloom within sixty days of his earning the crown, per an edict from the Boxing Commission. Red, however, couldn't get Rosenbloom to come to terms. That's because the Commission ruled that the fight should take place in Buffalo. Rosenbloom insisted the fight be held in New York City.

Slattery wanted to defend his title. He would need to. Fulfilling a lifelong dream, he built a brand new $23,000 home on North Drive, one of the most elegant streets in affluent North Buffalo. He and Betty were starting their new life together in style.

As the Rosenbloom talks dragged on, Slats accepted an invitation to come meet Pete Latzo at the "Madison Square Garden" that Rickard had built in Boston one year before he died. Latzo was a highly ranked light heavyweight who was most famous for having his jaw shattered by Jimmy Braddock. What happened at the Boston Garden in the spring of '30 was a travesty. Both Slattery and Latzo were tossed out of the ring for failing to adequately perform their punching duties. Fans jeered Slats throughout the match, plainly aware he was flicking faint love taps or dancing around. Latzo barely bothered to throw any punches. Both fighters had to forfeit their purses, a particularly harmful blow to Slattery, who had just taken out a hefty mortgage.

Slats and his archrival Rosenbloom were finally set to fight for the title—in Buffalo—on Wednesday June 25, 1930. The venue was Bison Stadium, which had been renamed Offermann Stadium. Following a three-week stay in Speculator, Slats returned to Buffalo on the Monday before the fight. Betty was the first to greet him when he arrived at the New York Central terminal. Slats wore a blue blazer and knee-high knickers, an outfit which made him look as if he were about to compete in a steeplechase event, not a championship fight. Evidently, Slats was not worried about beating Rosenbloom. The day of the fight, stories were going around town about how Slattery had stayed out the night before until 2:30 A.M. at the Palais Royale dance club on Main Street. A pair of busboys had to help put the drunken champion into a cab.

In what was the sixth meeting between the pair, Rosenbloom stripped Slattery of his crown, which he had worn for all of 135 days. In his heart, Slats thought he had won. Referee Patsy Haley voted for him. Two judges did not. Around 15,000 hometown fans roared with disapproval when the decision was announced.

The skirmish had been all mugging and grappling. Long gone was Slattery's clean, graceful swordsmanship. Instead, he relied on back-alley tactics. One of them involved grabbing Rosenbloom by the neck, pounding on his ear, and then ripping a shot to his face. Most writers described the bout as dreadful to watch. The closest thing to a knockout came in the 15th when one of Rosenbloom's wild swings accidentally struck the ref, Haley. Ultimately, Rosenbloom had been viewed as more aggressive with his whirlwind smacking and slapping. As the fans booed, the new, universally recognized champion strutted around the ring and posed for pictures.

Slats had vowed before the fight that if he lost he was quitting the game. Reneging on that pledge, he fought a few more times in 1930. That October, he was tossed out of a Syracuse ring for stalling against perennial whipping post Len Darcy. Even poorly conditioned, Slats, in three prior meetings, had never had any difficulty with Darcy. That Slats would carry him seemed suspicious.

Slattery's perilous financial situation led him to accept a match in November in Chicago against a 20-year-old fish monger named Harry Krakow, who fought as King Levinsky. His rise from Chicago's Jewish ghetto made him a popular draw. He was being touted as another Maxie Rosenbloom.

Slats lost. Newspaper accounts of the furor in the arena suggest hometown fans strongly felt Slattery should have been given the decision.

Slats would avenge his loss to Levinsky the following January. A few months later, Slats took on an aging but still respectable heavyweight, Tom Heeney. A former plumber from Gisborne, New Zealand, Heeney in 1928 had been the last challenger to face Tunney before the latter retired as champion. Heeney gave a valiant effort. Runyon gave him a moniker: "The Hard Rock from Down Under." As he was prone to do, Slats boxed circles around the slow, large man, turning in the kind of performance that suggested perhaps he was not washed up after all. But then, Heeney was 41; Slats was 26.

In between those two victories, Slats reached a truly monumental milestone, becoming a father. James Slattery, Jr. was born on February 4, 1931 at Millard Fillmore Hospital. A widely publicized photo of the prizefighter cradling his week-old son suggested Slats felt nothing but delight. However, his continual carousing during this period only showed there was indeed a limit to the extent to which his life had changed.

Slats had to provide for his family. Lucrative opportunities were fleeting. Crowds dwindled as post-Crash unemployment soared. Only marquee heavyweight fights could draw decent crowds. He had one last chance to get back on track.

In early August of 1931, Slats was matched once again with Rosenbloom, this time at Ebbets Field. Rosenbloom's title would be on the line. This marked the pair's seventh meeting. Slats had won four. Rosenbloom had taken two of the last three.

Slattery showed up at Stillman's Gym in New York on the day before the fight. Writers were amazed—by a conspicuous roll of fat around Slats' middle and his inability to show a decisive advantage against practice foes. Rosenbloom, rumor had it, was missing. No one seemed to care about either of them. Less than 5,000 people showed up for the fight. The $12,400 gate was one of the weakest hauls ever for a championship fight. It would be eight decades before Brooklyn hosted another.

The small crowd booed the entire time. Many walked out. Both fighters were listless and seemingly indifferent. They did little besides stall and clinch. Only a few half-speed love taps were thrown, almost as if each combatant had secretly wagered a bundle on the other. Rosenbloom won the decision, retaining the title.

Westbrook Pegler covered the fight for the *Chicago Tribune*. He seemed ready to give up the boxing beat. "Rosenbloom won . . . and Slattery lost but the patrons took the punishment," he wrote. "For those who sat through the monotonous waltz it will be a long time recovering from the horror of it all."

Added the *Police Gazette*: "The 5,000 or so fans who journeyed to Ebbets Field . . . would probably have gotten more thrills had they gone instead to the Brooklyn Botanical Garden across the street."

For his lackluster services, Slattery earned about $1,000. Ten times in his career Slattery had earned $10,000 or more in one night in the ring.

Rosenbloom made around $3,300, or what he could easily blow in an hour-long craps game. He said that he was giving up on the light heavyweight class. "I can't make a dime," he complained to reporters. "My title means nothing."

A few days after his defeat to Rosenbloom, Slats took part in an altercation outside the ring. The venue was 95 North Drive. The opponent was a neighbor, Bernie Naylon, a few years younger than Slats. The reason fists flew: a woman. Awakened neighbors rang the police. Overhearing the loud screaming and moaning sounds, one of the dispatchers at the Colvin Avenue station remarked, "It must be some battle."

"If you wanted to fight, you should have fought in Brooklyn!" Naylon was heard to scream as he pinned the former champion to the ground outside the home.

Slats took several heavy licks while under submission. When police came, he retreated inside. The officers waited patiently for Slats to come back out so they could arrest him for allegedly slapping the woman. Slats never came out and the policemen finally left. The woman, never identified, did not press charges.

Slats would stay out of jail. For now.

ELEVEN

HARD TIMES

N 1934, AMERICA WAS NEAR ROCK BOTTOM. Jimmy Slattery still had a long way to go.

By the latter part of that year, Slats was in Buffalo digging a sewer. When an AP reporter caught up with him, Slats, two years removed from his last real pro fight, seemed bewildered by his plight. How had he gone from Garden headliner to a city relief job earning $18 per week? "Just another ex-champ, I guess," he'd shrugged.

Boxing fans who spotted the item must have been shocked. But Slats wasn't the only fighter to fade out of the bright lights into a more humble existence. Paul Berlenbach was back driving a cab. Maxie Rosenbloom was roaming around the middle of the country fighting in nowhere towns for as little as $30 a night. Beloved Irish-American heavyweight Jimmy Braddock went on welfare for eight months in '34. One year later, Braddock upset Max Baer to become the world's heavyweight champion and an underdog hero celebrated by millions of empathetic countrymen.

Had Slattery simply held on to his shovel job, that would have been an accomplishment. Or even just his shovel—there's a hard-luck anecdote about Slattery breaking his, having leaned on it too heavily. As for his life, it had begun to fall apart in 1931.

After losing his fight at 95 North Drive, Slats lost the home to foreclosure. Betty and infant son Jimmy, Jr. moved in with her parents. Slats went to live with his mother. He still could walk into any bar in the city and have admirers and old pals buy him beers and shots. Slats was always talking of a comeback. His boasts got louder with each glass. Stablemate Roggie Lavin opened a restaurant and gambling parlor on the corner of Chippewa and Franklin, across from Newsboys' Gym. So Slattery's new home base was right near his old headquarters—and not too far from police headquarters, either.

Renewing his series with King Levinsky in Detroit in October of 1931, Slats dropped a ten-round decision and, seemingly, all further notions of continuing in the ring. Buffalo police arrested Slats that same month for driving while intoxicated. At the time, Slats had just finished racing with another driver on Niagara Street near the entrance to the Peace Bridge. He was later cleared of the charge when the arresting patrolman testified he never actually saw Slats driving drunk. "I'll dismiss the case," Judge Patrick Keeler said. "But if this charge had been substantiated, I would have sent you up to the state penitentiary for thirty days."

James J. Corbett had once yearned for a day when prizefighters would be more like him, refined gentlemen, and less like his whiskey-swilling, hell-raiser of a rival, John L. Sullivan. Slats had his cerebral side. Bob Hubbell, the famed Buffalo radio broadcaster, had a daily poetry program in the early 1930s. Hubbell recalled once how Slats had written into the station when he enjoyed a particular recital. When he wasn't listening to verse, Slats sure raised a lot of hell—drinking to excess, getting in bar brawls, blowing traffic signals and ditching out on cabbies. He never stopped chasing women. While still together with Betty, Slats brought another woman into their home. Betty caught him, which directly led to their separation. The house eventually sold at public auction. Slats hadn't made a single payment (loan, taxes, interest) since that July, before his seventh and final fight with Rosenbloom.

While in training (supposedly) for another comeback attempt, Slats, in March of 1932, sped through a red light in downtown Buffalo following a Friday-night drink-fest that had lasted into early Saturday morning. He was thrown in jail. Around noontime, Red came to bail him out. By Sunday morning the next day, Slats was back in police custody again after crashing his car into a vehicle parked on Main Street. On that following Monday, Slats, back in City Court for the second time in two days, pleaded guilty to a charge of being drunk and disorderly. Looking fresh-faced and sharp in his favorite blue chinchilla Chesterfield overcoat, Slats stood solemnly as grim-faced Chief Justice George Woltz lectured him.

"*You*," he said, "are your own greatest enemy. It's a pity a fellow of your type has allowed himself to so degenerate."

Judge Woltz was clear: the next time he saw Slats in his courtroom there would be consequences. Police were put on notice that because the hometown hero's record included not one but two convictions on public drunkenness charges, any subsequent charge would now have to come under state law, which carried a mandatory six-month sentence.

"Be a man," the judge said. "Stop your drinking."

Slats meekly nodded and paid his $25 fine in a crumpled roll of one-dollar bills. With this particular matter now closed—Slats was due back in court later that afternoon for running the light—Woltz pulled Slats aside, but not so far that a *Buffalo News* reporter couldn't hear them, apparently.

"Do you attend church?" Woltz asked.

"Yes, I do," Slats replied.

"See your priest."

Buffalo fans were more than a little curious when Slats climbed into a ring at the Bison ballpark in August of 1932 to face the light heavyweight champion of Canada, Charley Belanger. Slattery had declared he was starting a comeback campaign. Fans simply wondered: *How bad would he look?*

Belanger settled that issue one minute into the opening round with a right-hand smash to Slattery's jaw, knocking him down. Slattery fought at 166 pounds. Belanger, by now a heavyweight, was nearly 180 pounds. Slattery could no longer nimbly outfox a lumbering hulk. Belanger easily caught up with him and bashed him from one end of the ring to the other. He knocked Slats down again in the second. Slats did get up, but the referee stopped the fight. Slats didn't land a single punch. The bounce had vanished from his once spry legs. His arms wouldn't snap to his brain's commands. "He wasn't the twinkling will-o'-the-wisp anymore," wrote *Collier's* magazine. "But merely another flat-footed has been."

Buffalo boxing fans still had plenty to cheer about. That spring, West Side featherweight Tommy Paul won the N.B.A.'s crown, soundly defeating Johnny Pena of New York City. Buffalo had produced another champion to go with Erne, Goodrich, Kansas and Slattery.

After losing to Belanger, Slats hung up the gloves and set about to reinvent himself. That October he filled out an application for a policeman's job. Though he made his share of enemies, Slats also had a number of friends on the force. An old neighborhood pal, John Crotty, then rising up through the ranks, had always looked out for Slattery and would go to bat for him in his bid for a berth. The clerk at the Buffalo Civil Service Commission's offices accepted the paperwork without recognizing either the name at the top of the form, or the face of the 28-year-old who had handed it in. Slats passed the physical test. A written test, given every three years, was not scheduled for another year or so.

The country's economic nadir, as measured by the stock market, had come in July '32. At the bottom, $74 billion in share value had been erased as the Dow Jones Industrial Average plunged a jaw-dropping 89 percent over the nearly three-year period following the Crash of '29. By the time President Franklin Roosevelt took office in March of '33, the national unemployment rate hit 25 percent. Some 12 million American workers were unable to earn a living. Included in the ranks of the unemployed, according to a study of 54 colleges and universities, were roughly 22,000 degree holders. An estimated 25,000 families lost their homes. Many of them roamed the countryside, becoming "nomads of the depression." As many as 200,000 young men (ages 16 to 21) lived on the streets. Railroads reported a 50 percent increase in transient trespassing as well as a disturbing spike in related fatalities. Homeless wanderers—entire families—littered American highways. Such grim statistics at the end '32 represented an "index of insecurity," wrote Newton Baker, former mayor of Cleveland and a contender for the Democratic presidential nomination.

Shanty towns popped up in public parks. People dug holes and pulled tarps over them. Bread lines formed. Pregnant mothers took their place amongst elderly couples and middle-aged businessmen. Bond traders sold apples on the street. Thousands of unemployed war veterans marched on Washington, D.C. in the last days of the Hoover Administration which had genuine concern that a societal revolution was in the air. Financial ruin— abject poverty—pushed people to extremes. Normal, prominent, everyday citizens jumped out of buildings and took cyanide. Husbands murdered wives; mothers left newborns in doorways and parked cars with notes, such as one that read, "*I am a young widow, almost starving.*" There was the 38-year-old unemployed nurse from Babylon, Long Island, found covered in rags and old newspapers in a maple grove on a private estate. She was penniless and nearly starved to death. And the Mahwah, New Jersey man who killed his wife and then himself, leaving a note that read: "*My brain just cracked. I have had many financial worries. I'm terribly sorry.*"

Between 1930 and 1932, some 50 banks failed in New York State. As FDR was being sworn in, regulators in 22 states were temporarily suspending bank operations to stave off widespread runs. By 1933, 1.5 million New

York State residents, one-fourth of the workforce, were unemployed. What weighed on the souls of most people was the fear of being next, of joining a neighbor or relative in destitution. Roosevelt moved swiftly to inject confidence. He passed the National Recovery Act, which produced the short-lived Civil Works Administration, forerunner to the Works Progress Administration (WPA). The first CWA Project in Buffalo was underway by the spring of '33. Armies of relief-program laborers started digging sewer ditches around the city. These trenches, fortified by wood beams lining the earthen walls, were deep and wide, large enough to fit trucks filled with men, picks and shovels. It was brutal, hot, backbreaking work, but these were desperate times—and, as it turned out, the world really did need ditch diggers.

The toll of the times went beyond financial heartache. Diphtheria roiled the country, hitting small children the hardest. Slattery's nephews, James and Joseph, both under the age of two, died of the illness within a few days of each other in April of '33. Not long after, Slats' devastated older brother, John, father of the two stricken tots, was diagnosed with pulmonary tuberculosis. It was considered a death sentence.

The boxing world lost some irreplaceable figures right around then. Both Corbett and Muldoon had passed away. Commiserating over the telephone with Charlie Murray in June of '33, former Boxing Commission Chairman James Farley tried to put a positive spin on the dismal state of the sport. Attendance had dwindled as the Depression grew worse—"but boxing will come back," Farley predicted. "It's a human game. And human games will always appeal."

Murray had his own problems. The promoter was bedridden with a strange, severe muscular ailment. It is important to note here—Farley was one of the most influential political figures in the country right about then, having helped to mastermind FDR's rise to power.

"How is Slats?" Farley asked.

Discussing Slattery's decline pained them both.

"I never think of Buffalo without a pang of regret," Farley said. "At what might have been."

Slats would not fight at all in 1933. He stopped talking about comebacks. Joining him back at his mother's house on Abbott Road was his younger brother, Joe, who was then estranged from his wife and five-year-old daughter. Joe also struggled with alcoholism. One September night, he staggered out of the Roundhouse Tavern on the corner of what is today South Park Avenue and Elk Street. It all happened in a split second. Joe was so drunk he bounded out the door and stepped right in front of a street car. He was taken to Mercy Hospital in South Buffalo. Three days later, he died.

A few weeks later, in October of '33, Slats' old foe, and friend, William "Young" Stribling, was killed in a motorcycle accident in Macon, Georgia. He'd been on his way to a local hospital to visit his wife and newborn child. Same as Joe Slattery, Stribling was only 28.

That same month, the Buffalo Civil Service examination was administered at Bennett High School. Slats failed to show up. The next test would not be given for another three years. The age limit to be a policeman was 31; he was then 29. Slattery had had a fairly good shot to get on the force—and he blew it.

In December of 1933, two-thirds of the states ratified the Twenty-first Amendment to the Constitution, repealing the Eighteenth Amendment. Low-alcohol (3.2%) beer was made legal that prior spring. After nearly fourteen years, Prohibition was over.

Imposing his own personal ban on consumption of alcohol, Slattery in the spring of '34 launched yet another comeback. A hesitant Murray, keen to make sure Slats did not get himself killed, lined up a trio of inexperienced Polish heavyweights, a couple of whom had only recently obtained boxing licenses. The first two, Walter Kugel and Gus Flugel, proved to be easy knockouts. The Kugel K.O. came at the Broadway Auditorium. At 29, Slats was back fighting in warm-up bouts. Though his legs appeared scrawny and his stomach a bit flabby, Slats entered the ring to a ridiculous outburst of applause. Buoyed by the warm reception, Slats hooked and jabbed with the enthusiasm of a preliminary boy. It would be the last time he appeared at the Aud, capping one of the most thrilling eras in the history of Buffalo sports. Not long after, the Aud would be rendered obsolete with the construction of Memorial Auditorium, commissioned as a WPA project. The new building would host boxing, wrestling, concerts, college basketball and, eventually, professional hockey. It, too, became affectionately known as the Aud. The old Broadway Auditorium was closed and later repurposed as a parking barn for city snowplows.

The second and third Slattery comeback bouts that spring of '34 took place outdoors at the ballpark. The third one was against Eddie Kaminski, a wrestler taking part in his first-ever professional fight. Unable to disregard his grappling instincts, Kaminski kept rushing and tackling Slats into the ropes. In the fifth round, well behind on points, Kaminski blatantly shoved Slats into the ropes. When Slats got tangled up, the referee halted the action. Kaminski threw a few punches and was disqualified. Slattery's comeback tour—three wins—attracted little interest and promptly fizzled out.

Later that summer, Slattery's brother John was admitted to the J.N. Adam Memorial Hospital in rural Perrysburg, New York, south of Buffalo. Simply known as "Perrysburg," the hilltop sanatorium, surrounded by 500 acres of forest on either side, was the state's first and largest facility dedicated to treating T.B. patients. Thousands had come through since it had opened more than two decades earlier. Some sufferers of the lung disease recuperated, abetted by a steady diet of fresh air even in cold months. Most came to die. Slattery's niece, Patsy Kline, recalled vague memories of her father standing on a long front porch while she stood a safe distance away at the foot of a great stone staircase. Her only memory of her father is him smiling and waving from the porch.

John Slattery never left Perrysburg.

Slats enrolled in the city work-relief program in the latter part of 1934. He was assigned to one of the many sewerage projects ongoing around the city. He didn't mind it. For the most part, Slats enjoyed manual labor. If he wasn't feeling up for anything strenuous he could goof off with the best of them. One day, the foreman asked Slats to get him a box of chewing tobacco at a cigar store a few blocks away. Slats sped off in the foreman's truck. He didn't return until noon the next day.

Grieving his brothers, convinced that the grim reaper was stalking him as well, Slats lived for payday and for making the rounds—Cotter's tavern in the Ward, Crotty's on Niagara Street, Joey Joynt's on South Park and Lavin's on Franklin near Chippewa. As seedy as it was becoming, Chippewa was a busy, eclectic, neon-lit strip that had always been Slattery's favorite part of town. Some old pals were always around to buy him a steak and a glass of suds. He drank up, nightly, still dreaming of another comeback. Gradually, such talk subsided.

Slattery was floating along on an endless creek of screw-ups. He had turned thirty, an age when young men suddenly begin to feel the years slipping by. Slats had other meaningful ways to mark the passage of time. His idol, forty-year-old Babe Ruth, playing out his string with the Boston Braves, had finally called it a career in late May of 1935. Around the same time, a new heavyweight champion was crowned—Slattery's old rival Jimmy Braddock had completed his unbelievable underdog tale with a stirring triumph over man-killer Max Baer.

Braddock had knocked Slattery out in '29 when they were both in their mid-twenties and competing in the 175-pound class. To graduate to full-fledged heavyweight, Braddock literally had to eat like a horse following eight months of barely being able to feed himself and his family; a typical breakfast during his training for Baer included a half-dozen eggs and an entire loaf of toasted bread.

Slattery used to eat like a horse. For several years during his ascension, many boxing experts predicted Slattery would fill out at 185 pounds. But that extra bulk never did arrive. At his heaviest, Slats weighed 172.

Any money he came upon now went to feed his booze cravings. But he still had to eat. As a denizen of the downtown scene, Slats knew the best places to get cheap grub. One of his favorites was the Deco restaurant on Seneca Street, where downtown Buffalo brushes up against the First Ward. Gregory Deck's chain of miniature diners—Buffalo had about twenty locations—were beloved during the Depression because for a nickel you could get a decent (not watered down) cup of coffee; for a quarter you could get a quality hamburger. Though not hurting as badly as other parts of the country during the Depression, Buffalo was nonetheless still hurting. All types of people hung around these cozy diners, warm, inviting and open 24 hours. But, as mentioned, space was extremely tight, with only room for a small counter and about six stools. So if Slats got into a scrape inside a Deco—as he did one Sunday night in June of '35—it was an even bet either he or someone else was going through a window.

News clippings say it took four policemen to wrestle Slattery into handcuffs outside the Seneca Street Deco. Prior to their arrival, Slattery, as the result of some melee, had smashed through the window and was angrily refusing to pay for it when cops arrived. A judge later ordered him to make restitution.

"Do you have the $30?" the judge had asked.

Slattery just shook his head no. He pleaded guilty to drunkenness and was placed on probation.

His life was unraveling faster than ever.

A few weeks later, in July of '35, Slattery was involved in a serious auto crash across the border in Fort Erie. Police found and questioned Slattery after he left the scene to seek treatment for gashes on his face. The driver of the car that caused the accident was missing. A young woman riding in the other vehicle was in the hospital with a severe spinal injury. Police took Slats in on a public intoxication charge. Once again, Red bailed him out.

Later that same autumn, Slattery was racing down Abbott Road when a patrolman observed his recklessness and gave pursuit. Slats sped east toward the outskirts of South Buffalo, trying to escape. But he finally pulled over, a few miles away on Potters Road in the town of West Seneca. He was charged with speeding and fined $20. The judge ordered the fine paid on the spot. Slats didn't have the money. Red was not there to help. Slats was looking at actual jail time. But instead he received leniency. He pleaded for time to come up with the money, and the judge agreed.

At this point, it should be noted that Slats appears to have drifted into the transient class. By his own choice, he was flopping around town with no permanent address. At times, Slats gave the address of 153 Abbott. At others, he gave some fleabag Pearl Street hotel as his place of residence. He also was known to stay on Fulton Street with his sister, Mary, and her husband, Ed; or with his sister-in-law, Marion (John's widow) on Euclid. Slattery's separation from Betty became official. She was legally seeking a divorce, which would take a few more years to obtain. During this period, Slats would have only a minimal connection with her and their young son.

Somehow, Slats was able to stay out of jail. He even found steady work as a city laborer under the federal relief program. But he was growing increasingly desperate. Both his mother and younger sister, Helen, had been diagnosed with cancer. Slats put himself in charge of paying their medical bills. Red wasn't made of money, but he was still doing well representing a new local boxing star, George "Big Boy" Brackey, a popular Lackawanna heavyweight. When Slats was in need, he knew he could turn to Red, and to Charlie Murray. But there was only so much they could do.

At the end of February 1937, Slattery's mother lost her battle with breast cancer. Two weeks later, Slats was arrested on yet another public intoxication charge. Fed up, City Court Judge Peter Maul gave him thirty days in the state penitentiary in Attica, N.Y. A few days later, Red, unable to stand the thought of Slats being locked up, went to the judge and begged him to cut Slats a break. "Jimmy just lost his mother and it knocked the props from under him," Red explained. Judge Maul commuted the sentence and Slats was quietly released after serving less than a week. Slats swore to the judge he would resume his city laborer's job and take an oath of sobriety.

By this time, the federally funded sewerage project was nearly finished. Slats oiled the seepage pumps and occasionally drove a truck. It was a decent job. He held on to it all summer. For a while, Slats earned about $23 a week. But eventually, the program came to an end.

Later that year, in September of '37, Slattery's sister Helen succumbed to leukemia. She left behind a husband and an infant son.

In four years, Slats had lost his entire family except for his sister, Mary.

His boxing career had flamed out. His marriage had dissolved. His dream home had been taken. His once golden reputation had been severely tarnished. He'd had everything he could ever ask for in the palm of his hand and he had, as they would say in South Buffalo, *fucked it up.*

Slats may have had a right to sing the blues, but he seemed determined not to wallow. "Jimmy always went along on the assumption that a glass of beer was made to drink, not to weep into," journalist Quentin Reynolds wrote in the mid-1930s.

At age 34, Slats tried to get back in the game. Red was handling a new Irish boy, Paul Mahoney, and had asked Slats to help train the kid. In July of 1938, Jimmy Braddock came to Buffalo to pilot his friend, Walter "Popeye" Woods, a veteran middleweight from Sunnyside, Queens. Woods was set to fight at the ballpark against Jimmy Clark of Chicago. Slats agreed to meet Braddock at Singer's Gym to help prepare Woods for the outdoor bout and to pose for a few publicity shots. Singer's was packed to the stairwells. Fans wanted to catch a glimpse of the world-famous "Cinderella Man." Braddock was still treated like a champion even though he'd lost his title a year earlier to Joe Louis. What no one realized was that poor Braddock was broke again.

It happened to a lot of guys. That was boxing. For every hard-luck story there were successes. Jack Dempsey invested shrewdly in real estate and opened a thriving Broadway restaurant that grew into a Manhattan institution. Gene Tunney married into the Lauder cosmetics fortune and became a successful businessman in his own right. Tommy Loughran became a sugar broker and lived out of a room at the N.Y.A.C. Lou

Scozza opened a bowling alley. Retiring in Hollywood, Maxie Rosenbloom opened a popular nightclub, "Slapsie Maxie's."

Paul Berlenbach, on a good day, could take home $7 driving his taxi. His wife ran a newsstand in Union Square. They squeaked by.

Here was a guy who came from nothing, drove a taxi, rose to become champion, earned a fortune and had returned to driving a taxi again. Berlenbach once fought Jack Delaney at Ebbets Field in front of 60,000 people who paid nearly a half-million dollars to see it. Berlenbach now had nothing to show for his boxing career. A writer Berlenbach once picked up in his cab asked what had happened to his money. The ex-champ's response: "Oh, it just went."

Slats was hardly the only fighter struggling. That same week he was sent away to prison, Mike McTigue was sent to an insane asylum. Reportedly, the 44-year-old had been assaulted by some thugs who cracked his skull. He was never the same.

Dave Shade was shipped off to Bellevue in a straight-jacket following a violent outburst at a Bronx police station in 1933, although that appears to have been a one-off. Still, it seems fair to say that the man who first popped Slattery's bubble had some demons of his own with which to contend.

Braddock's woes were always financial. He'd lost thousands in the Crash of '29. Out of the ring with a hand injury during the winter of 1933–34, Braddock had to apply for relief aid, getting about $30 bucks a month. That welfare check wasn't enough to live on, so Braddock was always borrowing money from his manager and his friends. A large portion of the roughly $30,000 purse he earned the night he became champion was used to pay off a mountain of debts. Braddock didn't envision making a career out of handling fighters. But for now it was a nice little gig to have.

He was in a talkative mood when Billy Kelly, the *Courier-Express* sports editor, stopped by Singer's. With Slattery giving Woods pointers, Braddock took a break to sit down with Kelly to talk about the state of the game.

"Not an Irish heavyweight in sight," Braddock sighed. "Where are they? I feel like Tommy Loughran and I were the last ones."

Braddock paused and looked over at Slattery.

"He would have been a great heavyweight," Braddock said. "Twenty more pounds on his frame, with his speed and natural boxing ability . . . he would have been a world's wonder. I know."

Braddock would go on to tell Kelly how impossible he had found Slattery to hit that night at the Garden, how stupid he felt for nine rounds until he finally did catch up to him. He recounted how early in their meeting Slats struck him with a right that nearly caved in his head.

"I'll never forget him," Braddock said with a smile.

Winking, he added, "Nor will he forget me."

"Five dollars or five days."

The ruling had come from a criminal court judge in Washington, D.C. It was August of '38. Slats had traveled to the nation's capitol to see an important friend about a job. Afterwards, Slats, craving a drink, had stopped off in a public park to score a swig of whiskey. He made some new friends and helped them polish off their bottle. His timing couldn't have been worse. That night, police raided the park and hauled Slats and two other men off to jail. Some of the officers realized that they had busted the great Jimmy Slattery and tried to help him out. They offered him some money, which Slats refused. One of the cops suggested that Slats reach out to Jack Dempsey who just happened to be in D.C. as well. Slats was emphatic. He did not want to call Dempsey. He spent the night in jail.

Waiting to appear before the judge the next morning, Slats took a spot in a long line of drunkards and petty thieves. By his own estimate, Slattery made, and blew, nearly $500,000 in the ring, even factoring in Red's cut and taxes. The figure amounts to about $1.5 million in today's dollars. Now he was unable to produce five dollars from his pocket.

Slats steeled himself for incarceration. Right at that moment, according to newspaper accounts, a female reporter recognized the former golden boy and grabbed a hold of him. "Hell, Jimmy, this is on the press," she said, paying his fine.

The sadly uplifting incident made the national wires (*"Slats, who once wore $185 suits, thanked the reporter and shuffled away, his head high and his pockets still empty,"* wrote the UP); the *Washington Post*'s Shirley Povich, father of Maury Povich, interviewed Slattery for his morning column.

Some friends of Slattery's in Buffalo insisted it must have been a case of mistaken identity, because Slats had not been in D.C. A reporter in the Washington bureau of the *Buffalo Evening News* wrote "the local Boxing Writers' Association paid the $5 fine for a man identified as Jim Slattery."

Sammy Brindis in his saga added one extra detail—Slats strode out of the courtroom with the female reporter on his arm.

If that man was a different 34-year-old Jim Slattery, then he must have pulled a fast one on Povich.

Otherwise, here's what Slattery had to say for himself, according to Povich:

> It's the same old story, I guess. I didn't know how to keep my money. I went up fast and came down quick. When they gave the decision to Maxie Rosenbloom in 1930, that was the turning point for me. I thought I won that one. It was my last good fight. I drifted into work-relief jobs and then they petered out. I'm at rock-bottom now.

A few weeks after his bust in D.C., Slattery beat up a cabbie over an 80 cent fare. Slats spent the rest of the autumn trying to scrape together $70 to pay for the driver's chipped teeth so that he could stay out of jail. "Jimmy never harmed anybody but himself," Red had once told a judge.

During his early fighting days, Slattery's disinclination for violence was sometimes held against him. When he was rising to stardom, it was part of his charm. "He's just a good-hearted boy who wouldn't do a mean thing to a soul in the world," Murray told fellow sportswriters in the fall of '24. Back in 1930, when Slats was thrown out of the ring against Pete Latzo (for not giving a sufficient effort) his defense had been that he had tagged Latzo, hard, plenty of times, and there was no need to further hurt him during the late rounds.

So it was strange and deeply saddening when in December of '38 news broke that the former world's light heavyweight champion had been arrested for second-degree robbery, a felony. His downward spiral seemed completely out of control now. Maybe his brain just cracked.

According to police, Slats was at Quinn's Tavern in the old neighborhood on a Tuesday night when a Lehigh Valley railroad worker named Dennis Shea came in and pulled up a stool. Shea lived on Harvey Place in the heart of St. Stephen's Parish. The 31-year-old still looked up to Slats and bought him a few drinks. Shea had just cashed a $61 paycheck with the bartender. After settling an old tab, and his new one, Shea left to go home not realizing that someone was following him.

He would later testify that his idol stalked him to Harvey Place, came up from behind, punched him to the sidewalk and rolled him for the $37 he had left over in his pocket. Neighbors would corroborate his story. They told police it was Slats. Police arrested him a few hours later at a restaurant on Chippewa.

A notorious, trouble-making drunk—Slattery, sadly, was all that and then some. But a mugger? The news caught most people by surprise. When it came over the ticker, *New York Post* columnist Jack Miley telephoned Red. "Slats had a million-dollar noodle inside the ropes," the frustrated manager told him. "But outside of them he can't think his way through kindergarten."

Miley led his column about the robbery rap like this: "*Jimmy Slattery. Remember him? What a fighter he was! But all the poor fellow's brains were in his fists.*"

At the arraignment, on Wednesday, December 14, Slattery's bail was set at $2,500. He pleaded not guilty. His hair was slicked back perfectly like in his fighting days. He was clean-shaven and wore his top coat, still in decent condition. Shea looked awful. His left eye was blackened and swollen shut. His cheek was bruised. Former Buffalo councilman Andy Meaney put up his Louisiana Street home so Slats could walk free pending a hearing. The case went to a grand jury.

How Slattery managed to wriggle free from a lengthy jail term is something for a future investigation. But the episode had some positive effect. Slattery set about to reclaim his dignity as if launching one of his comebacks. He actually did launch another comeback and how he went about that in the spring of '39 warrants a brief probe. This next yarn involves the Boxing Commission, a world-famous trainer, a mysterious benefactor from Westchester County, and, oddly enough, goat's milk.

★★★★★

By 1939, Slats was staying in a flophouse above a Pearl Street stove company and subsisting on the charity of his friend Roggie Lavin. Growing up, Roggie (his actual name was Rodger Cleary) helped out his uncle, Paddy Lavin, in the retired boxer's thriving bootlegging business. Roggie and his brother Willie also became boxers, training out of Newsboys' Gym under Red's tutelage, often sparring with Slats. Both Cleary brothers took Lavin as their ring name. Roggie had his share of altercations outside the ring, as there was no shortage of enterprising competitors looking to encroach on the family business which Roggie inherited when his uncle Paddy was killed.

Some relatives suspect Paddy Lavin's car was bombed by a rival rumrunner. There's another story about a bomb, intended for Roggie, going off in a bar right before Roggie had luckily slipped out; and there was also the time three armed men walked into the Peacock Inn looking for Roggie, and wound up instead gunning down the Inn's 32-year-old proprietor, Michael George.

Lavin's Café on Franklin near Chippewa had a restaurant/cabaret downstairs and a gambling parlor up above. Some famous entertainers, most notably Bing Crosby, had performed there during the 1930s. Lavin's menu featured a porterhouse steak for a dollar. As difficult of a time Slats had been having, and as broke as he was, Lavin always made sure he didn't go hungry.

Red, likewise, was looking out for Slattery as best as he could. He invited Slats to work the corner when he took his top middleweight prospect, Paul Mahoney, to the New York Hippodrome to fight Braddock's boy, Popeye Woods. Slats in one corner, Braddock in the other—it must have seemed like old times. Mahoney, touted as another Slattery, bombed. Woods trounced him. Comparisons between Mahoney and a young Slattery struck ringsiders as ludicrous. But for Slats, it felt good to be back in New York, back in the game.

Holding court at Lavin's Café, Slats began to entertain the fanciful notion that perhaps he had one last comeback in him. Friends advised against it. Red would have no part of it. Many people feared Slats was going to get himself killed in the ring. But with enough of a support system, the 34-year-old believed he could pull it off. Luring him back into such contemplations was an offer from a mystery man of some means, Ed Boland of Larchmont, N.Y.

Said to be of social prominence, Boland had enough clout to help convince the Boxing Commission to issue Slattery a license and enough money to retain the services of Doc Robb, considered by many to be one of the best trainers in all of boxing. Robb was credited with resurrecting Braddock. The Catskills training camp Robb helped oversee was among the most grueling ever devised—Braddock went six rounds a day with a parade of four brawny, formidable contenders, all of whom had been instructed to unleash. Slats would go to Boland's estate in the Westchester countryside, breathing healthy air and chopping wood. It was widely accepted that Slats was the most naturally gifted boxer to come along since Corbett—maybe ever—and Boland's bet was that the last dregs of talent could somehow be extracted and brought to market for one more year, maybe two. What was Boland thinking? Slattery's physical condition had been wracked from a decade of heavy drinking. His legs were mush compared to the iron coils of his youth. A secret elixir would solve that, Boland told sportswriters. He had Slattery gulping down several pints of goat's milk a day, tapping into its supposed healing properties. But after five years away from the gym, a shadow of the shadow of his former self, Slats would need much more than goat's milk. If he could train his way back to even one ring appearance—it would be a miracle. Boland, it was said, approached the reclamation project with child-like enthusiasm. And apparently he believed in miracles.

While in Manhattan to take a physical required by the state, Slats met with Gayle Talbot, an AP reporter, to talk about his unlikely return. Ironically, right at that time, Billy Conn, a handsome Irishman from Pittsburgh, was shooting to stardom in the Big Town, much to the delight of the Garden old-timers who had been longing for another Jimmy Slattery. Little did they know, Slattery was seeking to be the next Slattery. No one paid much attention when he took in a few workouts—strictly shadow boxing—at Stillman's Gym on Eighth Avenue. He passed his test, although his license was granted on the condition that he pass another more rigorous physical exam before actually entering a ring. Sitting down with Talbot at a Midtown sandwich shop, Slats looked exhausted. He openly admitted he wasn't sure how this flyer would turn out.

"I won't try to fool you," Slats said. "Maybe I can get the old legs in shape again, and maybe I can't. If they don't come around, I'll give it up, as much as I need some money. I'm not going to let some young squirt knock my head off."

The legs never did come back. Slats would never fight professionally again. Nat Fleischer had tallied his record at a total of 108 wins (44 by knockout) and 14 losses.

But the time away from Buffalo, and perhaps even the experimental dairy intake, served him well.

That dash of publicity led to an offer from a wealthy Scranton man who enlisted Slats to train his pet heavyweight prospect, Hugh "Kid" Glynn, who would go on to appear as a preliminary boy at one of the first matches ever held at the new Memorial Auditorium.

Slats, always a popular figure in the northwest section of Pennsylvania, embraced the region. He trained Glynn and spent an enjoyable stint working as a greeter at a fancy hotel restaurant in Bradford, Pa.

Around this time, Sammy "Newsboy" Brindis, a 24-year-old former amateur boxer from Warren, Pa., befriended Slats and set about the task of restoring his reputation. An aspiring writer and devout worshipper of Slattery, Brindis spent several weeks getting to know his idol, discussing his story and retracing his "short hop from the Garden to the gutter." Brindis self-published a slim but thorough mini-booklet: *The Saga of Jimmy Slattery*. Resembling a brochure, its cover featured a photo of the wonder boy at seventeen, along with a claim that "this clean, authentic biography will help give courage and inspiration to every generation during these trying times."

Brindis, comparing Slattery to both Corbett and Casanova, declared (repeating a line others had used) that Slats was "the greatest fighter who ever lived, and the greatest liver who ever fought."

Brindis brought 500 copies of his booklet to Buffalo in 1940 and stayed in the city for several months, stocking cigar stores and newsstands. A generation of South Buffalo 10-year-olds who had soaked up second-hand lore of Slattery while growing up could now begin to more fully grasp his fabled existence. The older fans of Slattery's, the ones who now averted their eyes when they saw him, were at least able to see another side.

"It would probably delight reform characters if Slattery in these bleak days would at least bow his head in shame," Brindis wrote. "But he hasn't yet, and it's even money he never will."

"I wish Buffalo and the rest would remember the things Jimmy has done for this city," an unnamed friend told Brindis. "Too many people are ready to tear a man apart when he is down."

"Suppose I had invested my money?" Slats asked his narrator. "I'd only have lost it in the crash, wouldn't I? I have a hell of a good time. What the hell, Jack, one can't eat that stuff."

By the summer of 1940, Slats was living in a rooming house at 51 West Chippewa. His divorce had become final. He still got himself arrested for public drunkenness now and again. But the city court judges threw up their hands, letting him off with small fines. His life had become somewhat stable. It was not a short hop but, rather, a long way from, say, the Lake Placid Club or a suite at the Astor, but Slats wanted for nothing. He had his Chippewa world and to him that was plenty. Slats didn't need much—one dollar a day paid the rent. Acolytes still bought him drinks. Slats could always hop a trolley without having to pay. And when the trolleys were replaced, the bus drivers let him ride for free, too.

Hard times were cushioned by happy occasions. Sometimes on Friday evenings, Slats went back to the old neighborhood to have dinner with his sister-in-law, Marion, the widow of his brother, John. She and her young children scraped to get by, but the household was warm and friendly. Marion's daughter, Patsy, a first-grader in 1940, recalled how excited she'd get when she would see her uncle Jimmy come strolling down Euclid in his top coat. She knew nothing of his rise and fall, only that he was her favorite uncle who had a smile that lit up the block. Marion would never offer him a beer, but she would feed him and let him crash on the couch. Some nights, they and some other friends would go out dancing together. The swinging Big Band sound was all the rage ("Music Maestro, Please" by Tommy Dorsey was among Slattery's all-time favorite tunes), and dance halls had become the popular gathering places in South Buffalo. A heavyset woman who'd endured much and kept her mirthful spirit, Marion was also surprisingly light on her feet. Slats still could dance with the best. They were beautiful to watch.

Slats got arrested for disorderly conduct in the first week of September 1942. At his arraignment, the 38-year-old told the court he was feeling sick. He was admitted to Meyer Memorial Hospital.

Tests later confirmed his own worst fear. Tuberculosis. Slattery's long-anticipated death warrant had arrived.

TWELVE

JIMMY'S TOUGHEST FIGHT OF ALL

THEY SAY IT HAPPENED AROUND the first day of summer, 1943. Slats had caused a disturbance on Chippewa near Delaware Avenue. Three policemen arrived on the scene. For several minutes, their jowls took turns sampling the fists of the former light heavyweight champ. A crowd of a hundred or so pedestrians stopped to watch. An entire squadron arrived to grapple him to the sidewalk. But the onlookers were amazed—Jimmy Slattery still had some scrap in him.

In truth, Slattery was extremely ill. Following his initial diagnosis, doctors made plans to transfer Slats to the public tuberculosis institution at Perrysburg, but there was no way he was going. Slats believed once you went in, you never came out. He stayed at Meyer Memorial for a few weeks, and when he started to feel better, he skipped out and resumed his life of fleabag hotels and any gin mill that would have him. He grew worse. After his diagnosis, Slats went in and out of the hospital, while loved ones, including his sister Mary, and sister-in-law Marion, tried to stage an intervention.

Tuberculosis attacked lung membranes like ants on a dropped popsicle. For decades, doctors had struggled with how to treat T.B. patients, beyond the usual prescription of "heliotherapy," which involved pretty much nothing; the regimen consisted of little or no movement coupled with thin, dry air, allowing the lungs to rebuild. It was accepted that half of patients who got the virus would slowly suffocate to death within five years. Some people, even in a closely cloistered, poorly ventilated tenement environment, just had a natural resistance to T.B. and never got sick; some got it but were able to keep it in check. Others, such as Slattery's father and brother, got it and were rapidly consumed. Guinea pigs, scientists observed, had almost no resistance to the disease. Goats, on the other hand, were almost completely impervious. Had Slats gone to Perrysburg, he would have found goat's milk on the menu.

With each passing year, new treatments and drugs were tried, but as of 1943, the prognosis for an infected patient generally was not good. Because T.B. was so contagious, and so deadly, people were afraid to come into contact with anyone who had it; those who had it didn't want the guilt of giving it to someone else, so they avoided people altogether. Slats cordoned himself off in the Chippewa area, which almost by city ordinance had become Buffalo's skid row. It was the only place where he felt comfortable.

Red Carr sent a letter to the Husson family in Indian Lake up in the Adirondacks. A restful place and mountain air was Slattery's best hope. Might they consider taking Slats in?

Gerald Husson recalls the day as a teenager he overheard his parents having an intense discussion about it. His father, Earl, loved Slats dearly. But with young children in the house, Dora was adamantly against the idea. "They agonized over having to turn Slattery away," Husson recalled in 2012 at age 86. "At that time, people were very afraid of T.B."

On Monday, August 9, 1943, *The New York Times* published Slattery's obituary.

Erroneously.

The next day, the *Times* retracted the story and clarified the error—Slattery was alive in Buffalo; the AP had received incorrect information from a Brooklyn hospital superintendent who mistook a vagrant who had given his name as James Slattery—and who had claimed to be a former boxer—as the former titleholder from Buffalo.

Down but not out, Slats found sporadic employment as an iron worker. Each day he began to struggle more. He was wheezing and coughing up phlegm, beset by an overall feeling of malaise, which was only made worse by his drinking.

Slats could nil afford to have his constitution compromised by excessive drinking. Already his symptoms were worsening and his weak condition left him susceptible to other germs. He came down with a nasty sinus condition while his breathing became increasingly belabored. Slats knew if he wanted to live any longer, he would have to do something drastic.

On the outskirts of Tucson, Arizona, public health officials helped run a low-rent housing community of T.B. patients who had access to doctors specializing in the affliction. Aided by the generosity of his friends, Slats left Buffalo sometime around St. Patrick's Day of 1946. He moved to the outer fringe of South Tucson, taking up residence in a tiny, cement-wall cottage—a cinder block with a door, basically. His quiet street comprised nothing but these simple, look-alike dwellings, separated by dirt, scrub brush and the occasional cactus. Sitting out front, Slats had a view of the Santa Catalina Mountains. He was soon bored, miserable and lonely, though, with nothing to do except sit back and inhale the arid desert air. Tucson was 60 miles north of Mexico in the Sonoran Desert. Moisture from the Pacific Ocean was blocked by the San Bernardino Mountains; moisture from the Gulf of Mexico was blocked by the Sierra Madre. It was low in elevation. The area around his place at 2220 South Fourth Avenue was crawling with lizards, sidewinders and cockroaches. In summer, temperatures hit as high as 114 degrees. Even then, Slats was encouraged to do his heliotherapy, baking in the heat, wallowing in his own private purgatory. In those quiet moments, Slats would have heard white-winged doves rustling in the mesquite trees, perhaps the howl of a coyote and, very likely, the distant hacking of a germ-ravaged neighbor coughing up a lung.

Prescott, Arizona, in the higher-elevation, northern part of the state, had been the leading center for T.B. treatment for several decades. Now the entire state had become a destination for chronic sufferers. The only alternative to sitting in the sunshine that doctors allowed was taking a short, leisurely walk. Still, Slats was obviously free to break from regimen if he chose to do so. He could have found his way to downtown Tucson. It had bars. Whatever money he had, it went quick.

Word spread that Slattery was running low on funds. A group of sporting men, including members of the boxing fraternity and the Buffalo Athletic Club, staged a benefit dinner for him. On the Monday evening of October 28, 1946, about 500 men (and no women) attended "Jimmy Slattery Sports Night" in a plush ballroom at the Lafayette Hotel. "I've never seen more Irishmen in my life," joked one of three clergymen on hand to bless the $25-a-plate event. Special guests on the speaker's dais included Joe McCarthy, former manager of the Yankees (and a friend of Billy Kelly's), and Jimmy Braddock, former heavyweight champion.

"Everybody recalls Slats as a boxer," Braddock told the audience. "Funny part about that is Jimmy could punch. I found that out the hard way. He hit me during the third round at Madison Square Garden and I thought they had let the lights down on my head."

The night was filled with speeches and toasts. All of Buffalo's boxing greats were on hand: Lou Scozza and Frankie Schoell; Jimmy Goodrich and

Rocky Kansas; and Jackie Donovan, a handsome Irishman who became a popular attraction at the new Aud during the early 1940s. The gala event was a celebratory affair—it had been announced that $10,045 had been raised and would be placed into a fund for Jimmy. On the menu, a murderer's row of special dishes—Delaney Soup, Berlenbach Beef, Scozza Green Peas and, for dessert, Rosenbloom Baked Alaska. Even the rolls and butter were renamed (after Tommy Loughran). The evening culminated in a floor show, with two solo singers accompanied by a band. At the end of the night, attendees, equipped with printed lyrics in their event program, joined in a rousing tribute sung to the tune of "It's a Long Way to Tipperary."

> *Let us all shout for Jimmy Slattery*
> *We are all here to show,*
> *We are all here to prove our friendship,*
> *He was always on the go,*
> *Let us all join in celebration,*
> *For our pride from Buffalo,*
> *Let us join hands for Jimmy Slattery*
> *With a great big Hello!*

Sitting in his outdoor sauna, Slattery had at least one preferred way to pass the hours. He penned letters. If one has survived somewhere, this author has not found it—but there are *stories* about the letters. A few arrived at the old barber shop. Jimmy Kearns, one of Slattery's best friends and a local bookmaker, still got a shave there every day. "Any word from Slats?" he could be heard asking Angelo the barber. If a letter had come in, Angelo would excitedly read it aloud.

Lou Scozza also received a letter from Slats, according to his nephew, Jim Messina. Slats concluded the letter, according to Bob Caico, Buffalo boxing historian, by saying: "*Lou, I won the championship but you're the real champ.*" It was said that Slattery looked up to Scozza the person, not the warrior. Later in life, Scozza had adopted the orphaned triplets of a relative. The stand-up family man had also made a point to look out for retired boxers.

In late October of 1947, approximately one year after the benefit, some disturbing news reached Buffalo. Rumors and unsubstantiated reports put Slats in critical condition at an Arizona hospital, close to death. Slattery's sister, Mary, who had married a man named Ed Wilds, flew to Tucson to check on her brother. What she and her husband found surprised them both: Slats wasn't on death's door. In fact, he was doing much better. After nineteen months of living in the desert, Slats was trim, deeply tanned, alert and feeling well enough to take daily walks. They visited downtown Tucson and bought a cowboy outfit for Slattery's little nephew, Ed, Jr. Photos of Slats were taken that day. In them he wore a nice suit, if a bit worn-out, and stylish saddle shoes. His hair was slicked back. He had begun to wear rimless spectacles, giving him a mature look, though with his full head of jet-black hair and trim build—168 pounds, almost precisely his ideal fighting weight—he looked a lot younger than the typical 43-year-old. They had a happy visit. Mary had been preparing in her mind to retrieve her brother's body, but instead, she returned home a few days later with the wonderful news of his recovery.

The following summer, Slats returned to Buffalo for an extended visit. His symptoms were under control. He looked terrific. Mary had him out at her family's cottage in Crystal Beach one street away from the entrance to the amusement park. Friends flocked there to see him. Some fifty of them showed up on the day Slats arrived home. He was reunited with Red and Skitsy Fitzgerald and Joe Hickey. Red was working for the Buffalo Water Department. Skitsy ran a corner store on Potters Road in South Buffalo. Joe Hickey was working for a liquor distributor and living in a cheap hotel near Chippewa. He never married and, picking his spots, still loved to party. Babe Ruth had just died and so they all reminisced about the time back in the day that they met him and the entire Yankee team.

"Tough about the Babe," Slats said, his voice gravelly, the result of a wicked shot to the throat he once took from Scozza. "But when they ring that final bell, you go. That's all there is to it."

Thus began a migratory pattern that lasted several years; Slats would journey to Crystal Beach in the summer and go back to Arizona in the fall, and when the money ran out, his friends would throw a benefit boxing match or charity dinner to raise some more. Slats, feeling better, decided he had had enough of Arizona. Although experimental antibiotics had been used to treat T.B. with limited success during the 1940s, it wasn't until the 1950s that more effective drugs were being developed. Slats told friends he had been given an injection of a "wonder drug," which he claimed had cured him. He looked healthy. So he came back to Buffalo to stay. Perhaps his friends had also had enough of raising money for him. Many suspected he drank it up.

Slats rented a cheap room and found work with the Buffalo Parks Department. It was a no-show job, obtained from friends via the City Hall patronage system. His wages may have well been sent directly to his favorite haunt, which by 1952 was a Chippewa dive bar called the House O'Quinn. A saloonkeeper named Jimmy "Hoosier" Quinn had opened the place back in the 1930s. Over the front door was a green awning with a shamrock and the Gaelic phrase "Erin Go Bragh." The original old, faded sign out front had been retrofitted with BAR and GRILL in neon lights. Boxer Jackie Donovan, who also happened to be a talented artist, painted a mural on the wall behind the bar depicting Slattery in his glory days. The owner during the 1950s, Frank Brinkworth, was both a friend and an admirer of Slats, and made sure he was taken care of, which is not to say that Slats wasn't occasionally thrown out. People over the years have repeated stories heard from their fathers, stories that place Slats getting tossed out, or even refused entry; passed out on the sidewalk; pissing himself and puking; teetering along Chippewa, arms outstretched as if walking a tightrope. Up and down Chippewa were topless bars and seedy hangouts. These establishments mixed with offices, storefronts and restaurants, such as Gandy's and Your Host. Next to the House O'Quinn was the B&R Delicatessen, and in back of the deli was Cam Lee's Chinese laundry. The area was teeming with hustlers, losers, pickpockets, unemployed sailors, con artists and stone-cold drunks. Slats would not have been the only hard-luck ex-fighter hanging around. "It was the street of broken dreams," recalls Danny Redmond, a former Buffalo detective who spent the bulk of his childhood working at B&R and observing the characters that played cards in the back room, Slats among them. "Everybody had a story about how they ended up on Chippewa, how fate dealt them a bad hand—it was never their own fault. These guys were straight out of a Damon Runyon story."

Buffalo's skid row used to be on lower Main Street. Some of the world's filthiest flophouses were razed when the Aud was built in the 1930s. Going back decades, transient lake mariners and railroad workers could get a cot for pennies a day; and for a few pennies more, a man could even get his own "dormitory," which was really just a bed in a cramped space partitioned off by a few boards and chicken wire. Society's sludge eventually winnowed its way to Chippewa, which was attracting a surly crowd by the late 1920s. At that time, police made a point to crack down on "corner loungers and men of questionable character" loitering in the vicinity of

Main and Chippewa. It got so rowdy at times that women could not walk along Chippewa without being harassed or even accosted by some cretin. By the 1950s, drug dealing, prostitution, thievery and knife fights were becoming commonplace in the area.

Jimmy Slattery, Jr. certainly didn't expect to have any trouble the day he walked into the House O'Quinn looking for his father. He was mistaken.

★★★★★

Growing up in his grandparents' home, Jimmy, Jr. couldn't really recall much supervision. His mother worked and socialized a lot in the evening. He almost never saw his father.

Jimmy made it through high school without getting into too much trouble. But around the time he graduated in 1948, Jimmy began to butt heads with the police. He'd bought a 1935 Ford Roadster with money earned setting pins in a bowling alley. Caught drag racing on Main Street one too many times, Jimmy was given a strong warning from police disinclined to allow the son of Slattery to wreak havoc on the road the way his father had. Cops told him it might be a good idea for him to join the service— basically, get out of Buffalo. The speeding tickets piled up. Troopers would nail him on his way out to the lakeshore bars near Point Breeze in Angola. In December 1949, while on route to Boothbay Harbor, Maine, where his mother was remarrying a man named Gates Burgess, Jimmy was nearly killed while speeding around an icy corner somewhere near Brattleboro, Vermont. The car rolled 16 times, but the son of Slattery walked away with just some minor cuts and bruises. He never made it to the wedding.

In 1950, Jimmy joined the Air Force. America was in the midst of the Korean War and a lot of 19-year-olds were ready to do their part, having grown up in the ever-present shadow of the Second World War. He trained at Lackland Air Force Base in San Antonio, Texas, and later spent 18 months stationed in the Azores, an archipelago 900 miles west of Portugal. By the fall of '52, Jimmy was on leave and feeling good about himself in his uniform. He figured he'd pay a visit to the old man. Looking back on his childhood, he probably only ever saw his father twenty to thirty times total, if that much. They'd gone out to breakfast a few times. There was a vague memory of being on a beach together in Speculator. His father came by one day while Jimmy was hanging out with his next-door neighbor, Ray Notaro, who liked to mess around with the gloves. Slats could tell he had natural talent and taught him a few things. Jimmy, Jr. wasn't particularly adept, nor was he interested. He did, however, inherit his dad's love of automobiles. He was a natural mechanic who could take an engine apart and put it back together again. On the drag racing scene, no one was faster. Most cops couldn't catch him. But they all knew him, and, of course, all knew his father. Maybe he had been on a troublesome path as a teenager, but he had grown out of it. It wasn't as if Jimmy needed to show his father how sharp he looked in his Air Force uniform; soon enough his leave would be over and who knew when he would be home again. For all Jimmy knew, this could be the last time he ever saw the old man. And he knew exactly where to find him.

"Who the hell are you?" Slats growled in the darkness of the gin mill.

His voice was extra hoarse from the Pall Mall cigarettes he had resumed smoking after convincing himself of his new lease on life. He had a glass of Ballantine scotch on the bar accompanied by a Ballantine beer.

"It's me . . . I'm your son."

Slats looked at him irritably and waved him away.

"I don't know you," Slats grumbled, completely gassed.

He may have thought he was being trifled. Slats was often accosted by drunken Canadians who came to the bar on Sundays to circumvent Ontario's blue laws. They were always amazed when they entered the bar and realized that the drunk in the white tee-shirt near the window was actually the great Jimmy Slattery. However, upon approaching him and asking for an autograph, they would always get an angry rebuke.

Jimmy, Jr. tried one more time to explain himself.

"Don't you know who I am?"

Maybe Slats thought he was a cop. He shot over a hard right punch. Demonstrating he had indeed inherited his father's reflexes, Jimmy quickly ducked—and not a second too soon. The punch would have leveled him.

Jimmy, Jr. collected himself, bit his lip and walked out. A few days later, he reported to Eglin Air Force Base in the Florida panhandle. It wouldn't be long before he was called back to Buffalo.

★ ★ ★ ★ ★

With Slats having fallen back into his old habits, his health took a serious turn for the worse. He was so sick that he was sent to a T.B. ward. Some family members say it was Perrysburg, but there are also newspaper accounts of some ex-rivals sending Slats get-well cards to a facility called

Broad Acres near Utica, New York. Legend has it that Slats escaped from the premises and hitchhiked back to the House O'Quinn in his pajamas. By June of '53, Slats was back at Meyer Memorial. One lung had collapsed and the other was failing. In July, he took a turn for the worse. Doctors worked to give him repeated blood transfusions. Slattery was informed he was close to death. But he somehow staged a comeback. Waking up one morning after one of his near-death experiences, Slats found Red at his bedside.

"I was almost home," Slats joked to his old friend. "But they flagged me down at third base."

The only way Slats was going to survive was if he stopped drinking. What Red needed him to do now was to finally listen. He was in the fight of his life. He had to quit boozing. Slats agreed to be confined to Ward B1 at Meyer. He promised not to leave.

In that room he stayed, for the rest of the year. His toughest battle of all: the one he was waging against his addiction to alcohol. Slats fought as hard as he could. Each new day he resisted the urge to jump out of bed and go find some action. Somehow he never gave in.

By the start of 1954, Slats was back in good health. He walked out of the hospital a sober man.

THIRTEEN

LAST LEGS

"**O**FFICER, HELP!"

A frantic pedestrian could hardly get the words out—a man was hurt and bleeding terribly.

Yep, just another night on Chippewa, Tom Higgins thought.

For a rookie foot patrolman, there could be no more exciting beat than Chippewa between Delaware and Franklin on a Friday night. When Officer Higgins arrived on the gory scene near the House O' Quinn, he recognized the poor fellow on the ground—Slats.

Higgins grew up an altar boy at St. Stephen's Church. He had heard endless tales of the neighborhood hero. Now here was the great Jimmy Slattery sprawled out on the pavement, his forehead and nose busted open, blood squirting everywhere.

Higgins took a split-second look around. What he deduced caused an eruption of goose bumps along his neck and arms. Slats had fallen face first into a fire hydrant. The solid brass nut had met the 53-year-old squarely and to sickening effect.

Higgins used a curbside call-box to tell the station he needed an ambulance. Slats, barely conscious and groaning, was rushed to nearby Columbus Hospital. Its emergency room handled so many shootings, stabbings and beatings that the police department had commandeered a section of the nurses' station for their own makeshift booking area. The head nurse informed Higgins that unless Slattery was formally charged they would not treat him. Better, she said, that he be booked, because that way the hospital would be reimbursed by the City of Buffalo. The 27-year-old officer, just completing his first full year on the job, complied—the necessary forms and a typewriter were sitting right there. Although Higgins couldn't believe he was really about to arrest his idol, he knew it was for

Slattery's own good. So he charged him with the least serious offense he could think of: public intoxication.

Higgins finished his shift at midnight, had himself a few beers and went home to bed. At the time, he still lived with his parents, Irish immigrants who were tight with the Slattery family and who absolutely loved the former champ.

Awake and energized by the aroma of the breakfast his mother Madge was frying, Higgins told her about poor Slats bashing his face on the fire hydrant and the hysterical onlookers and getting him to the hospital in the ambulance and, *Oh yeah, due to some red tape with the city he actually had to arrest Slats . . .*

"You did WHAT?!"

Higgins had never seen his mother so appalled.

"Good heavens, how could you—how could you arrest Slats?!"

No matter how hard he tried to explain that he had no choice, Madge Higgins refused to speak to her son for the rest of the day.

★★★★★

The injuries Slattery suffered that Friday night in October of 1957 included a fractured skull, broken nose and damage to his ear. After emerging from Meyer Memorial remarkably healthy in the early part of 1954, Slats had returned with a variety of ailments. He'd had a mild heart attack; he required a hernia operation. He'd collapsed in a downtown drug store. Having a collapsed lung made his life a struggle. That precious eight-month detoxification was followed by a relapse that turned the tide of Slattery's battle with the bottle. The whiskey had him in its grip and wasn't letting go. All he could do now was play out his string.

By the mid-1950s, Slats was still known to the sporting world but purely as a tragic footnote to the golden age. When an arrest or hospitalization would come over the wires, some old-time sportswriter would inevitably publish a column about what a beautiful wizard in the ring Slats had once been. But a new generation of fans would have no reason to pay attention to a washed-up champ from thirty years before. As older writers retired, memories of Slats in his heyday went with them.

Slattery's niece, Patsy Kline, recalls visiting with him in the hospital. Slats was ready to be released, but had nowhere to go. She had just gotten married and was living in South Buffalo. She opened her home to him but he declined, muttering, "I'll figure something out."

He bounced from flophouse to fleabag hotel, eventually settling at the seedy Windsor Hotel at 234 Franklin Street. The rate was $10 a week.

One day, Patsy went to check on him. "It wasn't much," she said. "A single bed and a chair, maybe a small dresser—that's pretty much all there was. He didn't want me to see it . . . I remember he kind of hurried me out."

Slats resumed his job with the Parks Department. On the days he showed up, his official task was working in a spectacular Delaware Park garden, tending to the roses. However, he usually could be found at the House O' Quinn, blinded drunk, sitting by himself near the front window, sipping his beer and scotch. Sometimes Slats would start drinking first thing in the morning in the back room of the B&R Deli and move next door to the bar later when Frank Burns the bartender opened up. Bookies taking bets on horses were usually floating around the B&R and a dollar wager on a long shot was often the highlight of the day.

"Some afternoons, Slattery and I would sit and listen to the Yankee game on the radio," Danny Redmond said, remembering a childhood on Chippewa working in his father's delicatessen.

Redmond recalled:

> Slats liked me. I'd fetch the guys their coffee when they were in the back playing rummy. Joe Hickey used to hang around there, too. But sometimes it was Slats and me, just talking. He was a nice guy, intelligent, well spoken—when he wasn't drinking. When he was drinking you couldn't understand him . . . but when he was sober we'd sit and he'd talk about anything. Except boxing . . . unless you asked—and even then he didn't like it . . . Slats, he wasn't an ego guy. Never talked about himself . . . he wanted to talk about what was happening in the neighborhood. He loved Chippewa, the characters. He knew everyone. He liked to talk about what was going on. Who was in trouble, who won money on a horse, or who was in fight, that kind of thing . . . he got such a kick out of the neighborhood. He loved it down there.

Slats enjoyed the day in 1954 when Jimmy, Jr. married his sweetheart, Lois Griffin, a recent high school graduate from the Kensington section. Slats seemed to make peace with Betty. During the ceremony, which was held at St. Vincent de Paul's Church, Betty was escorted down the aisle by her new husband, Gates Burgess, on one arm, and Slats on the other.

Betty was the life of the party. After a modest daytime reception at the Westbrook Hotel—consisting of some snacks and punch—Betty and Slats and some other old friends kept the party going all night long, carrying on as if it were the '20s again, laughing and singing. Watching the two of them together, recalls Lois Slattery, it was apparent that for all of their differences and all of the tumult, they really had been kindred spirits. Betty had always held a special place for Slats in her heart.

When Slats' health took another turn for the worse, Jimmy, Jr. and Lois moved back to the area. He was able to get a posting in Niagara Falls, N.Y., helping to oversee a civilian air defense program. Father and son were geographically much closer, but as far as their relationship—there was distance. Still, each man now seemed increasingly willing to make an effort.

Jimmy and Lois soon had their first child, Joyce, in 1955. Around the time of her first birthday, Slats came to visit on the bus and brought her a ten-cent kewpie doll, a warm gesture that did not go unnoticed.

When Jimmy, Jr. was reassigned to a base in Frankfurt, Germany, he flew over first. Lois, Joyce and a second child, James Slattery, III, born in '56, joined him later. On the morning that Lois and her two tiny tots were due to leave, Slats showed up at the Buffalo Airport to see them off. "That meant so much to us," Lois recalled one afternoon in 2012 with a stray tear in her eye. "He was a good man."

Most people didn't see the sentimental side of Slats—most didn't see him at all. When the boxing community held reunions and charity events—a dais, some speeches, a chicken dinner—Slats never went. A group called the Old Time Boxers Association of Western New York organized a reunion event in '55, but Slats didn't bother to show.

"One of the reasons Slattery became so forgotten was because he dropped out of sight and had sunken so low," the late Bert Sugar said in 2008. The fedora-wearing former editor of *The Ring* conceded that, unfairly or not, Slats, had indeed wound up lost to one of history's blind spots.

If a roadmap to rock-bottom had existed, it probably would have included directions to the House O' Quinn at noon on a weekday. Slattery, when he least expected it, would be summoned from oblivion. On June 21, 1956, he received some unwanted attention—on television.

★★★★★

After his L.A. nightclub shuttered and the bit-part movie roles stopped coming, Maxie Rosenbloom reinvented himself as a stand-up comedian, performing in Vegas alongside Max Baer. Rosenbloom's humorous malapropisms ("I'd like that steak well to do") had always delighted sportswriters and show business people alike. He was a natural buffoon.

A sample of the Max & Max routine:

> BAER: "*Didn't you go to school, stupid?*"
> ROSENBLOOM: "*Yeah, I went to school stupid and I left stupid.*"

At the dawn of the television age in the early 1950s, Rosenbloom was the perfect guest for the advertiser-driven, vaudeville-inspired "variety" shows that aired on the networks, such as the National Broadcasting Co. and the Columbia Broadcasting System. When Milton Berle's hit show debuted in 1948 there were only about 6,000 homes with TV sets. By 1955, half of American homes had one.

On the night of June 21, 1956, Rosenbloom appeared on the *Arthur Murray Party* television program. During the telecast, the nutty ex-champion dropped a bombshell.

"I fought Jimmy Slattery [several] times in Buffalo," he told host Murray. "And beat him every time. But I was robbed on hometown decisions. I saw it was a hopeless case trying to beat him in Buffalo and I decided to make some money out of losing. So I bet $5,000 on Slats. Along about the fourth round, with neither of us doing anything in a dull bout, I said to Jimmy, 'Come on Slats, do something. I bet on you to win.'"

According to Rosenbloom, Slats then replied, "And I bet on *you*."

Twenty-five years after their last meeting in a ring, Jimmy Slattery and Maxie Rosenbloom were about to do battle again.

Aided by attorney William J. Flynn, Slattery sued Rosenbloom for $500,000 alleging defamation of character. Everyone knew Slapsie Maxie was flat broke, which is why Arthur Murray, CBS, and the Gillette Company, sponsor of the telecast, were all named as co-defendants in the suit.

In September of '57, a hearing was held at the New York State Supreme Court. At issue: whether Slats was required to state separate causes of action against each defendant in the suit. His attorney argued that the corporations were partners in the half-hour program, and thus, should all be held accountable for what aired, along with Rosenbloom.

"The defendants should have deleted the defamatory remark or interrupted the telecast before the words were spoken," Flynn argued. "Defamation by television is quite different than ordinary libel and slander. This telecast was heard by millions and sent out over the air to more than 200 TV stations."

Supreme Court Justice Carlton Fisher could not resist. "How many rounds will this motion take?" he asked at the outset.

Later on, Slattery's attorney invoked his own boxing reference to let his adversaries know that this suit was not going away.

"We'll still be punching at the bell," Flynn declared.

The case dragged on for many months. It would be Slattery's word against Rosenbloom's. There is no evidence that Slattery ever compromised his integrity in the ring. Also, several inconsistencies exist in Rosenbloom's comments (such as claiming that he never won against Slattery in Buffalo). Nevertheless, accounts of the seventh and final match between the two do little to allay suspicion that Rosenbloom's yarn may have held some element of truth.

★★★★★

When actor Tyrone Power emerged as a Hollywood heartthrob in the early 1940s, a lot of people saw in him the spitting image of Slats in his prime. In the early 1950s, still-handsome Slats, in his black hair and glasses, more resembled television star George Reeves, as Clark Kent in *The Adventures of Superman*. Slats never looked like a street bum. His hair was always cleanly combed. He was never scraggily or unshaven. Even at his most obliterated, he at least looked presentable. Slats used to take the bus back to the old neighborhood to get a shave and a haircut at Mordeno's.

One day, while Slats was returning downtown after visiting his Elk Street barber, a young boxer named Jackie Donnelly got on the bus and sat down next to him. Slats knew Donnelly from the neighborhood.

"Where are you heading?" Slats asked him.

"I'm going up to Buffalo General to get an EKG," Donnelly replied.

Slats knew. Donnelly was applying for his boxing license.

Squinting emphatically, Slattery issued a command: "Get off the bus right now *and go home.*"

Donnelly didn't. A few years later, while making his debut at Madison Square Garden, he was in one of the dressing rooms chatting with a grizzled old codger tending to the water buckets and towels. When it was revealed Donnelly was from Buffalo, the old-timer asked about Slats.

"I'll tell you something," the guy told Donnelly. "The greatest boxing match I ever saw in this place was Slattery against Loughran."

At some point, former boxer turned artist Jackie Donovan solidified the House O' Quinn's status as a standing monument to Jimmy Slattery by painting a colorful mural of the fighter above the bar. Slats barely seemed to notice it. When he left after a long day-night shift he would not so much walk around the corner to his hotel as he would teeter, slowly, his arms outstretched, hands fumbling for a street sign or storefront façade on which to steady himself, each step a perilous test of his damaged equilibrium. His demeanor, like his voice, had become increasingly coarse.

Sometime in the middle of 1959, Slattery's lawyers quietly settled with CBS for about $500.

Rosenbloom continued to be a regular on the early talk show circuit and performed his comedy act in Vegas nightclubs. He briefly owned a professional women's softball team, but mainly chased Hollywood starlets and bet on horses. One night he was struck on the head with a pipe during a mugging. He recovered physically but his brain never worked the same. Slapsie Maxie Rosenbloom eventually wound up in a Pasadena mental institution where he died in anonymity.

Slattery's health was going downhill fast and he did not help matters by spending every waking hour at the House O'Quinn. But the place, his routine, was all he had.

Donnelly:

Slats just sat quietly. He never paid attention to the mural, and he never talked about himself. A lot of ex-fighters would open up a bar or restaurant and always be hanging around, entertaining customers by telling stories, you know, reliving the glory days—Jack Dempsey did that. But Slats, he didn't want to be bothered. He came into the bar to drink. He never smiled. He didn't like talking to anyone. If someone tried to talk to him, he'd tell him to get the hell away. He could be a nasty guy. I came in there once in a while to see him. He'd talk to me because he knew me. Frank the bartender says to me once, "Jackie, you know, you're the only guy he'll speak to." Slats would sip his beer and grumble about boxing. "Get out," he would always tell me in his hoarse voice. "It's a lousy way to make a living."

One of the last known Slattery appearances at a public gathering was when he attended a wake held for another First Ward legend, Buffalo Police Lieutenant and St. Patrick's Day Parade organizer John W. Crotty, who had died unexpectedly at age 57. No matter how many times Slats got into trouble over the decades, Crotty, an old classmate at St. Stephen's, had always looked out for his old friend like he was his guardian angel. When Slats walked into the funeral home, recalled daughter Carol Ann Crotty Schlee, the crowd parted. An awed hush fell over the mourners. *"That's Jimmy Slattery,"* people whispered.

Slats approached the casket, knelt down and began sobbing uncontrollably. No one said a word.

Slats had been grateful for everything his friend had done for him, and he knew his own time was short.

In the summer of 1960, America was first hearing about a talented Olympic boxer named Cassius Clay who had a brash technique—he fought with his hands down. Writers marveled. They had never seen anything like it. Boxing in Buffalo was bottoming out. Friday night fights on TV killed the Queensberry Athletic Club. Charlie Murray had died back in 1950—some say of a broken heart after his failed attempt to bring professional football to town (it would take another decade for that to happen, but that is another story). Around the middle of August, Buffalo sportswriter Charley Bailey, who had taken the mantle from Murray and Billy Kelly, got a call from a friend. Apparently Slattery's health was rapidly deteriorating. It was no false or exaggerated report. Bailey sauntered over to Chippewa knowing he might never talk to the legend again.

"Do you have any regrets about your career?" Bailey asked Slats. "Would you do anything differently if you had another time around?"

"No," Slats replied. "I have no regrets. I had a lot of fun, saw a lot of sights, met a lot of interesting people. No regrets."

Around his 56th birthday, Slats got another visit. Jim Harkins, who helped organize an association to look after area ring veterans, as well as a few other members of Buffalo's boxing fraternity, got together to pay Slats a visit in his tiny room.

"We heard Slats was on his last legs," recalls Batavia-born Angelo Prospero, then a budding 30-year-old sportswriter. "He looked terrible," Prospero recalled. "Harkins asked him if he would do anything differently. Slats said no, but then he paused a moment. It was hard for him to speak. His breathing was labored. And then . . . he admitted, that yes, he did have a few regrets . . . about the kind of life he'd lived."

On Monday afternoon, August 29, 1960, one of the hottest days of the summer, Slats collapsed in the House O' Quinn. Frank Burns and some regulars were able to revive him and get him back to the Windsor. The next morning, when Slats didn't show up, Burns told the hotel manager they should check on him. When they opened the door to his stifling room, they saw Slats on the floor between his bed and a chair. His final bell had rung.

Slattery's death certificate lists the immediate cause of death as pulmonary tuberculosis. Chronic alcohol abuse surely also contributed, as had a lifetime of fights, car accidents and assorted mishaps. His body, a monument to resiliency, could take no more. His organs were spent. His brain had been battered, many times. So had his heart.

Once, after one of his sojourns to Arizona, Slattery spoke to the *Buffalo Evening News* about the way his life turned out: "What is it they say? When you dance, you have to pay the fiddler . . . that old fiddler always had his hand out. And I guess I did plenty of dancing."

EPILOGUE

JUST PRIOR TO SLATTERY'S DEATH, Jimmy Braddock was interviewed in a feature story by *Boxing Illustrated*.

"The greatest boxer in my time was Jimmy Slattery," Braddock said. "I know from experience."

Slattery had died five days after his 56th birthday and 33 years to the day on which he won his first championship. Tributes poured in from all over the country. "Slattery was more than just a great fighter—he was poetry in motion," said the *Joplin News Herald* on September 1, 1960.

Funeral plans were at first unclear, as Slattery's son waded through Air Force red tape to travel back from Germany to Buffalo. In the meantime, a well-attended memorial was held at a downtown cathedral, St. Joseph's. Three priests eulogized about frequently seeing Jimmy at mass during his last few months. Slats went to St. Michael's near the bus station and also to St. Joseph's. The priests used to point him out from the altar. They spoke about how the ex-fighter, though in poor condition and clearly suffering a great deal, never once complained. A wake was held. Red Carr, Joe Hickey and Skitsy Fitzgerald had an opportunity to share their favorite Slattery stories, such as the time a bewildered Tex Rickard came into the dressing room at the old Garden expecting the skinny Irish boy to be a wreck but instead finding Slats relaxed in a corner blowing on his harmonica; or the time Slats pulled $5,000 cash out of his pocket to buy a Lincoln he didn't even need, just to blow the mind of a snooty salesman who had disrespected him. "It was like sitting on an active volcano," Red commented more than a few times.

For the rest of his life—Red would live for a long time—he insisted that the Irishman from the First Ward was "the greatest fighter who ever lived."

The actual funeral mass, held at Holy Family Church in South Buffalo, was not well attended.

Jimmy, Jr. had made it home quickly, but didn't have much time, so there was only a small window in which to hold a service; Lois and the kids stayed back in Germany. One person in attendance was the former boxer Billy O'Day. He and Slats had once traveled to New York City together to fight as 16-year-old amateurs. They had also played on the same football team. Billy, now a widower, had been married to Skitsy Fitzgerald's sister. Slats attended the wedding. It was Billy who, when he gave up on boxing, gave the future champion his first decent pair of Everlast boxing shoes.

Or, rather, Billy had sold them. "That whole day," recalled Ellen Kolb, "my father kept repeating to himself, '*I should have given him the shoes.*'"

Many a young boy in the First Ward had been forbidden by their mothers to get into boxing. At the time—seeing Slattery's rise to fame and riches—there must have been some second-guessing and resentment directed toward the elders who tried to mold their lives. But after learning about how Slattery died penniless and alone, many of these now grown men had a different take—gratitude.

The Slattery family—only Mary remained—had a burial plot at Holy Cross Cemetery in Lackawanna. A family monument marked it; however, neither a headstone nor a plaque specific to Slats was placed upon the spot where the former champion's casket was interred.

Although Buffalo would soon experience sporting nirvana with a run of championships won by the Buffalo Bills of the upstart American Football League, the city was at the same time enduring a steady economic unraveling, due particularly to the opening of the St. Lawrence Seaway. This single, massive infrastructure project allowed grain-carrying freighters from Chicago to reach the Eastern Seaboard faster and without having to pass through Buffalo. The once-bustling waterfront section eventually became as quiet as a graveyard. Empty, rotting grain elevators still towered over the neighborhood, unmovable monuments to a bygone era.

In the world of sports, the legacy of the once nationally famous Slattery faded with each passing year. During the 1960s, banker Lewis Harriman, self-appointed sports scholar, oversaw the compilation of a thorough list of all-time greats. Known for his elephantine memory, Harriman knew, chapter and verse, the rise of the Buffalo phenomenon during 1925. He had strongly considered—but in the end, omitted—Slattery. His recklessness was held against him.

Not everyone discarded him, though. When films of Slattery's '25 bout against Paul Berlenbach surfaced in 1968, a boxing writer named Bob

Waters arranged for a screening and wrote a special feature in the October 1969 issue of *Boxing International*.

"I had read all those preposterous stories that implied he possessed some sixth sense which told him what an opponent was going to do next," Waters wrote. "But I had only read about those things. Last night, I saw Jimmy Slattery on movie film. Now I believe those things."

★★★★★

After getting out of the Air Force, Jimmy Slattery, Jr. drove a truck earning enough to provide Lois and his four children a comfortable life in the suburb of Amherst, N.Y., north of Buffalo. He became an Ironworker (Local 6) and also pruned trees for the City of Buffalo Forestry Department. Before long, young James E. Slattery, III, grandson of the legend, became something of a legend in his own right. A star basketball player at Bishop Neumann High School, the tall, handsome, magnetic teenager was marveled at regularly by the lovestruck friends of his three sisters, Joyce, Kim and Karen. He would get a full ride to the Catholic University of America in Washington, D.C.

In the early 1970s, the *Buffalo Evening News'* Frank Wakefield, who covered the 1927 Slattery-Rosenbloom title fight as a cub reporter for the Springfield, Mass. *Daily News* before moving to Buffalo, pointed out in his column that Slattery lie in an unmarked, grassy grave at Holy Cross.

It wasn't long before Jim Harkins, president of Ring 44 (the Western New York Veterans' Boxing Association), started a campaign to give Slattery a proper headstone. On Monday, August 30th, 1976, on the 16th anniversary of Slats' death, a group of ring veterans gathered for a ceremony and a graveside tribute led by Father Frank Kelleher, a former boxer and wrestler. Five years later, Kelleher, Harkins and about 150 others returned for another commemoration. Looking around that summer day in 1981, Harkins realized there were ten times as many people in attendance as there were at Slattery's funeral.

One year later, in the summer of '82, a young First Ward community leader named Peg Overdorf, trying to revive morale in a neighborhood decimated by two difficult, downhill decades—helped organize the "Jimmy Slattery Memorial Boxing Tournament" for neighborhood youths, many of whom would be fighting in the streets regardless.

A couple years after that, in a special column marking the re-opening of the Crystal Beach Ballroom, Frank Wakefield, by then retired as a local sportswriter, unearthed buried treasure: his memories of Slattery racing down from the Adirondack Mountains to enter, and win, a Charleston contest just prior to his first championship bout with Maxie Rosenbloom. "The slender, fun-loving Irish kid from the old First Ward was no less an idol here than other colorful super athletes of the celebrated Golden Age of Sports, including Jack Dempsey, Red Grange and Babe Ruth," Wakefield wrote under the headline, "Slattery Career Fit for Screen."

Meanwhile, in New York City, Jimmy Slattery's grandson, Jimmy Slattery, III, was living in a tiny walk-up apartment on West 56th Street in the Broadway vicinity near where Runyon once held court, and also close to where Rickard had once built his New Madison Square Garden, before yet another more modern, even more world-famous iteration of the Garden was built by Penn Station.

Jimmy Slattery III was working in finance and enjoying the bachelor's life. He was so good-looking that when he sat in the window of a bar or restaurant, women who passed by would sometimes stop dead in their tracks or go inside to try to meet him. "He was something to see," Jimmy, Jr. said of his son and idol.

All throughout his life, Jimmy Slattery, Jr. was asked whether he was the son of the great Slats, and for the most part, he grew tired of it. He'd made his own life. Being the son of a legend hadn't gotten him a thing—his own hard work had. Once in a while, though, over the years, he would hear a new story, some rich detail, giving him a slowly assembled mosaic of a man he barely knew.

In 1992, Jimmy Slattery was enshrined in the Greater Buffalo Sports Hall of Fame.

Two years later, on the occasion of his 100th birthday, Red Carr was interviewed by the *Buffalo News* and was still singing the praises of his idol. "There never will be another Slattery," Red said. "He was in a class by himself."

Paul R. "Red" Carr passed away on Wednesday, May 15, 1996, at Veteran's Hospital at the age of 101.

In 1997, a play about Slattery's life, *Jimmytown*, was written by Anthony Cardinale and produced by the Buffalo Ensemble Theater. Characters included a gambling parlor operator named Roggie and a young flapper named Betty. In attendance on opening night was Elizabeth Burgess, the ex-wife of Slats. She had helped Cardinale, a reporter at the *Buffalo News*, research his colorful tale.

"Betty" died a short time later.

In July of 1999, James E. Slattery, III, an executive at Citicorp with a wife and kids of his own, met his death at the age of 43. He'd battled leukemia—and lost. His family would never get over it. His parents and sisters still talk about him, in awe, the way many people discuss his famous grandfather. Jimmy, Jr. would never cease cherishing the wonder of his beloved hero in the flame of youth, as men are inclined to do, and as they should.

⭐⭐⭐⭐⭐

In June of 2005, Mike and Bernie Slattery were hanging around in the lobby of Graziano's Hotel in Canastota, New York, when the two lifetime boxing buffs spotted Hank Kaplan. A world-famous boxing historian, Kaplan was one of the luminaries who ran the International Boxing Hall of Fame, which was just down the road.

The Slattery brothers, retired steelworkers from Hamilton, Ontario, weren't sure exactly how they were related to the legendary Buffalo boxer, but their dad, John, had always insisted he had been a second or third cousin of the champ. Neither brother became a boxing fan because of this connection, but both were such enthusiastic followers of the sweet science that they had started making annual pilgrimages to Central New York each spring for induction weekend.

"Hank, how do you choose who gets in?" Mike Slattery asked after saying hello to Kaplan.

Kaplan explained that he was a member of the board which made the selections. They batted names around and debated, the way a jury might decide a court case.

"How come Jimmy Slattery isn't in there?" Slattery asked.

Kaplan glared incredulously.

"Well, he is in the hall of fame," he said.

No he wasn't, the Slattery brothers countered.

Kaplan told them to wait in the lobby and dashed up to his room to get the official register. He came back and opened it up. "Look here fellas," the Dean of Boxing History said, thumbing past Rosenbloom, Loughran, Delaney, Stribling, Greb, Braddock and others. And then Kaplan's voice trailed off in disbelief.

The Slattery brothers weren't trying to bust his chops; they just wanted to understand how it worked and to maybe put in a good word.

The following December, when the IBHOF Class of 2006 was announced, Jimmy Slattery, long overdue, was finally included. Kaplan himself was inducted that year. Shortly thereafter, Kaplan passed away.

During the entire summer that Slattery was inducted, Buffalo celebrated the achievement as its own. A resurgent section of South Park Avenue (near where Slats had once lived) was renamed Jimmy Slattery Place in his honor. The *Buffalo News* ran an extensive two-part series chronicling the fighter's rise and fall. Friday, August 25, 2006, was proclaimed "Jimmy Slattery Day," and was commemorated with a six-round exhibition boxing match. A special program was printed.

"*Generations later, Jimmy Slattery stories are still told by grandparents and parents throughout the City of Buffalo,*" the program noted, "*but primarily in South Buffalo where Slattery remains a boxing legend.*"

These days, a popular Halloween ghost tour has come to include Chippewa as one of its main stops. It is said that Slattery's ghost still haunts the strip near the corner of Franklin. The specter of a man staggering along just before dawn, arms outstretched, has supposedly been spotted several times over the years.

There's also the spooky tale of a young bartender who was once all alone at 4:00 A.M. closing up a tavern that stood where the House O' Quinn once did. Out of the corner of his eye, he caught a glimpse of a man sitting by the window staring out at the street. Startled to see he had company, the barkeep quickly turned his head, but no one was there.

That was Slattery alright: Here and gone, so fast so as to seem unbelievable—a flicker out over the bog—faintly remembered, and yet never forgotten.

—March 21, 2015

AUTHOR'S NOTE

So COLORFUL, OUTSIZED AND UNIMAGINABLY POPULAR were the athletic icons of the 1920s—Dempsey, Ruth, others—that it's not surprising some got overlooked. Arguing Slattery's place in the pantheon wasn't,
however, my inspiration for learning and relating his story.

That Slattery's rise and fall was destined for a book, and that I was the
one who would author it, were seeds sown by my father, Tom Blake, during my childhood. My father, who worked for the Buffalo Creek Railroad
and Buffalo Public Schools, spoke often and enthusiastically about his
idol. Anything he could get his hands on relating to the fighter and his era
was tucked away. My dad, born in 1931, missed Slattery's heyday. He never
saw Slats in action. But Slats' accomplishments in and out of the ring
reverberated throughout South Buffalo for years to follow. Coming of
age in the 1940s and '50s, my dad heard tales from Slattery's inner circle,
a special connection of which he was most proud; his uncle (his mother's
brother) was Skitsy Fitzgerald. During the 1950s, there was a deli on Potters Road, which, although owned by a woman named Woods, became
known for a time as "Skitsy's." Many people stopped in, picked up a few
items and made small talk with the little man behind the counter, never
suspecting the wild ride he'd once had during the '20s.

The lore soaked up by my old man during his younger days eventually
found its way to me in bite-size childhood increments. But then, 12-year-
olds have their own sports idols. Dad's silent-movie-era boxer could hold
my attention only up to a point. Still, I was intrigued by his old photographs of Slattery, sharply dressed, dashing; he seemed like an epic figure,
gregarious and always grinning.

My dad, spry from the physicality of working two or three or sometimes four jobs, used to imitate, in his own way, Slats, bouncing on his toes
and shooting jabs. He would allow himself to become swept up in some

distant excitement he had only heard about. "They called him the *will-o'-the-wisp!*" he would shout.

As a *Rocky* fanatic who had graduated to *Raging Bull*, I do recall being intrigued when the *Buffalo News* published, in 1984, an article titled, "Slattery Career Fit for Screen," which seemed to validate my father's claims over the years. I would have a few precious chances to sit with my dad, his friend Vince McNamara, and the legendary Red Carr at a café in the Holiday Inn on Delaware Avenue, but for the life of me I do not recall much of what Red had to say.

After college, and a few newspaper jobs, the notion of writing a book about Slats rerooted. But at the time, around 1995, while I thought the project's time had come, my father strongly *discouraged* me—I needed to get a job, gain some more experience. *Kid, you don't just write a book as a profession . . . most authors have day jobs, they do books on the side . . . these things can take years . . .* (that's the sensibility of what he said, if not his exact words). And so, for years, we talked about it. But I took no concrete steps, apart from picking his brain now and again and rifling through some old items he sometimes had scattered about his cluttered office in the basement of the Adult Learning Center on Elmwood Avenue, where he was stationary engineer.

After my father's sudden passing in 2002, I came across a large cardboard box at his cottage in Angola, N.Y. Neatly piled inside were scrapbooks and albums stuffed with his collection of Slattery photos, clippings and memorabilia. Resting on the front of the topmost black binder was a sheet of pale green paper. On it, in his chicken-scratch handwriting, my dad had underlined, <u>Slats</u>. He'd organized everything.

Yet it would *still be years* before I took up writing this book in earnest. The *Buffalo News'* well-researched two-part series in 2006 lit a fuse; I was suddenly petrified I had blown my literary birthright, certain that the sportswriter Tim Graham would follow that up with something larger in scope.

Slowly, starting in 2008, I began plotting the rollercoaster-ride of a story in fits and starts, patiently assembling a clearer picture. As it came into focus, I became even more drawn in and determined to see it through, to understand who this larger-than-life character was.

"In his heyday he was like the hero of some ancient Irish fable," wrote journalist Ed Dunn in 1945. "A ring-wise, black-haired Irish imp who carried man-made lightning in his gloves."

In committing to a book, the writer must decide: Is there a tale worth telling?

My hunch was absolutely there was; what began as a tribute to my father took on a life of its own.

Around 2010, a literary agent named John Wright instructed me to give up trying to snag a book deal by penning a masterful book proposal and instead to actually write the book, or, as he put it, "take the boat out to sea." Until I did, he cautioned, I would not know what I had. Agreeing to represent me several years later after reading some early chapters, Wright helped me shape a proper précis and brought my sample material to a major publishing house. Good news, he emailed. The publisher wanted a chance to consider the Slats proposal exclusively for one week. But after that week, a follow-up email came. Bad news—after some debate, they ultimately took a pass, describing Slats' story as more of a magazine feature, simply not important enough; the stinging rejection line my agent forwarded to me: "*Slattery strikes us as a has-been who never was.*"

When No Frills Buffalo agreed to put out the first edition, it seemed, honestly, like the smallest publishing deal imaginable, yet at the same time exactly right—a hometown focus, intimate.

I'd been warned not to engage in hagiography but let's face it—clearly, I was rooting for Slats; but I discovered, however, that his plummet was just as fascinating to explore as the ascension. Still, I won't deny the entire project was a labor of love. If that affection—for the characters, the city, the era—came through too strongly, then it is my hope that it was at least welcomed and not resented for having compromised the story. This is a first-edition Slats; keep it safe. My intention for future editions is to include extensive notes and footnotes and explanations of sources, but right now the opening bell of the printing schedule—the final deadline—approaches. And when the bell rings, that's all there is to it.

INDEX

ACKNOWLEDGEMENTS

WITHOUT EXTENSIVE HELP from numerous key collaborators, *Slats* would not have been possible. Foremost among them: Meryl P. Kaye, who provided support, encouragement, research assistance, editorial guidance as well as humor and perspective in times of distress and uncertainty. Meryl, thank you!!!

Thanks also to several researchers who selflessly rallied by my side over the years. A lake freighter load of gratitude is owed to librarian Grace Di Thomas–Di Virgilio, whose exhaustive scour of written sources—books, newspapers, magazines, websites, and a variety of other material—served as the historical backbone of the entire project. Thanks also to Laura Suttell for her help getting the ship out to sea, and to Brian Milligan who meticulously reviewed practically every *Buffalo Courier* and *Courier-Express* sports section between 1920 and 1930. Bob Caico at the Buffalo Veterans Boxing Association, Ring #44 was also extremely instrumental in the research, as was South Buffalo historian Gene Overdorf. A special thank you also to Angelo Prospero who opened up his encyclopedic knowledge of boxing lore and allowed me free roam. The always dependable and enthusiastic Jhon Usmanov at the Hank Kaplan Boxing Archive at Brooklyn College Library–Archives and Special Collections, likewise, can't be thanked enough.

Thanks also to Ty Wenger for his masterful edit, and to Tony Zajkowski for his world-class cover design.

Thanks to Slattery family members who gave me their time and who were patient with me as I saw this project through, especially Jim and Lois Slattery, and their daughter, Joyce Zygaj. Thanks also to Joan Slattery and to the late Alicia Imperi; and to Karen, Glenn and Patsy Kline, as well as the Hamilton, Ontario Slatterys, Mike, Bernie and Kim. Thanks to Tom "Luke" Carr and Judy Beecher for helping to bring Red's story to the page.

Thanks to my agent, John Wright, for inspiring me to steam ahead, even when the publishing community wasn't interested. Thanks also to Joel Gotler for his kind encouragement. Special thanks, as well, to Mark Pogodzinski at NFB, Tom McDonnell at Dog Ears and Joe Gannon at Mulberry Tree Press for helping to bring this project to fruition.

Thanks to the folks at the Historical Society of Lake Pleasant and Speculator—Bev Hoffman and Anne Weaver; the Town of Mohawk Town Clerk—Kimberly Sullivan; and the Montgomery County Department of History & Archives, County Historian—Kelly Yacobucci Farquhar. And a very special thanks to Jeff Brophy at the International Boxing Hall of Fame. Additionally, thanks to Dan Di Landro, archivist, E.H. Butler Library, Buffalo State College.

Thanks also to: Shawn Blake; Patsy Blake; Tommy Blake; Dan Blake; Patricia Blake; Noel Burke and the late Maureen Burke; Jackie Donnelly; Tom Higgins; Dan Redmond; Anthony Cardinale; Bertha Hyde; Ed Manning; Joe Marren; Patrick Kearns; Jimmy Joynt, Sr.; Jimmy Joynt, Jr.; Bill Zullo; Elaine Georgovich; Peg Overdorf; Jerry Collins; Shaun and Pat Cleary; Jay Tunney; Jim Messina; Jack Hirsch; Michael Cambria; John Honan; Robert Noonan; Kevin Hennigan; Chris Jacob; Allison Jacob; Mike Evans; Ben Wilson; Vince Brun; Kevin Keane; Pat Keane; Mike Keane; Tim Bohen; Mike Dwyer; Simon McLoughlin; Diane Alfano; Don Colpoys; Mary Sullivan Hake; John and Kristie Gallivan; Mary Walsh; the late Bert Sugar; Suzie Sugar; Bob Osborne and Bob Downey.

And finally, of course, thanks to the man who got this project started a long time ago—my dear father, Tom Blake.

CPSIA information can be obtained at www.ICGtesting.com
Printed in the USA
BVOW08s0126021215

429109BV00002B/7/P